JOSEPH CONRAD
THE MAKING OF A NOVELIST

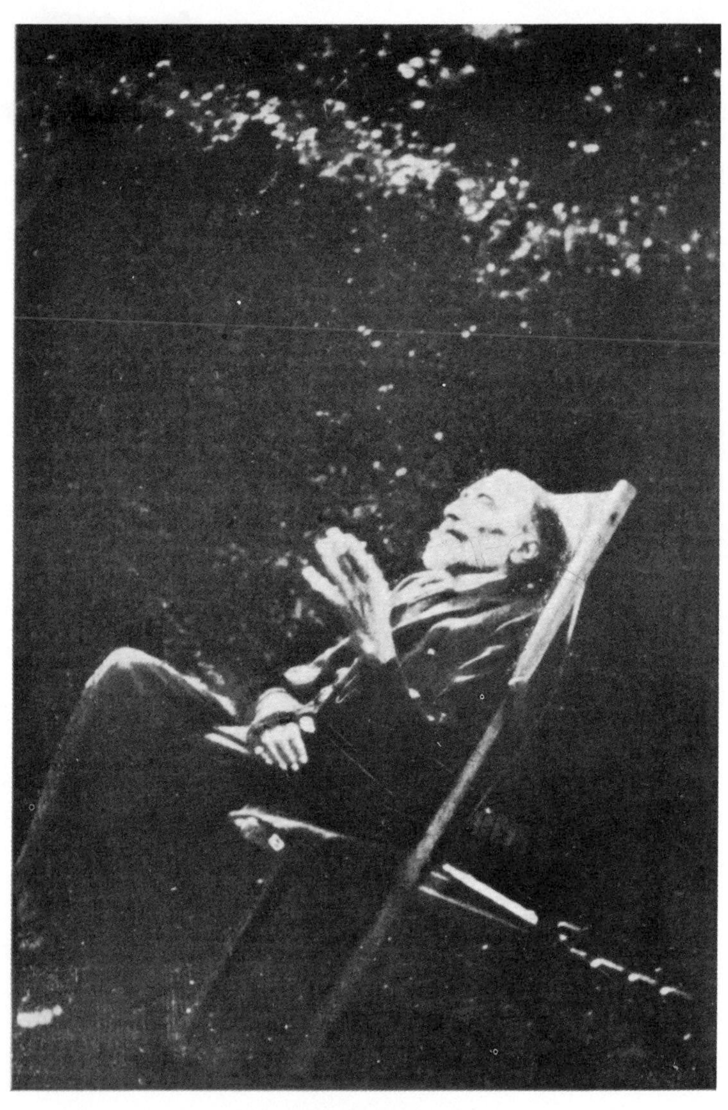

JOSEPH CONRAD
JUNE, 1924

JOSEPH CONRAD

THE MAKING OF A NOVELIST

BY

JOHN DOZIER GORDAN

NEW YORK

RUSSELL & RUSSELL · INC

1963

REISSUED, 1963, BY RUSSELL & RUSSELL, INC.
BY ARRANGEMENT WITH HARVARD UNIVERSITY PRESS
L. C. CATALOG CARD NO: 63—11031

PRINTED IN THE UNITED STATES OF AMERICA

TO ALL THOSE
WHO HAVE MADE THIS BOOK POSSIBLE
AND ESPECIALLY TO

MY WIFE
JOHN ARCHER GEE
HYDER E. ROLLINS
A. S. W. ROSENBACH

PREFACE

I AM most grateful for the help and cooperation which I have received in preparing this study. No one to whom I have turned for assistance or permission has refused my requests. Without such universal kindness I could never have published this book.

The late Mrs. Conrad allowed me to ask her questions about her husband's work. Mr. and Mrs. Andrew Gray of Malang, Java, Mr. V. A. Cools of Tandjong Redeb, Borneo, and Mr. Pangemanan of Bulungan, Borneo, provided me with invaluable information about Conrad's Bornean acquaintances. Professor Hyder E. Rollins of Harvard University read my manuscript and made countless helpful suggestions. Professor John Archer Gee of Yale University generously allowed me to use certain letters in the Keating Collection in the Yale University Library, which he and Dr. Paul J. Sturm are publishing as *Joseph Conrad's Letters to Marguerite Poradowska 1890–1920: Translated from the French and Edited with Introduction, Notes, and Appendices*, and to follow his datings. Miss Alice Evju, Mrs. Donald Goodfellow, Mrs. Homer Halvorson, and Mrs. Henry Zylstra have all patiently aided in the preparation of my manuscript for the press. My wife's encouragement and untiring assistance have been largely responsible for the completion of this book.

James B. Pinker and Son, Conrad's literary executors, have kindly granted me permission to quote from unpublished letters and manuscripts. Dr. A. S. W. Rosenbach's liberality in putting his magnificent collection of Conrad manuscripts at my disposal made possible a whole chapter of this study. Mr. Barnet J. Beyer of New York, Mr. E. Byrne Hackett of the Brick Row Book Shop, New York, and Mr. William B. Leeds of New York all generously allowed me to work on their collections of manuscripts, unpublished letters, and other documents. The Harvard University Library was most obliging in giving me access to its Conrad manuscripts, and the Yale University Library granted me the privilege of quoting extracts from unpublished material in the superb gift of Mr. George T. Keating. The British Museum has allowed me to use a manuscript which I had previously examined in the library of the late Mr. T. J. Wise. Mr. Henry S. Grew of Boston kindly lent me his first editions and rare Conrad items, and Mr. and Mrs. Howard Eric of New York have graciously allowed me to quote from a manuscript autobiography which they have privately printed.

I owe particular thanks to the following publishers for permission to quote:

George Allen and Unwin, Ltd., for *Almayer's Folly: A Story of an Eastern River* (1895) by Joseph Conrad.

Ernest Benn, Ltd., for *Almayer's Folly: A Story of an Eastern River* (1895) by Joseph Conrad.

Blackwood and Sons for *Lord Jim: A Tale* (1900) by Joseph Conrad.

The Bobbs-Merrill Company for *Letters from Joseph Conrad: 1895–1924* edited by Edward Garnett.

Coward-McCann, Inc., for *Men and Memories* by William Rothenstein.

J. M. Dent and Sons, Ltd., for *Last Essays* and *Youth and Gaspar Ruiz* by Joseph Conrad.

Doubleday, Doran and Company, Inc., for the works of Joseph Conrad, *Joseph Conrad as I Knew Him* by Jessie Conrad, *Joseph Conrad: Life and Letters* by G. Jean-Aubry, *A Conrad Memorial Library* edited by George T. Keating, *Conrad to a Friend* edited by Richard Curle, and *The Last Twelve Years of Joseph Conrad* by Richard Curle.

E. P. Dutton and Company, Inc., for *Joseph Conrad and His Circle* by Jessie Conrad.

Faber and Faber, Ltd., for *Joseph Conrad's Mind and Method* by R. L. Mégroz.

The First Edition Club for *Twenty Letters to Joseph Conrad* edited by G. Jean-Aubry.

Librairie Gallimard, Nouvelle Revue Française, for *Joseph Conrad: Lettres Françaises* edited by G. Jean-Aubry.

William Heinemann, Ltd., for *The Nigger of the "Narcissus": A Tale of the Forecastle* (1898) by Joseph Conrad.

Little, Brown and Company for *Joseph Conrad: A Personal Remembrance* by Ford Madox Ford.

Sampson Low, Marston and Company, Ltd., for *The Polish Heritage of Joseph Conrad* by Gustav Morf.

Studies in Philology for "The Rajah Brooke and Joseph Conrad" by John D. Gordan.

J. D. G.

CAMBRIDGE, MASSACHUSETTS
MARCH 19, 1940

CONTENTS

Introduction xiii

I. The Pattern of the Careers 3

II. The Four Sources 28

III. The Mood of Creation 75

IV. The Growth of the Text 96

V. A Chronicle of the Early Stories 174

VI. Conrad and the Public 269

Bibliography 311

Notes 333

Index 417

INTRODUCTION

THE fascination of a mariner with a story to tell was long ago immortalized. The spell was double, binding by the tale itself and by the personality of the man who told it. The character of Joseph Conrad is as absorbing as any of his novels. Astonishment at the Pole turned sailor and the sailor turned novelist becomes a profound curiosity as to the way Conrad's life shaped his stories. This study is focused upon the early years of his long career as a writer, when he drove himself to become a professional. It attempts to picture the dominant factors in his life and the way in which they affected his work. By bringing the problems of the creator into closer touch with the creation, it may supplement a reading of the stories themselves.

Without attempting to be a full biography, the study necessarily draws upon Conrad's reminiscences and letters, some of them unpublished, and upon biographical studies. The play of temperament in his development as sailor and writer, the influence of poverty and illness on his work could not otherwise be displayed. Without attempting to be a general criticism, the study analyzes the sources of his stories. It traces the evolution of plot and characterization through the manuscript and typescript, never before discussed in print, of three early novels. It compares manuscript, typescript, serial and book publication to show Conrad's unremitting care for style. The study tries to satisfy William McFee's desire for "a coherent and condensed account of the genesis of 'Almayer's Folly'. . . . Conrad himself – and this appears . . . to be generally overlooked in the essays written about him – was one of the most conscious and conscientious artists who ever lived. The technique, the manner, the fundamentals of writing, were an obsession with him." [1]

These broad aspects of Conrad's life and work are further illustrated by the record of each early story. Each, in fact, has a history of its own which can be followed in more or less detail from conception to publication. The pertinent facts have been here assembled in a source book for the future investigator. Even after publication the history of the stories did not end. Representative contemporary criticism has been collected to show Conrad's difficulties with the reading public; wherever possible his reactions to the criticism have been added. In a book such as this, documentation is essential and has been provided as unobtrusively as possible.

The study confines itself to the work Conrad had done by the time *Lord Jim* was published in October, 1900; it does not consider his collaborations with Ford Madox Ford. It is based fundamentally on *Almayer's Folly*, *The Nigger of the "Narcissus,"* and *Lord Jim* because these novels have most to reveal. In the first Conrad was a carefree amateur; in the second he made himself a professional; and in the third he wrote with the resolution of an established professional. The distinctions are not arbitrary. In 1896 Conrad himself spoke of "those fine days of *Alm: Folly* when I wrote with the serene audacity of an unsophisticated fool. I am getting more sophisticated from day to day. And more uncertain!" [2] The uncertainty increased so strongly that he was forced to put aside two novels, *The Sisters* and *The Rescue*. Then "the finishing of 'The Nigger,'" he admitted, "brought to my troubled mind the comforting sense of an accomplished task, and the first consciousness of a certain sort of mastery which could accomplish something with the aid of propitious stars." [3] *Lord Jim* was his first large piece of work after he accepted the career of a writer. In his next novel he felt "a subtle change in the nature of the inspiration." [4] *Almayer's Folly*, *The Nigger*, and *Lord Jim* were landmarks in the making of a novelist.

JOSEPH CONRAD
THE MAKING OF A NOVELIST

Chapter I

THE PATTERN OF THE CAREERS

MANY years before his death Joseph Conrad was recognized as one of the great English novelists of his generation. Yet serious discussions of his work were often marred by overemphasis on his romantic origin and sea life. He complained constantly that the critics treated him as a literary freak. In 1924, near the end of his career, even Virginia Woolf felt it reasonable to say in a lecture on Georgian and Edwardian novelists: "Mr. Conrad is a Pole; which sets him apart, and makes him, however admirable, not very helpful." [1] This was "a position," he found, "which outside the circus world cannot be regarded as desirable." [2] The extraordinary changes of his life naturally led incautious critics to misunderstand him.

Jozef Teodor Konrad Nałecz Korzeniowski, native of a country so unmaritime that he met only one other Pole at sea,[3] became first a French and then an English seaman and later an English novelist. A similarity is to be observed in his growth as a seaman and as a novelist. In each phase can be found the same talent developed by circumstance and the same transition from amateur to professional. The parallel provides a background for the present investigation of Conrad's early work from *Almayer's Folly* through *Lord Jim.* For nearly ten years he wavered between making his living by the sea and making it by fiction. His sea life provided him with much of the material of his stories and permanently affected his health and his character.

Conrad's ambition to go to sea was slowly achieved. When he first made the suggestion, it was received with anxiety by his family and with resentment by the society to which he was known. The boy, who was born on December 3, 1857, sprang from two old Polish families, the Bobrowskis and Korzeniowskis; they had connections in the Almanach de Gotha and were "land-tilling gentry." [4] Both families were ardent patriots in the apparently lost cause of Polish independence. The traditions of the army and politics were strong on each side, though the Korzeniowskis, of more initiative and less stability than the Bobrowskis, were also literary.[5] The generation of Conrad's parents had suffered for Poland. His mother's brother, Stefan Bobrowski, who was in the Provisional Polish Government, "died in a duel with a political enemy, in 1862." [6] His father's elder brother, Robert Nałecz Korzeniowski, was killed in the Polish rising against Russia that began on January 22, 1863.[7] The younger brother, Hilary Nałecz Korzeniowski, was exiled to Siberia in 1863 and died there ten years later.[8] In October, 1862, Conrad's father, Apollo Nałecz Korzeniowski, was deported to a distant part of Russia. His wife and only child, then five years old, were allowed to accompany him.[9] The hardships of exile were too much for Conrad's parents. His mother died on April 6, 1865, and his father some four years later, on May 23, 1869.[10] Conrad was with them both during their protracted illnesses. The funeral of Apollo Nałecz Korzeniowski was an occasion of national mourning for the citizens of Cracow, who in 1872 gave Conrad the freedom of the city.[11] The orphan was taken in hand by his mother's people, the Bobrowskis, of whom his uncle Tadeusz was the most devoted.[12]

To the Bobrowskis Conrad's desire to go to sea was disturbing. When he first mentioned the subject while in school in Cracow in 1873, they tried ineffectively to disregard it.[13] Conrad persisted. Tadeusz journeyed from the

Ukraine to Cracow to have a serious talk with his nephew. He must have found the ambition unintelligible. It was not in the tradition of either family. Probably Tadeusz regarded it as Korzeniowski instability, of which he left a frank account in his *Memoirs*.[14] He suggested that seafaring was not morally suitable for the son of two families who had sacrificed so much for a country without naval interests. He told the boy, Conrad later recorded, that he "must not only think of myself but of others; weigh the claims of affection and conscience against my own sincerity of purpose." [15]

Conrad's intention excited considerable comment in the society of well-born and patriotic Poles to which he belonged. "It stirred up a mass of remonstrance, indignation, pitying wonder, bitter irony and downright chaff," he admitted. "I could hardly breathe under its weight, and certainly had no words for an answer." [16] Undoubtedly it was looked upon as treachery to the cause of Polish independence. Conrad heard "men of unstained rectitude . . . murmur scornfully the word desertion"; he was "charged with the want of patriotism, the want of sense, and the want of heart too." [17] These reproaches were not lost on a boy already a little morbid. He never forgot them:

> But for a boy between fifteen and sixteen, sensitive enough, in all conscience, the commotion of his little world had seemed a very considerable thing indeed. So considerable that, absurdly enough, the echoes of it linger to this day. I catch myself in hours of solitude and retrospect meeting arguments and charges made thirty-five years ago by voices now forever still; finding things to say that an assailed boy could not have found, simply because of the mysteriousness of his impulses to himself.[18]

It would be illuminating to know Conrad's answers to the arguments and charges. Though he later ascribed his inclination toward the sea to a desire for "innocent adventure," even he felt it was "inexplicable." [19]

Since the maritime tradition was foreign not only to Conrad's family but also to Poland itself, the source of his interest in the sea was literary. He supplied plenty of grounds for such a conclusion. In recalling his mood when he decided to go to sea, he compared himself with Don Quixote, who read "so many romances he desired naïvely to escape with his very body from the intolerable reality of things." [20] Conrad also was a great reader, beginning at "the age of five." He recollected, "At ten years of age . . . I had read in Polish and in French, history, voyages, novels." [21] The abnormal life of exile intensified the boy's precocity. He gave a pathetic account of his dependence upon books during the winter of 1869 when he was in Cracow with his dying father: "I don't know what would have become of me if I had not been a reading boy. My prep finished I would have had nothing to do but sit and watch the awful stillness of the sick room flow out through the closed door and coldly enfold my scared heart. I suppose that in a futile childish way I would have gone crazy. But I was a reading boy. . . . I read! What did I not read!" [22] Much of the reading was connected with the sea.

His "first introduction to the sea in literature" [23] was just after his mother's death. Apollo Nałecz Korzeniowski had recently completed his Polish translation of Victor Hugo's *Toilers of the Sea* and, being ill in bed, had his young son read the proofs to him. The unhappy conditions of grief and exile, the responsibility of his task, must have impressed the story indelibly on Conrad's mind. Perhaps the impression, reinforced by family friendships in Marseilles, later made him choose the French merchant marine.[24]

As a boy, Conrad probably read Polish or French translations of English sea stories. The article, "Tales of the

Sea," published in 1898, discusses Cooper and Marryat, whom he called "the enslaver of youth," with "irresistible power to reach the adventurous side in the character, not only of his own but of all nations." [25] A Christmas note to young David Garnett showed that Conrad knew Cooper's Leatherstocking Tales in his own boyhood.[26] "Tales of the Sea," which mentions characters and ships in *The Pilot, Homeward Bound, The Sea Lion*, and other novels,[27] suggests that he knew several of Cooper's sea stories. The effect of such fiction on his imagination is plain from one of the omniscient author's generalizations so common in his novels: "We are the creatures of our light literature much more than is generally suspected. . . ." [28]

Conrad's interest in the sea did not come entirely from fiction. When he was ten, he read a French translation of Sir Leopold McClintock's *Voyage of the "Fox" in the Arctic Seas*, the story of the last days of Sir John Franklin. The boy's enthusiasm was instantaneous. "The great spirit of the realities of the story sent me off on the romantic explorations of my inner self; to the discovery of the taste for poring over maps; and revealed to me the existence of a latent devotion to geography which interfered with my devotion (such as it was) to my other school-work." [29] He took up next the annals of Mungo Park and James Bruce,[30] probably Park's *Travels in the Interior Districts of Africa* (1799) and *Journal of a Mission into the Interior of Africa in 1805* and Bruce's *Travels to Discover the Source of the Nile in the Years 1768–73*. At this time Conrad must first have read Heinrich Barth and David Livingstone.[31] Barth's *Travels and Discoveries in North and Central Africa 1849–55* had been published in 1857–58 and Livingstone's *Missionary Travels and Researches in South Africa* in 1857 and his *Narrative of an Expedition to the Zambesi and its Tributaries* in 1865. In imagination Conrad lived with the great explorers: "They and not the characters of famous fiction . . . were my first friends." [32] A strain of inherited restlessness must have been strongly affected by tales of adventure. An incident which he repeated three separate times shows how reading fired his ambitions. "It was in 1868 . . . that while looking at a map of Africa of the time and putting my finger on the blank space then representing the unsolved mystery of that continent, I said to myself with absolute assurance and an amazing audacity which are no longer in my character now: 'When I grow up I shall go *there*.' " [33]

Jean-Aubry first suggested that an unhappy love affair helped make Conrad a sailor.[34] The girl whom he loved just before he left Poland in 1874 lay behind the character of Antonia Avellanos, the heroine of *Nostromo*, and behind canceled passages in the First Note of *The Arrow of Gold*. Later Morf emphasized that this early love was the character to whom the First Note was addressed and to whom the whole *Arrow of Gold* was supposed to be sent as an account of the life of the hero, her childhood friend, after he left his native country.[35] In real life, according to the Author's Note to *Nostromo* and the canceled passage in *The Arrow of Gold*, Conrad had been too disturbed to voice his love to this girl. For in the summer of 1873 he had been fascinated by another girl who had treated him so badly that after thirty-five years he remembered her as "particularly wicked and even devilish." [36] The unhappiness of these two affairs must have contributed to his desire to leave Poland.

More fundamental to Conrad's departure was the political history of the Bobrowskis and the Korzeniowskis. Both families were well known to the repressive Russian authorities. A boy whose parents had given their lives to Poland and who had an uncle in Siberia would be under the secret surveillance of the police all his life. It has not been sufficiently emphasized that Conrad must have been oppressively aware of his position. His bitterness can be surmised from *Under Western Eyes* (1911) in which the hero Razumov found himself, like Conrad, through no action of his own, suspect to the Russian secret police. He realized that life in Russia was over for him and left for Switzerland. Conrad showed the paralyzing effect of the word *suspect* by repeating it at least seven times [37] during the fateful hours when Razumov grasped his situation. He became aware of "the incarnate suspicion, the incarnate anger, the incarnate ruthlessness of a political and social régime on its defence." [38] The meaning of such suspicion overwhelmed him: "Razumov sat up in anguish. Was he to remain a political suspect all his days? Was he to go through life as a man not wholly to be trusted – with a bad secret police note tacked on to his record? What sort of future could he look forward to?" [39] The only future in which he would not be "menaced by the lawlessness of autocracy . . . and the lawlessness of revolution" [40] lay outside his native country. Razumov's decision grew from Conrad's own predicament.

Tadeusz Bobrowski's understanding of his nephew's position kept him from coercing Conrad. He did not try to override the boy's refusal to consider the naval training school at Pola and a career in the Austrian navy. Conrad wanted not "a naval career, but the sea." [41] His uncle, he afterwards said, "concluded that he would not have me later on reproach him for having spoiled my life by an unconditional opposition." [42] Instead, during the late spring and summer of 1873, he sent the boy with his tutor Mr. Pulman on a tour of Western Europe.[43] On the trip Mr. Pulman was to dissuade his charge from a life at sea. Conrad left the story of the victorious moment when he realized he would be given his way. The reiterated arguments and persuasions of his tutor had nearly broken his determination. Then the sight of a vigorous old Englishman at the top of the Furca Pass revived his spirit of adventure and silenced his tutor. "And indeed," he declared, "there was no more question of my mysterious vocation between us. There was to be no more question of it at all, nowhere or with any one." [44] Soon after, he saw the sea for the first time, from the Lido at Venice. The struggle was over, and he was ready to take up the profession toward which unusual influences had directed him. On October 14, 1874, he left Poland for France and the sea.[45] He was within two months of seventeen.

For a long time Conrad remained an amateur seaman. The Mediterranean, which he later called "the nursery of the craft," [46] was the scene of his first experiences with the sea. During his four years at Marseilles he did not hurry to complete his apprenticeship. He was at an irresponsible age and independent for the first time. He was befriended by the Corporation of Pilots and spent many hours out in their boats.[47] At last, through family connections, he was employed by Delestang and Sons, bankers and shippers.[48] His first deep-water voyage, on the *Mont Blanc* to the West Indies from June to December, 1875, was undertaken in the spirit of high adventure because he "had to go there. It was a sort of mystic conviction – something in the nature of a call." [49] When he returned to Marseilles, he was in no haste to find another ship, but in seven gay months ran heavily into debt.[50]

Probably at this time he met the conspirators who wanted to put the pretender Don Carlos on the throne of Spain.[51] He later described them as "the most casual assemblage of irresponsible young men (all, however, older than myself) who, as if drunk with Provençal sunshine, frittered life away in joyous levity on the model of Balzac's *Histoire des*

Treize qualified by a dash of romance *de cape et d'épée.*" [52] His more responsible friends warned him "*à ne pas gâter sa vie.*" [53] After one more voyage to the West Indies, on the *Saint Antoine* from July, 1876, to February, 1877,[54] he returned to Marseilles and definitely joined the Carlists. He had already been trained in the ways of lost causes in Poland.

Conrad was connected with the most dramatic of the Carlists' activities. He was on their balancelle the *Tremolino,* with which they smuggled guns into Spain, when they sank her to evade the Spanish coastguards.[55] On his return to Marseilles he became the lover of the beautiful and unusual woman, perhaps once the mistress of Don Carlos himself, who was financing the gun-running.[56] The love affair ended almost in tragedy. Another admirer insulted Conrad, who challenged him to a duel and was so seriously wounded that Tadeusz Bobrowski had to be summoned from Russia. When he recovered, the Carlists one and all had vanished. The boy was not yet twenty-one.[57]

From the fall of 1874 to the spring of 1878 Conrad had enjoyed his nautical experiences like an amateur. He drifted into various berths and did not try seriously to advance himself. With genuine disapproval his uncle Tadeusz now took him to task for his dilatory spirit: "You wanted to be a sailor, and you must be responsible for the consequences; you have forfeited my confidence. Work now to regain it; you will win it back if you apply yourself steadily and pull yourself together." [58] His nephew followed the advice. Only after four years in the French merchant service did he try to make himself a professional seaman.

Conrad's mature sea life began on April 24, 1878, when he found a berth in a British ship, the *Mavis,* which eventually took him to Lowestoft, England.[59] Now he decided, "If I was to be a seaman then I would be a British seaman and no other. It was a matter of deliberate choice." [60] For nearly three months he served on a North Sea coaster. Apparently he considered that here his nautical education began in earnest; whereas he referred to the Mediterranean as "the nursery of the craft," he called the North Sea the "school-room of my trade," the "academy of seamanship," the "finishing school of seamanship." [61] Next he went to London to find a ship that would give him more deep-water training.[62] Without influence this time, he used a regular seaman's agent. He was working toward a definite goal: "I was pursuing a clear aim, I was carrying out a deliberate plan of making out of myself, in the first place, a seaman worthy of the service, good enough to work by the side of the men with whom I was to live; and in the second place, I had to justify my existence to myself, to redeem a tacit moral pledge." [63]

Before achieving his aim, Conrad suffered moments of hopelessness and of longing for other occupations, as he later did with his writing. He was torn with the desire to return either to Marseilles or to his uncle in Russia. He considered a job as secretary to a Canadian businessman and politician in 1880. In the summer of 1886 he thought of entering business.[64] He declared himself "sick and tired of sailing about for little money and less consideration." [65] Yet while suffering from these periods of reaction, he turned himself into an accomplished seaman. In 1880 he passed his examination for third mate, in 1883 for mate, and in 1886 for master.[66] At last he had become a professional and redeemed his "tacit moral pledge" to his uncle and to Poland. His certificate as master had for him an "ideal significance. It was an answer to certain outspoken scepticism, and even to some not very kind aspersions. I had vindicated myself from what had been cried upon as a stupid obstinacy or a fantastic caprice." [67]

Conrad's literary offers many parallels to his nautical career. There is the same interplay of influences, the same protracted period of amateurism, the same resolution to vindicate himself, and the same dissatisfaction with his new life. Conrad's inclination to write was not so strong as his intention of going to sea. "My first novel," he confessed, "was begun in idleness. . . . It was not the outcome of a need – the famous need of self-expression which artists find in their search for motives. The necessity which impelled me was a hidden, obscure necessity, a completely masked and unaccountable phenomenon. . . . I was not at all certain that I wanted to write, or that I meant to write, or that I had anything to write about." [68] In an autobiographical sketch given Garnett in 1900 he carefully added "tentatively" to a brief account of his literary beginnings:

> tentatively
> . . . he began to write his first *book* * novel ALMAYER'S FOLLY. . . .[69]

Gustav Morf's explanation that Conrad's writing arose from a sense of guilt about his self-exile from Poland seems extravagant.[70] Whatever its origin, the impulse did not alter his life so immediately as did his sea ambitions. His desire to ship before the mast had changed the whole direction of his life. Nearly a decade passed before he gave up all thought of the sea and fell back upon writing as a career. Again circumstances changed his occupation. Of his life at sea he admitted in 1919: "I was content with it; . . . I would have been perfectly content with it to this day." [71]

Unlike his going to sea, Conrad's impulse to write accorded with family tradition. Literary dilettantism was a social grace of the Korzeniowskis. Conrad's grandfather,

* In the quotations from Conrad's manuscripts his cancellations are shown by italics.

Teodor Nałecz Korzeniowski, wrote "a tragedy in 5 Acts, verse, privately printed and so extremely dull that no one was ever known to have read it through." His father, Apollo Nałecz Korzeniowski, was of marked literary bent: he translated Victor Hugo and Shakespeare into Polish, wrote a verse comedy in five acts, and was interested in journalism.[72] His uncle, Tadeusz Bobrowski, wrote his memoirs in two volumes, published in 1900.[73] The tradition of writing was so familiar to Conrad that his own attempt at a novel had no special significance for him.

It is surprising that he had not long since begun the pastime which led to another career. There was the example of his family; there were also other writers to emulate. Conrad declared that he was "a reading boy." He continued the habit; only an inveterate reader would have taken a complete Shakespeare to sea or would have been reading Trollope the day before he began his own first novel.[74] In conversation he once acknowledged that he had excelled in composition at school.[75] A childhood friend remembered that Conrad, at eleven or twelve, used to write and act little comedies with his playmates.[76]

Yet it would be far-fetched to suppose that he sailed before the mast to get material for fiction. He left specific warnings against any such assumption: "La vie que j'ai passée à travers le vaste monde se trouve dans mes livres. Je ne cherchais pas à faire une carrière; mais il se peut que, sans le savoir, je cherchais des impressions." [77] It seems unlikely that Conrad ever took notes of these impressions. "Till I began to write that novel," he declared of *Almayer's Folly*, "I had written nothing but letters, and not very many of these. I never made a note of a fact, of an impression or of an anecdote in my life." [78] Though the statement must be qualified, like much of Conrad's autobiographical information, it appears on the whole true. Yet Captain Craig of the *Vidar*, under whom he served as first mate in 1887–88 on voyages from Singapore to Borneo, stated that Conrad was constantly writing.[79] Possibly he was keeping a diary, as he did two years later in the Congo, though he always spoke of himself as one of "those . . . who have never kept a diary or possessed a note-book in our lives."[80] In 1881 he disregarded Tadeusz Bobrowski's recommendation to send travel letters to a Warsaw newspaper, the *Wedrowiec*, but in 1886 he submitted a short story, "The Black Mate," unsuccessfully for a prize competition in *Tit-Bits*.[81]

Conrad's imagination and impressions in these days must have gone into yarns and musings. All his friends testified to his amazing ability as a raconteur.[82] A personal trait as well as a literary convenience lay behind Marlow's long monologues in *Youth*, *Lord Jim*, and *Chance*. Conrad was so given to "pensive habits (which made me sometimes dilatory in my work about the rigging)"[83] that he was once appointed night watchman of his boat. The observations of the long sea days may have found their way later into fiction.[84]

Conrad was entirely amateur in spirit and intention when he began *Almayer's Folly* in 1889. All too frequently critics have assumed that he deliberately abandoned the sea for writing. He did not take his work with the slightest seriousness. "The conception of a planned book was entirely outside my mental range when I sat down to write; the ambition of being an author had never turned up amongst these gracious imaginary existences one creates fondly for oneself at times."[85] Any other attitude would have been surprising. Not quite three years before, he had established his professional seamanship with a certificate as master. He had just returned from his first command, the *Otago*, of which he had been captain from January, 1888, to March, 1889.[86]

To all appearances he was in the early stages of a nautical success. Because of the disapproval under which he had left home and because of his distance from Poland ever since, he felt a strong dependence upon the sea.[87] He thought of himself as a member of the great British merchant marine. "I had elected to be one of them very deliberately, very completely, without any looking back or looking elsewhere," he announced not quite accurately in *Notes on Life and Letters*.[88] "The circumstances were such as to give me the feeling of complete identification, a very vivid comprehension that if I wasn't one of them I was nothing at all." During the next decade his attempts to get a command or even a fair berth do not indicate that he considered writing as an alternative career.

In the latter part of 1889, just after he had begun *Almayer's Folly*, and in 1890 he worked for the Société Anonyme Belge pour le Commerce du Haut-Congo. He had been recommended by Mme. Marguerite Poradowska, a woman of literary and social influence in Brussels and Paris, a distant connection of his. From the Société he desired the command of an ocean-going boat but received only the berth of second mate on a Congo river steamer. Africa seriously undermined his health. From January to November, 1891, when he was recuperating from tropical fever and resulting gout, he kept on writing without any thought of gain.[89] He went to Glasgow in February, 1891, in a vain hunt for a ship, before a serious relapse.[90] On March 30 he wrote Mme. Poradowska that he had been in bed a month and had declined the command of a Newcastle steamer on account of ill health.[91] During his convalescence he was manager of Thames-side warehouses, numbers 1 and 2 Dyers' Hall Wharf, 95 Upper Thames Street, E.C. 1, belonging to Barr, Moering and Company. He did not begin work until August 4.[92] On August 5 he wrote Mme. Poradowska:

J'ai commencé a travailler hier. Pour le moment je dirige l'entrepot appartenant a MM. Barr Moering.

Si je vois que je peux me faire a cette vie je resterai a Londres.

J'ai un peu de fièvre encore tous les jours; rien de serieux — seulement cela empêche de regagner les forces.[93]

The lingering fever and the demands of the position tired him so that he wrote little.[94] He began to fear that he was caught in London for good.[95]

As soon as health and opportunity permitted,[96] he went to sea as first mate on the *Torrens* from November 25, 1891, to July 26, 1893.[97] In his last voyage out on the *Torrens* Conrad showed the manuscript of *Almayer's Folly* for the first time; W. H. Jacques told him that the story was " 'distinctly' " worth finishing.[98] Commenting on the incident in 1919, Conrad appraised his ties with writing and the sea in 1892–93:

I had already then (though I did not know it myself) lived one of my lives. I was content with it. . . . I had no conception of what a literary ambition may be and I don't know that I understand it even now. . . . I didn't think of writing then. I really did not care what he [Jacques] might say. But I imagine that if he had said 'No' I would have gone on and finished that piece of writing, simply because . . . I did not care.[99]

Conrad's maritime career was over when he left the *Torrens*: "I took a long look from the quay at that last of ships I ever had under my care, and, stepping round the corner of a tall warehouse, parted from her for ever, and at the same time stepped (in merciful ignorance) out of my sea life altogether." [100]

If Conrad never went to sea again, it was not for want of seeking a berth. In the fall of 1893 he was searcning anxiously.[101] From November 29, 1893, to January 14, 1894, he was second mate of the *Adowa*, chartered to carry emigrants from France to Canada. She went no farther than Rouen.[102] When he saw that she was fated never to sail, he began immediately to look for another ship. "Je suis fort ennuyé d'avoir a quitter l''Adowa,' " he remarked. "C'etait bien commode d'avoir une occupation près d'Europe. J'ai bien peur que je serai forcé de partir pour un long voyage dans très peu de temps." [103] In December, 1893, he asked Mme. Poradowska to use her influence again to get him a job as a pilot in the Suez Canal.[104] Though he repeated the request in March, 1894, nothing came of it nor of his attempt to join the fleet of pearl fishers in Australia.[105] The *Adowa* was Conrad's last professional connection with the sea.

The search for a command was still his constant preoccupation and writing his pastime. For the last four years he had amused himself with *Almayer's Folly*. His attitude toward professional writing is suggested by his note on the novel: "My best remembered sensation about it is the perpetual surprise that I should be able to do it at all." [106] It was finished on April 24, 1894, and submitted to T. Fisher Unwin on July 4.[107] The manuscript was sent from the offices of the Shipmasters' Society, where Conrad looked for berths from Captain Froud, who had placed him on the *Adowa*.[108] On July 12, 1894, he told Mme. Poradowska:

> J'ai envoyé mon manuscript a Fisher Unwin. . . . Pas de reponse encore. Elle viendra sans doute dans la forme de renvoi de ce chef d'oeuvre en vue de quoi j'ai envoyé les timbres-poste nécéssaires. —
>
> A Vous dire toute la verité je n'eprouvre aucun interet au sort d' "Almayers Folly." — C'est fini. Du reste dans tous les cas cela ne pouvait être qu'un épisode sans conséquence dans ma vie.[109]

Conrad was so little interested in writing and so desperate that he was even willing to risk his small capital for a command:

> Vous me faites des offres de service a Bruxelles chez Pechet ou autres. Je vous dis franchement que mes ressources sont presque epuisées et qu'il faut absoluement que je trouve une occupation bien vite. . . . Si pour commander il faut y mettre de l'argent je pourrai bien deposer 12,000 fr au *premier mars 1895* PAS AVANT.[110]

He was ready to leave on a moment's notice,[111] but nothing came of his offers or Mme. Poradowska's efforts. Though he began *Two Vagabonds*, the first title of *An Outcast of the Islands*, it could have been only to while away time, for he had not yet received Unwin's acceptance of *Almayer's Folly*.[112] In the very letter of October 4 in which he announced the acceptance of *Almayer's Folly*, he added, "Les 2 Vagabonds chôment. Je suis trop occupé a courir après les navires. Rien encore de ce coté là."[113] This is not the letter of a man who sees a new way of life opening before him. He complained towards the end of the month, "A vrai dire je suis preoccupé de mes plans pour partir et comme ils n'ont pas l'air de se realiser je suis dans un état d'irritation qui ne me permet pas de m'oublier dans mon récit – par consequence le travail ne vaut rien."[114] In mid-November he denied any interest in seeing *Almayer's Folly* through the press. "Moi j'espère de . . . toute mon âme que je ne serai plus a Londres a cette époque," he insisted. "Si je reste plus longtemps a terre tout se gatera."[115]

Though Unwin's acceptance of the novel suggested another way of earning money, Conrad did not give up the old profession to develop the new. "The only doubt I suffered from, after the publication of '*Almayer's Folly*,'" he declared, "was whether I should write another line for print. . . . Neither in my mind nor in my heart had I then given up the sea."[116] At his first meeting with Edward Garnett in November, 1894, he announced almost immediately that he intended to stop writing and to go back to sea.[117] " 'You have the style,' " Garnett replied, " 'You have the temperament; why not write another?' . . . Had he said, 'Why not go on writing?' it is very probable he would have scared me away from pen and ink for ever." [118] Despite Garnett's encouragement, Conrad continued to look for a berth on the Continent as well as in England: "Rien encore d'Anvers. Je suis en negotiations avec des gens de Liverpool. Ils ont un si joli petit navire – et il a un si joli nom! 'Primera.' – Je pense que cela aboutira mais je ne suis sur de rien." [119] He even turned to the new world for an opportunity: in the winter of 1895 he was planning a business trip to Newfoundland.[120]

When his second novel, *An Outcast of the Islands*, appeared on March 16, 1896,[121] Conrad was making every effort to get to sea. He was again ready to invest capital. In February, 1896, he tried unsuccessfully to get a position as captain-sharer through Edward Garnett.[122] He also journeyed to Grangemouth to buy the barque *Windermere* and found her impossible.[123] His marriage on March 24, 1896, doubled his responsibilities.[124] Dependence upon writing for a living made creation all the harder. His excessive difficulty with *The Sisters* and *The Rescue*, both begun in 1896,[125] reflected his appalled state of mind when he realized that "only literature remains to me as a means of existence." Even when he was offered a command in early March, it was so unpromising that he refused.[126] "I was never one of those wonderful fellows," he later admitted, "that would go afloat in a wash-tub for the sake of the fun." [127] He denied in May, 1896, that "my seagoing days are over. It is not my feeling. I do hanker after the sea – it's only the want of opportunity that keeps me on shore." [128]

Opportunity continued to be wanting. Meantime Conrad published *The Nigger of the "Narcissus"* in 1897. On January 15, 1898, his situation was complicated by the birth of a son.[129] Towards the end of the month he left home to investigate a small boat with which to trade in the East.[130] In a letter of January 31 to R. B. Cunninghame Graham he confessed: "Last night a heavy gale was blowing and I lay awake thinking that I would give ever so much (the most flattering criticism) for being at sea, the soul of some patient faithful ship standing up to it, under lower topsails and no land anywhere within a thousand miles. Wouldn't I jump at a command, if some literary shipowner suddenly offered it to me!" [131] Perhaps a hint was intended, for in the summer of 1898 Cunninghame Graham tried to place him with the Union Line. The only hope was a tramp or a collier, which never materialized. Even this "shadow of possibility to go to sea" made Conrad "almost frantic with the longing to get away." [132] He had meanwhile written the five stories that were published in *Tales of Unrest* in March, 1898.[133] Towards the end of September, 1898, he went to Glasgow, and was helped by another Scotchman, Dr. McIntyre. Though he felt that "a command will come out of it sooner or later – most likely later, when the pressing need is past," he was again disappointed.[134] He wrote Cunninghame Graham, who had used his influence for him: "I had a most enjoyable trip to Glasgow. I saw Neil Munro and heaps of shipowners, and that's all I can say. The fact is from novel writing to skippering *il y a trop de tirage*. This confounded literature has ruined me entirely." [135] According to Jean-Aubry, Conrad made no further attempt to return professionally to the sea.[136]

Yet there is evidence that his purpose was not forgotten. Mrs. Conrad said, "The sea called with an insistent voice, and I should never have been surprised to find myself left alone while he made one or two more voyages before he finally settled down." [137] On October 16, 1898, he planned:

"Early next year, when that torment [*The Rescue*] is over (and I am hardly able to realise that such a time will ever come), I will without scruple use and abuse everybody's goodwill, influence, friendship to get back on the water. I am by no means happy on shore." [138] Apparently Cunninghame Graham and Dr. McIntyre continued their efforts, but Conrad was no longer expectant.[139] A momentary hope sprang up in 1905 but faded away.[140] From 1898 on his letters referred to the sea as forever in the past. His career as a professional seaman ended in deferred hopes, not in a clear decision to abandon seamanship for writing.[141]

Once Conrad gave up his first command, he never received another and had to sign on as mate. To a certain extent he had brought his difficulties on himself. He refused to "hunt up some of my old skippers" because "it would be giving up everything to begin life for the third time." [142] In the sketch of his life written for Edward Garnett, he touched on his adventurous carelessness:

> firm *never at-*
> He never *attached himself to any regular employ* or line of
> *taching him* *never attaching*
> ships; seeking variety in *his* the pursuit of his profession.[143]

Conrad left Poland primarily because of his desire to go to sea but he left the sea for want of a ship.

Maturity helped him accept the drastic change. His ideas of nautical life had been modified since he came inexperienced to the Mediterranean in 1874. Then they had been romantic, derived from nineteenth-century fiction. Conrad learned the cruelty of the sea on one of his West Indian voyages when he helped rescue the crew of a wrecked brig:

> Already I looked with other eyes upon the sea. I knew it capable of betraying the generous ardour of youth as im-

placably as, indifferent to evil and good, it would have betrayed the basest greed or the noblest heroism. My conception of its magnanimous greatness was gone. And I looked upon the true sea — the sea that plays with men till their hearts are broken, and wears stout ships to death. . . . Open to all and faithful to none, it exercises its fascination for the undoing of the best. To love it is not well.[144]

The sea's fascination for a boy born inland was transformed into an affection for ships, nobly expressed in *The Mirror of the Sea*:[145] "Indeed, I suspect that . . . the love of the sea, to which some men and nations confess so readily, is a complex sentiment wherein pride enters for much, necessity for not a little, and the love of ships – the untiring servants of our hopes and our self-esteem – for the best and most genuine part." His disillusionment probably made authorship more acceptable.

Ill-health was another reason for Conrad's taking up a new career. He confessed to Cunninghame Graham that he had "felt overtasked ever since the age of 28."[146] Probably he fixed the time by an accident which occurred in 1887, just before he was thirty.[147] He was on the *Highland Forest*, bound for Samarang, and "a piece of one of the minor spars . . . flew against [his] back, and sent him sliding on his face for quite a considerable distance along the main deck. Thereupon followed various and unpleasant consequences of a physical order . . . inexplicable periods of powerlessness, sudden accesses of mysterious pain." A doctor in Samarang told him, " 'It may be very serious for your whole life,' " and ordered him to leave his ship for three months.[148] Conrad had to stay in a hospital in Singapore for "some weeks." His illness probably accounted for his next berth, an easy one on the *Vidar*.[149]

His constitution had already been impaired before he went to the Congo in 1890. He sickened within the first month.[150] On his way up the river he had four spells of fever and at Stanley Falls an attack of dysentery that lasted five days.[151] Captain Duhst, a Dane who met Conrad in the interior, noted in his diary on October 23, 1890: " 'He is continually sick with dysentery and fever.' "[152] His condition became more and more serious. In "Heart of Darkness" he recorded how nearly fatal his illness was. When he started back to Europe he was "too sick to care" whether or not he died on the way.[153] After his arrival in England in January, 1891, he had his first attack of gout, from which he was a constant and agonized sufferer all the rest of his life. During February and March, 1891, he was in the German hospital in London, and his convalescence was so slow that he went to Champel, near Geneva, for hydropathic treatment.[154]

The Congo changed Conrad mentally and physically. Tadeusz Bobrowski now reproved him for being a pessimist,[155] and he referred to himself as "neurasthenic."[156] His stamina was so weakened that he almost declined a berth on the *Torrens* from "doubts of . . . fitness for the post, from the point of view of health."[157] Though he was on the *Torrens* for two years, the sense of unfitness persisted. It weighed heavily on his conscience and helped to reconcile him to leaving the sea. In 1893 he was sick for two weeks during his last voyage out to Australia.[158] A canceled passage in the autobiographical sketch discloses his increasing doubts:

> His health was *so* seriously *affected* and as it turned out permanently affected. After two more years at sea he *concluded* that in *common honesty* to his *employers — whoever they may*
>
> physically *decided to*
>
> be — *he was no longer fit for the sea* he *must* leave the sea. He judged himself no longer to be physically fit for the life of his choice. . . .[159]

Conrad's ability to write a book was undoubtedly an influence in separating him from the sea though not enough by itself to alter his way of life. The loosening of his ties with ships appears in a reaction against writing after he completed *Almayer's Folly*: "Neither in my mind nor in my heart had I then given up the sea. In truth I was clinging to it desperately, all the more desperately because, against my will, I could not help feeling that there was something changed in my relation to it. '*Almayer's Folly*' . . . had left the memory of an experience that, both in thought and emotion was unconnected with the sea, and I suppose that part of my moral being which is rooted in consistency was badly shaken." [160] He had established a new pattern which could be followed when the old failed. Looking back across a quarter of a century, he decided that "from the moment I had, in the simplicity of my heart and the amazing ignorance of my mind, written that page [the first page of *Almayer's Folly*] the die was cast." [161]

Conrad began writing as an amateur. The leisurely five years he spent on *Almayer's Folly* do not suggest an earnest author. *An Outcast of the Islands* was begun and continued with the same unconcern, though towards the end he became more aware of the difficulties of creation. Shortly after the publication of the second novel he mentally accepted the new work into which he had drifted. "Only literature remains to me as a means of existence," he admitted. "You understand . . . that if I have undertaken this thing, it is with the firm resolution to make a name – and I have no doubt that I shall be successful in this connection." [162] The conviction must have been only theoretical. He would not be professional until he was emotionally convinced of his ability to produce work undertaken in seriousness and completed despite difficulty.

Conviction came to Conrad when, after abandoning *The*

Sisters and *The Rescue*, he completed *The Nigger of the "Narcissus."* The novel represented a supreme effort, of which he was moved to say, "By these pages I stand or fall."[163] With *The Nigger* he reached an emotional independence declared in the Preface: "After writing the last words, . . . in the revulsion of feeling before the accomplished task, I understood that I had done with the sea, and that henceforth I had to be a writer. And almost without laying down the pen I wrote a preface, trying to express the spirit in which I was entering on the task of my new life."[164] It may seem inconsistent that, although *The Nigger* had appeared in serial and book form by November, 1897, Conrad was trying strenuously to get a command as late as September, 1898. Perhaps he was reluctant to commit himself to a life that exacted such nervous penalties. After this last effort, he made no serious attempts to escape to sea. *Lord Jim*, his next novel, with its complex conception and technique, was achieved with the determination of an established professional.

In the development of any great writer, there are always mysteries which cannot be penetrated. These are the workings of genius, the impulses which elude analysis. Their existence Conrad himself admitted: "I dare say I am compelled, unconsciously compelled, now to write volume after volume, as in past years I was compelled to go to sea, voyage after voyage. . . . I do not know which of the two impulses has appeared more mysterious and more wonderful to me. Still, in writing, as in going to sea, I had to wait my opportunity."[165] He indicated the final mystery. An urge towards certain activities has to grow in the imagination and to reach fulfilment through unpredictable influences. Conrad's two careers cast light upon each other, if only enough light to suggest the unexplainable ways of genius.

By a series of parallel driftings he became first a seaman and then a writer. His desire for the sea, fostered by reading, made him leave Poland. Family tradition, an interest in literature, and his own impressions made him write. The potential seaman was influenced by peculiar conditions in Poland that cut off any satisfactory life, and the potential novelist by failure to find a position at sea that would support him. A slow growth from amateur to professional was characteristic of Conrad in both his careers. Until he was forced by misadventures to leave the Mediterranean, he was an amateur seaman. Until he was forced to accept his dependence on writing, he was an amateur writer. But once the necessary stimulus moved him, he had the power to achieve his highest aims, to become a master seaman and a master novelist.

Chapter II

THE FOUR SOURCES

CONRAD was seldom at a loss for material. In the Preface to *The Nigger of the "Narcissus"* he asserted his absolute moral freedom to select any subject. He felt free to send "a passing glance of wonder and pity" into the dark and the splendid experiences of life.[1] He was not afraid of the pathological, though he did not dwell upon it.[2] "Morbid psychology, be it always understood," he wrote Galsworthy about the character of Hilary Dallison in *Fraternity*, "is a perfectly legitimate subject for an artist's genius." [3] Conrad's first eight books contain unshirking studies of human disintegration. Unfalteringly he traced the decay of Almayer and Willems, the more subtle deterioration of Lingard and Mrs. Travers in *The Rescue*, the sinister corruption of the Belgian agents in "An Outpost of Progress" and "Heart of Darkness." In "The Idiots" he treated actual mental disease. Yet he could also show men rising above the influences that might have led to degeneration. The seamen on the *Narcissus* kept their integrity despite the Nigger and Donkin. Karain emerged from the shadow of madness. Lord Jim established his ideal of himself on the ruins of his past life and died to defend it.

Conrad depended upon instinct to guide him toward the right sort of subject. He tenaciously believed in "that mysterious, extraneous thing which has nothing to do with the theories of art," inspiration.[4] In describing the evolution of *The Secret Agent*,[5] he revealed his instinctive recognition of what Henry James called the germ:

There must have been, however, some sort of atmosphere in the whole incident because all of a sudden I felt myself stimulated. And then ensued in my mind what a student of chemistry would best understand from the analogy of the addition of the tiniest little drop of the right kind, precipitating the process of crystallization in a test tube containing some colourless solution.

Once inspiration presented a subject, his judgment made strict demands. "The necessary preliminary assumption," as he said of *Lord Jim*,[6] was that the subject should be "interesting." He always stressed this vital characteristic which some writers have found so easy to forget. Interest was to him "the quality without which neither beauty nor, I am afraid, truth are effective. . . ."[7] A story had to contain "the telling, representative facts, helpful to carry on the idea, and, at the same time, of such a nature as not to demand an elaborate creation of the atmosphere to the detriment of the action." A story could not become "wearisome in the presentation of detail and in the pursuit of clearness."[8] After more than a decade of practice as a professional writer, he summed up his experience for Norman Douglas, who was then a beginner. "Try and make it a novel of *analysis* on the basis of some strong situation,"[9] he advised. The circumstances of Conrad's life provide a quick explanation of the formula. Analysis came naturally to the Slav who from boyhood had brooded over a family tragedy. The strong situation appealed to the man who had adventured in Marseilles and sailed the seven seas.

The subjects of the stories were not the product of an energetic inventive faculty, such as Jules Verne or Poe possessed. Time after time Conrad confessed: "I am not a facile inventor. I have some imagination, – but that's another thing."[10] When in "The Informer" and "An Anarchist" he exercised his inventive faculty,[11] the result left much to be desired. His power lay not in invention but in recollection. "One's literary life," he declared, "must turn frequently for sustenance to memories and seek discourse with the shades. . . ." [12] Creation came to him easily – at times came only – when he had some personal experience or some observation to elaborate. He gave a defense of his practice in a comment on "Gaspar Ruiz," which he called

> truly fiction, by which I do not mean that it is merely invented, but that it is truly imagined from hints of things that really happened and of people that really existed. . . . That sort of work is of course of a creative (not reminiscent) nature. . . . I need not say that such knowledge as I had was used throughout with a scrupulous regard to the truth of it. No incident was introduced arbitrarily but only as a necessary touch in the general picture. In this arrangement consists the art of story telling as distinguished from the style.[13]

Dependence upon memory added to his difficulties. Sometimes his personal knowledge of a subject prevented his altering fact to fit the purposes of fiction. In the early days of *An Outcast of the Islands* he grumbled: "Ce qui m'ennuie le plus ce que mes personnages sont si vrais. Je les connais si bien qu'ils m'entravent l'imagination." [14] More often his memory was slow to supply him with suitable material. During his first attempt at *The Rescue*, a novel not stemming from memory, he envied the propagandist whom he usually despised.[15] "Other writers," he complained to Edward Garnett in June, 1896,

> have some starting point. Something to catch hold of. They start from an anecdote — from a newspaper paragraph (a book may be suggested by a casual sentence in an old almanack) They lean on dialect — or on tradition — or on history — or on the prejudice or fad of the hour; they trade upon some tie or some conviction of their time — or upon the absence of these things — which they can abuse or praise. But at any rate they know something to begin with — while I don't. I have

had some impressions, some sensations — in my time: — impressions and sensations of common things. And it's all faded. . . .[16]

The impressions did not remain faded forever, and Conrad soon discovered that, without becoming a theorist, he could use some of the theorist's sources. Yet the disadvantages of recollection lasted into later years. In 1905 he confessed to Gosse: "Acutely conscious of being neither the interpreter in any profound sense of my own epoch nor a magician evoker of the past either in its spirit or its form, I have often suffered . . . with my work from a sense of unreality, from intellectual doubt of the ground I stood upon . . . especially in the periods of difficult production." [17] But difficulty or no, he depended for his subjects preponderantly upon memory.

Conrad felt a certain delicacy about the exploitation of the past. The repugnance showed clearly when, after writing *The Mirror of the Sea* and *A Personal Record*, he was "remonstrated with for bad economy; as if such writing were a form of self-indulgence wasting the substance of future volumes." The advice distressed him. He could not "bring himself to look upon his existence and his experience, upon the sum of his thoughts, sensations, and emotions, upon his memories and his regrets, and the whole possession of his past, as only so much material for his hands." [18] Sometimes he felt almost dishonorable. "It's an odious thing," he said, "to have to write in 'descriptive' fashion of men with whom one talked like a friend and had found acceptance as one of themselves." [19] Yet his memory was responsible for his being a writer.[20] He turned to the past, not to exploit, but "to snatch in a moment of courage, from the remorseless rush of time, a passing phase of life. . . ." [21] *Almayer's Folly* was a commemoration, *The Nigger* and "Youth" were valedictions.[22]

At times Conrad fought the charge of specialization. Vainly he emphasized the general appeal of his "subjects, which are not too specialized as to the class of people or kind of events. . . ."[23] He was niched as a writer of exotic adventure stories and tales of the sea. Though he himself admitted that from "the Eastern Seas . . . I have carried away into my writing life the greatest number of suggestions,"[24] he maintained that other aspects of his work were ignored.[25] Reviewers and readers unfortunately insisted, as William McFee complained, that Conrad was "a two-fisted shipmaster who wrote nothing but tales of adventure in the Orient, tales of brave men rescuing beautiful white girls, or equally brave men falling in love with island princesses."[26] On his visit to America in 1923 the press played him up as a " 'Spinner of sea yarns – master mariner – seaman writer,' and so forth. . . ."[27] His efforts to correct the misunderstanding were futile.[28] At the very end of his life he suggested to Curle an article pointing out that "his stories expand far beyond their frame and appeal to no special public – looking for exotism, or adventure, or the sea. . . ."[29] The labeling has endured so constantly that the manuscript of *Nostromo* was catalogued in 1938 as "Conrad's Great Sea Story."[30] The persistent classification hurt his sales all his life.[31]

In handling actual past experience, his own or another's, Conrad felt unconstrained. A few preliminary conditions had to be fulfilled. The subject – one of the many "subjects of which a writer of tales is more or less conscious within himself . . ."[32] – had to be ready for treatment. He had to await "the right moment . . . the positive feeling of it, which is a thing that cannot be discussed."[33] The right moment was unpredictable. He once explained, "*The Arrow of Gold* is a subject which I had in my mind for some eighteen years, but which I hesitated to take up till now. . . . I won't attempt to apologize for my opinion that work is not to be rushed at simply because it can be done or because one suffers from mere impatience to do it. A piece of work of any sort is only fully justified when it is done at the right time. . . ." [34] When the material matured through the chemistry of the imagination, he was seldom hampered by its connection with the actual past. "I do not write history, but fiction," he told Jean-Aubry shortly before his death, "and I am therefore entitled to choose as I please what is most suitable in regard to characters and particulars to help me in the general impression I wish to produce." [35]

The general impression often necessitated deviations from fact. Conrad commented on his adaptations of autobiographical material. "Heart of Darkness," he declared, was "experience pushed a little (and only very little) beyond the actual facts of the case for the perfectly legitimate . . . purpose of bringing it home to the minds and bosoms of the readers." [36] *The Shadow Line*, too, was "a piece of as strict autobiography as the form allowed, – I mean, the need of slight dramatization to make the thing actual. Very slight." [37] If Conrad was so unrestricted in dealing with his own experience, he must have felt even freer with the experience of others.

His freedom can be gauged from his reminiscences. "Initiation" in *The Mirror of the Sea*, written in 1905, described a rescue which took place a quarter of a century earlier.[38] The boat on which Conrad was serving "in mid-Atlantic . . . took off the crew of a Danish brig homeward bound from the West Indies." [39] The captain, a Dane, gave a long account of the wreck and a funeral oration upon his ship in the most idiomatic English.[40] In all literalness, the captain would not have spoken English, and Conrad would not have understood or remembered what he said. If the incident took place in 1875 or 1876, Conrad was on a French boat and did not yet know a word of English.[41] Since he felt so unconstrained when writing unofficial history, he could adapt his material at will to the purposes of fiction. It is consequently idle, in a study of the origins of his subjects, to look for exact correspondence. The value of such a study lies not in identification but in an understanding of Conrad's use of his raw materials.

All the ingredients which crystallized in any one story can never be reduced to a formula.[42] Yet some distinctions must be drawn between the various sources of Conrad's material. He himself believed that in the broadest sense "every novel contains an element of autobiography – and this can hardly be denied, since the creator can only express himself in his creation. . . ."[43] At once the danger of oversimplification is apparent; probably Conrad saw it more clearly than anyone. His own statement prevents misinterpretation: "The nature of the knowledge, suggestions or hints used in my imaginative work has depended directly on the conditions of my active life. It depended more on contacts, and very slight contacts at that, than on actual experience. . . ."[44] Here he made a fundamental distinction. His material was derived generally from situations and people with whom he had had no intimate connection and sometimes from personal experiences and relationships. As he himself put it, some stories, like "The Secret Sharer," grew from "facts gleaned from hearsay or experience in the various parts of the globe"; others, like "Youth," were "a record of experience in the absolute sense of the word."[45] Conrad was but affirming his own practice when he told Norman Douglas: "A man like you, who has seen things and known many people, has got only to descend within himself for material."[46] He might find subjects in another man's life or in his own, but each was capable of imaginative transformation into fiction. If memory yielded nothing, Conrad drew upon another source: the printed page.[47] He was to mine all lodes as instinct moved him.

He began with subjects that he had found in observation of other people's lives. Soon afterwards he made use of his own experience – "experience in the absolute sense of the word." [48] Before the end of the century he turned to hearsay and books for inspiration. The three novels emphasized in this study may not be derived exclusively from one source. Yet predominantly *Almayer's Folly* was based upon observation, *The Nigger of the "Narcissus"* upon more personal experience, and *Lord Jim* upon hearsay and reading.

The indelible impression made by one personality was responsible for Conrad's career as a writer. "But if I had not got to know Almayer pretty well," he insisted, "it is almost certain there would never have been a line of mine in print." [49] He met Almayer in Borneo during his voyages out of Singapore on the *Vidar* in 1887–88.[50] The supposed facts about Almayer were set forth in *Joseph Conrad: Life and Letters* by Jean-Aubry, who apparently obtained them from Captain Craig of the *Vidar*, under whom Conrad had served as first mate.[51] Almayer – for such his name was believed to be in real life also – was a Eurasian, a Dutch half-caste, living in Bulungan up the Bulungan River in East Borneo. Married to a full-blooded Malay, he had one son. He died of a wound received on a python hunt.[52] When Captain Craig talked to Jean-Aubry in 1924, he was seventy and had been a seaman for half a century.[53] He was naturally somewhat confused in his recollections. His memory failed him on many of the facts about Almayer, and unintentionally Jean-Aubry preserved the mistakes in print.

In the summer of 1939 I visited Bulungan to inquire about the people whom, according to Captain Craig, Conrad met there and later introduced into many of his Malayan stories. I discovered that the originals of the characters had lived not in Bulungan but in Berouw (sometimes called Tandjong Redeb) on the Berouw River. The manuscript of *Almayer's Folly* contains a clue for this discovery. Though Conrad called the river in the novel the Pantai, he referred to it twice in the manuscript as the Brow, a mistake which he corrected before the typescript was made.[54] And Sambir, the name of the village in the novel, was once called Brow in the manuscript, a slip allowed to stand in the typescript and the published text.[55] The differences in the spelling of Berouw are of no account, for Western phonetic renderings of Malay differ greatly.

In Bulungan I learned that one of Almayer's surviving children was Mrs. Andrew Gray of Malang, Java. I obtained an interview with her and Mr. Gray. What she and her husband could remember about Conrad's acquaintances in Borneo I was able to supplement with the records of the Peneleh Cemetery in Sourabaya, Java, with a letter from Mr. V. A. Cools, a resident in Berouw since 1904, and with the recollections of Mr. Pangemanan, now of Bulungan, a resident of Berouw from 1919 to 1925.

Kaspar Almayer of *Almayer's Folly* was drawn from William Charles Olmeijer of Berouw, where Conrad knew him in 1887–88. It is impossible to tell why Conrad altered the name when he kept so many real names in the same novel. Usually he found it hard to call a character drawn from life by any but his actual name. Writing to Mme. Poradowska in 1894 about one of her stories, he confessed: "Du moment que Vous *voyez* le personnage comme Wojtek il est impossible de changer le nom. Je comprends cela très bien."[56] In "Heart of Darkness" when the sinister Mr. Kurtz was first introduced, Conrad called him Klein, the real name of the Belgian agent at Stanley Falls,[57] and corrected it immediately:

meet Kurtz
In the interior you will no doubt *Monsieur* Mr. *Klein*. . . .[58]

Twice more on the same page he corrected Klein to Kurtz, which he then followed throughout. In *The Shadow Line* he gave the first mate, drawn from life, the name Burns, but the man's real name, Born, slipped once into the manuscript:

sensations urns
. . . my own *thoughts* which were not those of Mr. B*orn*.[59]

Though the change of Olmeijer to Almayer was almost as slight, Conrad did not betray the name in the manuscript.

William Charles Olmeijer was born in Sourabaya, according to Mrs. Gray, who did not remember the year or the names of her grandparents. She referred me to the Peneleh Cemetery which contains a whitewashed brick vault, number B821, bearing a single plaque: Carel Olmeijer, born in Grissee, October 16, 1799, died in Sourabaya, "Deeply regretted by his children." The records of Peneleh Cemetery state that he died on November 17, 1877, aged 78. Grissee is some thirty miles northwest of Sourabaya. The children were presumably those listed in the cemetery records as also buried in the vault: two daughters and three sons, including [William] Charles Olmeijer. The records also mention a Casper Olmeijer, who died in 1875 and who is not buried in the vault. Mrs. Gray believed that the Olmeijer family settled in Java probably in the eighteenth century, but she was not sure whether they originated in Holland or Germany.

The cemetery records reveal that William Charles Olmeijer was born in 1848. If he was Eurasian as Captain Craig declared, the family had been in the Indies long enough to intermarry with natives or Eurasians. Mrs. Gray recalled that her father left Java for Borneo when a young man, and, according to Mr. Cools, he arrived in Berouw in 1870. His daughter believed that he married at about the age of twenty-six – therefore in 1874; Mrs. Olmeijer's maiden name was Johanna Cornelia van Lieshout. There is little doubt that she was at least Eurasian. Mr. Pangemanan called her a Malay, and Mr. Cools, a Javanese and Olmeijer's concubine. Photographs show her and her daughters to be decidedly native in appearance. The Olmeijers had eleven children, five sons and six daughters. The oldest child was named William Charles Carel, after his father and grandfather, and the third child and first daughter, born in 1876, was named Johanna Elizabeth, now Mrs. Gray.

According to the Grays, Olmeijer was a trader in guttah, rattan, and rubber and shipped his "produits forestiers," as Mr. Cools called them, through Captain Lingard. The two men shared trading interests. Olmeijer made and lost a fortune in rubber. Mr. Gray emphasized the respect felt for his father-in-law by everyone, particularly the Dyaks, who used to call him Rajah Dyak. But, Mr. Gray added significantly, the Dutch authorities, who were stupid and venal, were always against Olmeijer and mistrusted his friendship with the Dyaks.

Olmeijer died in Sourabaya after an operation for cancer, according to his daughter. His convalescence was impeded by fits of coughing which prevented the incision from healing. Though the Grays could remember only that he died about the turn of the century, the Peneleh records establish the date as September 2, 1900, and Olmeijer's age as fifty-two. Mr. Gray cleared his estate and became guardian of the children.

In *Almayer's Folly* Conrad used what facts he wanted from Olmeijer's life and altered or discarded the rest. He made Almayer a native of Buitenzorg and of pure Dutch parentage, which increased the humiliation of his marriage and that of his daughter with Malays. Here Conrad completely disregarded the normal Dutch tolerance for Eurasians and laid himself open to Sir Hugh Clifford's charge that he did not understand Malayan life. Almayer came to Borneo as a young man to be Lingard's agent in the handling of forest products which the English Captain exported on his brig. In later life Almayer got into trouble with the Dutch authorities for his intimacy with the natives, to whom he was suspected of selling gunpowder. Though Olmeijer had a large family, Conrad allowed Almayer only a daughter, the focal point of her father's affection, ambition, and final disappointment. The change was fundamental to the conception of the story, which in its melodramatic development illustrated the drastic changes wrought by Conrad's imagination on the facts of Olmeijer's life. Olmeijer did not die until the novel had been out five years, and his death was very different from Almayer's fatal degeneration.

Clearly *Almayer's Folly* was not a record of the life of William Charles Olmeijer but an expansion of the impression made upon the novelist by the man's personality. In *A Personal Record* Conrad left a non-fictional account of the psychological and physical impression Olmeijer made upon him at their first encounter in Berouw. He still called the man Almayer, and *A Personal Record*, it must be remembered, was written long after *Almayer's Folly*. Almayer the character may well have colored Conrad's supposedly untouched recollections of Olmeijer the man. Yet to compare the two Almayers casts light on the novelist's imaginative use of his recollections. Captain Craig of the *Vidar*, who knew Olmeijer much longer than Conrad and who became an enthusiastic reader of the work of his old first mate, called Almayer "an exact moral and physical portrait." [60] The moral impression made by Olmeijer Conrad stressed in fiction and the physical in *A Personal Record.* The comparison brings out Conrad's selection of the morbid side of Olmeijer's character, which, though apparent to the novelist and the officers of the *Vidar*, was naturally not the side emphasized by the Grays and Mr. Cools.

In *A Personal Record* [61] Almayer's face was "round and flat"; his hair was long and black "and a curly wisp of it strayed across his forehead." The years added to his age in *Almayer's Folly* brought with them gray hair, and the forehead lock was shorn. Perhaps its place was taken by "the long white beard" of his old age.[62] The "flapping pyjamas of cretonne pattern (enormous flowers with yellow petals on a disagreeable blue ground) and a thin cotton singlet with short sleeves," which Olmeijer wore when Conrad first saw him on a misty Bornean morning, were transformed in the novel into something more native, "a white jacket and flowered sarong." [63]

Though most of the details of Olmeijer's life were altered, the morose aspects of his disposition seem to have been elaborated for the novel. Even the physical characteristics which suggested his sullenness were emphasized. Conrad was so impressed by the actual man's "heavy, pained glance" that he made his creation "sulky-looking." [64] Olmeijer's suspicion, elaborated in the novel, was noted in *A Personal Record.*[65] His "deep-seated mistrust" grew from his desire for success. He appeared "ambitious, aiming at the grandiose," full "of some deep scheme, of some diplomatic plan, of some hopeful intrigue." [66] Almayer revealed just such a personality. His "dream of wealth and power" [67] was ambitious and grandiose, built on a fantastic desire to discover an inexhaustible El Dorado. Olmeijer hinted to Conrad about his " 'very large interests . . . very important interests . . . up the river.' "[68] These vague references to vast wealth were defined in *Almayer's Folly* as a gold mine in the interior.

Olmeijer's pretensions were treated as a joke by the officers of the *Vidar*, where Conrad heard his name frequently and derisively mentioned.[69] General laughter at Olmeijer's expense was perhaps echoed in the amusement which Almayer inspired in the Dutch officers visiting Sambir.[70] Conrad minimized Olmeijer's claims to distinction. He ridiculed his flock of white geese, " 'the only geese on the East Coast' " of Borneo. Olmeijer sent a goose to the officers of the *Vidar* "as if it were a sort of Court decoration."[71] Perhaps the disparity between the man's conception of his greatness and the means whereby he showed it impressed the incident on Conrad. In the novel when the officers from the Dutch gunboat came to Almayer's house, he said to them, " 'I can give you a goose. Look at my geese – the only geese on the east coast – perhaps on the whole island.' " The phrase, " 'the only geese on the east coast,' " must have been used by the actual man: Conrad employed it again towards the end of the novel.[72]

Olmeijer's house was described by Mr. Gray as unusually large for Berouw and as old-fashioned, with numerous guns in the wall racks. It must have been pretentious because it was nicknamed Olmeijer's Folly by the captain of the *Vidar*.[73] In the novel much was made of the ruinous condition of the mansion which Almayer built to house his future splendor and where he hid his destitute old age. Indeed Almayer's Folly, "his new but already decaying house – that last failure of his life," was symbolic of the futility of his dreams. The nickname in the novel was bestowed upon the house by the officers of the Dutch gunboat, whom Conrad patterned upon the officers of the *Vidar*.[74]

Olmeijer hated his surroundings and was "always complaining of being lost to the world. . . ." [75] Similarly Almayer was always dreaming of escaping from Sambir to the Europe he had never seen.[76] Conrad twice described the attitude of the actual man as "aggrieved." " 'Nothing was ever quite worthy of you,' " he explained to him in an imagined conversation in *A Personal Record*.[77] " 'What made you so real to me was that you held this lofty theory with some force of conviction and with an admirable consistency.' " Conrad's imagination expanded Olmeijer's self-pity for the latter part of the novel. A sense of grievance caused Almayer's final repudiation of Nina and drove him to burn his old house, to segregate himself in Almayer's Folly from the rest of Sambir, and to drug himself to death.[78] On the lack of "faith, hope or pride," the "absence of any sort of sustaining spirit," [79] which Conrad noticed in Olmeijer, he based Almayer's psychological and moral degeneration. Obviously Conrad selected the aspect of Olmeijer which appealed to his imagination and developed it as if it were the whole man. It is indeed necessary to distinguish not so much between the Almayers in *A Personal Record* and *Almayer's Folly* as between Olmeijer and Conrad's Almayer.

Of the other figures in *Almayer's Folly* Conrad had little to say, and that little was somewhat ambiguous. *A Personal Record* [80] implied that each character was suggested in some measure by a personality he encountered in Berouw. Yet a study of "the rest of that Pantai band" shows that their origin was complex.

Mrs. Almayer of Sambir, a full-blooded Malay, bore slight resemblance to Mrs. Olmeijer of Berouw, who was a Malay or a Eurasian. Both women were married young, but Mrs. Almayer lived to old age,[81] whereas Mrs. Olmeijer died at thirty-five, according to Mrs. Gray. Conrad provided Mrs. Almayer with a background of violence for which no similarity in fact can be discovered, and the manuscript of the novel reveals changes in details made as he worked out the characterization. He referred first to "the romantic story of some child – a girl – rescued from a piratical prau." Probably the implication that the girl was held against her will prompted him to correct it in the manuscript to "the romantic tale of some child – a girl – found in a piratical prau." [82] She was called the granddaughter of the Sultan of Sulu, and in the manuscript had originally been the daughter of the captain of a Sulu piratical prau, though in the final reading her exact paternity was canceled.[83] As a young girl she sailed with Sulu pirates on their raids, until Lingard exterminated them. He adopted her, had her educated in a convent in Java, and then married her to Almayer.[84] The convent moved elusively around the island to Java. First it was mentioned unspecifically as "some convent in Java"; next it was declared to be in Sourabaya and then in Samarang.[85] Mrs. Almayer's conventual education was perhaps derived from the experience of five of Olmeijer's daughters, who were sent to a convent in Sourabaya, according to Mrs. Gray, herself brought up as a protestant in Macassar. No closer connection between fact and fiction can be traced.

The origin of Nina Almayer is even more obscure. Mrs. Gray never heard of a Nina in her family. The Olmeijers had six daughters, of whom the eldest could not have been more than twelve in 1887–88; it is unlikely that Conrad had one of them in mind as his heroine. Nina Almayer was sent away from Borneo to be educated, and this possibly reflected the education of Olmeijer's daughters. By allowing Almayer one child and that a girl Conrad increased the isolation of his hero. Nina's love affair with Dain Maroola gave an extra pang to " 'the very anguish of paternity' " [86] stressed in the characterization of Almayer. Nina's crossed strains of Malayan and European provided a heroine of a type that attracted Conrad during his experiences in the East. Years after he completed the novel he confessed, "A dash of Orientalism on white is very fascinating, at least for me; though I must say that the genuine Eastern had never the power to lead me away from the path of rectitude; to any serious extent – that is." [87] The temptation to see in Nina the reflection of a particular personal experience must be firmly repressed.

Lingard played an increasingly important role in the three novels in which he appeared. The Tom Lingard of *Almayer's Folly* and *An Outcast* was apparently founded upon a Captain Tom Lingard whom Conrad met at Berouw. The actual Lingard was a Scotchman, according to Mr. Cools, a trader of considerable consequence. He paid the Sultan of Sambaliung, who ruled Berouw, a relatively large yearly tax of seven hundred florins. He had business connections with the Getle Company of Singapore, and Captain Craig remembered him as "the captain of a schooner which traded between Singapore, Benjarmassim, Cottu, Bulungan, and other Dutch places to the north." [88] Lingard and Olmeijer shared many commercial interests. Mrs. Gray recalled that her father shipped his goods by Lingard's schooner when there was no direct line between Borneo and Java and all shipments had to go via Singapore. Mr. Cools added that before coming to live at Berouw Lingard represented Olmeijer in Bulungan. Lingard's voyages brought him high renown. He was called Rajah Laut by the Malays and he discovered a channel for ships in the Berouw River still called on the official chart "Baak van Lingard."

It is easy to see what Conrad was inspired to borrow for

the Tom Lingard of *Almayer's Folly*. An English trader called Rajah Laut by the Malays, he sailed everywhere in the Dutch East Indies. In Borneo he discovered the channel of the dangerous Pantai River. He guarded the secret jealously, became rich on the trade monopoly, and was a power in the little native state, Sambir. He took Almayer on his schooner as supercargo and then established him as land agent in Sambir to collect goods for shipment. Marrying Almayer to his adopted Malay daughter, Lingard treated him like a son.

The connection between Lingard and Almayer suggests a relationship Conrad observed in Berouw. The actual Captain Lingard, according to Mrs. Gray and Mr. Pangemanan, married a sister of Olmeijer's, but the couple was childless. Lingard had a nephew, Jim Lingard, whom he took as an associate on his ship and later helped to set up as a trader in Berouw. Another nephew, Joshua Lingard, brother of Jim, suspected that Conrad was the author of the stories in which the inhabitants of Berouw appeared as characters. "I had a visit from a man out of the Malay Seas," Conrad wrote Pinker in 1909. "It was like the raising of a lot of dead – dead to me, because most of them live out there and even read my books and wonder who [the] devil has been around taking notes. My visitor told me that Joshua Lingard made the guess: 'It must have been the fellow who was mate in the *Vidar* with Craig.' . . . And the best of it is that all these men of 22 years ago feel kindly to the Chronicler of their lives and adventures." [89]

Jean-Aubry suggested that another inspiration from Conrad's past experience went into Lingard, "traits . . . borrowed from Dominic Cervoni, who, from Conrad's first seafaring days to the end of his literary life, was a sort of familiar demon of his imagination." [90] Perhaps to some extent Cervoni directed Conrad's imagination when he was creating any intensely masculine figure. Yet the characters admittedly modeled on Cervoni [91] all exhibit a grave, ironic, experienced personality in direct contrast with the violent, sentimental and naïve Lingard. Another influence can also be traced. The conception of Lingard in *The Rescue* apparently owed much to the diaries and letters of the Rajah James Brooke of Sarawak,[92] of whom more will be said in connection with *Lord Jim*.

Conrad modeled some of the minor white characters upon his acquaintances. He gave old Hudig, the great merchant of Macassar who at one time employed both Almayer and Willems, the name and possibly the personality of a Dutch merchant whom he knew in Amsterdam during the winter of 1887 just before he went to Borneo.[93] The account of the actual man can be found in *The Mirror of the Sea*: [94] "Mr. Hudig . . . was a big, swarthy Netherlander, with black moustaches and a bold glance. He always began by shoving me into a chair before I had time to open my mouth, gave me cordially a large cigar, and in excellent English would start to talk everlastingly about the phenomenal severity of the weather." Though Conrad nowhere described the appearance of the fictional Hudig, he seems to have borrowed mannerisms from the actual man. The cordiality was heightened for the merchant's boisterous way with visiting captains, whom he pushed into his inner office and plied with liquor and tobacco.[95] Though in *Almayer's Folly* Hudig spoke in broken English, in the first draft his English was far less foreign than it was after Conrad worked on it.[96] The broken English was completely abandoned in *An Outcast*.[97] Probably Conrad always thought of the character as speaking "excellent English," like the original. In outline, the Hudig of Macassar seems to have sprung directly from the Hudig of Amsterdam.

Another figure who apparently stood for a thumbnail

sketch in *Almayer's Folly* was the captain of the *Vidar*, who appeared as Captain Ford. The *Vidar* was a steamer, owned by an Arab, like Ford's boat in the novel.[98] Both Conrad and Jean-Aubry were reticent about the captain's true name: in *A Personal Record*[99] Conrad called him Captain C– and Jean-Aubry followed the disguise even after an interview with him. From an inadvertent reference in one of Conrad's letters he can be identified as Captain Craig.[100]

Conrad's connection with the *Vidar* provided him with many of the arresting natives in *Almayer's Folly* and *An Outcast*. The *Vidar* "belonged to an Arab called Syed Mosin Bin S. Ali Jaffree,"[101] a descendant of Mohammed, as the designation Syed shows. His actual son Abdulla[102] appeared in *Almayer's Folly* as "the great trader of Sambir." Conrad supplied the fictional Abdulla with a nephew, "Syed Reshid, returned from his pilgrimage to Mecca, rejoicing in . . . the proud title of Hadji."[103] He created his fictional Arabs by moving the actual Arabs forward one generation. In the manuscript of *Almayer's Folly*[104] is a passage which referred originally to "Syed Abdulla, then establishing *his* a trading post for his venerable father Moshin – the richest Arab in Singapore." In the printed text Moshin was completely dropped, and his place taken by Abdulla who owned the steamer that corresponded to the *Vidar*.[105] The fictional Reshid, who had no existence in real life, was put into the generation of the actual Abdulla, upon whom he was modeled. Reshid did not appear in *An Outcast*, where the career of Abdulla bore a close resemblance to the career of Reshid in *Almayer's Folly*. "Son of the rich Syed Selim bin Sali, the great Mohammedan trader of the Straits," Conrad said of Abdulla in *An Outcast*,[106] "he went forth at the age of seventeen . . . to the Holy Shrine." In *A Personal Record*[107] Abdullah bin Selim of Berouw was mentioned as Almayer's enemy, and in the novels he was the cause of Almayer's financial ruin. Conrad saw the owner of the *Vidar* only "once, quite accidentally." Syed Mosin was standing on the wharf "having his hand severely kissed by a crowd of Malay pilgrims to whom he had done some favour, in the way of food and money."[108] The episode was so fixed in Conrad's mind that before he used it in *The Shadow Line* he applied it to Abdulla in *An Outcast*.[109]

Other native figures owed their origin to some suggestion that came to Conrad from his *Vidar* days. In *Almayer's Folly* the Chinaman Jim-Eng seems to have derived his name from a Sing Jimmung of Singapore to whom Babalatchi shipped goods on the *Vidar*.[110] In *An Outcast of the Islands* Daoud Sahamin, Hamet Bahassoen, and Mahmat Banjer may have been taken from Abdulla Bahasoean of Singapore and Sahamin Orang Banjar of Berouw who used the *Vidar* to trade with each other.[111] According to Mr. Cools, Patalolo, the name given the old Rajah of Sambir, was taken from Patalolo, Sultan of Dongala, Celebes, where the *Vidar* touched.[112] Conrad described him, without mentioning his name, as a "fat, dingy Rajah" who "came on board in a friendly way with only two attendants, and drank bottle after bottle of soda-water on the after-skylight."[113] At Dongala Conrad saw Babalatchi and probably Lakamba, "merchants . . . much respected by the inhabitants, and their remarkable appearance attracted [his] attention."[114] Though he left no other account of them to compare with the descriptions in *Almayer's Folly*, these are sufficiently remarkable to be direct portraits. The fictional Lakamba had a "portly form," "small eyes," "a satisfied and furtive smile"; he wore a "green turban and gold-embroidered jacket." Babalatchi "was perfectly repulsive, possessing only one eye and a pock-marked face, with nose and lips horribly disfigured by the smallpox."[115] Lakamba was transformed into the Rajah of Sambir, or Sultan as he was sometimes called, and Babalatchi into Lakamba's "prime minister, harbour master, financial adviser, and general factotum." [116] The manuscript of *Almayer's Folly* [117] shows that Conrad once considered making Babalatchi "of Chinese origin" but substituted Sulu.

Dain Maroola, Nina's romantic lover, owed his name, according to Mr. Cools, to Dain Marola of Berouw.[118] Marola was a Bugis who acted as Bornean agent for Syed Mosin Bin S. Ali Jaffree, the owner of the *Vidar*, and hence Conrad as mate must have seen much of him. His store, a large building eighteen by thirty-six meters, is now Mr. Cools' home. Conrad did not decide at once upon the place from which Maroola should come. In the manuscript he came from Lombok; in the typescript from Bali.[119] Yet Lombok remained in Conrad's imagination as the home of Maroola: Babalatchi spoke of sending him back to his father the rajah in Ampanam, the principal city of Lombok.[120] As Conrad apparently never visited Lombok or Bali, there was no apparent reason for the change. He was not sure of the geography of either island, for at first he described Bali as dominated by several mountain peaks and then corrected it to one supreme peak.[121]

Conrad's free use of past associations extended even to the geography of *Almayer's Folly*. His four months on the *Vidar* gave him first-hand knowledge of many places in the East Indies that provided a setting for his stories. The trading steamer, according to Jean-Aubry, traveled from Singapore through Carimata Strait to Banjarmassim on the south coast of Borneo; then through Pulo Laut Strait, with a stop at the island of Pulo Laut for coal, and across the Strait of Macassar to Dongala on the west coast of Celebes; back across the Strait to Berouw and Bulungan on the east coast of Borneo.[122] To these ports of call Richard Curle, who must have been informed by Conrad himself, added "Palawan in the Sulu Sea and Palambang in Sumatra," [123] and Mr. Cools added Samarinda.

In *Almayer's Folly* Conrad gave a general geographic setting but avoided specific identification of places. In all his later stories he followed the same principle. He wished to stimulate, not limit the reader's imagination. The names of countries and large cities were sufficiently general, he believed, to be given without danger from the reader's associations. Yet exactness in the names of small villages and districts might be dangerous because of discrepancies between the description and the actual spot. He made his point of view plain in rebuking Richard Curle:

> Didn't it ever occur to you . . . that I knew what I was doing in leaving the facts of my life and even of my tales in the background? Explicitness . . . is fatal to the glamour of all artistic work, robbing it of all suggestiveness, destroying all illusions. . . . In "Youth," in which East or West are of no importance whatever, I kept the name of the Port of landing out of the record of "poeticized" sensations. The paragraph you quote of the East meeting the narrator is all right in itself; whereas directly it's connected with . . . it becomes nothing at all . . . is a damned hole without any beach and without any glamour, and in relation to the parag. is not in tone. Therefore the par., when pinned to a particular spot, must appear diminished — a fake. And yet it is true! [124]

Of the islands Conrad visited on the *Vidar* Borneo was the most important for *Almayer's Folly*, and it is revealed as the general setting of the story in the eighth paragraph.[125] Though Almayer lived on the east coast, the identification is not too exact, since Borneo is the second largest island in the world and the east coast some eight hundred miles long. The reader is able to associate with such a broad background all he may have imagined about the East Indies.

In treating the specific scene of the novel Conrad was more cautious. Since he met Almayer and many of the other characters up the Berouw River in the little settlement of Berouw, the actual place-names might be expected. Yet he never mentioned them in *A Personal Record* or the Author's Note of *An Outcast of the Islands*, in which he discussed the origins of the characters. For the river in the novel he borrowed the name Pantai from the southern mouth of the Berouw, a disguise that half reveals. In the manuscript he twice referred to the fictional Pantai as the Brow, inconsistencies corrected by the time the typescript was made.[126] He took greater precautions to prevent the identification of Berouw with Sambir, the name of the settlement in the novel. Yet he slipped once into calling the place Brow, a blunder that stood in the manuscript, typescript, and printed text.[127] In the manuscript the settlement was sixty miles from the sea, but in the typescript the distance was only thirty miles.[128] Perhaps he remembered that Berouw lay up river "forty miles . . . more or less." [129] Though no Sambir can be found on the map of Borneo, he may have adopted the name from Tandjong (or Point) Sambar, which the *Vidar* passed just east of Carimata Strait, or from an abbreviation of Sambaliung, a name for Berouw on some maps. At Berouw the Berouw River forks; the northern branch is called the Sega and the southern, the Kelai. In the novel the division was mentioned as "the two branches of the Pantai" – "the main stream of the Pantai" and "the Sambir reach." [130] The settlement of Berouw itself is composed of two main villages, Gunung Tabur and Tandjong Redeb, sometimes called Sambaliung. Sambir itself was divided into two settlements: Almayer lived on one side of the river and Lakamba on the other.[131]

Conrad first used and later discarded material that he must have picked up by direct contact. The young man whose indecorous attentions produced Nina's rift with Mrs. Vinck was described in the manuscript as " 'that young fellow from Katz's Brothers' " and "the employé of Messers: Katz Bthers";[132] in the printed text he was called " 'that young fellow from the bank' " and "the young man from the bank."[133] Possibly Katz Brothers was then so well known in the East that Conrad decided to avoid the name. Of the Vincks he made an inconsistent double use. Mr. Vinck was first a clerk of old Hudig's in Macassar.[134] Later the Vincks were reintroduced as "good friends" of Lingard's in Singapore with whom Nina went to live.[135] At some time Conrad must have been strongly impressed by people named Vinck.

Somewhere in Celebes and Borneo he probably came upon a political assassination. Sketching the background of *An Outcast of the Islands*, he describes Sambir as "un petit etat malais, dont le dernier mot est: empoisonnement."[136] There is no poisoning in *An Outcast*, and it has been removed from *Almayer's Folly*, although at first the old Rajah of Sambir was murdered. The manuscript, typescript, and first edition differ from the final version:

> Lakamba's visits had ceased when, by a convenient decree of providence and the help of a little scientific manipulation, the old ruler of Sambir departed this life.[137]

> Lakamba's visits had ceased when, by a convenient decree of Providence the old ruler of Sambir departed this life.[138]

Much talk of poisoning remains in the definitive edition.[139]

In his first novel Conrad was trying his imagination upon characters and situations with which he had not been intimately connected. He took actual people and added to their experiences and personalities. He felt free to borrow names, traits of character, events, and backgrounds from his own observation and to shape them as his creative instinct dictated. Such selection was natural to his method of building up a story. Since he never planned his work as a whole, there was every opportunity to add to his original conception. Consequently in any analysis of the sources of his work many of the stories must appear under two classifications and a few under three.

Some stories were so fundamentally the product of observation that minor contributions from other sources must not be exaggerated. *An Outcast of the Islands*, like *Almayer's Folly*, arose primarily from Conrad's acquaintance in Borneo.[140] The Grays recalled that a Dutchman named De Veer lived with Olmeijer in Berouw and that no one else was a regular dependent. De Veer had a broken wrist and a weakness for alcohol. Whether or not De Veer suggested Willems, Conrad had first-hand knowledge of Willems' passion for Aissa – "l'esclavage physique de l'homme par une femme absolument sauvage j'ai vu ça!" [141] It has been briefly noticed in print that the material of the immediate action of *The Sisters* provided the antecedent action of *The Arrow of Gold*.[142] In the later and professedly autobiographical [143] *Arrow of Gold* Conrad recounted his love affair with the Rita who was the heroine of both stories. He must have based *The Sisters* upon observation of Rita and upon the account of her past, in which he played no part but which he probably had directly from her. "The Idiots" was inspired by a glimpse of the unfortunate children themselves.[144] Amy Foster was a servant in the Conrad household for years and impressed the writer with "her animal-like capacity for sheer uncomplaining endurance." [145] Some of the personages in *The Secret Agent* [146] and "The Partner" [147] were drawn from real people and possibly also in "Falk" [148] and "Because of the Dollars." [149] The Author's Note of *Victory* [150] emphasized the importance of observation for Heyst, Lena, Pedro, Ricardo, and Mr. Jones. And glimpses as brief as snap-shots lay behind parts of *Lord Jim*[151] and "Prince Roman."[152]

In *The Nigger of the "Narcissus"* Conrad first used a subject from his own experience. Unlike many authors, who unburden themselves in an autobiographical novel, he left to his sixth story events in which he had played an active part. Even so, he himself was not the center of interest in *The Nigger*, as he was later in "Youth" and "Heart of Darkness." In contrast to his earlier work, *The Nigger* must be considered "a record of experience in the absolute sense of the word." Conrad, as an officer of the *Narcissus*, lived through the storm and the sickness and death of the Nigger, whereas he had no share in the lives of Almayer, Willems, and the others.

A curious inconsistency makes it apparent that Conrad was writing about personal experience. At the beginning he did not appear as a character but told the story omnisciently. On the thirty-third page he entered the story in describing how incidents happened to *us*.[153] Though he was included in this collective *we*, he was not second officer of the *Narcissus*, as he was in actuality,[154] but one of the crew. He took part in the rescue of Wait during the storm: five men went to look for the Nigger, and since four of them were mentioned by name as the boatswain, Belfast, Wamibo, and Archie,[155] Conrad himself must have been the fifth, who told what occurred. At the very end of the novel, he emerged from the collective *we* into his own person as *I*.[156] Whatever may explain the inconsistencies in point of view, they bring Conrad into the novel as an actor and confirm the autobiographical quality of *The Nigger*.

Conrad left information about *The Nigger* which shows how his imagination turned personal experience into fiction.

In 1914 he implied that the novel was founded on an actual voyage,[157] and in 1923 he allowed Richard Curle to state in an article that "the story of 'The Nigger of the Narcissus' is founded on an actual voyage from Bombay to England made by the author in a ship of that name." [158] Conrad signed on the sailing ship *Narcissus* as second officer at Bombay late in April, 1884, after giving up a berth on a steamer of the British India Line because he was charmed by the beauty of the *Narcissus*.[159] On the voyage he was "acting mate of her (the proper mate crazy – melancholia). . . ." [160] His instantaneous affection for the ship was also felt by the characters in *The Nigger*.[161] The actual *Narcissus* left Bombay on April 28 and reached Dunkirk on October 16.[162] The voyage of more than five months was reflected in the comments on the "long passage" of the *Narcissus* of fiction, though Conrad cut it by a month.[163] The principal events of the real voyage – "an awful gale in the vicinity of the Needles, south of the cape," and the death of a Negro member of the crew [164]– were incorporated into the novel. Conrad altered the sequence of events, for the death of the Negro of the actual *Narcissus* took place "just" after the storm south of the Cape. Conrad said nothing of a near mutiny over the illness of the Negro such as occurred in the story. He remembered that a sailor brought some coffee to the Negro's berth shortly before he died, and in the novel the cook brought Wait " 'a pot of cold tea for your night's drinking' " on the evening of the mutiny.[165] The real Negro died between five and six o'clock in the morning, and James Wait just at dawn.[166]

Into his experiences on the *Narcissus* Conrad wove memories of other passages. The actual ship docked at Dunkirk in Northern France, but "from other voyages . . . made under similar circumstances" he introduced into the novel a superb description of the progress of the *Narcissus* down the Channel, up the Thames, to her pier in London, and also a last glimpse of her crew as they were paid off in the Board of Trade Office on Tower Hill.[167] Sailing up the Thames so stirred him that he amplified the description in *The Mirror of the Sea*.[168] Into the crew of the *Narcissus* he introduced "the two Scandinavians from associations with another ship." [169]

"Most of the personages . . . ," Conrad told Jean-Aubry, "actually belonged to the crew of the real *Narcissus*, including the admirable Singleton (whose real name was Sullivan), Archie, Belfast, and Donkin." [170] All through the manuscript he called "the admirable Singleton" by his real name, Sullivan, though in the serial the pseudonym Singleton was given him, perhaps because of the presence of another Irishman, Belfast, in the novel.[171] Of the officers Conrad made no mention.[172] The character of the Nigger in the novel was modeled closely upon the Negro in the crew of the *Narcissus*.[173] "I had much to do with him," Conrad declared in the preface entitled "To My Readers in America." "He was in my watch. A Negro in a British forecastle is a lonely being. He has no chums. Yet James Wait, afraid of death and making her his accomplice was an impostor of some character – mastering our compassion, scornful of our sentimentalism, triumphing over our suspicions." [174] He visited the Negro in the sick-bay a little before he died, just as Donkin did, though certainly not with the same intent.[175] The Negro's name Conrad had forgotten, and he took the name James Wait from "another nigger we had on board the *Duke of Sutherland*." [176] From the arrival of the actual James Wait aboard the *Duke of Sutherland* he contrived the dramatic opening scene of the novel.[177] *The Nigger of the "Narcissus"* shows how his imagination worked on his "experience in the absolute sense of the word," how he adapted and added until he had produced those pages by which he was willing to " 'stand or fall.' "

In later years Conrad took other subjects from his personal experience. "Youth" and "Heart of Darkness" were far more intimate than *The Nigger* in their revelation of autobiography.[178] They dealt with incidents of great importance in the development of his character. Yet in neither of these stories did he speak in his own person. He invented Marlow, to whom he attributed his own experiences and who tells them to the reader. So pleased was Conrad with Marlow that he used him in stories that were not created from his own "experience in the absolute sense of the word." In "The End of the Tether," which he said was "also the product of experience . . . [belonging] to the time before I ever thought of putting pen to paper," [179] he sank himself in Captain Whalley. In "Falk," which contained a great deal of personal history,[180] he wrote in the first person, as he did in the autobiographical "Smile of Fortune" [181] and *Shadow Line*.[182] Though *The Arrow of Gold* [183] was also autobiographical, he disguised himself this time, not as Marlow, but as Monsieur George, of undetermined nationality. The alterations were part of what Conrad called "the need of slight dramatization" [184] of personal experience.

Lord Jim is the best example of the complex sources of Conrad's material. Its origin was fourfold, in observation, personal experience, hearsay, and reading. Though the first two influences were incidental, the last two were of great and equal importance. Hearsay and reading were aspects of Conrad's inspiration scarcely present in *Almayer's Folly* and *The Nigger of the "Narcissus."*

Once more the observations can be traced back to *Vidar* days. At Berouw he met Jim Lingard, who acted as a trader in Captain Lingard's interest.[185] Perhaps the connection was carried over into the novel for Stein's friendly interest in Jim and Jim's becoming the representative of Stein and Company in Patusan.[186] According to Mr. Cools, Jim Lingard was called Tuan Jim and, according to Captain Craig, Lord Jim by the officers of the *Vidar* " 'thanks to the swaggering manner he assumed.' " He made several voyages to Singapore in the *Vidar* while Conrad was mate.[187] Here the novelist found the title of his story and his hero's somewhat aggressive carriage, emphasized in the manuscript and toned down in print. Perhaps he also found Lord Jim's romance with Jewel, the beautiful half-caste, in Jim Lingard's marriage with a Malay who, Mr. Cools stated, was half-Chinese. Mr. Cools and Mr. Pangemanan supplied considerable information about the Lingards' numerous children. Two boys and a girl were educated in Singapore. The sons entered the English army and disappeared in the first World War; the daughter became a shop assistant. Another son, Tambi Lingard, was born completely "black face," as Mr. Pangemanan expressed it, and, never recognized by his father, lives like a native in Berouw at present. Jim Lingard himself became well-to-do by lending money to Po Eng Sing, a Chinese trader of Berouw, and lived on the interest. He died about 1923, and his widow married a Malay. His children and career were not to the novelist's purpose. Jean-Aubry and possibly Captain Craig, too, felt that "of course, the real Jim Lingard and the Lord Jim of Conrad's novel have nothing in common except their name and physique." [188]

The picture of Lord Jim was rounded out by a brief glimpse of another man. "One sunny morning in the commonplace surroundings of an Eastern roadstead," Conrad remarked in the Author's Note, "I saw his form pass by – appealing – significant – under a cloud – perfectly silent.

Which is as it should be. It was for me, with all the sympathy of which I was capable, to seek fit words for his meaning. He was 'one of us.'"[189] The impression apparently found its way into the story through the eyes of Marlow:

> The third was an upstanding, broad-shouldered youth, with his hands in his pockets. . . . The young chap, making no movement, not even stirring his head, just stared into the sunshine. This was my first view of Jim. He looked as unconcerned and unapproachable as only the young can look. There he stood, clean-limbed, clean-faced, firm on his feet, as promising a boy as the sun ever shone on. . . . He had no business to look so sound.[190]

Conrad added a few touches to the novel from his own experience. When his back was injured by a loose spar on the *Highland Forest* in 1887, he had to stay for weeks in the hospital in Singapore. Instead of sailing home on the *Highland Forest*, he remained in the East and took a berth on the *Vidar* trading to Borneo.[191] Jim also was "disabled by a falling spar" and forced "at an Eastern port . . . to go to the hospital." His "recovery was slow," and, instead of returning to his ship, he stayed in the East and took a berth on a local steamer.[192] Another detail throws light on Conrad's literary preferences. When he was second mate on the unfortunate *Palestine* in 1881, he had with him "a five shilling one-volume edition of the dramatic works of William Shakespeare."[193] Conrad might be said to give the book – in a slightly cheaper edition – to Jim. Jim carried to Patusan "a thick green-and-gold volume – a half-crown complete Shakespeare."[194] Another incident was taken from Conrad's African experiences. In the Congo he was once nearly sucked under by river mud and fainted from his efforts to extricate himself.[195] Jim was stuck in the mud of the Patusan River during his escape from Rajah Allang and fell asleep exhausted after he pulled himself free.[196]

"Facts gleaned from hearsay" shaped the first twenty chapters of *Lord Jim.* In the Author's Note Conrad outlined the growth of the novel and admitted that his "first thought was of a short story, concerned only with the pilgrim ship episode; nothing more." [197] He did not reveal the source of the episode, but in 1923 two letters to the London *Times Literary Supplement*, occasioned by Curle's "History of Mr. Conrad's Books," disclosed it while Conrad was still alive. He never publicly denied his debt. The pilgrim ship incident took place in the Gulf of Aden in August, 1880, and "created a good deal of interest at the time." [198] From October, 1878, to October, 1893,[199] Conrad was continually making voyages to Australian and Eastern ports where he would surely have been told the details of such a notorious event. The letters from Sir Frank Swettenham and from Alfred Holt and Company are full enough to show what Conrad took over entire and what he altered.

In the summer of 1880 an old steamer called the *Jeddah*, carrying about nine hundred pilgrims from the Dutch islands, left Singapore for Jeddah, the port of Mecca.[200] The novel made here no fundamental change. The name of the ship was altered to *Patna*, but she was still a steamer "as old as the hills." [201] In the manuscript of *Lord Jim* [202] the number of pilgrims, which never reached nine hundred, was raised from six hundred to eight hundred. The fictional pilgrims also came "from the outskirts of the East, . . . crossing in small canoes from island to island . . ." until they reached the port of embarcation. Although Conrad did not name the port, the evidence points to Singapore. The place was "a thoroughfare to the East," and in this "Eastern port" Jim was laid up in hospital and joined the *Patna,* a reflection of Conrad's own experience in Singapore.

The identification is strengthened by the course of the *Patna*: "She cleared the Strait, crossed the bay, continued on her way through the 'one-degree' passage. She held on straight for the Red Sea. . . ."[203] To this account should be added a canceled sentence from the manuscript:[204] "She went on heading westward across the Bay of Bengal." This identifies the Strait as the Strait of Malacca, the route between Singapore and the West.

Now Conrad began to deviate from the original episode. On August 7, 1880, near Cape Gardafui, the *Jeddah* was abandoned at night during heavy weather by all her officers except one. The old boat was heavily insured, and her owners, the captain himself and Seyyid Muhammad Alsagoff, a Singapore Arab, wished to collect on her.[205] Conrad made the management of the *Patna* more polyglot. She was "owned by a Chinaman, chartered by an Arab, and commanded by a sort of renegade New South Wales German." The disaster took place some six hundred miles beyond Cape Gardafui, past the Island of Perim at the mouth of the Red Sea. Though the *Patna* was deserted at night, there was no rough weather: the mysterious accident occurred in the midst of great calm, and the rain squall did not arise until afterwards. The motive for desertion was not a fraudulent insurance scheme, but animal fear that possessed the white men after the accident.[206]

The *Jeddah* was towed to Aden by a ship of the Ocean Steam Navigation Company, "commonly called the Blue Funnel Line," and the deserters reached Aden in a lifeboat.[207] In the novel the *Patna* was towed into Aden by a " 'French gunboat homeward bound from Réunion.' "[208] Conrad seems to have transformed the Blue Funnel Line into the "Blue Star Line" for which Brierly worked,[209] and the Ocean Steam Navigation Company emerged years later as the Oceanic Steam Navigation Company of *Nostromo*.[210]

In *Lord Jim* the deserters from the *Patna* were picked up by another ship, the *Avondale*,[211] and taken into a port which Conrad never identified.

This "Eastern port" was the scene of the official inquiry about the *Patna*.[212] In the original incident after the deserters from the *Jeddah* reached Aden, a brief inquiry was carried on there and later a detailed investigation in Singapore.[213] Conrad telescoped the trials into one. The investigation in the novel was certainly not held in Aden, for the officers of the *Patna* were informed that she had been " 'towed successfully to Aden' ": [214] there would be no reason for telling them the name of the port if they too were at Aden. The deserters were also on the *Avondale* several days,[215] too long for the short trip from the island of Perim to Aden. The details given about the "Eastern port" do not fit Singapore so well as Bombay, which Conrad himself visited in 1884.[216]

The "Eastern port," like Bombay, was " 'over six thousand miles' " [217] from Australia. The town had an Esplanade, with decorative grass-plots and a band-stand, just back from the water, and behind the Esplanade was the Harbour Office and the Malabar Hotel.[218] Bombay has a similar plan: the Esplanade has grass-plots and a band-stand, faces the water, and is backed by various government offices and hotels. Though no record of an actual Malabar Hotel can be found, the most distinctive landmark of Bombay is Malabar Hill. Along the Esplanade in the "Eastern port" were gharries and their Tamil drivers.[219] Webster defines a gharry as a wheeled cart or carriage native to India and comments that Tamils are "numerous throughout southern India." [220] In Conrad's port there were Parsee shipping firms and bazaars; rupees were the currency, and the natives had caste-marks; the attendants in the court of inquiry wore Indian dress.[221] Beyond doubt Conrad transferred the scene of the inquiry from Singapore to Bombay, perhaps to give Jim's retreat "towards the rising sun" [222] a more dramatic extent.

Conrad made a striking change in the character and adventures of the one officer of the *Jeddah* who did not leave the ship. He was a junior engineer and remained behind "because he was not quick enough to get into the boat or boats with the other deserters." [223] When the *Jeddah* was picked up, he was made a hero and "taken to Singapore where he found work in a ship chandler's store, grew fat and prospered. That was how he really 'worked out his salvation.'" [224] From a tale of undeserved success Conrad created the early chapters of his hero's disillusionment. Jim, who was chief mate in the novel, jumped with the other deserters. He was with them outside the Harbour Office when the Captain made his false report on the *Patna*. There Marlow first saw them after the falsehood had been exposed.[225] In the *Jeddah* anecdote Captain Bragg, who salved the *Jeddah*, "entered the Consulate to report the salving, just as the master of the Jeddah was leaving after reporting his vessel lost with all hands." [226] In both cases the Captain got away.[227] Jim faced the inquiry alone. Afterwards he too became a ship-chandler's clerk [228] but not to grow fat and prosper. The way he finally worked out his salvation in a remote Malay state was not inspired by the incident of the *Jeddah*. The Patusan sequence introduced the fourth of the sources of *Lord Jim*.

The first part of *Lord Jim* was not the only story in which Conrad drew upon "facts gleaned from hearsay." He had already used them in "An Outpost of Progress." [229] Later he found in anecdote the source of part of "Typhoon," [230] "Falk," [231] "Amy Foster," [232] *Nostromo*,[233] *The Secret Agent*,[234] "The Brute," [235] *Under Western Eyes*,[236] "Il Conde," [237] "The Secret Sharer," [238] "Freya of the Seven Isles,"[239] "Prince Roman,"[240] "The Planter of Malata,"[241] and "The Tale."[242] No other suggestions crystallized in Conrad's imagination more readily than anecdotes.[243]

Jim's adventures in Patusan were apparently influenced by Conrad's reading. The fourth inspiration came late in the development of the story. Conrad recorded that his "first thought was of . . . the pilgrim ship episode; nothing more." After writing "a few pages" and putting them aside in discontent, he "perceived that the pilgrim ship episode was a good starting-point for a free and wandering tale. . . ."[244] At this time he may have taken from certain books the material for Jim's destiny in Patusan. Two hundred and fifteen pages were based on the *Jeddah* incident; the remaining two hundred were devoted to Patusan. The book seems halved with a knife. Conrad was himself well aware of the break. In November, 1900, he admitted to Garnett: "You've put your finger on the plague spot. The division of the book into two parts. . . ."[245] The latter half recalls the two earlier Malayan novels. The Lord Jim of Patusan is the reverse of the Jim of the *Patna*: he is now the romantic in the triumph of fulfilling his dreams instead of the romantic in the despair of disproving them. Countless details confirm the probability that the Patusan episode derived from Conrad's reading about the Rajah James Brooke of Sarawak.

Apparently he had read widely about Brooke, in whom he must have become interested in Borneo, though he never visited Sarawak. No direct mention of the Englishman can be found in any of Conrad's published work or correspondence, but there are indirect references to him in *Almayer's Folly*, *An Outcast of the Islands*, and *The Rescue*. When Conrad began *Almayer's Folly* in September, 1889, several important volumes dealing with Brooke were available. In

1846 appeared Captain the Hon. Henry Keppel's *Expedition to Borneo of H.M.S. Dido for the Suppression of Piracy: with Extracts from the Journal of James Brooke, Esq., of Sarawak (Now Agent for the British Government in Borneo)*, and in 1853 his *Visit to the Indian Archipelago, in H.M. Ship Maeander: with Portions of the Private Journal of Sir James Brooke, K.C.B.* In 1848 was issued Captain Rodney Mundy's *Narrative of Events in Borneo and Celebes down to the Occupation of Labuan: from the Journals of James Brooke, Esq. Rajah of Sarawak, and Governor of Labuan; together with a Narrative of the Operations of H.M.S. Iris.* In 1853 John C. Templer edited *The Private Letters of Sir James Brooke, K.C.B. Rajah of Sarawak, Narrating the Events of his Life, from 1838 to the Present Time.* And in 1876 the first long biography was published, Gertrude L. Jacob's *Raja of Sarawak: An Account of Sir James Brooke, K.C.B., LL.D., Given Chiefly through Letters and Journals.* The titles of these volumes indicate that they are largely composed of extracts from the unofficial writings of Brooke himself. The books repeat one another in parts, and as Conrad made no reference to them anywhere, it is impossible to tell exactly which he knew. He may have known them all equally well.[246]

After an unsuccessful career in India and England, in 1839 Brooke came to Kuching, the capital of the province of Sarawak on the west coast of Borneo, and helped the governor, Muda Hassim, uncle of the Sultan of Borneo, to put down a local rebellion. In 1841 he was officially created Rajah of Sarawak. The rest of his life he devoted to his new people. He fought the pirates; he mastered the treachery of the Bornean princes; he overcame the suspicions of the English government. He gave Sarawak security, justice, and prosperity, and won the confidence and love of the natives. When he died in 1868, he left his nephew to carry on the traditions and the dynasty, still extant, of the only white rajahs in the world.[247]

Such an achievement would have made an incalculable impression on Conrad. His imagination would have turned to good account any knowledge of the English Rajah. The evidence that Conrad supplemented current gossip about Brooke by careful reading is strong not so much in any single point as in the aggregation of small details.[248] The probability of this literary influence is nowhere more apparent than in *Lord Jim*, as my article, "The Rajah Brooke and Joseph Conrad," attempts to show:

The Patusan of *Lord Jim* was not given a definite position in the Malay Archipelago, but all implications put it in northern Sumatra.[249] Yet Borneo may have supplied much of the topography. In August, 1844, the English Rajah wiped out a pirates' nest up the Sakarran River at Patusan – the very name Conrad gave his settlement.[250] When Brooke helped Muda Hassim suppress the Sarawak rebellion, he had to blast the rebels from their forts on "Sarambo, a high detached mountain . . . with a notch in the center." Sarambo was apparently transplanted to Conrad's Patusan, where "there can be seen rising above the level of the forests the summits of two steep hills very close together, and separated by what looks like a deep fissure" so that "the appearance . . . is of one irregular conical hill split in two." From the top of Sarambo Brooke had a magnificent view over "mountain, and vale, and hillock, rivers and sea." From the Patusan twin hills Jim could see " 'the grey spots of villages, and . . . far off, along the coast, the empty ocean. . . .' " The visualizing imagination of the creator seems to have turned the bare statements of the original into pictures.

Much of the background and many specific incidents in *Lord Jim* suggest Brooke. When he arrived in Sarawak, he found the country distracted. His letters recounted the extortion of the chiefs: the poor man "labours, but is robbed of his produce, by some chief, who gives him a mere nominal price for the most valuable articles. . . ." ". . . for the last ten years there has been no government [and] intrigue and plunder form the occupation of all the higher classes. . . ." Affairs in Patusan bore a noticeable resemblance to Sarawak, except that one man, Rajah Allang, was made specifically responsible for them. "Villages were burnt, men were dragged into the Rajah's stockade to be killed or tortured for the crime of trading with anybody else but himself. . . . The penalty for the breach of the monopoly was death; but his idea of trading was indistinguishable from the commonest forms of robbery." It is little wonder that Brooke – and Jim in his turn – found a rebellion in progress.[251]

If general conditions in Sarawak and Patusan have similarities, the particular events of the war in each country form closer parallels. Muda Hassim, who for four years had tried in vain to suppress it, appealed to Brooke for help. The rebels were in forts on Sarambo mountain, and Brooke constructed fortifications nearby, brought up guns, including two six-pounders, and bombarded the rebel strongholds until they were ready to fall apart. But he could not get his cowardly native soldiers to advance. After nearly three months of intermittent fighting, in which the Malays, to the Englishman's disgust, would not follow up their bombardments by attacks, the rebellion was concluded by negotiation. Brooke now became the nominal rajah of Sarawak and in less than a year was formally invested. In the Englishman's difficulties and success Conrad's selective sense apparently recognized the very train of action to carry Jim to triumph. There are differences of detail, which heighten the dramatic values of the novel. The Patusan scene was further complicated by the existence of two rival factions against Rajah Allang: the party of Sherif Ali, the half-caste Arab, who had started the civil war; and the Bugis party, headed by old Doramin, whom Jim aided in the attempt to restore peace to a distracted state. Ali had a fort on one of the twin Patusan hills. With difficulty Jim prevailed over the Bugis' fears and planned a surprise attack. Bringing two seven-pounders up to the summit of the other hill, he constructed a battery there, all under cover of night. At dawn he pounded Ali's fort to splinters, led his forces into the breach at once, and was completely victorious. As a result " 'he became the virtual ruler of the land.' " It is almost as if Conrad refought Brooke's campaign, taking advantage of the errors committed before. The guns were a little larger; the natives' courage was screwed to the sticking-point; the bombardment was followed up immediately; and the war was over in a day instead of three months.[252]

Conrad's reading may also have suggested to him the intrusion of the outside world on the adventurer's domain, from which he built up Gentleman Brown's raid on Patusan.[253] Brown blundered into the river while Jim was in the interior, had his eyes opened " 'as to the home affairs of Patusan,' " and determined to share with Jim. But the unscrupulous ruffian was disappointed in his hopes, though Jim did give him safe passage down the river. On the way down, however, Brown destroyed a party of natives under Dain Waris, Doramin's son and Jim's particular friend. Tamb' Itam, Jim's loyal retainer, brought his master news of the slaughter of Dain Waris. A number of these details seem traceable to Brooke. The idea of an unexpected raid up the Patusan River was perhaps inspired by the Englishman's accounts of sudden raids of pirates up Borneo rivers. Furthermore one of the charges brought against Brooke by his foes in Parliament was that he did not allow other interests in Sarawak, and he did turn down offers of help from strangers. Once Brooke, who was absent at the time, was much disturbed by a visit to Brunei of the American frigate *Constitution* to obtain trade concessions from the Sultan. In his letters he confessed that the Americans might have been successful if they had been "better versed in native politics." And Jaffer's announcement to Brooke of Budrudeen's death seems to make its familiar appearance in Tamb' Itam's tale.[254]

By far the most suggestive similarities between the Brookiana and *Lord Jim* lie in characterization. Sometimes it is only a name, again it is the basic psychology of a character that carries the resemblance. Keppel's *Indian Archipelago* may have bestowed the name Kassim on the chief counselor of Rajah Allang. Mundy's *Borneo and Celebes* may have provided many: Elliot for the Master Attendant of the Harbour Office; Matheson for Matherson who first owned the *Fire Queen;* McNeil for M'Neil, the Scotch merchant who befriended Stein. Further evidence indicates that Conrad borrowed the last two names and that he was aware of the influence of his reading. In the manuscript in the Rosenbach Collection [255] they were originally spelled Matheson and McNeil as in Mundy and then corrected to Matherson and M'Neil. . . .

Other characters in *Lord Jim* had probable relationships to personages in Brooke. Muda Hassim, for instance, the uncle of the Sultan of Borneo, "a remarkably short man, and slightly built," seems to have had a sort of literary practical joke played upon him: he may have been caricatured as the miserable Rajah Allang, " 'the worst of the Sultan's uncles, . . . little, . . . wizened,' " and with a

" 'frail old body.' "[256] Conrad apparently appropriated the Sultan of Borneo with few changes. The man Brooke knew was over fifty, an imbecile, with "an extra diminutive thumb" on his right hand. In *Lord Jim*, the Sultan was " 'an imbecile youth with two thumbs' " on his left hand. All the details which can be duplicated in Brooke and Conrad, however, are not freakish. Though Stein, who gave Jim his chance in Patusan, had no definite model, Conrad may have borrowed two picturesque episodes from the Englishman's life for the German's. On his visit to Celebes Brooke had been warmly received by an old rana who wanted to adopt him as her son. And when Brooke was about to leave Sarawak forever, according to the Jacob biography, he summoned the nobles and chiefs and made the country formally over to his nephew, Captain Brooke. Stein, in his turn, had been definitely adopted in Celebes by old M'Neil, the trader, " 'a privileged friend' " of a Wajo rana there. Feeling himself about to die, M'Neil made over his trading privileges to Stein before the rana and her court. In contrast to Stein, Doramin may owe a good deal to a Bugis mentioned in Mundy's *Borneo and Celebes*. During his voyage to Celebes, Brooke was much impressed by "the nakodah Pelewo, a man of upright mind and liberal principles. . . . He is, for a Bugis, very rich, and may be considered the head of the middle class which has arisen in Wajo from the wealth acquired in trade." Pelewo had many sons and daughters whom he married to nobles. Now Doramin, too, was a Bugis, an immigrant from Celebes to Patusan, and " 'of the *nakhoda* or merchant class.' " His wealth made him the head of the two hundred Bugis traders and hence the only power for law and order in Patusan. He was the husband of a woman of noble birth and the father of many daughters and one son, his beloved Dain Waris. The two nakhodas have enough in common to suggest how Conrad could fashion a figure on the skeleton of a few suggestions.

The clearest example of Brooke's possible influence on Conrad might naturally be expected in the character of Lord Jim: not the Jim of the *Patna* but Tuan Jim of Patusan. The romantic aspiration and energy of the English Rajah were of the sort to fire the novelist's imagination. The great work the Englishman had accomplished in the teeth of danger, far off the map of Western civilization, was material after Conrad's heart. And in Brooke's achievement in Borneo he seems to have found the perfect pattern for Jim's rehabilitation and fulfilment. . . .

Brooke and Jim shared many parallel experiences. The former had four sisters and a brother: the latter four brothers and presumably a sister. That both were named James and both were called Tuan by the natives who worshipped them must not be entirely discounted by the fact that Conrad knew in Bulungan a Jim Lingard who was called Lord Jim on account of his swaggering manner. Perhaps the ring that Budrudeen sent Brooke in farewell suggested the silver ring that Doramin had given Stein and that Jim brought to Patusan as a token of authority. Each man won his place with the Malays by suppressing civil dissension, and each was rewarded with supreme authority in the state. As might have been expected, Brooke was supposed by the natives to have charmed the dangerous bore in the Serebas River. To Jim also were ascribed supernatural powers: had not the tide in the river " 'turned two hours before its time' " to help him up to Patusan? Another popular superstition in *Lord Jim* seems to have been worked up from a suggestion in Brooke's letters. The Rajah found a large and fine crystal which he hoped was a diamond – "the (is to be) celebrated 'Brooke Diamond.' " From this Conrad may have elaborated the natives' story that Jim possessed a fabulous emerald, a story which grew out of his name for the girl he loved – Jewel. Certainly the subordinate part Jewel played in the novel could have been conditioned by the lack of sentimental interest in Brooke's life. *Lord Jim* is essentially the story of a man in a man's world. Jewel was not introduced until the novel was two-thirds completed. And the love affair was a subsidiary, not an indispensable, factor in the action.

It was Brooke's position in Sarawak that seems to have most inspired Conrad. The inspiration, if such it was, was more of the spirit than of the events of the English Rajah's life among his people. After the suppression of the Dyak rebellion Brooke refused "to have the blood of conquered foes shed" and with difficulty restrained Muda Hassim. Similarly Jim would not let the Bugis " 'pay off old scores' " or depose Rajah Allang when the Patusan civil war was brought to a close. Both men were constructive. Brooke set about improving the chaotic condition of Sarawak according to his ideals. In a passage in his letters he summed these up succinctly: "to establish and encourage the good, to punish the evil-doer, to develop the resources of these countries by personal inspection, to inspire confidence in the native mind, to afford security for property, to prevent the oppression of the poorer and productive classes." And he did travel about his country. He established peace and prosperity upon a foundation of justice for all so successfully that the population of Kuching grew in five years from fifteen hundred to twelve thousand. The responsibility and the work he took squarely upon himself: he was accustomed to "dispense justice for four or five hours a day." By a similar procedure Conrad had Jim find his own rehabilitation in the rehabilitation of Patusan. Lord Jim went to work. " 'Whole villages, deserted, rotted on their blackened posts' " no longer. Of such conditions he admitted simply to his friend Marlow, " ' "I've changed all that." ' " He too traveled about his little state and dispensed justice to a grateful people: he " 'could settle the deadliest quarrel in the country by crooking his little finger' "; " 'his word decided everything.' " [257] In Patusan the new " 'social fabric of orderly, peaceful life, when every man was sure of tomorrow,' " was " 'the edifice raised by Jim's hands.' "

For their efforts both Brooke and Jim were rewarded by the trust and love of their people. Brooke was able to say: "The confidence of the natives in me personally is astonishing." The affection of Sarawak for him was so great that he wrote home: "Though it may appear vain, I must say that the attachment of the people is to my person, as well as to my government." And what could Jim say? He confided to Marlow: " ' "If you ask them who is brave – who is just – who it is they would trust with their lives? – they would say, Tuan Jim." ' " As Marlow put it, Jim had taken " 'the leap that landed him into the life of Patusan, into the trust, the love, the confidence of the people.' " [258]

Conrad's habit of drawing inspiration from his reading lasted throughout his life. Before *Lord Jim* he had probably used the Brookiana in *The Rescue*.[259] Into *The Rescue* [260] he also worked the krissing of a Balinese girl by her relations for giving a flower to a foreigner, an incident taken from Alfred Russel Wallace's *Malay Archipelago*,[261] his "favorite bedside book." [262] He returned to books for part of the inspiration of *Nostromo* [263] and *The Secret Agent*.[264] "Falk" owed something to "a short paragraph in a newspaper." [265] Two books and a letter from a friend provided the subject of "Gaspar Ruiz." [266] "The Duel" sprang from a newspaper paragraph.[267] The greatest amount of reading went into preparation for the Napoleonic novel which Conrad left incomplete at his death. He began reading for it during his stay in Capri in 1905; he worked in the public library in Montpellier in 1907; he was still reading during a vacation at Ajaccio, Corsica, in the winter of 1920, and later that year at the British Museum.[268] "The Warrior's Soul" sprang from the same researches.[269] In a letter to the London *Times Literary Supplement* [270] Miss Mildred Atkinson made a brief but revealing comparison of *Suspense* and the *Memoirs of the Countess de Boigne.* Of *The Rover*, which grew out of *Suspense*, Conrad said: "The first notion of this story originated in the reading of Napoleon's dispatch to the Admiral commanding in Toulon in 1804. . . ." [271]

The origins of Conrad's novels and short stories can generally be traced to four main sources of inspiration. There remain stories about which he left no information and of which the origin has not yet been discovered. Some stories belong under more than one heading. Research and Conrad's own disclosures reveal the importance of first-hand contact with life. The contact was sometimes mere observation of other men, sometimes his own "experience in the absolute sense of the word." Curle declared, "His creative imagination can only work at its best when it is attached . . . to a remembered incident. . . . This sense of contact with life . . . gives to his pages the feeling that things happened so and no otherwise." [272] Yet this judgment leaves out the vital inspiration of anecdote and reading. Only abstractions failed to stimulate Conrad: he was unable to clothe a point of dogma in the flesh and blood of fiction. Taking inspiration from one source at a time or merging all four, he was seldom at a loss for material.

Chapter III

THE MOOD OF CREATION

THE events which turned the seaman into the novelist reveal the emotional pressure under which Conrad wrote. Though composition is generally laborious, except for the fortunate few like Trollope and Arnold Bennett, it need not involve all Conrad's mental and physical complications. At first he suffered from poverty and ill-health. Of the two poverty was less demoralizing, though it caused him many agonized hours, for he eventually achieved prosperity. He never escaped from ill-health. The work considered in this study was accomplished under the most acute suffering from both difficulties. They affected his habits of writing and induced moods injurious to creation. His confidence in his ability and productions and his control over his imagination were seriously impaired. A study of his physical and mental condition is essential to an understanding of his work.

Though Conrad's financial difficulties were the lesser of his two troubles, they were a continual disturbance. From 1896 on, money was of great importance to him. Early in February he became engaged to Jessie George.[1] He had in reserve a legacy left him by his uncle and invested in a South African gold mine.[2] About two weeks before his marriage the company failed, and he began married life with only "a few hundred pounds."[3] He gave an unexpectedly optimistic account of his frame of mind at this time in the autobiographical sketch, where he spoke of losing

after another
all his money in the South African slump *an* exciting experience
slight yet
which *he does not regret* except for the *obvious* inconvenience of the thing, he does not regret. . . . With no money and in uncertain health the position seemed desperate. Mr. Conrad married a woman who was not afraid to face it with him. This was the most *reckless* dangerous *reckless* the most reckless and
he had
the most fortunate adventure in his life.[4]

When attempts to find an acceptable command fell through, he was forced to admit, "Only literature remains to me as a means of existence. . . . If I have undertaken this thing, it is with the firm resolution to make a name – and I have no doubt that I shall be successful in this connection. . . . The question is only to earn the money '*qui est une chose tout-à-fait à part du mérite littéraire*,' yet I am not sure of it – but my needs are very moderate and I can wait. I therefore look towards the future rather calmly."[5] The change from the active life of a seaman to the sedentary life of a writer demanded delicate psychological adjustments. Conrad set about a new existence under a financial disadvantage that was to grow heavier with the years.

The very optimism of his early "resolution to make a name" may have increased the strain later. He made his resolve clear when at their second meeting Edward Garnett encouraged him to write: "His tone," Garnett remembered, "was emphatic. 'But I *won't* live in an attic. . . . I'm past that, you understand? I *won't* live in an attic!' "[6] His expectation of success developed apparently into the belief that he was morally obligated to be successful. At the turn of the century he made this impression on Ford Madox Ford, his collaborator. "Conrad had very strongly the idea of the Career," Ford remarked. "A career was for him something a little sacred: any career. It was part of his belief in the shipshape."[7] Conrad wanted to make a competent living by his exertions. Even during his sea days he was constantly dissatisfied with the small payment for so much hard work.[8] Though his schemes to improve his fortune were generally not put into action, he believed in his business ability. His friends have confirmed the practical force of his mind.[9] He was able to handle his affairs with publishers and agents to advantage.[10] Because of his ambitions and his ability he was acutely disappointed when he was unable to make even a living. He pressed himself harder and added to the intolerable tension under which he worked so long.

Not until 1912 did Conrad's writing support him.[11] In October, 1896, he wrote his publisher Unwin: "I can't afford to work for less than ten pence per hour and must work in a way that will give me this magnificent income."[12] He must have worked for far less. He depended primarily on the sale of serial rights, though they did not bring him enough to live on. The *Savoy* paid him forty guineas, two guineas a page, for "The Idiots,"[13] but the *Cornhill Magazine* only twelve and a half guineas, a guinea a page, for "The Lagoon."[14] *Cosmopolis* gave him £50 for "An Outpost of Progress."[15] Though he sold the serial rights of *The Rescue* for £250 to McClure, the £100 received in advance of completion became a back-breaking debt, since he was unable to finish the story for more than twenty-three years.[16] Toward the end of the century *Blackwood's Magazine* gave him only a little more: £40 for "Karain," the first story he sold them, and thereafter forty-five shillings a thousand words.[17] Considering the unpredictable time he took to produce a story, the payment was definitely less than ten pence an hour.

For book publication Conrad was receiving even smaller

amounts: £20 for *Almayer's Folly*,[18] £50 for *An Outcast of the Islands*,[19] £50 promised when *The Rescue* appeared in America,[20] and £50 or £60 for *Tales of Unrest* in advance of royalties.[21] Unwin's terms for royalties were ten percent of the published price on the first two thousand copies, twelve percent on the next two thousand, and fifteen percent after four thousand.[22] The royalties hardly existed, for the books were slow to run into more than one impression. *Almayer's Folly* (1895) reached a second impression in 1896, a third in 1902, and a fourth in 1908; [23] *An Outcast* (1896) a second in 1907, a third in 1916, and a fourth in 1919; [24] The *Nigger* (1897) a second in 1898, and a third in 1914; [25] *Tales of Unrest* (1898) reached a second impression in 1909; [26] *Lord Jim* (1900) a second the same year, a third in 1904, a fourth in 1905, and a fifth in 1914; [27] *Youth* (1902) a second in 1903, and a third in 1909.[28] The figures do not compare favorably with the popularity of Sarah Grand's *Heavenly Twins* (1893), of which Conrad wrote in 1894 with envious scorn: "Le livre a passé par 10 éditions et l'auteur a empoché 50,000 francs. Le monde est un sale endroit." [29] He clung to a desperate philosophy of compensation: "The opinion that in 'art alone there is a meaning in endeavour as apart from success' . . . [is] the truth that saves most of us from eternal damnation." [30]

Conrad was constantly aware that he was working for the barest necessities of life. It was his writing "upon which depends the daily bread of the house (literally – from day to day)." [31] The fear of destitution haunted him as an immediate reality. He was unable to keep pace with the expenses of even the most modest household. In 1899 he admitted, "It is years and years since I first began to afflict and exasperate my friends with these dark allusions to a perfectly clear matter, my inability to work fast enough to get my living. It is ridiculous and sad and wearisome, and that . . . does not make it any less offensive."[32] Dark allusions color his letters for nearly two decades.

If Conrad had been a bachelor, the situation would have been disheartening. As a married man he found it appalling. The birth of his first son, Borys, on January 15, 1898, filled him with apprehension.[33] Not only daily bread depended upon his writing but "(I dare hardly think of it) the future of my child, of those nearest and dearest to me, between whom and the bleakest want there is only my pen – as long as life lasts."[34] The years increased his worry. Mrs. Conrad's severe injury to an already "invalid knee" which, after November, 1904, required a series of operations, did not improve his peace of mind.[35] Amputation seemed inevitable twice.[36] His responsibilities grew with the birth of a second son, John, on August 2, 1906.[37] Various illnesses of the two children's, especially a threat of tuberculosis to the elder boy, heightened Conrad's tension. At the worst of the difficulties, he wrote John Galsworthy, "The state of worry in which I am living, – and writing, – is simply indescribable. It's a constant breaking strain. And you know that materials subjected to breaking strain lose all elasticity in the end, – part with all their 'virtue' on account of profound molecular changes. The molecular changes in my brain are very pronounced."[38] His own letters were corroborated by Ford Madox Ford: "And to so admirable a family man as was Conrad, half of whose mind at least was given to the matter of securing comfort and permanent provision for those dependent on him, whose agonies over this department of his life were sempiternal and overwhelming, the mere illness of a member of his family was sufficient to maim his working mind for long periods."[39]

Conrad was a great contriver of schemes to relieve his necessity. The schemes must have distracted his attention and added new anxieties. Ford Madox Ford recorded "the agony of mind Conrad would be in over his debts or his complication of affairs" and his "crises of rearrangement." [40] His methods of rearrangement extended from the simplest and most temporary to complicated and would-be permanent solutions. Ford recalled a poignant picture of Conrad's "leaning over a counter, persuading the stolid Mr. Dan West, grocer of Hythe, to grant him credit unheard of in that market town." [41] In moments of bitter lightness Conrad longed for a millionaire who would subsidize him.[42]

His serious attempts to improve his finances met with obstacles. Acting on the advice of Edward Garnett, he tried to induce his original publisher, T. Fisher Unwin, to increase the advances for the proposed *Tales of Unrest* from £50 to £100, and Unwin refused. The refusal so infuriated Conrad that he declared: "Nothing would induce me to go back to F. U." [43] The incident preyed upon his mind: as he wrote Unwin at the time, "It has interfered fiendishly with the work upon my last story." [44] Next, with an introduction from Garnett, he tried a new publisher, Smith Elder and Company, who disappointed him in the end. Once more Garnett came to the rescue with an introduction to S. S. Pawling of William Heinemann, Limited. Pawling took an immediate interest in Conrad and, like Unwin, seems to have acted much as a literary agent for him. By the end of November, 1896, Conrad was sending his work to him.[45] In February, 1897, he told Garnett, "I feel very safe in his hands," and in November, "I am immensely relieved. I hope I've done with the *selling* business for life." [46] At once Conrad became dependent upon what he could persuade Pawling to advance him. In March, 1897, he seems to have asked for £25 and received £30.[47] In November he borrowed £50 from Unwin for six months at three percent.[48] But he was in need of more than small advances.

By the first of the year he confessed to Edward Garnett that he "must borrow money somewhere" and broached a plan whereby Pawling was to lend it to him on the security, apparently, of his literary promise. Garnett seems to have discouraged the idea, and the difficulties continued.[49]

Conrad's literary affairs became more and more complicated. Pawling's firm, William Heinemann, Ltd., published *The Nigger* in 1898, but the next few books had to go elsewhere. Conrad had promised *Tales of Unrest* to Unwin, who brought it out in 1898.[50] Blackwood published *Lord Jim* in 1900 and *Youth* in 1902; the stories had appeared in their magazine.[51] As his relationships with publishers demanded more and more time, Conrad turned to a literary agent, J. B. Pinker, who approached him in August, 1899. At first Conrad refused his assistance:

> My method of writing is so unbusinesslike that I don't think you could have any use for such an unsatisfactory person. I generally sell a work before it is begun, get paid when it is half done and don't do the other half till the spirit moves me. I must add that I have no control whatever over the spirit—neither has the man who has paid the money. . . . I live in hopes of reformation, and whenever that takes place you and you alone shall have the working of the new Conrad.[52]

Though the reformation never took place, he soon gave Pinker the working of the old Conrad.

The relationship with his literary agent, though not without disturbances, was of the greatest aid to Conrad. He still worried extravagantly over his finances but he had a resource to which he could always turn. Richard Curle recorded that it was "Pinker, his literary agent since the beginning of the century, who financed him through the lean years. . . ."[53] Unforeseen accidents made the lean years leaner. Early in 1904 Watson and Company, bankers, who had treated Conrad with consideration, failed. He lamented: "I've lost a good friend, for he [Watson] did back me up through all these years. Of course, I shall be bothered now about my overdraft and so on." [54] He had to depend upon Pinker all the more. By the first of January, 1908, Conrad owed him £1572.[55] About a month later he was seriously alarmed at the condition of Pinker's affairs, which he described as "gatées." [56] If his agent failed, Conrad realized he too would be ruined. Yet both survived the crisis.

By the middle of July, 1909, he must have owed Pinker considerably more. The two had quarreled, and Conrad was trying to raise £2250 to pay off "old liabilities." [57] The quarrel seems to have arisen over the amount of work sent Pinker, the sale of which would decrease the debt. Towards the end of 1908 Conrad had been much incensed over "a letter from P. telling me he hopes to have manuscript sent regularly. That I've given him nothing to sell for two years, and threatening to stop short if he don't get end of R.[azumov: i.e., *Under Western Eyes*] in a fortnight. If he does that I shall fling the MS of Raz in the fire and see how he likes that." [58] Both sides of the disagreement can be understood. Conrad's royalties from all his books in 1908 had been under £5.[59] Pinker had just been in serious financial difficulties. As Curle put it, "At one time Mr. Pinker stood to lose thousands of pounds that he had advanced to Conrad, and as book followed book with little sign of enhanced popularity the investment must have seemed an extremely poor one." [60] The misunderstanding reached a climax with the completion of *Razumov*.[61] During a conference the two men lost their tempers, and Pinker, in a deliberate attempt to wound Conrad, "turned upon him with a sharp demand that he should speak English, if he could!" Conrad was preparing to destroy the manuscript when his wife hid it. Immediately afterwards he came down with a severe attack of gout.[62]

Around this time his friend Perceval Gibbon suggested a scheme to relieve the tension of Conrad's debts, particularly to Pinker, by a number of life insurance policies.[63] The plan came to nothing. Even when peace was made by October, 1909, Conrad accounted for his work to Pinker with savage defensiveness.[64] His popularity received a great impetus just before the war, and Pinker was eminently successful in placing his work.[65] At Pinker's death in February, 1922, he keenly felt the loss of a "friend of twenty years' standing, whose devotion to my interests and whose affection . . . were the greatest moral and material support through nearly all my writing life." [66]

In addition to his poverty Conrad was extravagant. As Curle put it, he was "utterly incapable of saving." [67] He was given to imploring Pinker: "You must help me settle down now on an economical basis." [68] When he was in Marseilles in 1876, he spent money in a lavish way and was severely reprimanded by his uncle Tadeusz.[69] In his early writing days he underestimated his expenses. When he assumed that he could live on £360 a year, he was actually spending about £650.[70] He received an allowance of £20 a month "for a year or two" from Frank N. Doubleday and William Heinemann as an advance on *The Rescue*,[71] but the advance was insufficient and only increased his financial worries. Before he was given a Civil List pension, a group of friends, Hugh Hammersley, Henry Newbolt, W. P. Ker, Gilbert Murray, and William Rothenstein, "helped to relieve Conrad of some of his pressing difficulties." [72] They tided him only over a crisis. Even the pension of £100 presented to him in 1905 did not remove the strain of debt.[73] Though he became prosperous just before the war, in 1919 he was demanding of Pinker, "Shall I ever get into real smooth water and you have no longer to stand by ready with ropes and lifebuoys . . . ?"[74] To the very end of his life, when he was paying a "tax and super-tax . . . of nearly £1,800," he was still finding it hard to provide what he considered sufficient for his family.[75]

Conrad was often to deplore the way "money difficulties . . . interfere with one's mind in a sort of sterilizing way, driving all images and expressions clean out of it."[76] Once he lamented to John Galsworthy, "You don't know what an inspiration-killing anxiety it is to think: 'Is it salable?' There is nothing more cruel than to be caught between one's impulse, one's act, and that question, which for me simply is a question of life and death. There are moments when the mere fear sweeps my head clean of every thought. It is agonizing, – no less. And, – you know, – that pressure grows from day to day instead of getting less."[77] Conrad's trouble with *The Rescue*, according to Ford, was due to the hypnotizing effect on his will of advance payment.[78] If writing for money killed inspiration, so did writing without commercial success. As Conrad confessed to Wells in 1903, "A paper-success (as I call it) is not a strong enough tonic."[79] Craving relief from financial anxiety, he was for seventeen years its constant prey.

If he had had to worry only about money, he would have been fortunate. Great as it was, his financial difficulty was less troublesome than his ill-health. His recurrent illnesses were largely the aftermath of his service in the Congo in 1890. He was subject to intermittent malaria.[80] In his letters to Mme. Poradowska he successively complained of "rheumatisme de jambe gauche et neuralgie de bras droit"; "jambes dans mauvais état et estomac aussi"; "nerfs desorganisés . . . palpitations de coeur et des accés d'étouffement"; "une attaque de malaria sous forme de dyspepsie"; "un peu de fièvre encore tous les jours."[81]

The worst ailment was intense gout of which he had the first attack in January, 1891, as soon as he returned from Africa.[82] Despite his attempts to cure it at Champel in 1891, 1894, and 1895,[83] it continued to incapacitate him. It "disabled [him] physically and mentally" and left him "always . . . demoralized and gloomy."[84] In 1923 he spoke of his "gout (the most obscure of diseases) of thirty-two years' standing . . . not to be driven off by the Medicine-men incantations. . . . I consulted people in France (Montpellier) and in England, in Switzerland. I have tried all sorts of treatment and diet."[85] These maladies afflicted him with what Richard Curle called "more than thirty years of auto-intoxication. . . ."[86] When chronic illnesses were reinforced by some common ailment, he collapsed. He wrote, for instance, in February, 1900, while working on *Lord Jim*: "I've been ill since the 26th of Jan. . . . Malaria, bronchitis and gout. In reality a break-down."[87]

The legacies from the Congo were not all physical. While Conrad was in Africa, he became mentally sick. He was "tant soit peu demoralisé"; he felt "la nostalgie de la mer, l'envie de revoir ces plaines d'eau salé . . . sous le ciel sombre de Decembre."[88] He referred to himself as "neurasthenic" on his return to Europe.[89] He described his nervous condition figuratively in May, 1891: "Moi je suis encore plongé dans la nuit la plus épaisse et mes rêves ne sont que cauchemars. . . ."[90] In 1908 he compared his condition with a friend's:

I have been in a state resembling yours, some time after my Congo experience. It was not the convalescence from the fever. The convalescence was over for a year, and I was apparently as well as ever, when that sort of weakness stole over me. I couldn't move *my fingers* (not hand, *fingers*) without sending the pulse up an incredible number of beats. I lay on my back in dismal lodgings and expected to go out like a burnt-out candle any moment. That was nerves, and it was a six-months' job.[91]

During the years of writing he frequently complained of his nerves. In 1894 he lamented, "Ma maladie des nerfs me torture, me rend malheureux et paralyse action, pensée, tout! . . . Même dans les intervalles – quand je suis censé d'être bien – je vis dans la peur du retour de ce mal tourmentant." [92] He was never able to forget himself. Nervous tension found vent in fits of violent irritation which, in their turn, affected his health. Mrs. Conrad used to "maintain that in nine cases out of ten the irritation produced the gout." [93] Once in 1899 Conrad himself admitted that he was lame from gout "brought on by – by – by agitation, exasperation, botheration." [94] Insomnia accompanied the nervous crises, probably as both cause and effect.[95] The aggregation of strains kept him constantly wrought up. "I suspect," he said in June, 1896, "that I am getting through a severe mental illness." [96] Later letters echoed the same suspicion. When the effort of creation was added to his other difficulties, it is miraculous that he did not finally break down.

Such chronic ill-health inevitably hurt Conrad's work. It interrupted his writing routine. He deplored his "habitudes luxueuses en matière de maladie qui me mettent à sec périodiquement." [97] He estimated that of the years between 1895 and 1909 "a full third must be taken off for illness alone, – not speaking of other pieces of bad luck." [98] And in 1912 he longed to be free of his malaria, his gout, his nerves for "a clear twelve months. I've never had that in all my writing life." [99] His letters substantiate these melancholy claims.[100]

Conrad's correspondence shows how much his writing

suffered from sickness in the family. He was unable to write when Mrs. Conrad was sick in April, 1896, and in June, 1897.[101] The illnesses of the children also interrupted him.[102] Defending himself to Pinker, he analyzed the effect of domestic emergencies on his concentration:

Of course you may say that I ought to disregard all the complications and peg away with my eyes shut to domestic affairs. I know some men are capable of that sort of thing; and with an organized household one could perhaps abstract oneself for six hours per day. It's another matter with me. You understand that my wife was pretty helpless and required some attention; the child too. For me to have to lay down my pen ten times in the course of the day is fatal. I wish there had been something of a hack-writer in my composition.[103]

And Conrad was anything but a hack-writer.

Poverty by itself, illness by itself, would have been strain enough. The combination made him hopeless. While he was writing *Lord Jim*, he let himself go in a letter to E. L. Sanderson:

I am now trying to finish a story which began in the Oct. No. of *Blackwood*. I am at it day after day, and I want all day, every minute of a day, to produce a beggarly tale of words or perhaps to produce nothing at all. And when that is finished . . . I must go on, even go on at once and drag out of myself another 20,000 words, if the boy is to have his milk and I my beer (this is a figure of speech,—I don't drink beer, I drink weak tea, yearn after dry champagne) and if the world is not absolutely to come to an end. And after I have written and have been paid, I shall have the satisfaction of knowing that I can't allow myself the relaxation of being ill more than three days under the penalty of starvation: nor the luxury of going off the hooks altogether without playing the part of a thief regarding various confiding persons, whose desire to serve me was greater than their wisdom.[104]

All the difficulties of Conrad's existence – ill-health, responsibilities towards his family and his creditors – contributed to the despair in this outburst. For years conditions did not improve.[105] About ten years later, he confessed that despite a two weeks' illness he had not called in a doctor: "The mere thought of the bill by and by makes me shudder." [106] Even near the end of his life, in November, 1923, he mentioned that a bad heart, "strain and worry" had produced in him "an unshakeable despondency." [107]

At their worst his miseries interrupted his writing completely. When he was working on *Almayer's Folly* as a pastime, he was frequently too exhausted to continue.[108] Sometimes his mind felt powerless:

> Il y a des moments ou la pensée s'endort, les mots s'enfuient, ou l'espoir lui même semble mort. . . . Il me semble que je n'ai rien vu, que je ne vois rien, que je ne verrai jamais rien. . . . Certainement ceci ressemble au commencement d'une imbécilité incurable.[109]

Though *An Outcast of the Islands* was also partly a pastime, he burned much of it in September, 1894,[110] and later reached a standstill. On May 1, 1895, he confessed: "Seriously, I find I can't work. Simply can't! I am going to try what mountain air combined with active fire-hose (twice a day) will do for divine inspiration." [111] Although Champel helped him,[112] he could not afford continual cures. The next February, when he was facing marriage, disappointment in his sea life, and the prospect of a literary career, he acknowledged: "My horrible inability (for the last fortnight) to write a line imbued me with a sense of insecurity." [113]

Conrad was later moved to almost hysterical outbursts. Few utterances match the accounts of his trouble with *The Rescue*. On June 19, 1896, he admitted to Garnett:

> Since I sent you that part 1st (on the eleventh of the month) I have written one page. Just one page. I went about thinking and forgetting — sitting down before the blank page to find that I could not put one sentence together. To be able to think and unable to express is a fine torture. I am undergoing it — without patience.[114]

Though he had already faced pages that remained stubbornly blank in *An Outcast of the Islands*,[115] he had yet to learn just how fine the torture could be. Early in August he was in frightful condition:

> I have been living in a little hell of my own; in a place of torment so subtle and so cruel and so unavoidable. . . . There is 12 pages written and I sit before them every morning, day after day, for the last 2 months and cannot add a sentence, add a word! I am paralyzed by doubt and have just sense enough to feel the agony but am powerless to invent a way out of it. . . . I had bad moments with the Outcast but never anything so so ghastly nothing half so hopeless. When I face that fatal manuscript it seems to me that I have forgotten how to think — worse! how to write. It is as if something in my head had given way to let in a cold grey mist. I knock about blindly in it till I am positively, physically sick — and then I give up saying — tomorrow! and tomorrow comes — and brings only the renewed and futile agony. I ask myself whether I am breaking up mentally. I am afraid of it. . . . The only certitude left to me is that I cannot work for the present. . . . The darkness and the bitterness of it is beyond expression.[116]

His difficulties were never so poignantly expressed as on March 29, 1898:

> I sit down religiously every morning, I sit down for eight hours every day — and the sitting down is all. In the course of that working day of 8 hours I write 3 sentences which I erase before leaving the table in despair. . . . I assure you . . .

that sometimes it takes all my resolution and power of self control to refrain from butting my head against the wall. I want to howl and foam at the mouth but I daren't do it for fear of waking that baby and alarming my wife. . . . After such crises of despair I doze for hours still half conscious that there is that story I am unable to write. Then I wake up, try again — and at last go to bed completely done-up. So the days pass and nothing is done. At night I sleep. In the morning I get up with the horror of that powerlessness I must face through a day of vain efforts. . . . I seem to have lost all *sense* of style and yet I am haunted, mercilessly haunted by the *necessity* of style. And that story I can't write weaves itself into all I see, into all I speak, into all I think, into the lines of every book I try to read. . . . You know how bad it is when one *feels* one's liver, or lungs. Well I feel my brain. I am distinctly conscious of the contents of my head.[117]

Throughout his career Conrad was the victim of "moments of cruel blankness when one's writing life seems to come to an end," and he lived "in the constant dread of these visitations."[118] Paralysis of expression was to recur, most noticeably, during and after the composition of *Chance*, during the war, and while he was engaged on the uncompleted *Suspense*.[119] In his depressed condition he looked upon each moment of blankness as "the end of Conrad." He was well acquainted with what he called by a phrase of Baudelaire's, " '*les stérilités des écrivains nerveux*' . . . that anguished suspension of all power of thought that comes to one often in the midst of a very revel of production, like the slave with his *memento mori* at a feast."[120] On New Year's Day, 1920, he was driven to a characteristically ironic statement: "I've done nothing for the last six weeks and I feel that I'll never do anything any more. Somehow I don't feel so happy about it as I ought to — for what could be more soothing than a sense of impotence?"[121] Despite the exaggeration Conrad suffered intensely. Mrs. Conrad provided the corroboration of an eye-witness: "It was the days, weeks, even months, when he could not write a line, that held for us the greatest worry and stress." [122] Ford believed that "few men can so much have suffered." [123] Only the discipline of his sea life must have kept him persistently at his desk during these months of barrenness.

Such sterility was not constant, yet there were many intermediate stages between writing nothing at all and writing freely. Conrad had difficulty with concentration. Complaints of "inability to concentrate" [124] vary the other laments in his letters. Summarizing his bad habits of work, he confessed that at times he could not write "till the spirit moves me. I must add that I have no control whatever over the spirit. . . ." [125] He reiterated that he was working at "nothing like the rate I ought to keep up to make things look better." [126] Though a slow rate was better than " 'les stérilités des écrivains nerveux,' " it was far from ideal.

Conrad was always a severe critic of himself, a perfectionist, ruthless in destroying what cost him superhuman effort. When eight hours on *The Rescue* produced only three sentences, those pitiable sentences were erased. During later struggles with the story he informed Garnett, "I've destroyed all I did write last month. . . ." [127] In speaking of *Nostromo*, for which he " 'wrestled with the Lord,' " he mentioned the "wounded, dead pages that would be burnt at the end of the day." [128] While writing "A Smile of Fortune" in August, 1910, he was as rigorous as ever with himself: "I did not really start till July. June's work was mere fooling, – not on purpose, of course. I was still too limp to grasp the subject and most of the pages written then have been cancelled in type-script. It was strangely nerveless bosh." [129]

Conrad's frequent exhaustion was another sign of physical

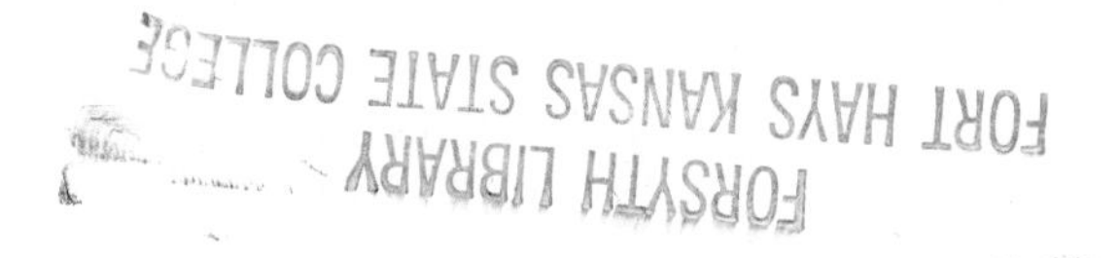

and psychological strain. Already tired from constant attacks of gout, he was quickly wearied by the effort to stimulate his imagination and to concentrate. He grumbled from time to time. "I am weary of the difficulty of it," he complained in October, 1899. "The game is not worth the candle; of course there is no question of throwing up the hand. It must be played out to the end. . . ." [130] Sometimes, after the exertion of completing a story, he had to go to bed. "I have been in bed two days," he wrote after terminating *The Nigger*, "A cheap price for finishing that story." [131] When he concluded *Chance* in 1912, he admitted, "J'en suis resté assomé pendant une quinzaine. Je commence à me réveiller. Naturellement je me sens stupide encore." [132] After the publication of his last completed novel, *The Rover*, he collapsed for ten weeks.[133]

Conrad was apt to call exhaustion indolence. Almost always he mentioned laziness in connection with other physical or mental difficulties.[134] When he began *Almayer's Folly*, while recuperating from Congo fever, he declared that he was "steeped deep in the indolence of a sailor away from the sea . . . the mood of absolute irresponsibility tasted to the full." [135] Convalescence more than holiday spirit must have induced the mood. Certainly he could not be charged with irresponsibility, when in 1924 after a bout of asthma he complained of "a certain mental languidness." [136] The feeling of laziness often accompanied difficulty in writing.[137] Perhaps what he called laziness was the fear of a future dependent on writing. At Montpellier in 1907 he admitted, "Il fait paresseux surtout ici. Ce que je n'ai pas envie de travailler!! . . . mon horreur de la plume." [138]

Conrad constantly dreaded the future. His fear was nourished by all the circumstances of his life. When he found that he was committed to the pen for a living, he confessed, "I am appalled at the absurdity of my situation – at the folly of my hopes, at the blindness that had kept me up in my gropings. Most appalled to feel that all the doors behind me are shut and that I must remain where I have come blundering in the dark." [139] Early difficulties destroyed his confidence. From 1898 he was "haunted by the idea I cannot write. . . . The harm is in its haunting me. For the last six months, I have not known a minute's real peace of mind." [140] In 1905 he summed his situation up bitterly: "I've been abominably ill. . . . And to-morrow I must start another short story. And I shall, of course, but I dread the to-morrow all the same. And in another 20 days or so, the same thing shall turn up again, the same powerlessness of body, the same anguish of mind." [141] He branded himself in 1909 as "a failure from the worldly point of view . . . knowing well that there can be no change, – that this must go on *usque ad finem*." [142] Until his unexpected success with *Chance* and *'Twixt Land and Sea* he felt no confidence in the future.

Anxiety produced in Conrad a horror at being behind with his work. The matter seems to have begun with the advance sale of *The Rescue*. "I am awfully behind," he remarked in June, 1898, "and though I can work my regular . . . I cannot make up for the lost three months. I am full of anxiety. Here, I have already had a 100 pounds on acct/!" [143] Again in 1899 he worried over not writing "quick enough to make up for the frightful leeway." [144] From time to time he found the strain too great. He feared in 1899 that "I have not the capacity and the power to go on, – to satisfy the just expectations of those who are dependent on my exertions." [145]

Sometimes pressure moved Conrad to the bitterest resentment against his profession. It demanded so much and for years did not even provide a living. Writing as an occupation turned out to be different from writing as a pastime: the amateur learned this lesson as he became a professional. In December, 1896, he admitted: "I used to write and to write ceaselessly, but now the sight of an inkpot and a penholder fill me with rage and disgust." [146] The bitterness of his tone increased with the years. "J'écris avec peine, lentement, raturant sans cesse," he declared in 1903. "Quel métier de chien! 'C'est un art trop difficile' comme ce cher et bon Henry James me dit. . . ." [147] Ford Madox Ford remembered Conrad's comparing his life to rowing up stream in a fog, not knowing whether he was advancing or falling back.[148] He likened his existence to a prison sentence: "There's neither inspiration nor hope in my work. It's mere hard labour for life – with this difference, that the life convict is at any rate out of harm's way – and may consider the account with his conscience closed. . . . I envy the serene fate and the comparative honesty of the gentlemen in grey who live in Dartmoor. I do really. . . ." [149]

A Personal Record [150] gives the most elaborate account of Conrad's loss of "the common joys of life that fall to the lot of the humblest on this earth. . . . It is difficult to characterize . . . the intimacy and strain of a creative effort in which mind and will and conscience are engaged to the full, hour after hour, day after day, away from the world, and to the exclusion of all that makes life really lovable and gentle – something for which a material parallel can only be found in the everlasting sombre stress of the westward winter passage round Cape Horn." There is always the suspicion that Conrad was exaggerating. But just how removed he was from the world and the common joys of life he described to Galsworthy in 1909. "In the last 23 1/2 months, I have written 187,000 words. . . . I sit 12 hours at the table, sleep six, and worry the rest of the time, feeling age creeping on and looking at those I love. For two years I haven't seen a picture, heard a note of music, had a moment of ease in human intercourse. . . ." [151] He spoke with bitter conviction in advising Mme. Poradowska in 1910 about a young literary protégé of hers: "Quand a moi je ne conseillarais jamais la carrière des lettres a personne." [152]

Conrad seems to have suffered more and longer than any author who has left an account of his labors. His poverty, his debts, his constant ill-health, his responsibilities would have been hard to bear without the sterility, the exhaustion, the fear. Cause and effect became so confused in his mind that he attributed all his troubles to the life of a writer.

Chapter IV

THE GROWTH OF THE TEXT

THE physical act of writing was complicated for Conrad by lack of privacy and of established routine. The pressure of poverty, ill-health, and imaginative stiffness unavoidably molded his habits of work. His author's notes, essays, letters, and especially his manuscripts display his method of writing.

When he was an amateur writing for amusement only, he was indifferent to the discomforts of his quarters. He worked on *Almayer's Folly* wherever he happened to be: in London, Poland, the Congo, Switzerland, and possibly at sea. He was not troubled by his surroundings at Champel and 17 Gillingham Street, London, S.W., while writing *An Outcast of the Islands*, since he had not yet accepted literature as a profession. The simplicity of the room in Gillingham Street proved that he did not crave luxury.[1] His bachelor quarters provided what seems to have been his chief need, privacy.

Apparently Conrad's fears and tensions caused him to object to his environment. His Gillingham Street quarters had nothing to do with his abandoning *The Sisters*, which he gave up on the advice of Edward Garnett.[2] After his marriage he wrote easily at Ile Grande in Brittany, where his house was roomy and comfortable.[3] During his six months there [4] he composed "The Idiots," "An Outpost of Progress," and "The Lagoon" and began *The Rescue* and *The Nigger*. He was so satisfied, despite some difficulties with *The Rescue*, that he considered remaining on the Continent indefinitely. Only fear for his health sent him back to England.[5]

On his return Conrad began to have chronic trouble with his work. The expense of life in England, family responsibilities, and ill-health provided such interruptions and worries that he tried to get back to sea. At once he became more aware of his environment. The slightest inconvenience irritated him out of all proportion. He could not control all distractions, though he refrained from opening his mail.[6] Because rent was high, his house was too small to give him a really private study.[7] He required "perfect silence" and freedom from even the smallest disturbances,[8] which for years he could not afford. Without any regular study he worked anywhere the inspiration seized him – in the bathroom, at the dining-room table, on the front porch, out of doors – and his wife tried to protect him from interruption.[9] He always worked untidily, accessible to all the interruptions of a growing family.

The Conrads were especially unlucky with their first English homes. In September, 1896, they went to live at Stanford-le-Hope in Essex.[10] They remained for six months in a "semi-detached villa," which Mrs. Conrad called superlatively uncomfortable and Conrad a " 'damned jerry-built rabbit hutch.' "[11] Here he began "Karain" and completed *The Nigger*. By the middle of March, 1897,[12] they could stand it no longer and moved to Ivy Walls, an Elizabethan farm-house in the neighborhood. Though an improvement over the house they had left, it was not large enough to give Conrad seclusion.[13] At Ivy Walls, where he lived some eighteen months, he wrote "Karain," "The Return," and "Youth," began *Lord Jim* and "Heart of Darkness," and went through his worst struggle with *The Rescue*. Finally it became impossible for him to work there. If he had not blamed his surroundings for his difficulty, he could not have endured the strain. It eased the burden to feel that the low situation of Ivy Walls prevented creation.[14]

Conrad began negotiations with Ford Madox Ford to rent his Pent Farm at Stanford, near Hythe, in Kent. At the end of September, 1898, he told Garnett, "When I feel sure of Pent Farm I shall be comparatively happy." [15] Late in October he moved to his new home.[16] "The mournful house under the bare downs," according to Ford, exercised "a great fascination over him." [17] Conrad liked it because it was "near the sea, though not absolutely in sight of it . . . (but I still have *la nostalgie de la mer*). . . ." [18] The farmhouse had literary associations; its pictures and furniture, which had come to Ford from Ford Madox Brown, Christina Rossetti, and other Pre-Raphaelites, appealed to Conrad.[19] He liked the Pent from the first. After a few days he announced, "The place is a success." [20] Here he stayed almost nine years,[21] and here he completed *Lord Jim* and "Heart of Darkness" and composed many other novels and short stories.

Even at the Pent he had no private room. He was a prey to intrusions. When W. H. Hudson paid an unexpected visit, he surprised Conrad at work in the living-room, frightened half to death because he mistook Hudson for a bailiff come to arrest him for debt.[22] Once while working on *Nostromo*, he was interrupted by a visitor. He felt "stunned and dazed, every nerve quivering with the pain of being uprooted out of one world and flung down into another. . . ." [23] His language probably does not exaggerate: Ford declared, "The occupation of writing to such a nature as Conrad's is terribly engrossing. To be suddenly disturbed is apt to cause a second's real madness." [24]

The need of a change of climate finally drove Conrad from the Pent. He confided to his friend Harriet Capes in the summer of 1907, "A dead set had been made at me by two doctors and half a dozen friends — the object of it being to force me away from the southern counties altogether. . . . Its so important that for the next couple of years I should keep well! All the future hinges on that. So we are going to try find something inland. . . ."[25] His health as well as his finances increased his trouble in finding the right place to work.

He had not been a year at his new home, the Someries, at Luton, Bedfordshire, before he found the environment impossible. "It's here that the pen is clogged," he complained. "I have a positive horror of this place. . . ."[26] The next house at Aldington, near Hythe, in Kent, to which the Conrads went in the spring of 1909, was even worse.[27] Soon Conrad was declaring, "This hole is growing more odious to me every day."[28] "I *must* have space and silence – silence!"[29] he repeated. From the spring of 1910 he established himself for nearly a decade at Capel House, Orleston, near Ashford, in Kent, where he found he could "certainly . . . write."[30] He moved to Spring Grove, Wye, for a few months in 1919 and there he finally completed *The Rescue*.[31] Though he stayed five years at his last home, Oswalds, Bishopbourne, near Canterbury, he was constantly restless. At the time of his death he was planning to move.[32] Curle, who met him in 1912, believed that it was not until Conrad lived at Oswalds that "he ever had a study."[33] But he was dependent upon his home even when the atmosphere made writing difficult. He did not adapt himself easily to temporary changes. His attempts to work at Capri and in London were not successful.[34] He regarded the isolation of his own home as a protection.[35]

Though Conrad attempted to work out some sort of routine, he was noticeably unsuccessful. He acknowledged to Wells: "As to working regularly in a decent and orderly and industrious manner, I've given that up from sheer impossibility. The damned stuff comes out only by a kind of mental convulsion lasting two, three or more days – up to a fortnight – which leaves me perfectly limp and not very happy, exhausted emotionally to all appearance, but secretly irritable to the point of savagery." [36] At times his way of writing can only be described as volcanic. He explained in another letter to Wells: "For me, writing – *the only possible writing* – is just simply the conversion of nervous force into phrases." Conrad's letters heap up proof that nervous force cannot be precisely harnessed. "In your case," he continued, "it is the disciplined intelligence which gives the signal – the impulse. For me it is a matter of chance, stupid chance. But the fact remains that when the nervous force is exhausted the phrases don't come – and no tension of will can help." [37] His reliance upon instinct put him at the mercy of his nerves. Mrs. Conrad commented on "the element of chance" in his work which "grew infinitely worse as he grew older." [38] His writing was dominated not by a will that disciplined his imagination efficiently but by an inefficient, painful bondage to time.

The element of chance entered Conrad's work not in the quality of what he wrote but in the unpredictable time he took tɔ complete a story. He always took too long. As he said of *A Set of Six*: "I've spent over these stories more time than they are worth; but this is true, I fear, of all my work." [39] Yet he was rigorous in his efforts to control the ungovernable element of time. He held himself firmly to his desk even when things were not going well with *An Outcast*. "J'ai ecrit fort peu," he admitted, "mais l'inspiration me vient en regardant le papier. Puis ce sont des echappées a perte de vue; la pensée s'en va vagabondant dans des grands éspaces remplis des formes vagues. Tout e[s]t chaos encore mais – lentement – les spectres se changent en chair vivante, les vapeurs flottantes se solidifient et qui sait? – peut-être quelque chose naitra dans le choc des idées indistinctes." [40]

Discipline did not always reward him with a completed page. During his honeymoon on Ile Grande, when he was having great difficulty with *The Rescue*, he devoted "every morning, day after day," [41] to the manuscript, to which he was unable to add a word. Before long he was speaking of a "working day of 8 hours." [42] So many of these hours were fruitless or productive only of nervous frenzy that he could not depend upon set times for work. He began to write "not only throughout the day but even far into the night." [43] Mrs. Conrad remembered how he would work late at night alone and also with Ford on their collaborations.[44] He was under the strain of composition almost twenty-four hours a day. The less he could write because of worry and ill-health, the more relentlessly he held himself at his desk. Though the discipline produced the short stories and novels by slow accumulation, the nervous cost can be reckoned from the bitter protests in the letters.[45]

The work done at almost phenomenal speed merely underlines Conrad's inconsistency. "The Idiots" was completed within a month in 1896, and "Youth" in a few days at the end of May, 1898. He even turned out "a 10000 or perhaps 12000 words story done in 10 days." [46] On rare occasions, spurred by the need for money, he produced an article with miraculous rapidity. He wrote once for the *English Review* and once for the *Daily Mail* under such circumstances.[47] Sometimes he could conclude a long piece of work at an amazing clip. He ended *Lord Jim* "with a steady drag of 21 hours," after he sent his family away from home and had absolute privacy.[48] He finished "The End of the Tether," *Nostromo*, and *Victory* with a volcanic overflow.[49] Possibly these whirl-wind conclusions were not good for his work: Ford suggested that Conrad would abandon some of his aims in order to ease the strain of writing.[50]

Conrad could write next to nothing, he could write in a torrent, but he could never count upon regularity. He tried to accept his irregular pace as indispensable to his temperament. The explanation was cold comfort to one who squandered time and accomplished little: "I have always that feeling of loafing at my work, as if powerless in an exhaustion of thought and will. Not enough! not enough! And yet perhaps those days without a line, nay, without a word, the hard, atrocious, agonizing days are simply part of my *method* of work, a decreed necessity of my production. Perhaps! But if it is so, then nothing can repay me for such a sombre fate. . . ." [51]

His method of shaping a story was largely to blame for the strain upon his imagination. Dependence upon memory for his subjects "frightened" him.[52] He needed long periods of brooding to assemble the material and to develop it. He discussed the process in the Preface to his "Shorter Tales." "However spontaneous the initial impulse," he declared, "not one of the stories . . . was achieved without much conscious thought bearing not only on the problems of their style but upon their relation to life as I have known it, and on the nature of my reactions to the particular instances as well as to the general tenor of my personal experience." [53] In the Author's Note to *Typhoon* [54] he reiterated that behind each of his creations lay all his past life and "a conscientious regard for the truth of my own sensations." He could never fuse his complex conceptions rapidly.

If Conrad's dependence upon instinct had not given him a distrust of notebooks and preliminary sketches, he might have mastered his ideas more easily. He denied, somewhat forgetfully, that he ever "made a note of a fact, of an impression or of an anecdote in my life." [55] The diary he kept in the Congo was a ship's log, not a literary notebook, and was not used for "Heart of Darkness." [56] The list of short-story subjects sent to Garnett [57] and the jottings in the Polish souvenir album now in the Harvard University Library [58] came closest to conventional notes. The outline which Conrad and Ford drew up for *Romance* was necessary in a collaboration.[59] In October, 1897, Conrad wrote out "a long epitome" of *The Rescue* for Pawling which, he said, "brought me to terms with myself." [60] The epitome, coming some twenty months after he began the novel, was hardly advance preparation; rather it resulted from absence of a preliminary sketch. The nearest approach to a plan can be found in the Harvard album, which contains a seven page skeleton of a play: act one, scenes one, two, and three, and the beginning of act two. Though the piece would have been a costume romance laid in what seems to be Renaissance Italy, it was apparently never developed. Conrad did not build his stories from any sort of writer's blueprint.[61]

His method of working out a story was instinctive and hazardous. As he showed in his comments on *Almayer's Folly*, he usually started with a strong impression of a character and situation and only a general conception of the events to be connected with them.[62] The details of the story depended upon the inspiration of the moment.[63] " 'You will discover, if you read my books,' " he explained to Mégroz in conversation, " 'how I am writing towards some fixed event or scene I can see, but I do not know how I shall ever get there.' " [64] Sometimes he began writing without a definite idea of the most important events. The Author's Notes to *Nostromo* [65] and *The Secret Agent*,[66] like Henry James' famous prefaces, accounted for the way the germs of the novels developed. The growth of *An Outcast of the Islands*, described for the most part while Conrad was actually writing, best illustrated how he built up a story.

An Outcast grew from the impression of a man whom

Conrad met at Olmeijer's house in Berouw. Though the man's name may have been De Veer, the novelist called his character Willems. Two days after he began to write he gave Mme. Poradowska a shadowy outline of the story and admitted he had not yet thought out the plot:

Je veux decrire a grand traits — sans ombres ni details — deux epaves humaines comme on en rencotre dans les coins perdus du monde. Un homme blanc et un Malais. . . . Le blanc c'est un ami d'Almayer le Malais c'est notre vieil ami Babalatchi. . . . Mais une catastrophe dramatique me me manque.[67]

For a considerable time he could not fill in the details of the action.[68] "Les idées ne viennent pas," he confessed. "Je ne *vois pas* ni les personnages ni les evenements." [69]

Then his conception of the story expanded. The character of Willems assumed definite shape:

Le motif d'abord c'est une vanité effrenée, feroce d'un homme ignorant qui a du succés mais n'a ni principes ni d'autre ligne de conduite que la satisfaction de sa vanité. — Aussi il n'est même pas fidèle a soi même.

As the personality of Willems emerged, so did the events of the story.

D'ou chute, degringolade subite jusqu'a l'esclavage physique de l'homme par une femme absolument sauvage. . . . La catastrophe sera amenée par les intrigues d'un petit etat malais, dont le dernier mot est: empoisonnement. Le denoument est: suicide par vanité encore.[70]

A new character had entered Conrad's imagination to alter the original idea. The woman, Aissa, supplanted Babalatchi, who, though now in the background, was used to bring about the hitherto missing catastrophe. Conrad had apparently not yet conceived of the way in which Babalatchi was to make Aissa his tool for controlling Willems. Willems did not commit suicide but was murdered by Aissa as the logical outcome of the intrigues, Malay and white, of the little native state, Sambir. The denouement of the novel came to Conrad much later.[71] Yet the death of Willems was the event towards which he had all the time been working; the details he was slow to imagine. The idea was plainly fluid in his imagination even after he began writing.[72] The pattern of action was altered in the course of composition. As he put it while writing the novel, "Une fois l'idée generale arretée il faut Vous laisser guider par l'inspiration du moment." [73]

Once Conrad had a preliminary notion, he went through a dramatic adjustment to it. As he wrote, he seems to have thrown himself into a story as an actor throws himself into a play. Mrs. Conrad disclosed how he acted out the startling first appearance of Wait in *The Nigger* and how he required her to rehearse with him scenes from the novels.[74] He projected a story on the screen of his imagination and deliberately went through the emotional reaction he expected of his audience. "In order to move others deeply," he remarked in *A Personal Record*,[75] "we must deliberately allow ourselves to be carried away beyond the bounds of our normal sensibility – innocently enough, perhaps, and of necessity, like an actor who raises his voice on the stage above the pitch of natural conversation. . . ." Just what his work cost Conrad in time and energy, just how thoroughly he experienced his own stories, was displayed in his advice to Edward Noble in 1895:

Imagination . . . should be used to create human souls: to disclose human hearts. . . . To accomplish it you must cultivate your poetic faculty, — you must give yourself up to emotions (no easy task). You must squeeze out of yourself every sensation, every thought, every image, — mercilessly, without reserve and without remorse: you must search the darkest corners of your heart, the most remote recesses of your brain, — you must search them for the image, for the glamour, for the right expression. And you must do it sincerely, at any cost: you must do it so that at the end of your day's work you should feel exhausted, emptied of every sensation and every thought, with a blank mind and an aching heart, with the notion that there is nothing, — nothing left in you. To me it seems that it is the only way to achieve true distinction — even to go some way towards it.[76]

The letter explains the strain of his surrender to creation.

So vivid were his conceptions that Conrad frequently drew little pictures of them. The manuscript of the Congo diary contains sketches of the river or the country side on almost every page.[77] Mrs. Conrad once saw a drawing of Nina Almayer in red and black ink, perhaps intended as an illustration for the novel.[78] In the manuscript of *Almayer's Folly* [79] is a plan of a compound beside a river, with a large house, a smaller house, several outhouses, and trees. Mrs. Conrad remarked on the skill with which he drew a picture of Karain when he had just begun the story.[80] In the manuscript of *The Laugh*,[81] which later grew into *The Arrow of Gold*, is a drawing of a floor plan, apparently of the house in Marseilles which belonged to Doña Rita and in which Mr. Blunt and Monsieur George lived. Conrad also made a sketch of Doña Rita herself and one of Old Peyrol, the hero of his last completed novel, *The Rover*.[82]

When he had worked himself into the mood of the story, he was unwilling to break it – "to get out of tune." [83] He told Mme. Poradowska, "Je regrette chaque minute que je passe loin du papier." [84] He resented any interruption: "Il me serait insupportable de quitter un ouvrage qui me tiendrait au coeur." [85] It was his destiny to be the prey of almost all the interruptions that can beset a writer.

If the pictorial or dramatic tone of a story faded in his imagination, Conrad worked strenuously to recall it. Often he had to refresh his impressions of *The Rescue* by reading over the manuscript and visualizing the forgotten scenes. In 1910, when he planned to resume that troublesome story, he declared, "It will take me a week to read and think myself into a proper frame of mind." [86] Before he finished the novel, he was not so sanguine. He feared to be taken "out of the mood for *The Rescue*, which I have been cultivating most earnestly for the last six weeks and have in a measure attained now." [87] The difficulty of the actual writing may have prolonged his imaginative reflections. "J'ai la paresse de tous les Polonais," he admitted, "je prefère rêver un roman que l'écrire. Car le rêve de l'oeuvre est toujours beaucoup plus beau que la réalité de la chose imprimée. Et puis l'Anglais m'est toujours une langue étrangère qui demande un effort formidable pour être maniée." [88] The letter suggests that his knowledge of Polish and French complicated his English style and prevented his concentrating on the narrative. His devices for creating the atmosphere of a story, though they delayed him, were psychologically necessary.

Sometimes the evocations of mood could not prevent indecision and change. Conrad did not consider his "first plans" final. Mrs. Conrad declared, "I don't think Conrad ever conceived his books as wholes before he began to write." [89] Lack of clear intention was responsible for a great deal of his procrastination and despair, especially with *The Rescue*. "Now I've got all my people together," he lamented, "I don't know what to do with them. The progressive episodes of the story *will* not emerge from the chaos of my sensations." [90] Indecision accounted for the unexpected length of some of his stories. From *An Outcast of the Islands* to *The Rover* he was never sure that his short stories might not grow into novels. The classic example was *Lord Jim*, which he intended to treat in twenty thousand words [91] and which developed into some hundred and twenty thousand.

Conrad's early approach to writing was altogether emotional. He was guided by impulse; he depended upon spurts of inspiration; he lacked objective standards. In a comment on Mme. Poradowska's *Mariage du Fils Grandsire* he discounted himself as a critic and revealed the source of his judgments:

> Mon appreciation de Votre livre — de tout livre — est purement émotionale. — De l'ouvrage, du travail, de la ciselure — si je puis m'exprimer ainsi — je ne peux guère juger; et comme l'emotion est une affaire personelle mon jugement ne peut qu'être incomplet et bien souvent incorrect. Vous voyez donc que je perd la joie de "celui qui sait" et voit l'oeuvre d'art dans son entier. — Mais il m'est permis — heureusement — de m'oublier dans la contemplation des images charmantes, d'écouter la musique des mots écrits; de vivre la vie, de respirer dans l'air, de partager les joies et les douleurs, les espérances, et les regrets qui remplissent ce coin de l'Univers que Votre plume de magicienne a crée.[92]

Unconsciously he disclosed the attitude he must have taken while working on his own stories. He experienced all the disadvantages and advantages of the instinctive artist: inability to grasp the whole, want of confidence, waste motion in contrast to individual rhythm and the power to create vivid pictures and living characterizations.

With a seaman's ingenuity Conrad set about to correct the lack of economy in his method. The first remedy was to work on two or more stories at once. When he began the habit, he was having much trouble with *The Rescue*. Acting on a visual suggestion, he wrote "The Idiots." Shortly thereafter he began *The Nigger*. It, in turn, was put down while he went back to *The Rescue*, which he again dropped to write two other short stories, "An Outpost of Progress" and "The Lagoon." After the summer of 1896 alternation became almost a principle. To work on new material when the old became stale was a great relief. A novel would form the chief project, which would be laid aside periodically for a short story or essay. While he was primarily concerned with *Lord Jim*, he also wrote "Youth" and "Heart of Darkness" and collaborated with Ford on *The Inheritors* and *Romance*. When at work on *The Secret Agent*, *Chance*, *Under Western Eyes*, and *Victory*, he produced countless short stories, articles, and books of reminiscence. *The Rescue* occupied him intermittently for nearly a quarter of a century. At the end of his life he was working on *Suspense*, which he had put aside to write a short story that grew into a novel, *The Rover*. Except for *The Sisters* [93] he apparently meant to complete every piece of work he had once begun. As he said of *The Rescue*, "I wanted the deck cleared before going below. As to leaving any loose ends hanging over the side, I couldn't bear the thought of it!" [94]

Dictation, another practice to increase efficiency, grew out of Conrad's habit of writing two things at once. He seems to have first resorted to it early in 1904 when he was working on *Nostromo* and *The Mirror of the Sea*. On February 7 he told Wells, "I've started a series of sea sketches and . . . I've discovered that I can dictate that sort of bosh without effort at the rate of 3,000 words in four hours. . . . So in the day *Nostromo* and, from 11 to 1 A.M., dictation." [95] The change of material and of method provided a double respite. Dictation enabled Conrad to continue working far into the night. As an alternative means it was not always successful: in that portion of *The Mirror* called "The Inland Sea" he dictated "five typewritten pages, then finding I did not get on wrote the paper to the end."[96] Towards the end of his life he fell back upon dictation to a great extent: *The Arrow of Gold* and *The Rescue* in its final phase were largely dictated.[97] Curle remarked that the double system of writing and dictating gave Conrad "the visual sense of what he was doing while enabling him to have the benefit of that clear contemplation which comes from dictating."[98] But he implied that Conrad never took to it whole-heartedly. Though it must have helped during illness, it was not entirely satisfactory to a writer who labored over details and insisted on perfection.

Conrad was a perfectionist in both philosophy and practice, an exacting combination. He respected writers like Maupassant who had "the power of artistic honesty, one may say of artistic virtue. The inherent greatness of the man consists in this, that he will let none of the fascinations that beset a writer working in loneliness turn him away . . . from the vouchsafed vision of excellence."[99] With entire sincerity Conrad felt himself "under the obligation of a more scrupulous fidelity to the truth of my own sensations."[100] He set about his writing with "a quite ridiculous scrupulosity and an absurd seriousness."[101] His exactness was vividly illustrated in his minute corrections of his friends' writings. He would enter into the most intricate discussion of conception, structure, and expression. He devoted some five hundred words to a criticism of an article by Norman Douglas.[102] He wrote a thousand words to Hugh Clifford about a short story.[103] Once he made a fifteen hundred word study of the rough draft of Galsworthy's *Fraternity*.[104]

Conrad's thorough attention to other men's work emphasized his demanding scrutiny of every line of his own. He was so "extravagantly nervous about details" that he would "go mad over a sentence."[105] He pondered each word in each sentence before he put it into his manuscript. In 1896 he spoke of "the wear and tear of my writing. . . . I write in doubt over every line. I ask myself – Is it right? –Is it true? – Do I feel it so? – Do I express all my feeling? And I ask it at every sentence. I perspire in incertitude over every word!"[106] "*Every* word," he cautioned Galsworthy in 1899, "is an object to be considered anxiously with heart searchings and in a spirit of severe resolution. Don't write them (words) hurriedly."[107] His considerations were almost philosophic: "Give me the right word and the right accent," he once remarked, "and I will move the world."[108] Compelled by such a belief, he felt all too frequently that he had "lost all *sense* of style and yet [was] haunted, mercilessly haunted by the *necessity* of style."[109] He would "dream for hours, hours! over a sentence and even then [be unable to] put it together so as to satisfy the cravings of my soul."[110]

Though Conrad asserted occasionally that he was too lazy to work over what he had once written,[111] he tested each word severely even after he had put it in the manuscript. He was continually reworking. "It's no use parting with stuff which may require weeks of correcting work," he explained to Pinker, who had asked for manuscript. "Moreover, when I have it [the manuscript] by me a lucky idea occurs and is set down in its place; whereas when the MS. is not there it is lost because my brain has no storage room."[112] His letters reported his labor on manuscript, typescript, serial, and even galley proof.[113] His intense absorption in revision was illustrated by an anecdote of Ford's:

We had finished . . . "Romance" after an all-night sitting and were taking the manuscript up to London. . . . We went on correcting and correcting the manuscript in the train. . . . The train jostled frightfully. My collaborator in his exasperated haste over his corrections lay down on the floor and wrote and wrote, swearing frantically at the motion. The train went into Charing Cross, the terminus, and stopped. He still wrote and wrote — when I disturbed him . . . he sprang straight from the floor at my throat. He had been in the Cuba of our "Romance" among the pirates.[114]

Conrad's repeated correction of his work led Curle to estimate that "some of it is extant in at least six different states – the manuscript, the corrected typescript, the serial form, the American book form, the English book form, and the collected edition book form." [115] In addition Conrad worked on states which, though not extant, can be traced.

In the period with which this study is concerned, the six states mentioned by Curle cannot all be followed for any important story, either because the story never existed in all six or because some have been lost. The manuscript, typescript, serial, English, American, and definitive book forms of the stories completed by 1900 show Conrad's methods of composition. A representative analysis can be safely based on *Almayer's Folly*, his first production, *The Nigger*, with which he dedicated himself to literature, and *Lord Jim*, which marked the climax of his early period as a novelist.

Never published serially, *Almayer's Folly* exists in the other five states mentioned by Curle. The survival of the typescript allows a study of Conrad's method impossible with *The Nigger* and *Lord Jim*, of which the typescripts have almost entirely disappeared. The differences between the manuscript and the typescript show that the novel must have existed in an intermediate state; the differences between the typescript and the first edition show that the proofs must be regarded as a separate state. Two more states of *Almayer's Folly* must be considered, further evidence of Conrad's exacting care with his work even before he had accepted literature as a career.

The manuscript in the Rosenbach Collection, of which chapter nine is missing, is the earliest existing state of the novel. It is probably the first draft. The manuscript often contains sentences not found in the published text: [116]

The risks were great, and Almayer thought more than once with a slight thrill of apprehension of the silent, poisoned darts, the favorite arm of the river Dyak. But Maroola was brave. . . .[117]

The dangers were great, but Maroola was brave. . . .[118]

Similarly the manuscript lacks sentences:

Almayer stepped homewards with long strides and mind uneasy. Was Dain also going to play him false? — Wherefore talk with Lakamba? . . . At this point in his meditations he found himself at the foot of the steps leading to the verandah of his home.[119]

Almayer stepped homewards with long strides and mind uneasy. Surely Dain was not thinking of playing him false. It was absurd. Dain and Lakamba were both too much interested in the success of his scheme. . . . At this point in his meditation he found himself at the foot of the steps leading to the verandah of his home.[120]

Aside from subtractions and additions, the passages contain minor alterations of wording. The novel was not set up from the manuscript.

Examination reveals that the Rosenbach manuscript and the typescript in the Leeds Collection differ strikingly. There is evidence that an intermediate typescript was made and carefully corrected, of which the Leeds typescript is probably a fair copy. Clearly Conrad showed the story to Mme. Poradowska in an early typescript which he revised in detail.[121] He mentioned specifically his revisions of the early chapters, and a comparison of the Rosenbach manuscript and the Leeds typescript shows the sort of stylistic changes carried out in the intermediate typescript. The manuscript uses words and phrases not found in the typescript:

Having no will of his own he was however gifted with an active and unruly imagination.[122]

He was gifted with a strong and active imagination. . . .[123]

The typescript adds words and phrases to the manuscript:

Turning round he beheld the pretty little house, the new godowns built neatly by an army of chinese carpenters, and felt that the world was his.[124]

When, turning round, he beheld the pretty little house, the big godowns built neatly by an army of Chinese carpenters, the new jetty round which were clustered the trading canoes, he felt a sudden elation in *of* the thought that the word was his.[125]

The first five chapters in the manuscript, though they show important differences from the Leeds typescript, do not reveal so many physical signs of correction as do later chapters in the manuscript. The textual alterations in these early chapters were surely made in the intermediate typescript. Yet differences in text are by no means confined to the early chapters: Conrad once spoke of "practically rewriting" the story.[126] In chapter eleven the Rosenbach manuscript runs:

. . . she laid her head on his bronze shoulder with a sense of defiance to all the world in the encircling protection of that *arm* strong arm her arm. All of him was hers. His bravery and his *cunning* [?] strength, his recklessness and his cunning his virtues and his faults, his thought — the very breath of his life was hers.[127]

The Leeds typescript reads:

> . . . she laid her head on his shoulder with a sense of defiance to all the world in the encircling protection of that arm. He was hers all his qualities and all his faults. His strength and his courage, his recklessness and his daring, his simple wisdom and his savage cunning — all were hers.[128]

The highly important changes in plot, though they too are most noticeable in chapter one, run through the whole story.[129] All the evidence points to a non-extant intermediate typescript in which the stage of the story found in the Rosenbach manuscript was altered to the stage found in the Leeds typescript.

The first edition did not exactly follow the existing typescript, which was apparently the one submitted to Unwin.[130] Of course some passages in which the typescript agreed with the manuscript were corrected on the typescript itself to the form they bear in the printed text:

> eat
> "Do not let him see on your face the pain that will *make* your heart *sick*." [131]

Such corrections abound, showing that Conrad availed himself profitably of Unwin's permission to work on the story before it was set up.[132] Yet the typescript contains uncorrected passages that differ from the printed text. There are variations in sentence structure:

> . . . with a shining mass of black long hair falling in heavy tresses over her shoulders, making her pale olive complexion look paler. . . .[133]

> . . . with a shining mass of long black hair that fell in heavy tresses over her shoulders, and made her pale olive complexion look paler. . . .[134]

Most of the discrepancies are merely verbal:

A sigh full of unspeakable sorrow passed over the land in the last effort of the dying breeze, and in the great silence which succeeded, the earth and the Heavens were suddenly hushed. . . .[135]

A sigh as of immense sorrow passed over the land in the last effort of the dying breeze, and in the deep silence which succeeded, the earth and the heavens were suddenly hushed. . . .[136]

Conrad must have worked in detail on the proof sheets which Unwin promised to print off quickly for him [137] and which mark another state of development.

Though the American edition of *Almayer's Folly* did not come to Conrad's attention until November, 1919, he revised the English in April, 1916, for the definitive edition.[138] Working on a copy which he afterwards presented to J. B. Pinker, he cut several hundred words from the text. Occasionally he altered only a word, cut only a phrase:

"Will come to-morrow, he said." [139]

"Promised to come to-morrow." [140]

Usually he excised entire sentences. The excisions were sometimes of description:

A general air of squalid neglect pervaded the place. Great red stains on the floor and walls testified to frequent and indiscriminate betelnut chewing. The light breeze from the river swayed gently the tattered blinds. . . .[141]

A general air of squalid neglect pervaded the place. The light breeze from the river swayed gently the tattered blinds. . . .[142]

Sometimes they were of analysis:

Thenceforth there was slavery in the far countries, amongst strangers, in unknown and perhaps terrible surroundings. Being fourteen years old, she realised her position and came to that conclusion, the only one possible to a Malay girl, soon ripened under a tropical sun, and not unaware of her personal charms, of which she heard many a young brave warrior of her father's crew express an appreciative admiration. There was in her the dread of the unknown; . . .[143]

Thenceforth there was slavery in the far countries, amongst strangers, in unknown and perhaps terrible surroundings. There was in her the dread of the unknown; . . .[144]

He was intent, even after twenty years, on quickening the pace of the story.

In view of Conrad's emphasis on the comparative ease with which he wrote his first novel, the amount of correction is surprising. "The conversion of nervous force into phrases" left its physical traces on the manuscript of *Almayer's Folly*. The first five chapters, especially chapters two and three, are less worked over than the rest of the novel. The sixth, seventh, and eighth chapters abound in modifications; the tenth and eleventh are the most heavily corrected. Mrs. Conrad remarked on her husband's discontent "at the second reading of anything he had written."[145] The manuscript of *Almayer's Folly* proves that he had always been discontented.

Apparently Conrad worked his wording out on paper. When he decided against a word, he usually scratched it out and did not rewrite the entire sentence up to the point of cancelation. He wrote the new word or phrase sometimes above the cancelation, sometimes immediately after it, as the following example reveals:

care to ask
He did not *dare question* awed by the calm impassiveness of her face, by those *great eyes* solemn eyes. . . .[146]

On occasion he superimposed the new word directly on the discarded one, mostly with technicalities of language, changes in tense, in preposition, and in construction.[147] Frequently words were added above the line when there was no cancelation to fill out:

> move to destruction!
> Why? Not likely! [148]

Parts of sentences were interchanged by brackets and arrows indicating the new positions.[149] The varied conditions under which Conrad wrote the novel were reflected in a trivial but interesting way. Though most of the manuscript was written in ink, pages eleven through fifteen of chapter five were done originally in pencil and then retraced in ink; the first seven and a half pages of chapter eight remained in indelible pencil.

Although Conrad seems to have made it a habit to destroy the false starts of composition,[150] a few traces of them survive. A page that escaped destruction contains the first version of the opening of chapter eleven, some two hundred and fifty words; [151] the extra page suggests other abandoned attempts. On the versos of completed pages are fragments of unsuccessful phrasings. The first draft of page seventeen, chapter four, for instance, can be found on the verso of page twenty-two, chapter four. Sometimes Conrad saved the discarded sheet to use the fair side. One curious example allows several explanations. The first version of page five, chapter three, appears on the verso of page three, chapter three. Perhaps he rewrote the first five pages (at least), using the fair side of one abandoned page. Perhaps he began by accident to write page five on the fair side of page three without noticing his previous use of the sheet. The rapid cancelations and corrections fitted his moods of worry and spurts of nervous action.

The states of *Almayer's Folly* reveal that Conrad constantly sharpened his prose. The changes in the manuscript condensed the material, although there were many additions intended to increase the vividness of impression. The picture of Mrs. Almayer on the riverbank was enlarged for greater distinctness:

She stopped *listening intently* straining her ears to catch the slightest sound. . . .[152]

Generally he was intent upon reducing redundant impressions:

. . . over the sunlit solitude *of that path generally usually so full of the awakening of daily life* of the settlement.[153]

The corrections in the typescript for the most part continued the search for the exact word and did not affect the length of the novel:

trodden
heavy
. . . the *rotten* grass of the courtyard.[154]

In reworking the first English edition he cut scores of words at a time. Nina's return to Sambir was originally treated thus:

. . . contempt from white people for her mixed blood. She had tasted the whole bitterness of it and remembered distinctly that the virtuous Mrs. Vinck's indignation was not so much directed against the young man from the bank as against the innocent cause of that young man's infatuation. And there was also no doubt in her mind that the principal cause of Mrs. Vinck's indignation was the thought that such a thing should happen in a white nest, where her snow-white doves, the two Misses Vinck, had just returned from Europe, to find shelter under the maternal wing, and there await the coming of irreproachable men of their destiny. Not even the thought of the money so painfully scraped together by Almayer, and so punctually sent for Nina's expenses, could dissuade Mrs.

Vinck from her virtuous resolve. Nina was sent away, and in truth the girl herself wanted to go, although a little frightened by the impending change. And now she had lived on the river for three years. . . .[155]

The four full sentences were cut in the definitive edition because they repeated in analysis what had already been advanced in dialogue.[156] The alterations in the entire novel led to greater exactness and condensation.

Because Conrad did not rewrite a sentence whenever he changed a word, the evolution of some of the heavily worked passages can be traced. His imagination can be caught selecting, discarding, piecing together. The opening of chapter eleven provides a valuable example because it exists in more states than any other part of the novel. In the manuscript the abandoned page of chapter eleven contains his preliminary attempt to describe Dain Maroola in Bulangi's clearing on the night of his escape from Sambir. It reads:

sigh
He turned over with an impatient *sighs*, and pillowing his head on his bent arm lay*d* quietly with his face to the *fire* dying fire. The glowing embers shone redly in a small circle and
ting a and
put gleam into his *eyes* wide open eyes, *and his steady breathing*
left by of bygone fires light cloud
at every deep breath the fine white ash rose in a *small puff* from before his parted lips and danced *upward into the* [indecipher-
to lose itself in the moonbeams
able] away from the warm glow *into the cold moonlight The*
Bulangi's
great flood of moonlight pouring down upon *the* clearing.[157]

The corrections did more than remove such grammatical mistakes as *sighs* and *layd* and vary the sentence structure by the change of *put* to *putting*. Conrad continually added to the picture, by turning a non-visual phrase like *small puff* into *light cloud* and by qualifying *eyes* as *wide open eyes*. The cancelation of *cold moonlight* destroyed the too obvious contrast with *warm glow*. The style was tightened when the unnecessary *left by* was condensed into *bygone* and *the great flood of moonlight* into *pouring*.*

Conrad was dissatisfied with the whole passage, of which these two sentences were only a part. He discarded it and tried again. This time he began with two paragraphs describing the clearing itself and worked up to the description of Dain Maroola:

> He turned over on his side with an impatient sigh and, pillowing his head on his bent arm [indecipherable] *again he sighed and changed his position lying now on his back, both his hands under his head, his face turned to the stars. His* lay
> *embers*
> quietly, with his face to the dying fire. The glowing embers shone redly in a small circle throwing a gleam into his wide-open eyes and at every deep breath the fine white ash of bygone
> cloud
> fires rose in a light before his parted lips and danced away from the warm glow into the moonbeams pouring down upon Bulangi's clearing. His body was weary. . . .[158]

The nervousness of Conrad's corrections is worth noticing: after beginning the second sentence he suddenly cut the first sentence in half and gave it a new ending. The deleted phrases merely repeated what preceded and left Dain Maroola looking at the stars. With Maroola in such a position Conrad could not use the description of the fire. He eliminated the useless *from* and *to lose itself* of the first

* In the quotations from the manuscripts and typescripts the words in italics were canceled by Conrad. In my analyses of these quotations words are italicized to distinguish them.

version and exchanged the neutral *putting* for the more active *throwing*.

After these corrections he was satisfied with the passage and with a few changes in punctuation let it stand in the typescript and in the first edition.[159] For the definitive edition he condensed it. The final version reads:

> He turned over on his side with an impatient sigh, and, pillowing his head on his bent arm, lay quietly with his face to the dying fire. The glowing embers shone redly in a small circle, throwing a gleam into his wide-open eyes. His body was weary. . . .[160]

It would be interesting to know Conrad's reasons for the deletion. Was it to shorten one of the shortest of his novels? Or did he visualize the scene so minutely that he saw Dain Maroola not only raising a cloud of ashes when he breathed out but also choking from the ashes he drew down into his lungs?

Conrad's habit of leaving his first attempt on the page with his ultimate choice reveals his unexpected economy with word, phrase, and sentence. He could never irrevocably reject anything that he wrote until he tried every possible way of including it.[161] Perhaps his frugality arose from nautical neatness and efficiency. Continuous financial worry, the slow evolution of even his first phrasings, and the dread of prolonged inactivity may also have made him afraid to discard so much as a word.

Sometimes he was thrifty only in the rearrangement of a sentence. There are examples of redistribution in which not an idea or a word was lost:

Then in the hot nights of the s.w. monsoon she slept

dreamlessly under the bright stars on the platform built outside
well *outside on the platform built over the river under*

the house and over the river
the bright stars.[162]

The rearrangement, which he allowed to stand in the typescript, the first, and the definitive editions,[163] removed *under the bright stars* from its awkward position at the end of the sentence and attached it to *dreamlessly* and the verb *slept*. Not a phrase was wasted.

Sometimes Conrad tried his preciously hoarded words in different settings before he fitted them to his satisfaction.

as of the traces *of* left by a desperate
The appearance *of a violent* struggle *having taken place* was
which
accentuated by the chairs *that lay about* seemed to have been
scattered place
flung about violently all over the *verandah* and now lay about
the verandah
[indecipherable] with a ludicrous suggestion of inebriety in
big
their helpless attitudes. Only Nina's rocking chair *towering*
furniture
above the chaos of demoralized stood on its high runners stand-
black and the
ing motionless *and black* on *its* high runners towered above the
chaos of *demoralized furniture dignified in its patient readiness*
in
to take up its burden with all the dignity of unflinchingly and
upright and [*read*]*y*
grave readiness to take up its burden in demoralized furniture,
patient
unflinchingly dignified and *upright*; waiting for its burden.[164]

In the first sentence *violent* reappeared as *violently*, and possibly because of alliteration *verandah* was changed to *place*. *Lay about* was removed from the first clause only to be worked into the second. *Flung about* was changed to *scattered*, perhaps to avoid the repetition of *about*. In the second sentence *Towering above the chaos of demoralized furniture*, though *towering* was altered to *towered*, haunted Conrad's imagination until he disposed of it. *Black* shifted its position in relation to *motionless*, perhaps for the rhythmic effect of the unaccented syllables. *Dignified* was altered to *dignity* and then restored to its original form. *Readiness to take up its burden*, twice introduced, was twice abandoned in a general condensation. The whole phrase was metamorphosed into *waiting for its burden*; the implication was reinforced by the final choice of *patient* instead of *upright*. *Upright* was cast out for the second time, and *unflinchingly*, once cut, was restored.

The typescript [165] introduces a few changes that satisfied Conrad with the passage. *Ludicrous suggestion* was crossed out and *lamentable aspect* written above, possibly to avoid over-emphasis on a somewhat dubious comic touch. In the phrase *on the high runners* the change of *the* back to *its*, as the manuscript first read, removed one of Conrad's characteristic mistakes in English. The version finally printed, with punctuation probably not his own, reads:

> The appearance as of traces left by a desperate struggle was accentuated by the chairs, which seemed to have been scattered violently all over the place, and now lay about the verandah with a lamentable aspect of inebriety in their helpless attitudes. Only Nina's big rocking-chair, standing black and motionless on its high runners, towered above the chaos of demoralized furniture, unflinchingly dignified and patient, waiting for its burden.[166]

At times Conrad showed on a larger scale his desire to save anything worth preserving. Whole sentences were canceled only to be incorporated later into the novel. An instance is found in Almayer's dream on the night Nina left Sambir forever:

er
He got a firm foothold and stiffened his muscles in heroic resolve to carry his burden *to all eternity. And now the mysterious Power that laid upon him the giant task seemed to seek his his destruction. With terror he felt an irresistible hand shake him by the shoulder, while the voices swelled louder into an agonized prayer to go! go! before it is too late*; to all eternity.[167]

The cancelation was wholesale but not permanent. A few lines later the printed text contains the discarded sentences in almost identical form.

He got a firmer foothold and stiffened his muscles in heroic resolve to carry his burden to all eternity. And ages passed in the superhuman labour, amidst the rush of circling worlds; in the plaintive murmur of sorrowful voices urging him to desist before it was too late — till the mysterious power that had laid upon him the giant task seemed at last to seek his destruction. With terror he felt an irresistible hand shaking him by the shoulder, while the chorus of voices swelled louder into an agonized prayer to go, go before it is too late.[168]

With unimportant additions and a few minor changes in construction the canceled passage has been carefully restored.

Almayer's Folly illustrates the gradual evolution of Conrad's plots. A comparison of the manuscript and typescript with the printed text gives the rough and smooth sides of the material. He began the story with the central theme clearly stated on the first two pages of the manuscript. Almayer was presented in a state of financial and domestic decay, dreaming of the gold he intended to get somehow before he died.[169] Yet in the opening pages of the manuscript there was no mention even by implication of the two most important agents in Almayer's life: his daughter Nina and Dain Maroola, her lover. They were mentioned at the opening of the typescript and the printed text.[170] Between the Rosenbach manuscript and the Leeds typescript Conrad rewrote the first two pages to introduce important conceptions not in his mind when he began.

The idea of Almayer's fierce love for Nina came slowly to Conrad. Paternalism was not a reason for Almayer's wanting to make a fortune and leave Sambir in the opening pages of the manuscript as it was in the typescript and book form.[171] It did not appear in the manuscript version of Almayer's first conversation with Nina, though it was present in the typescript and the printed text.[172] Most of the changes involve passages too voluminous to compare in full.[173] Brief evidence will show how the addition of paternal love altered the whole tone. When Almayer first spoke to Nina, in the manuscript his mood was expressed thus:

> Almayer spoke peevishly and dropped heavily into the nearest armchair by the table.[174]

In the printed version the incident reads:

> Almayer spoke jovially and dropped with a contented sigh into the armchair nearest to the table.[175]

When he introduced Dain Maroola into the action on the opening night of the story, Conrad had no clear conception of his relationship to Almayer. In the manuscript the young Malay and the Dutchman had no enterprise in common nor even an understanding.[176] The published novel reveals that between the Rosenbach manuscript and the Leeds typescript Conrad rewrote the conversation to fit his new conception of Dain's and Almayer's relationship. Now Almayer had a definite understanding with Dain, for he had been " 'waiting for [him] every day and every night.' " He implored his friend " 'not . . . to abandon me now, when all is ready.' "[177] The two were engaged upon an enterprise involving Dain's brig, which had run afoul of the Dutch authorities, an occurrence not even suggested by the manuscript.[178] In the manuscript,[179] before Conrad thought of the powder-running activities of the brig, four men brought Dain up the river. In the typescript[180] they were reduced to two; the other two had been killed in the brig's fatal fight with the Dutch coastguard.[181]

The evolution of Almayer's enterprise brings out the vagueness of Conrad's original plans. A correction in the manuscript shows that the secrecy of the Pantai River was an afterthought:

Into that river whose entrances himself only knew
was
That where Lingard used to take his assorted cargo.[182]

The disaster which disclosed Lingard's secret was not at first clearly conceived.[183] Though he corrected himself in the manuscript, originally he may have planned to have the secret surprised by the English traders who were Lingard's rivals:

> Almayer struggled with difficulties in the midst of Arab intrigues, *white competition* (for the river had been found out by those indefatigable traders). . . .[184]

Conrad did not plan minutely the scheme whereby Lingard and Almayer hoped to recoup their fortunes after losing the trade monopoly. The opening chapter shows how the gold hunt was worked up. Almayer's conversation with Nina about Dain revealed in the manuscript that Almayer had " 'the means of getting away [from Sambir] almost within my reach,' " but did not suggest that he had yet broached any plan to Dain. He intended to approach

Dain with his project on the next day.[185] In the typescript version of the conversation Almayer mentioned an expedition that he and Dain were to start upon " 'the day after to-morrow.' "[186] According to the manuscript Conrad intended the expedition to be highly melodramatic.

> Guided by the scraps of information contained in old Lingard's book he was going to seek for the big diamond and the gold nuggets, the old seaman had buried. . . .[187]

The conception of a buried treasure, in the tradition of a boy's book of adventure, was toned down in the Leeds typescript:

> Guided by the scraps of information contained in old Lingard's pocket-book he was going to seek for the rich gold mine; for that place where he had only to stoop to gather up an immense fortune and realise the dream of his young days.[188]

The buried treasure died hard. Conrad had to remove it from later pages of the typescript:

> gold was to be found
> . . . where the *treasure was supposed to be buried* was a sore point. . . .[189]

The diamonds were never entirely eliminated. Though the manuscript reads, "Expedition! Diamonds!," the typescript and published version read, "Expedition! Gold!"[190] But the diamonds can still be found on page twenty-four of the definitive edition.

Conrad may have intended to elaborate his plot. After discovering the riches of the interior, Lingard went back to England to raise money to develop them. From home he wrote according to the manuscript, "saying he was ill, had only found one relation living – a young man – but little else besides."[191] Perhaps Conrad meant to introduce a rival claimant or a helper who would ultimately steal the treasure from the unfortunate Almayer. Such a supposition is borne out by an abandoned passage earlier in the manuscript:

> Was Dain also going to play him false? . . . Who ever looks for honesty in a Malay. A white man was what he wanted. But there was no white man![192]

He may have planned also to use the young man as an actor in the love story. The mysterious young man had disappeared in the typescript: the letter came from Lingard "saying he was ill, had found no relation living – but little else besides."[193] The awkwardness of *but little else besides* betrays the elimination.

The love affair of Nina and Dain Maroola was another important strand not clearly worked out in advance. Almayer's first conversation with Dain contained in the manuscript[194] no allusion at all to Nina. In the typescript Dain's first speech alluded to his passion for her:

> "Nothing could have stopped me from coming back here" — said the other almost violently — "Not even death" — he whispered to himself.[195]

The idea of the love affair must have occurred to Conrad quickly: in all versions Nina's first conversation with her father suggested her interest in Dain.[196]

The manuscript and the typescript show that Conrad's imagination worked constantly on the details of the story while he wrote. Slowly he felt his way toward the right instruments for bringing about Almayer's ruin. Although energy may have been wasted, the story must have remained alive in his mind because of his freedom in altering work already done.

The Nigger of the "Narcissus" introduces a stage of development never existing with *Almayer's Folly*, the serial. The Rosenbach manuscript, which is complete, is the earliest extant and probably the original state of the story. The typescript has disappeared; nothing is known about it at the office of William Heinemann, Ltd., who published the novel, or of James B. Pinker and Son. At one time it must have existed. *Almayer's Folly* shows that Conrad submitted his work to editors typewritten, and the manuscript of *The Nigger* is too illegible for any publisher's reader. With the manuscript is one unnumbered typewritten page beginning, "The cook wrung his hands . . . ," and ending, "Why not cried a voice": the passage can be found on pages 128–130 of the manuscript and on pages 118–119 of the Canterbury Edition. The typewritten page follows the corrected manuscript and is identical with the printed text except for one sentence omitted from the definitive edition.[197] It may be one of the pages of the missing typescript. Probably it is an additional copy typed intentionally or by mistake when the typescript was made. The serial and book publications present no mysteries.

The examination of *Almayer's Folly* indicated Conrad's careful correction of each state in turn. *The Nigger* need be analyzed only enough to show that he continued the habit. One example from each existing stage will suffice, though many are available. Differences between the manuscript and the first printed text, which appeared in the *New Review*, can be observed from the beginning:

Ever since five in the afternoon the carpenter had finished battening down the main hatch. . . .[198]

The carpenter had driven in the last wedge of the main-hatch battens, and, throwing down his maul, had wiped his face with great deliberation, just on the stroke of five.[199]

The alterations must have been made in a missing typescript. The changes in the published text show even more care than those in *Almayer's Folly*. Though seven copyright copies were "struck off from type set up for the *New Review*," Conrad later revised the serial for the first English and American editions, which appeared almost simultaneously;[200] for example:

At night, instead of the cheerful yell, "Turn out! Do you hear there? Turn out! . . ."[201]

At night, instead of the cheerful yell, "One bell! Turn out! Do you hear there? Hey! hey! hey! Show leg! . . ."[202]

Finally he subjected the text of the first edition to extensive alterations for the definitive:

The night was clear, with a gentle breeze. The ship heeled over a little, slipping quietly over a sombre sea towards the inaccessible and festal splendour of a black horizon pierced by points of flickering fire. Above the mastheads the resplendent curve of the Milky Way spanned the sky like a triumphal arch of eternal light, thrown over the dark pathway of the earth.[203]

The night was clear, with a gentle breeze. Above the mastheads the resplendent curve of the Milky Way spanned the sky like a triumphal arch of eternal light, thrown over the dark pathway of the earth.[204]

The manuscript has been so worked over that it looks almost indecipherable in an astonishing number of places.[205] Considered chapter by chapter,[206] Conrad's increasingly meticulous revisions become a lesson in patience. Though the first six or seven pages have not been much corrected,[207] the rest of chapter one abounds in alterations. In chapter two there is a conspicuous increase in the number of corrections, which are here as numerous as in the most revised parts of *Almayer's Folly*. The third chapter of *The Nigger* surpasses the second: some pages are almost solid black with rewriting. The greatest amount of work has been done on the fourth chapter, the longest of the five. Chapter five has been altered at least as much as chapter three.

The corrections were made by the quick methods of *Almayer's Folly*. New words followed cancelations in the middle of a sentence without the sentence's being begun afresh; new words were written above cancelations and on top of old words; new words, unconnected with cancelations, were written above the line. Page 175 even contains a new way of making a cancelation: the regular page has been pasted over a fragment of several canceled lines that constituted a first phrasing of the material.[208]

The manuscript of *The Nigger* abounds in signs of hasty writing. On a few lines an initial word or two is followed by a pen stroke across to the opposite side of the page.[209] In many passages an incoherent repetition and mixture of words testify to the speed at which Conrad's imagination worked while he struggled to put his idea on paper:

But *one or two*
several   one
One or two motionless on their backs, and with *a* hand grip-
with
ping hard the edge of the bunk, smoked nervously, *in big*
staring upwards;   immobilized
quick puffs, *with great avidity; for peace. They were extenu-*
by
ated by *now with the vague fear hard work or vague fear but*
an
by the unceasing turmoil of the unrelenting violence filled the
world, wearied their hearts [indecipherable] *with a craving*
disturbed and passive like men
for peace. *They were waiting for something inconceivable.*
The end of that and withering and unearthly uproar darkness

and violence. never ceasing inextinguishable uproar of that everlasting darkness, of that unearthly violence, in a great craving for peace.[210]

The passage gives graphic meaning to his confession that "for me, writing – *the only possible writing* – is just simply the conversion of nervous force into phrases."

The appearance of the manuscript shows that while writing *The Nigger of the "Narcissus"* Conrad became a professional. He learned the meaning of an artistic conscience; he was continually aware of effects he could never quite achieve. The scarred pages present the efforts of the amateur corrected by brilliant strokes into the successes of the professional writer. The corrections illustrate what Conrad called "la note vibrante, la phrase révélatrice; le mot, le cri de la situation, qui vous persuade de la réalité des évènements." [211]

The brilliant strokes can be found in description, as in the passage about the whaling expeditions of Captain Allistoun of the *Narcissus*:

restless
When he spoke of that time his *steely* blue eyes *became*
became still and cold like the loom of ice
dreamy.[212]

When Conrad balanced *restless* against *still* and for *dreamy* substituted *cold* backed by the sailor's term, *the loom of ice*,[213] a chill wind seems to blow over the sentence and freeze it into perfect form. Passages of narration were imaginatively reshaped. The behavior of Donkin with the dying Nigger makes a vivid example:

looking away
Jimmy's chest heaved. Donkin
The rattle stopped. Donkin bent his ear to Jimmy's lips and

rustle dry
heard *a sound* like the *rustling* of a single leaf *dancing on the*
driven along the smooth sand of a beach.
sand.[214]

The death rattle has been made audible by the perfected simile. The addition of Donkin's *looking away* while he determined that Wait was dying has great psychological force. The same psychological force is revealed in the emendation of a word used to introduce dialogue. During the storm, when the Nigger was trapped in his sick-bay and the rescuers had just cut a small hole through the wall, Wait

whispered
put his lips to it, *yelled* "Help!" . . .[215]

In no other way could Conrad have conveyed the Nigger's exhaustion. The dramatic implication that he could put behind dialogue appears in another inspiration. At Wait's funeral, his self-appointed guardian, Belfast, sprang into action when the corpse refused to slip into the ocean:

be a man!
"Jimmy — *go*" he shrieked passionately.[216]

Conrad's ability to imply a philosophy in a phrase is illustrated by the officers' behavior when the *Narcissus* was righting herself after the storm. Mr. Creighton, the second mate, had broken his leg, and though the men crawled all over him in the confusion, he bore the pain

the
without a moan, without a sigh. The master's ardour,
cries of that silent man
inspired us.[217]

The inserted phrase added a whole code of endurance. Such additions and changes are the measure of Conrad's growth at the time of *The Nigger.*

Unlike *Almayer's Folly*, the manuscript of *The Nigger* was augmented by alterations. Conrad seems to have used his first phrasing as a rough sketch to which he added details. Yet it must not be assumed that he could not cancel a word once he had set it on paper. In the heavily corrected manuscript, though he added more than he cut, he cut copiously. Sometimes the excisions were of a word only. When Donkin spread mutinous sentiments among the crew, Conrad said the men "listened to the *interesting Donkin* fascinating *and contemptible* Donkin." [218] Probably he was dissatisfied with a word so overtaxed as *interesting*; to improve the sentence he added two adjectives before seeing that *contemptible* belonged more to the author's point of view than the men's. He could be ruthless in eliminating entire sentences that would have delighted most writers. Much was cut from the description of the *Narcissus*' progress up the Thames:

The reach narrowed. from both sides the land approached the
a dark blue ridge [indecipherable] *high up in the pearly sky*
ship. *The Kent hills showed above the sky pearly sky.*
Upon the low level mists of the tops of scattered
scattered
Above the mist of the marshy flats clumps of trees stood in
floated like puff balls in feathery clusters
[indecipherable] *black clusters.* She went steadily up the river.[219]

Perhaps he felt that he had too many details in his picture and could most easily sacrifice the hills and the trees. The excision is all the more worthy of respect because the sentences had been carefully worked over during psychological and domestic distress.

Though Conrad's exacting standards resulted in many omissions, more frequently they led him to develop his ideas. It may be roughly estimated that he wrote the novel twice over, though he by no means retained all the additions to his original conception. The pace was set by the first two sentences, which at first read:

> Mr. Baker the chief mate of the ship "Narcissus" came out of his cabin on to the dark quarter deck. It was then just nine o'clock.[220]

Then in the manuscript itself they were expanded to the form in which they remained:

> Mr. Baker the chief mate of the ship "Narcissus" stepped in one stride out of his lighted cabin into the darkness of the quarter deck. Above his head on the break of the poop the night watchman rang a double stroke. It was nine o'clock.[221]

In the first draft the sentences were mere statements of fact; in the second they created a picture and gave a feeling of reality. The neutral *came out* became active in *stepped in one stride*. Light flooded the picture from the contrast of *lighted* and *darkness*. From the additional sentence the reader learns the time and also hears the bell. Perhaps for the first time Conrad was working consciously on the principles which, after finishing *The Nigger*, he formulated in the famous Preface. He was sparing no effort "to make you hear, to make you feel . . . , before all, to make you *see*."[222]

Sometimes a phrase added reality, as in the boatswain's reaction to the storm:

[The] boatswain swung quickly, gripping things with a fist hard
and remembering suddenly snatches of the last letter
as iron.[223] [from his "old woman."

The irrelevance lent the utmost psychological conviction. Many of the additions were single words that stamp an idea indelibly on the reader's mind. Sometimes the supplementary words overplayed an effect. No one would deny that the adjectives spoil this sentence:

noisily,
The tug that would come paddling and hissing *noisily*
hot and smoky, in the pellucid, cool quietness of the
in the quietness of the early morning.[224]

Yet the following figure was much improved by the inserted adjective.

a timid at the foot of a
. . . like *a* creature *stopped by a* wall.[225]

One of the most revealing psychological touches of the novel was achieved by an extra pronoun. After the crew risked their lives to save Wait from drowning in his sick-berth during the storm, the superb Nigger remarked:

myself
"Now, after I got out from there!" [226]

Conrad's success in practising the creed of the Preface owed much to additions.

A comparison of the serial and the first edition shows careful revision of the earlier state and discloses that the text was neither augmented nor diminished by the changes. The additions sometimes had real bearing on the story. At the beginning of the storm, according to the *New Review*,[227] "the watch then on duty began to struggle up the rigging." To emphasize the sterling quality of the officers of the *Narcissus*, Conrad added in the book form: "The watch then on duty, led by Mr. Creighton, began to struggle up the rigging." [228]

The elaborations were balanced by many cuts. Some excisions cast light on the workings of Conrad's mind. The *New Review*[229] speaks of "the certitude that lurks in doubts, the essential logic of accidents, the realm of safety and peace beyond the frontiers of sorrow and fear." When Conrad revised the text, he turned "the essential logic of accidents" out of his philosophy.[230] There were many exchanges of an unapproved for an approved word. The *New Review*,[231] for instance, reads, "Captain Allistoun scrambled . . ."; and the book form, seeking an effect more consistent with the dignity of the master, runs, "Captain Allistoun struggled. . . ."[232] The correction of *rumour* to *murmur* was another frequent change: "the rumour of voices" became "the murmur of voices,"[233] though on occasion *rumour* slipped through, as in "a deep rumour of excited men."[234] Conrad went over the serial at William Heinemann's request to extirpate *bloody*.[235] Belfast's indignant " 'bloody nigger,' " for example, was emended to " 'cursed nigger,' "[236] but Donkin's " 'bloody thing' "[237] eluded a not too vigilant search.

The differences between the first and the definitive editions show that Conrad sheared away all redundancy. He worked in longhand on a reprint issued by Heinemann in 1910 as the Popular Edition, and he gave James B. Pinker the copy containing his emendations and deletions, which he had completed by April, 1919.[238] Some of the alterations made in the reprint he discarded before the definitive edition went to press. The Popular Edition was corrected thus, but the correction was not adopted in the final text:

officially
The cook (*technically* a seaman . . .)[239]

There was one cancelation that was eventually rejected:

. . . the *dull* peace of resumed routine.[240]

One long correction went through two stages. The first change ran:

. . . through the profound impertinence of his large eyes that
in a melancholy stare of disdain
stood far out of his head *like the eyes of crabs.*

Then Conrad canceled the whole for the reading:

. . . through the impertinent mournfulness of his languid and enormous stare.[241]

Though in the accepted corrections the excisions are most noticeable, there were other changes. Words and phrases were altered. "Threatening a shadowy vengeance" became "promising a shadowy vengeance,"[242] with a loss of sinister implication. The aural effect was increased by the change of "the cook's lips moved inaudibly" to "the cook's lips moved without a sound."[243] The phonetics of Donkin's cockney pronunciation were corrected. Conrad sought out the incorrect initial *h's*. Donkin said in the first edition, " 'Hit's a blooming himposyshun . . . but hit don't tyke me hin.' "[244] In the definitive edition the *h's* have been removed: " 'It's a blooming imposyshun . . . but it don't tyke me in.' "[245] Conrad did not catch all the inappropriate aspirates; many can still be found, as in Donkin's " 'I cleared hout 'ere,' " and his reference to Belfast as " 'a bandy-legged little Hirish chap.' "[246] Conrad worked on other sounds in Donkin's phonetics. Sometimes he removed the initial *h's* and also altered the *o* sound: " 'hignorant hass' " became " 'ignerant ass.' "[247] He was not consistent with the *o* or other sounds. In one of Donkin's speeches appears the following mixture of pronunciation:

"I've been airing yer clothes. . . . Giv' us the key of your chest, I'll put 'em away for yer. . . . You can do it, unless you *are* sick. . . . if yer can look after yer clothes, yer can look after yerself." [248]

His attitude towards phonetics was summed up in a brief exchange of letters early in September, 1920. C. S. Evans of William Heinemann, Ltd., criticized *minnyt* and *hymposed* and the indiscriminate *you's* and *yer's*.[249] Conrad replied:

> A. I don't know really how Donkin pronounces *minnyt*,—but I know that the phonetic spelling of the Oxford Dictionary is a mere phantasy: for no one says *minit*, giving exactly the same sound to both "i's" in that word.
>
> B. All the phonetics of Donkin's speech are wrong, alas! A real Cockney drops his aspirates,—but he *never* adds one. It's the country people who do that. I have for this the undeniable authority of Mr. Edwin Pugh. A cockney will naturally say "ome" for *home*, but he would *never* say (for instance) *hoperation* for *operation*. What I ought to have done was to take *every* initial *h* out of his speeches, since I called him a cockney. But God only knows what Donkin is! It's too late now to chase all those *h's* out of the text, I fear.
>
> Yer-you should be adhered to as printed in my first Ed.[250]

Though such changes did not affect the length of the novel, others made the definitive shorter than the first edition. Descriptive touches were lopped off:

> He slept at last. He breathed heavily, high-booted. . . .[251]
> He slept at last, high-booted. . . .[252]

Distracting generalizations were lifted out of the text:

> Through the perfect wisdom of its [the sea's] grace they are not permitted to meditate at ease upon the complicated and acrid savour of existence, lest they should remember and, perchance, regret the reward of a cup of inspiring bitterness, tasted so often, and so often withdrawn from before their

stiffening but reluctant lips. They must without pause justify their life. . . .[253]

Through the perfect wisdom of its grace they are not permitted to meditate at ease upon the complicated and acrid savour of existence. They must without pause justify their life. . . .[254]

Condensation increased the narrative value of the definitive edition.

The many states of the story make it possible to trace the evolution of representative passages. On the back of the unnumbered typewritten page included with the manuscript is a sentence in longhand more worked over than any other in *The Nigger*. Conrad was trying to convey the isolation of James Wait confronting the idea of death before the entire crew during the near mutiny. The first attempt runs:

surrounded
He did not appear to be aware of anyone and *surrounded*
by the eagerness of excited men
by eager men in the entr of men's eagerness he stood *as if*
and *alone* utterly alone in the im-
facing something terrible; *in the impenetrable solitude of his*
penetrable solitude of his fear.
fear.

Conrad seems to have considered introducing a picture of the crew "in the entr[ance]" of the sick-bay. He worked hard to express the curiosity of the men and the loneliness of the Nigger.

Possibly because of its awkward second clause, the sentence did not please him, and he tried again:

appear in the midst of
He did not *seem* to be aware of anyone; *surrounded by the*
and he made an effort *singlehanded* to
eager looks *of* excited men *he stood facing something terrible,*

confront
meet singlehanded something terrible that was coming at him
[in the
and utterly alone in the impenetrable solitude of his fear.

The new version kept the essentials of the old, though Conrad tried another presentation of the eager and excited men. He added to the isolation of Wait by *singlehanded*, and he tried to make the fear more suggestive with *that was coming at him* and more dignified by changing *meet* to *confront*.

The order still displeased him, for he altered it in the third version:

In the midst of eager faces and excited men he did not
near him
appear to be aware of anyone and singlehanded he faced something terrible that confronted him in the impenetrable solitude of his fear.

He tightened his style. *In the midst*, etc., was transferred to the first clause to balance a transposed *singlehanded* in the second. The second clause was cleared of the somewhat childish *that was coming at him*, while the sense of approaching doom was more imaginatively conveyed by *near him*. The emphasis on Wait's loneliness was tempered, and perhaps the excisions or the repetition of *face* dissatisfied Conrad.

Far from exhausted by three failures, he worked over a fourth version that really amounted to two rephrasings:

near him; he stood
He did not appear to be aware of any one *and singlehanded*

singlehanded amidst the faces of men
in the midst of eager looks and excited whispers he faced

facing standing and utterly alone in the
something terrible, that confronted him in the impenetrable solitude of his fear.

silent battling singlehanded with a
near him; he stood for a moment *gasping, and singlehanded*
nameless
legion of terrors *terrors*
faced the name[*less*] and the eager looks of excited men watched him far off, utterly alo[ne] in the impenetrable solitude of his fear.

At first he followed the third version closely, except for the much altered phrase beginning *in the midst,* which was restored to the second clause of the compound sentence. The unbalanced combination of *eager faces* and *excited men* was improved to *eager looks* and *excited whispers.* Perhaps this was the best phrasing of Wait's terror. But Conrad was not satisfied with it. He canceled the second clause; above the cancelations he wrote in words from earlier versions – *near him, he stood, utterly alone;* he confused himself again in a repetition of *faces of men* and *faced.* Then he abandoned this corrected second clause and constructed what was practically a fifth version. Like all the preceding attempts, it contained *he did not appear to be aware of anyone* and *in the impenetrable solitude of his fear.* It used many effects formerly discarded: *near him, stood, eager looks, excited men, utterly alone,* all can be found in fresh combinations. In the fifth version Wait's isolation and fear were intensified by the addition of *silent for a minute* and *battling . . . with a legion of nameless terrors.* The conception was overcrowded at the last, and Conrad's haste to include everything resulted in incoherence.

The incoherence had been corrected in the sixth or serial version.

He did not appear to be aware of any one near him; he stood silent for a moment, battling single-handed with a legion of nameless terrors amidst the eager looks of excited men that watched him far off, utterly alone in the impenetrable solitude of his fear.[255]

The changes were minor: *amidst* was introduced before *eager looks* and *that* before watched. When in the first and definitive editions *that* was changed to *who*,[256] a seventh version appeared. Surely there is no more convincing evidence of Conrad's excessive effort than those seven versions of the same passage.

The important part of the corrections just discussed lies in the manuscript. Instructive changes may also be found in the printed story. The *New Review*,[257] in describing the Azores, begins: "That day, just before dark, land had been reported from aloft. . . ." Conrad must have decided that *day* was too general, for in the first edition he altered the word to suit the time: "That evening, just before dark. . . ." [258] Since the definitive edition eliminates all unnecessary details, it reads: "That evening land had been reported from aloft. . . ." [259] Conrad focused his impression in a single word.

A passage studied in its manuscript and printed versions shows how he built up and then cut down a conception. The passage is especially significant for its illustration of Edward Garnett's influence. In depicting Donkin's sensations after he had done Wait to death, Conrad wrote in the manuscript:

And the immortal sea stretched away, immense and hazy, like the image of life, with a glittering surface and lightless depths; *the sea restless fei unforgiving fateful* [?], *cruel, entrancing and terrible ever changing and always the same.*

at the sea but
Donkin shivered slightly. He gave a defiant look round and

slinked slunk noiselessly he had felt himself suddenly starting off slinking away forward as if if condemned and cast out by its by the anguished silence of the waters. the

exacting

sea wringing tears and toil; promising, empty, inspiring and ter-

gave

rible — ever changing and always the same. Donkin *stoo* it a

judged

defiant glance and slunk off noiselessly as if *condemned* and cast out by the august silence of its might.[260]

He wished to express the indefinable majesty of the sea in contrast with the contemptible Donkin. Indulging excessively in adjectives, he used eight in his first draft and six in his second. In the margin beside the succession of adjectives Garnett [261] wrote "Cut?" and in the serial Conrad cut:

And the immortal sea stretched away, immense and hazy, like the image of life, with a glittering surface and lightless depths; promising, empty, inspiring — terrible. Donkin gave it a defiant glance, and slunk off noiselessly, as if judged and cast out by the august silence of its might.[262]

He sacrificed ten words to his respect for Garnett's opinion: *exacting tears and toil, . . . ever changing and always the same.* The adjectives were now reduced to four. Ultimately he carried out Garnett's moderation to the letter. Though the first edition was like the serial, the definitive edition lacked *promising*, *empty*, *inspiring*, and *terrible.*[263] The evolution of any passage was complete only when the definitive edition had gone to press.

Now that he was committed to literature for his livelihood, Conrad's frugality with words, noticeable in *Almayer's Folly*, became more prominent. The much corrected sentence on the verso of the typewritten page shows the same words or some metamorphosis of them running through all versions. His care in fitting a discarded sentence back into the text is clear in Donkin's feelings after the death of Wait. In these instances Conrad used the abandoned material at once, but frequently he delayed. In describing the men after the mutiny, he wrote:

a
in negligent poses, or, bending *one*
Men sprawled about on the deck, sat *with bowed heads,* [knee,
leaned drooped with one shoulder against
leaned carelessly against bulkheads. The air was oppressive like
thundery noon. All the lips moved but
the languid air of thunder storms. *Donkin*
crouching arched a narrow
crouched by the bowsprit bending his with his meagre back
humped
arched raised his peaked shoulders as high as his ears and
hanging his *pointed face*
with hanging fa head *resembled a sick vulture with ruffled*
plumes. . . . Knowles sat subdued with one shoulder against a bulkhead.[264]

Though he canceled the description at the moment, he was too much taken with his picture of Donkin and too economical to abandon it permanently. He used it again in perfected form on the next page:

Donkin, crouching all in a heap against the bowsprit, hunched his shoulderblades as high as his ears, and hanging a peaked nose, resembled a sick vulture with ruffled plumes.[265]

The manuscript of *The Nigger* does not exhibit as much alteration in plot as the manuscript of *Almayer's Folly.* One or two details were changed, and the ambiguous question of the Nigger's relationship with death was twisted now one way, now another. At first several of the new members of the crew taken on at Bombay came from an American ship,[266] but this was later altered to Donkin's being a deserter from an American vessel,[267] possibly to throw the shiftiness of his character into higher relief. Another change bore upon the stoical acceptance of a sailor's life. When Donkin promoted insurrection among the sailors, their interest was at first in " 'the same wages as the mates.' "[268] This was afterwards changed to " 'the same grub.' "[269] Conrad avoided the larger social aspect of the mutiny and ridiculed Donkin as a breeder of class hatred.

One of the most dramatic scenes in the novel and most subtly brutal in all literature may have been an afterthought. The third climax of the story is the death of the Nigger, and Conrad seems to have been uncertain of the best means of bringing it about:

> somebody
> "Dead calm" said *a man* quietly. *The murmur of talk died out. Men began to descend the ladders looking grave. Belfast went last to Jimmy give Jimmy the knows* [sic]. *He sat chatting in the cabin for a long time and in his excitement forgot himself so far as to mention a doctor. "Who wants a doctor?" asked Wait in a strong offended voice. "Well! for your cold"*
> And chaffed at
> *muttered Belfast To* Donkin the peace, *the sea*, the ship, the sea. . . .[270]

The manuscript continues with the cruel scene in which Donkin frightened Wait to death. The cancelations may mean that the devoted Belfast was at first intended to cause the death – surely inadvertently – of his beloved Nigger by talk of doctors. Perhaps Conrad was then inspired to use Donkin's vindictive greed as the instrument. Perhaps the scene with Belfast had no significance except as preparation for Donkin's work. The original intention will never be known.

Conrad gradually built up the character of Wait as the exploiter and victim of illness. Originally he wrote "the legend of his death" and corrected it in the manuscript to "the imposture of his ready death."[271] He altered "Jimmy's existence" to "Jimmy's sham existence."[272] A change in the manuscript suggests that at first he meant Wait to be aware of his approaching death and then made him ignorant of it. The Nigger's self-deception was substantially increased by a cut in the account of his attitude after the storm. This read at first:

> *appeared*
> *He was very weak. It was manifest that that the night*
> *the night on the*
> *on the poop had "done for him." He observed a greater reticence as to his intimate relations with the invincible death, and at the very time when we all began to see it plainly enough standing*
> *intervals and as though if inadvertently he put*
> *by his side he at times affected to ignore its presence. He asked*
> *by and stealthily anxious*
> *often and anxiously "Any wind? Has she got steerage way?*
> *buried or cured*
> *I want to go home to be cured — or buried" his intimate rela-*
> *through*
> *tions with the invincible death. And times and as if through inadvertence he seemed to ignore his old friendship.* He affected the languour of extreme weakness so as to make it manifest to us that our delay in hauling him out from his horrible confinement, and then that night spent on the poop among our selfish neglect of his needs, had "done for him."[273]

The passage implied that Wait recognized a certain truth in his vaunted relationship with death and was no longer so eager to boast of his illness. The cancelations left the confident Nigger unaware that he was dying. Conrad's opinion was summed up in corrections of the manuscript of "To My Readers in America," dated 1914:

Yet
But James Wait afraid of death and making her his
only accomplice an impostor of some
companion was *a man of* character. . . .[274]

He decided Wait must have no idea that he was playing in earnest the part of the dying man which he had assumed for convenience.

The reworking of other details helps to prove that the Nigger was really fooling himself while trying to fool the crew. Two corrections in his admissions to Donkin arouse suspicion by their understatement:

now and again
"Been out of sorts this year" he mumbled. . . .

as well as ever"
Jimmy coughed violently. "I am *better*. . . .[275]

The sentence on the verso of the typewritten sheet shows Wait facing his fear before the officers and men. By the addition of *nameless* his *terrors* were left vague to him no matter how the reader is meant to understand them. Captain Allistoun understood them to be the terror of death, for, in the much corrected passages in which he explained his sudden pity for Wait, his opening words were emended:

so
standing there three parts dead and scared
"When I saw him *standing there*. . . ."[276]

According to Conrad's original intentions, the Nigger himself was meant to realize at the end that he was dying:

promptly *and at once went*
"Ten days" he said *very quick and very low and went off in-*
off back directly to roam again to roam *and*
stantly to roaming *in the delightful past*
remote could not distinguish from the smiling *He*
which he mistook for the near future future that was so near
felt quiet, safe,
now. Death was coming at last easy, beyond the reach of
the slightest
any incertitude. He wished that fellow Donkin would keep
quiet. . . .[277]

Perhaps Conrad cut the mention of death because he never intended it for part of Wait's thoughts and realized it might be misinterpreted. Perhaps he at first meant it to be part of his thought and then recognized that it would mar the Nigger's ignorance that he was the dupe of his own fraud. Whatever Conrad's reasons may have been for the cancelation, James Wait was consistently presented.

Lord Jim is extant in the same states as *The Nigger of the "Narcissus."* The manuscript exists in a divided and imperfect condition. The typescript has been lost, according to William Blackwood and Sons, though seven typewritten pages, which cover the first four and a half pages of chapter fourteen, are laid in with the Rosenbach manuscript.[278] A corrected copy of chapters thirty-one through thirty-five of the serial publication in *Blackwood's Magazine* exists, which shows how Conrad revised for the first edition. A comparison of the first and the definitive editions completes the study of his imagination at work on *Lord Jim*. Again one example from each state will prove that he continued the system of revision begun with *Almayer's Folly*.

The manuscript of *Lord Jim* is incomplete and is divided

into two very unequal portions, of which the smaller is in the Harvard University Library and the larger in the Rosenbach Collection. The Harvard fragment, twenty-eight pages long, is in a small ornamental notebook, which once belonged to Teofila Bobrowska.[279] It consists of two chapters that more or less correspond to the first two chapters of the printed text. The first chapter in the manuscript is but the opening two pages and a half of the seven pages of printed text; the second manuscript chapter begins with the same sentence as the printed text, roughly matches paragraph for paragraph and even contains some analysis cut from the text. Clearly the story was much rewritten before publication. Though some of the changes were merely of a word, others involved considerable passages:

Imagination the enemy of man the father of all terrors must
have something to feed upon, otherwise it sinks to rest *from in*
admits the possibility
in the dulness of exhausted emotion. One *may or may not be*
of being struck
struck from behind, in sleep, or in the dark, but one does not
believe in it till the blow comes. It is otherwise when meeting
a
danger with brain, eye and hand. Then it is only *an* serenity of
combined with of for
temper, *and a* contempt not *for* death but *of* a life [indecipher-
meet efficiently
able] that can *face* the aimed blow. Jim saw nothing. . . .[280]

The fear grows shadowy; and Imagination, the enemy of men, the father of all terrors, unstimulated, sinks to rest in the dulness of exhausted emotion. Jim saw nothing. . . .[281]

Obviously the serial was not printed from the text of the Harvard notebook. The stages between the notebook and the published version can never be known: the Rosenbach manuscript does not cover the opening chapters.

The manuscript in the Rosenbach Collection consists of three hundred and fifty-six pages. Yet it, too, is fragmentary. It is incomplete at both ends: it begins at page forty-six (page thirty-six of the Canterbury Edition) and ends on page six hundred and forty (page three hundred and eighteen of the Canterbury Edition, ninety-nine pages before the end of the novel). Throughout the manuscript are gaps which total two hundred and forty pages.[282] Examination proves that the serial was not printed from the Rosenbach manuscript; for example:

He stared into the sunshine of the empty esplanade. Here and there the slender figure of a native was striding on dark long
vivid european of some sort
legs across the light of the big space; a *white man* was walking briskly towards the quay, a white speck moving in the distance under the trees near the band stand; a ramshackle gharry pulled
his right foot
up short opposite the group and the driver putting *a foot* over his knee began to examine his toes critically.[283]

"He stared across the empty Esplanade. A ramshackle gharry, all dust and venetian blinds, pulled up short opposite the group, and the driver, throwing up his right foot over his knee, gave himself up to the critical examination of his toes." [284]

As Conrad observed to Garnett in March, 1900, he had been "cutting and slashing whole parts out of Jim." [285]

From the existing typewritten pages it is difficult to guess the condition of the text in the lost typescript. Perhaps the changes between the manuscript and the serial readings were made at this stage. A letter of August 11, 1900, to Galsworthy shows that a typescript did exist and that Conrad worked hard over it:

The corrected type went off five days ago. . . . I've done nothing except, as I said, getting the end of *Jim* fit for print. There was a good deal to do to it, as a matter of fact.[286]

The fragmentary typescript follows exactly the final reading in the manuscript. The typewritten pages bear many corrections in Conrad's hand that changed the text to the version found in print:

chocolate coloured

The plaintiff who had been beaten, *a* an obese man with shaved head, *chocolate coloured, with* one fat breast bare and a bright

the bridge of in pompous immobility

yellow caste-mark above his nose sat *like an idol in a barn.*[287]

Sometimes the text, though uncorrected in the fragmentary typescript, appears in an altered form in print:

Other natives sat picturesquely under the shade of a lonely tree in the courtyard, the villagers connected with the assault case looking like a chromo lithogra[ph] of a Camp in a book of Eastern travels. One missed the obligatory thread of smoke and the animals grazing. A blank wall rose behind them overtopping the tree, reflecting the glare.[288]

"Under the shade of a lonely tree in the courtyard, the villagers connected with the assault case sat in a picturesque group, looking like a chromo-lithograph of a camp in a book of Eastern travel. One missed the obligatory thread of smoke in the foreground and the pack-animals grazing. A blank yellow wall rose behind overtopping the tree, reflecting the glare." [289]

The extant typewritten pages clearly do not represent the final state of the text before publication. The typed fragment supplies what was probably on the missing page 313 of the manuscript, though Conrad cut the passage from the serial:

I don't know what was the matter with me that morning but *all the people there*, the ex-officio stainless trio behind the desk, the natives in court, the people who did not understand anything, the few — besides myself — who understood the words read out; those who not having been tried were called to judge,

listened and

and those who did not care — they all seemed to me strange, foreign, *as if* belonging to some order of beings I had no connection with. It was only when my eyes turned towards Jim that I had a sense of not being alone of my kind, as if we two had wandered in there from some distant regions, from a different world. I turned to him for fellowship. He alone seemed to look natural. The magistrate read on in a low distinct and careless voice.

By Jove. For all my foolishness about scaffolds and heads rolling off — I assure you it was infinitely worse than [beheading].[290]

Of this long analysis not a trace can be found in the published text except " 'in an even, distinct, and careless voice.' " [291] Possibly it was out of tone with the impersonal dignity of the inquiry and the personal misgivings of Brierly. Few though they are, the typewritten pages reveal that Conrad took an exact copy of the manuscript, frequently corrected the typescript by hand, and later altered the typewritten version of the text before he allowed it to appear in print.

Conrad gave the entire serial text a careful revision for book publication. There were countless alterations of individual words:

". . . the oars rose and fell once, twice." [292]
". . . the wet oars flashed and dipped once, twice." [293]

The most abundant changes were excisions:

"I liked him well enough, though some I know—meek, friendly men at that — couldn't stand him at any price. The serenity of his confidence in himself was intolerable. He had the selfish conceit of a clever boy, bound in the thick hide of a rhinoceros. I haven't the slightest doubt he considered himself vastly my superior. . . ." [294]

"I liked him well enough, though some I know—meek, friendly men at that—couldn't stand him at any price. I haven't the slightest doubt he considered himself vastly my superior. . . ." [295]

Conrad disclaimed responsibility for the first American edition. In Richard Curle's copy he wrote: "Set up probably from English proofs but neither revised nor in any other way corrected by me. It is probably much nearer the text of *B'wood's Maga.* than the first English Ed. of book form." [296]

The five chapters from *Blackwood's Magazine* in the Beyer Collection, corrected by Conrad, are direct indication of his method. He worked in long hand on pages extracted from the magazine as if revising a manuscript or typescript. He made many changes in the serial text that were not followed in print. The second and third sentence of the following passage were marked for deletion:

> "How does one kill fear, I wonder? How do you shoot a spectre through the heart, slash off its spectral head, take it by its spectral throat? It is an enterprise you rush into while you dream, and are glad to make your escape with wet hair and every limb shaking." [297]

Finally he decided to keep the sentences, for they can be found in the first edition.[298] The Beyer chapters show that he sometimes indicated an addition to the serial that was not used in book form:

for a time
". . . I seemed to have lost all my words. . . ." [299]

The first edition did not incorporate the emendation.[300] A few corrections were further altered when they appeared in the first edition. The serial, for instance, had " 'his timidity baulked him,' " which Conrad corrected to " 'his timidity kept him off.' "[301] The first edition reads, " 'his timidity had kept him back.' "[302] Clearly he changed his corrections of the serial either in a fair copy or in the proofs. On the whole he abided by his alterations in the Beyer chapters and presumably in the rest of the emended serial. The mastery of his revisions is demonstrated by the description of Marlow's last sight of Jim:

> "The twilight lay over the east, and the coast, turned black, ex-
> that
> tended infinitely *from north and south*: its sombre wall seemed
> the very stronghold of the night; *only* the western horizon was
> *long since* one dazzling blaze of luminous
> *a great blaze of* gold *and crimson* in which a big detached cloud
> dark and still
> floated *sleepily*, casting a slaty shadow on the water beneath,
> and I saw Jim. . . ."[303]

North and south was eliminated perhaps because it gave the reader too many directions when *western* alone was important. *Long since* may have been cut because it brought the night a little too close. The most expert touch of all was the alteration of *sleepily* to *dark and still*, which completed in the sky the color that the cloud cast upon the sea. The Beyer chapters show that the care which Conrad gave the manuscript was lavished upon the text even after it had been published.

The conscientious revision of the serial satisfied him that the first edition was as perfect a text as he could achieve. The definitive edition differed from the first scarcely at all. Aside from corrections in punctuation[304] and in typographical errors,[305] the changes were negligible.[306] Conrad considered the first edition of *Lord Jim* his final word.

The manuscript of *Lord Jim* discloses in its corrections that the professional had already emerged from the amateur. In *The Nigger of the "Narcissus"* Conrad had successfully waged a struggle for artistic maturity that left its mark on almost every page. In *Lord Jim* he was more master of his imagination. Yet he was not satisfied easily, for both the Harvard and Rosenbach manuscripts were much worked upon. The novel cannot be considered chapter by chapter, as could *Almayer's Folly* and *The Nigger*, because *Lord Jim* is too long and because the chapter divisions are hopelessly confused. An examination of individual pages reveals Conrad's exacting corrections. A few pages [307] are almost untouched; many [308] are as corrected as the pages of *The Nigger;* the majority [309] are abundantly revised.

Conrad used the same methods of correction as in *Almayer's Folly* and *The Nigger.*[310] He canceled words in the middle of a sentence without recopying it. He canceled words and wrote the new words on top or just above. He added words above uncanceled passages. In *Lord Jim* first occur noticeable additions at the top of the page and in the margin. False starts appear on the versos of two pages.[311] In the Harvard notebook facing the first page of the manuscript of *Lord Jim* is a page of disconnected jottings which read in full:

his
Afterwards when *he disappear — The Malay red* [sed?] *from a* perception of the intolerable drove him away from the haunts of white men, the Malays of the village where he *he buried* [found?] *himself free from the intolerable* without ex-
added
ercising his perceptive faculty *called* him Tuan Jim — as one *might* [say]

Lord Jim

had had been
He never to my own knowledge *born his* [indecipherable]
being only
guilty of an assault. This provoking and brutal stare *was the*
the
result of an exquisite sensibility.

The passage does not connect with either page one or two of the manuscript, which follow each other consecutively. It was not worked into any one paragraph in the printed text: the phrase *exquisite sensibility* is found in the second paragraph, and the idea of the first sentence and the phrases *perception of the Intolerable* and as *one might say Lord Jim* in the third.[312] Similarly the Rosenbach manuscript contains an extra page which Conrad numbered A225, though it is not connected in context with 224, 225, or 226, which follow one another consecutively.[313] The material of page A225 was redistributed later in the story. The two extra pages were not plans made in advance of composition. They seem to be first attempts at phrasing part of the narrative.

The manuscript offers other signs of nervous haste. Some passages are incoherent.[314] Certain pages were doubly numbered;[315] he may have cut a page and in condensing have given one page two numbers, or he may have forgotten to number consecutively. The chapter divisions were also inconsistent. Chapters two and eighteen, for instance, were marked at the first writing.[316] Fifteen and twenty were arranged plainly during a revision.[317] Many, like seven and thirty-one, were not marked at all.[318] Twenty-one was first introduced where there was no reason for it.[319] Possibly he felt that disregard of chapter divisions gave him "more freedom."[320] Possibly he expected *Blackwood's Magazine* to make its own divisions.

The manuscript of *Lord Jim* contains a rarity not found in *Almayer's Folly* or *The Nigger*. One page begins a scene broken off in an unfinished sentence:

> In the evening I strolled towards the band-stand. There were
> small
> carriages moving slow in a circle *an* inner ring of white people
> on
> and a large *outer* ring of natives indistinct and wavering *in*
> edge of the lamps
> the outer darkness. The new established electric *lights* jumped
> high
> and spluttered above all that as [321]

The broken sentence occurs at the bottom of page 107, and the following page was first numbered 109 and changed to 108; obviously the scene was continued on a missing page: no trace of it appears in the printed text. Another abandoned scene can be found in the manuscript of "Heart of Darkness." Conrad devoted four pages to Marlow's experiences during one day in "the seat of the government" at the mouth of the Congo River; he cut the scene from the printed text.[322] There is also a reference to a rejected scene in a letter about *The Rover*.[323] His economy in using material once shaped makes it most unusual to find discarded scenes in the manuscripts.

The corrections in the manuscript of *Lord Jim* enlarged the text, though such a long manuscript necessarily contained many excisions.[324] Sometimes a word was expanded into a phrase:

> backed away from the
> The Patna *left the* wharf.[325]

A phrase was frequently lengthened:

> he made me sign a chit for
> ". . . and *he charged me* ten dollars. . . ." [326]

A simple sentence developed into a compound:

> *The rain began to fall again.* He never moved and said not a word. The rain began to fall again and the *sound* loud, gentle uninterrupted *sound* a little mysterious sound *of the sea* with *with* which the sea receives a shower arose on all sides in the night.[327]

In each instance the addition followed the principles of the Preface to *The Nigger*: the reader receives the impression with an extra vividness.

The number of words cut from the serial for the first edition is unexpectedly large. Though there were a few additions, phrases and whole sentences vanished at a time:

> ". . . I only remember that he managed wonderfully to convey the brooding rancour of his mind into the bare recital of events. They stood before me indubitably true, but a little distorted, as if seen by the sinister glow of his burning contempt. It fell on the sky, on the earth, on the ship, on the men — on himself too — oh yes! on himself too: only he seemed honestly confident of his erect attitude in the general wreck of decent appearances. Twice, he told me, he shut his eyes. . . ." [328]

In the first edition the second and third sentences had been cut ruthlessly from the text.[329] Even whole paragraphs were extirpated.[330] The changes of the first for the definitive edition were negligible.

A comparison of certain passages in all the states of *Lord Jim* shows that Conrad constantly revised his thought and expression. In the Harvard manuscript the first analysis of Jim's reactions to a bad storm runs:

The passive
The exhausted courage is the result of exhausted emotion and
in the
when the body rest motionless body, imagination, the enemy of

man and the father of terror, rests in a slumber that resembles the peace of conscious resignation.[331]

Canceling the entire passage, possibly because it was only an incoherent attempt to discipline his thought, he began a second time:

In the motionless body the imagination, that enemy of man and the father of all terrors, sank into a slumber that resembled the peace of resignation.[332]

Though the sentence had now been compressed into grammatical form, he made a third start:

The fact is he did not see, he had not to exert himself and passive courage is easy since it is a sign that imagination, the enemy of man, the father of all terrors is asleep in a motionless body.[333]

The sentence had been augmented by new ideas and by old ones from the first version. The third arrangement was also revised:

As he had not to look menace in the face, as he had not to exert himself the danger became only a matter of faith, and imagina-
man
tion the enemy of may the father of all terrors.[334]

The fourth attempt remained unfinished because Conrad reached the bottom of the page. Abandoning certain grandiloquent phrases, he worked out a fifth phrasing:

when has
The danger not seen had the vagueness *of the impossible* of our imperfect thoughts. Imagination the enemy of man the
must
father of all terrors *has* must have something to feed upon, otherwise it sinks to rest *from in* in the dulness of exhausted emotion.[335]

With this synthesis of earlier versions he stopped in the Harvard manuscript. By the time the passage appeared in the serial it had been considerably altered:

> The danger, when not seen, has the imperfect vagueness of human thought. The fear grows shadowy; and Imagination, the enemy of men, the father of all terrors, unstimulated, sinks to rest in the dulness of exhausted emotion.[336]

The first sentence had been rephrased. A new second sentence had been added somewhat redundantly. The last sentence had been condensed. With this sixth version Conrad remained content.[337]

He worked as hard on the Rosenbach manuscript as on the Harvard. At least one passage, which does not offer all the variant readings of the Harvard manuscript, carried the corrections beyond the serial into the first edition. Marlow analyzed Jim's reactions to the "wretched cur" incident:

> Perhaps he looked to that hammering he was going to give me for rehabilitation in his own eyes. The eye of man can't follow nor the mind of man can conceive the crooked ways of another man's thought, *He was naive enough to expect anything, and I should think desperate enough. He was confounded humiliated and baffled. He had given himself away for nothing. It was*
> *the most* the
> *pitiful thing you can imagine. these* naive perversities of reason-
> and
> ing inspired by the ardour of self love guided by preposterous hopes to some astonishing conclusion. Who can tell what relief he expected from this chance? [338]

The analysis was much worked upon, in either the typescript or some other intervening state, before it appeared serially:

"Perhaps he looked forward to that hammering he was going to give me for rehabilitation, for appeasement? The eye of man can't follow nor the mind of man conceive the crooked ways of another man's thoughts; these naive perversities of reasoning, inspired by the desperation of self-love, kept up by preposterous hopes, arriving at astonishing, at incredible conclusions. Who can tell what relief he expected from this chance of a row?" [339]

In the first sentence the limiting *in his own eyes* was cut and two additions made: the redundant *forward*, and *for appeasement* which extended the thought to show what *rehabilitation* would mean to Jim. The awkward negative in the second sentence was smoothed out and the appositional phrase polished. The canceled *desperate* reappeared as *desperation*, a word more tense than the discarded *ardour*. In the last sentence *chance* was rendered more specific by the added *of a row*. Despite all his work on the passage Conrad was dissatisfied. In the final version the overweighted second sentence was discarded:

"Perhaps he looked forward to that hammering he was going to give me for rehabilitation, for appeasement? Who can tell what relief he expected from this chance of a row?" [340]

The corrected fragment of *Blackwood's* presents the evolution of Conrad's thought in a state not extant in the other novels. The gradual shaping of the following passage can be traced through the manuscript, the serial, the corrected serial, and the first edition. Marlow's feelings during his conversation with Jewel were built up thus:

But no matter. It was only a moment; I went *in* back into my shell directly — One *must — don't you know — and I was safe even if I did seem to have lost all my words in the dark chaos outside. But they too came back to me so that when I heard her whisper to herself — or perhaps to me — "He swore when we were alone* must — don't you know — though I seemed to have lost all my words in the dark chaos of dark thoughts I had contemplated for a second or two outside beyond the pale.[341]

The differences in the serial were very slight:

"But no matter. It was only a moment: I went back into my shell directly. One must — don't you know? — though I seemed to have lost all my words in the chaos of dark thoughts I had contemplated for a second or two beyond the pale." [342]

The Beyer fragment of *Blackwood's Magazine* introduced a change not carried out in the first edition and failed to show emendations that later appeared. In his corrections Conrad added *for a time* between *to have lost* and *all my words.* But the first edition reads:

"But still — it was only a moment: I went back into my shell directly. One must — don't you know? — though I seemed to have lost all my words in the chaos of dark thoughts I had contemplated for a second or two beyond the pale." [343]

The version lacks *for a time.* The opening phrase was also altered: *But no matter* became *But still.* Slight as they are, these changes illustrate the constant perfecting of *Lord Jim* from the manuscript through the first edition.

The care with which Conrad still hoarded words has come out indirectly in the analysis of other aspects of the manuscript. One further example will show that he continued in *Lord Jim* to treasure abandoned fragments. The picture of Jim fighting his grief in Marlow's room at the Malabar House was at first discarded:

. . . he stood with his face to it [door] having a hard *time all to himself.* time with all possible privacy. *He was as if rooted*

to spot but like a tree in a gale the upper part of him was restless;
was swayed; he had convulsive shudders pass down his back;
at him
his shoulders shook and heaved. I *glanced* slanted a glance or two with my nose down on the paper.[344]

More than a hundred and fifty words further along in the paragraph the figure was reintroduced and perfected:

"At times I stole a sidelong glance. He was rooted to the spot, but convulsive shudders ran down his back; his shoulders would heave suddenly." [345]

The manuscript of *Lord Jim*, like *Almayer's Folly*, reveals how Conrad groped his way at times towards the handling of action. Like *The Nigger*, it brings out his indecisions about the development of a central character. There was considerable alteration in plot. After the accident to the *Patna* Jim discovered a bulging plate. While he was visualizing the madness that would follow when eight hundred pilgrims began to fight for seven boats, one of the pilgrims spoke to him. The man only wanted water for his sick child, but, in a panic lest the others should be aroused, Jim fought him off by dashing a lantern in his face. In the manuscript the account of their struggle runs:

The glass jingled, the light went out, but there were other lamps hanging under the fore-derrick and I could see a great stir below the awnings [where the pilgrims were sleeping]. They were getting up and chattering all about me. The blow
man belonged made the man let go. Somebody called out my name from the bridge and yelled "Keep them back". I ran off — I wanted to get at the boats. . . .[346]

Though the passage was not canceled in the manuscript, it is not in the printed text:

" 'The glass jingled, the light went out, but the blow made him let go, and I ran off — I wanted to get at the boats. . . .' "[347]

Even in the manuscript the scene did not develop into the murderous scramble it promised to be, but ended without any one's being aroused.[348] Perhaps Conrad intended at first to justify the white men's desertion by creating a deadly fight for the seven boats.

The additional page, numbered A225, in the Rosenbach manuscript shows that he probably changed the order in which he released information. The page reads:

After
When the first of the squall had passed *it was* the boat was too far and the night remained too dark for the hull to be *seen.* made out. The ship was turning her back on them. She was lying with her head to the *Sou* south-west with the lights still
as as a sheep pen
burning in sunshine and her decks packed close with brown
above a mass of H
heads *and* variegated rags *with h*undred of eyes staring at the
stared
French gunboat *staring* at a homeward-bound French gunboat that had swept slightly out of her course to find out what was the matter with that steamer so much out of trim *and with the*
at and
red ensign flying half mast Union down. and with a signal of distress flying at the main gaff. The serang had the sense to hoist the ensign at daylight Union down at daylight. *The rai*
e
The nativ*es* cooks were were cooking in the fire boxes forward. The rails, the boats, the

Here the incoherent page ends. It has already been observed that page A225 is not connected in context with the pages around it. Therefore it is not impossible that it was incorrectly numbered and actually belonged with the subsequent portion of the manuscript dealing with the rescue of the *Patna*. A comparison cannot be made, unfortunately, since the manuscript lacks pages 241–307, where the rescue would have its place. As A225 is numbered in Conrad's hand, it is necessary to consider it as evidence for a change in the course of the narrative. If Conrad did intend at this point to tell his readers that the *Patna* remained afloat, he changed his mind and kept them in suspense. The information contained on page A225, enlarged and differently worded, appeared in the definitive text exactly twenty pages later than the information contained on manuscript page 225:

"Being thus out of trim, when the squall struck her a little on the quarter, she swung head to wind as sharply as though she had been at anchor. . . . But she turned her back on them [the deserters] as if in disdain of their fate. . . . At about nine o'clock next morning, a French gunboat homeward bound from Réunion [sighted them]. The report of her commander was public property. He had swept a little out of his course to ascertain what was the matter with that steamer floating dangerously by the head upon a still and hazy sea. There was an ensign, union down, flying at her main gaff (the serang had the sense to make a signal of distress at daylight); but the cooks were preparing the food in the cooking-boxes forward as usual. The decks were packed as close as a sheep-pen: there were people perched all along the rails, jammed on the bridge in a solid mass; hundreds of eyes stared. . . ." [349]

Conrad also introduced two other important factors in the plot, suppressed them in the interest of suspense, and reintroduced them several pages later. The manuscript contains an analysis of Jim's condition when he first went to Patusan that begins:

> this would cast the complexion of a upon
> Strange, fatality that *attaches the idea of* flight *to his per-*
> all his acts
> *son.* . . . [350]

In the analysis mention was made of the destiny that "caused him to set about making peace in Patusan. . . ." [351] The phrase was not used in the printed text, and the fact that Jim introduced peace into Patusan was not revealed directly for another thirty-two pages in the definitive edition.[352] The analysis mentioned "his love," not found in the printed text at this point but forty-six pages further along in the definitive edition.[353]

The manuscript also reveals the development of suspense in individual scenes, as in Jim's abrupt departure from Egström's employ. Egström told Marlow of the conversation about the cowards on the *Patna* and Jim's sudden announcement, " 'I must leave now.' " Then Egström continued:

> Thinks
> " '*Says I to myself: you want a rise in your screw* I to myself:
> "Oho! that's the trouble — is it? "All right" says I "You want
> No that
> a rise. very well need of fuss Jimmy. Just mention your figure.
> Anything in reason. "He *looks at me very resolute and steady.*"
> *'ve been*
> *I am the mate of the Patna*" *he says.* . . . looks at me as if he
> wanted to swallow me only I was too big. "I can't stop" ' " [354]

Conrad must have seen at once, for the correction was immediate, that it would never do for Jim to announce his past. It was entirely out of character; it also released the information too soon and destroyed the dramatic enlightenment of Egström. The end of the scene was built up according to the new conception. Egström asked Marlow:

"And where might you have come across him captain, if it's fair to ask?" — "He was the mate of the "Patna", I said.[355]

As in *The Nigger*, Conrad did not always achieve at first the right impression for his chief character to make on the reader. The manuscript is full of improvements. Sometimes they involved merely expository material, sometimes the alteration of analysis. Jim's background and training-ship experiences, which make up most of chapter one in the printed text, are not found in the Harvard manuscript. Conrad first planned to introduce the facts of Jim's home life much later in the story. They did not appear until pages 470–471 of the Rosenbach manuscript:

As a matter of fact he was born in an Essex parsonage which had been in the family for generations and he may have inherited that and never *been perplexed; but* known a doubt or a

youngest

perplexity if he had not been the *last of many boys.* youngest of many boys. Its peace and serenity missed him. . . .

Though the passage was not canceled in the manuscript, it is not found in this place in the printed text.[356] At some time after he completed the Rosenbach manuscript and before the serial was printed, Conrad must have used this passage as a basis for the fourth paragraph of the novel.[357] He now gave from the start the contrast between Jim's background and his plight.

Ingenious changes in the manuscript and even in the serial show Conrad's anxiety to win sympathy for Jim. Some alterations affected the hero's appearance. In the manuscript and serial he was " 'not yet six-and-twenty,' " in the first and definitive editions " 'not yet four-and-twenty.' "[358] His size and manner were toned down:

He was over six feet and stared downwards at one with an *overbearing* air of overbearing watchfulness. You felt
sometimes were you the
that *if you happened* to say something, *some* one special thing which he did not want to hear, he would [indecipherable] knock you down *and* without more ado.[359]

The description in the printed text was much less combative, even to the loss of several inches of height:

He was an inch, perhaps two, under six feet, powerfully built, and he advanced straight at you with a slight stoop of the shoulders, head forward, and a fixed from-under stare which made you think of a charging bull. His voice was deep, loud, and his manner displayed a kind of dogged self-assertion which had nothing aggressive in it.[360]

After Jim attained success in Patusan, Conrad was alert to keep his appearance youthful. At one time he considered aging him a bit:

. . . he was like an old portrait that had been renovated; The
a trifle more added
expression *more* mature perhaps, but not an wrinkle on that *round* beardless face which remained fundamentally boyish.
The had become
with the red *comp* and tan complexion *more* florid; the eyes seemed of darker and more vivid blue; the *clustered*
curly
clusters of fair hair had gleams of deeper auburn and he bore
assurance
himself with an unassuming *carelessness* not devoid of dignity. That was my last view of him. . . .[361]

The description was a little over-ripe; the touch of middle age had begun to coarsen him. Conrad realized at once that part of Jim's charm was his immortal youthfulness. The heavier, and more realistic, description had to go.[362]

Even more carefully Conrad reshaped unsympathetic aspects of Jim's temperament. His deterioration through contact with the sailors in the Eastern port where he was hospitalized was softened:

Jim listened for days to *their* the endless professional gossip, *to the jealousies* of these men who as seamen seemed at first to him *as thin as shadows* unsubstantial as shadows. Then some responsive chord in his nature was struck and he let himself go. There was a charm in seeing all these men well clothed well fed and knowing so little of danger or toil. And after a few days instead of going home he secured a berth as chief mate of the *steamer* 'Patna' [?].[363]

In the printed text the *responsive chord* and the *charm* were removed, and the *original disdain* was emphasized:

To Jim that gossiping crowd, viewed as seamen, seemed at first more unsubstantial than so many shadows. But at length he found a fascination in the sight of those men, in their appearance of doing so well on such a small allowance of danger and toil. In time, beside the original disdain there grew up slowly another sentiment; and suddenly, giving up the idea of going home, he took a berth as chief mate of the *Patna*.[364]

A description of the demoralizing result of the days on the *Patna* was entirely eliminated from the printed text:

decks
The awnings covered the *ship* from stem to stern with a white roof Jim kept his watch. He felt himself, melted [wilted?],
an insidious languour
overcome conquered by *a feeling of* of safety and rest. It was

sailoring reduced to its simplest expression. *Only the engineer* There was nothing to do, nothing but a little navigating. Watchfulness such an *To look out* even seemed unnecessary in *this* empty universe.[365]

While Jim was fleeing from his reputation, the effect of the flight on his character was diminished. In the manuscript, "he had lost much of that elasticity which had enabled him to rebound back into his uncompromising position after every *throw he got* heavy throw." [366] In the printed text he had lost only " 'some of that elasticity.' " [367] When he got a final chance from Stein, his reactions were at first those of a schoolboy:

[Jim] bolted out calling goodbye over his shoulder *joyously* with a joyous ring he could not *get* keep out of his voice like a youngster hurrying to join in a jolly lark. I heard him. . . .[368]

Later Conrad made him appropriately serious and eliminated the "youngster on a jolly lark" from the printed text.[369] Conrad wanted a hero with a youthful appearance and a mature attitude toward life. In keeping with this rein upon enthusiasm was the careful shading of Jim's enjoyment of his romantic career. The serial runs:

"Jewel he called her; and he would say this as he might have said 'Jane,' don't you know, with a marital, homelike, peaceful effect. The romance applied to everyday uses. Oh, he was set afloat in a sea of romance, disported himself, darted here and there, rested immersed in it, with the unconscious ease of a first-rate swimmer. I heard the name for the first time. . . ." [370]

The passage with its over-emphasis had been taken from the first and definitive editions.[371] The most important change occurred in Jim's final reactions to the *Patna* disaster. In the manuscript he first told Marlow:

"'. . . only I know I can talk to you. I talk about forgetting but perhaps I don't want so very much to forget. "Hang me
has
if I know! I can think of it quietly. After all what *does* it
I *know* suppose you
proved? Nothing. *If you were capable to make it clear to their minds they wouldn't even know what you were driving at. I made a confounded fuss about it. I am ashamed of it now. What was it after all? A trifle.*" don't think so". . . .[372]

Jim's cavalier dismissal of the *Patna* episode was not true to his character.

The study of Conrad's habits of composition substantiates his claim that he wrote first and theorized later.[373] His perseverance against unfavorable environments, his worry over health and money, his periods of nervousness and sudden spurts of creation are reflected in the copious corrections of the manuscripts. The cancelations, new attempts, economies, incoherence, and sudden changes of those blackened pages are evidence of his perplexities. He felt his way towards the plot of his stories and towards the best presentation of his material. The labor with which he evolved some of his most moving passages explains his dissatisfaction with the rewards of his work. One is able to see through Conrad's eyes that writing is "un art trop difficile."[374]

Chapter V

A CHRONICLE OF THE EARLY STORIES

THE facts about Conrad's early writing are widely scattered. Some of the material is spread throughout many published volumes: the author's notes in the collected edition, the collections of letters, bibliographies, and the reminiscences of Conrad's circle. A good deal is in still unpublished correspondence and documents and in the manuscripts themselves. All this disseminated information has never before been united and arranged around each story to which it belongs. The history of the individual stories, in chronological order, gives a further understanding of Conrad's attitude towards his work, his habits of writing, and his literary plans.

Conrad left a mass of contradictory statements, and his friends have added their quota. His inability to remember the facts about his work [1] has led to confusion in his own assertions and in those of his commentators. A careful comparison of the discrepancies and the data upon which they are based will clarify many inconsistencies. Though Conrad's recollection must frequently be accepted for want of more exact information, the evidence must be checked as carefully as possible.

"The Black Mate"

The history of Conrad's stories opens, appropriately, with a double problem. In his reminiscences he always reckoned his literary life from *Almayer's Folly*. Yet a short story, "The Black Mate," questions the priority of the first novel. Does the existence of "The Black Mate" disturb the accepted chronological order of Conrad's work? Is the existing version of "The Black Mate" the first version of the story?

His two statements about the chronology were made in 1922, nearly forty years after the possible composition of the story. On January 19 he asserted to Pinker: "I wrote that thing in '86 for a prize competition, started, I think, by *Tit-Bits*."[2] Somewhat later he was not so definite. "My memories about this tale are confused," he admitted, "I have a notion that it was first written some time in the late eighties and retouched later."[3] Uncertain as Conrad's memory was, his recollection of writing a story called "The Black Mate" in 1886 must stand in the absence of any substantiated contradictions. Jean-Aubry accepted the date for the official *Life and Letters*.[4]

Because the story was not accepted by *Tit-Bits*, there arises the second problem of whether or not "The Black Mate" published in 1908 was written in 1886. Conrad admitted the story was "retouched later." Mrs. Conrad insisted that it was an entirely new story. She was emphatic in what she wrote for George T. Keating in a copy of *Tales of Hearsay*:

> This is one of the two stories written by Joseph Conrad that he liked least. Yet curiously enough it holds a prominent position because of a misleading statement made by Conrad himself. I was amazed one day to hear him assuring Mr. Curle that it was the first thing he had written. My mild protest called forth such a violent excitement that I forebore to insist. This was to be regretted as it caused Mr. Cunninghame-Graham to make the misleading statement in his Preface to this book. I gave my husband the facts and matter for the tale but he received it in such a manner that my astonishment was great when I saw the 'bones' I had given clothed in the story and heard his unexpected claim that it was his first story.[5]

Though Cunninghame Graham referred to the story in *Tales of Hearsay* [6] as Conrad's first, antedating *Almayer's Folly*, Curle did not accept it. He was "inclined to think that he [Conrad] may twice have had much the same idea and that the first story is lost." [7] Jean-Aubry concurred with Curle's opinion.[8]

Though Conrad may have thought at times that the two stories called "The Black Mate" were one and the same, the evidence indicates that the version published in the *London Magazine* for April, 1908,[9] shared at most its title and theme with the version of 1886. By 1922 the manuscript of the story was in the hands of T. J. Wise. Probably Wise acquired it in 1919 when, according to Richard Curle, he began to collect Conrad.[10]

The story did not occupy Conrad's attention again until 1922 when he planned another collection of short stories. He was reluctant to use "The Black Mate" for the proposed volume, since he was aware that it would confuse his literary history, which he had always dated from *Almayer's Folly*. On January 19, 1922, he informed J. B. Pinker, his literary agent, "It would complicate my literary history in a sort of futile way. . . . It is an extraneous phenomenon. My literary life began privately in 1890 [1889] and publicly in 1895 with *Almayer's Folly*, which is regarded generally as my very first piece of writing. However, the history of the 'Black Mate,' its origin etc., etc., need not be proclaimed on housetops, and *Almayer's Folly* may keep its place as my first serious work." Apparently he had forgotten the magazine publication of the story, for he went on to say: "I can [procure the manuscript] through Wise. . . . My feeling about it is that there will be nothing actually disgraceful in its inclusion in my collected editions (for that is what its publication in book form would ultimately mean). . . . Therefore I agree to your proposal, with the proviso that should *The Rover* turn out a longer piece of work than we anticipate, we will try to do without the 'Black Mate.' "[11]

When *The Rover* grew into novel length, the publication of the collection of short stories was not pressed. Conrad's interest in "The Black Mate," however, had been sufficiently aroused for him to agree to a private printing of fifty copies in February, 1922.[12] Though the edition bears the legend "Printed for the Author," T. J. Wise was behind the publication. In Richard Curle's copy were inserted "2 specimen leaves for this story of different sizes. On one Mr. T. J. Wise has written '*This will make 64 pp.*' and on the other, '*This will make 96 pp. but I have decided upon it.*' "[13] The story here appeared for the second time in print.

The third and last appearance of "The Black Mate" is as the fourth story in *Tales of Hearsay*, published a year after Conrad's death. The title was selected by Curle who had often heard Conrad mention it as excellent for some future collection.[14] R. B. Cunninghame Graham wrote the preface. There was no dedication. The volume was issued in 1925 by T. Fisher Unwin in England and by Doubleday, Page and Company in the United States.

Almayer's Folly

Once the chronological position of "The Black Mate" is established, *Almayer's Folly*, with which Conrad's literary career really began, may be considered. He made many incorrect statements about his first novel, and his errors led his friends to add to the misinformation. The most accurate account of the time at which he began *Almayer's Folly* was his memorandum for John Quinn who bought the manuscript: "Commenced in September 1889 in London."[15] The season, though not the month, was confirmed by *A*

Personal Record,[16] which said that the novel was begun on "an autumn day." The exact day entirely slipped Conrad's memory. The date was corroborated by Jean-Aubry's research. After a stay of more than two years in the East, where in Borneo he met the original of Almayer and other characters in his stories, Conrad returned to London in late May or early June, 1889. While he sought a new berth, he spent the summer and autumn in lodgings in Bessborough Gardens, Pimlico.[17] There, to pass away the time, he began writing.[18] "I had been treating myself to a long stay on shore," he remarked, "and in the necessity of occupying my mornings, Almayer (that old acquaintance) came nobly to the rescue." "For many years he and the world of his story had been the companions of my imagination. . . ."[19] Yet "the first manuscript page . . . (it contained about two hundred words and this proportion of words to a page has remained with me . . .)"[20] led not only to a novel but, by unexpected circumstances, to a new way of life.

The history of *Almayer's Folly* after its casual beginning has been confused by the activity of Conrad's life during the next five years. The story progressed slowly. In the autobiographical sketch given to Garnett, he asserted:

> *a few chapters*
> [*were written*
> . . . some chapters were written in London *some* in Poland
> *a few* the
> and *couple* in Africa — in *the Congo* — Belgian Congo. . . .[21]

Apparently he began the fifth chapter while staying with his uncle in the Polish Ukraine in the late winter of 1890;[22] on the verso of page one of chapter five is a letter in Polish which reads in part: "I very much regret that circumstances will not permit me to return by way of Cracow. I came here by way of Warsaw in order to get to my uncle as soon as possible and now I must return by that same route to see my family in Radon." It is impossible to tell how much of the story preceding and following the first page of chapter five may have been written during this visit to Poland. He affirmed that he had seven chapters with him when he was carried ill down the Congo on his way to Europe in December, 1890.[23] He over-estimated by one chapter; the first few pages of the seventh chapter were written at Champel, near Geneva, where he was convalescing from May 21 to June 14, 1891.[24] On the verso of page one of chapter seven [25] of the Rosenbach manuscript is a series of computations in pounds and the words: "Can it be done. – 1891. Anno Mirabilis." On the verso of page six of chapter seven [26] is a computation of 536 francs for four weeks' board and the words: "Genéve . . . Receive from London 375 fr." Unless Conrad worked at most unusual speed, he could not have completed the chapter before leaving Champel.[27]

Conrad continued to write after he returned from the continent. "The events of the ninth [chapter]," he declared, "are inextricably mixed up with the details of the proper management of a waterside warehouse owned by a certain city firm whose name does not matter." [28] Actually the warehouse was numbers 1 and 2 Dyers' Hall Wharf, at 95 Upper Thames Street, and belonged to Barr, Moering and Company.[29] Though Conrad expected to start work there in July, he suffered a feverish relapse and could not begin until the fourth of August.[30] Perhaps he was living in the "shabby, sordid lodgings on the bank of the river Thames, in the little village of Greenhythe," [31] just outside London, where, he told his wife, some of *Almayer's Folly* was written. By the middle of September he had moved to 17 Gillingham Street, S.W., which was his home off and on until his marriage nearly five years later.[32] It is impossible to be sure how far the manuscript had advanced when on November 25, 1891, he left for his first voyage to Australia on the *Torrens*.[33]

During his second voyage on the *Torrens* from October 25, 1892, to January 30, 1893, he impulsively showed the manuscript to a passenger, W. H. Jacques, who assured him that it was " 'distinctly' " worth finishing.[34] The novel made little progress while Conrad was mate of the *Torrens*.[35] It was still in chapter nine in the summer of 1893 when he nearly lost all the manuscript on his way to visit Tadeusz Bobrowski in Poland.[36] While staying with his uncle, he may have completed chapter nine before his departure in early October.[37]

More is known about the history of the last three chapters than about any other part of *Almayer's Folly*. On his return from Poland Conrad was apparently slow to take up the novel again, complaining in November of idleness and melancholy.[38] He began the tenth chapter at Rouen where, as second officer of the *Adowa*, he waited from December 4, 1893, to January 10, 1894, for the ship to sail for Canada.[39] Since the *Adowa* was his last professional connection with the sea, the final chapters were written much more rapidly than the earlier. Leisure to write brought the nervous tension that was to grow with the years. By the end of the winter he was working on the eleventh chapter with difficulty:

Je suis en train de lutter avec Chap. XI; une lutte a mort Vous savez! . . . Je regrette chaque minute que je passe loin du papier. Je ne dis pas de la plume car j'ai ecrit fort peu, mais l'inspiration me vient en regardant le papier. Puis ce sont des echappées a perte de vue; la pensée s'en va vagabondant dans des grands éspaces remplis des formes vagues. Tout e[s]t chaos encore mais — lentement — les spectres se changent en chair vivante, les vapeurs flottantes se solidifient et qui sait? — peut-être quelque chose naitra dans le choc des idées indistinctes.[40]

Despite trouble with his material, he still enjoyed the act of writing.

The novel was completed with a rush. Probably on April 10 he went to stay with Launcelot Sanderson at Elstree, Herts, where on the sixteenth he finished chapter eleven, 9000 words in all, "plus long mais bien plus mauvais que les autres. Je commence le XII dans un quart d'heure."[41] Returning to London on April 20, he wrote Mme. Poradowska in triumph at eleven o'clock on the morning of the twenty-fourth:

> J'ai la douleur de vous faire part de la mort de M. Kaspar Almayer qui a eu lieu ce matin a 3*h*
>
> C'est fini! En grattement de de plume ecrivant le mot de la fin et soudain toute cette compagnie des gens qui ont parlé dans mon oreille, gesticulé devant mes yeux, vécu avec moi pendant tant d'années devient une bande des fantômes qui s'eloignent, s'effacent se brouillant; indistincts et palis par le soleil de cette brillante et sombre journée —
>
> Depuis que je me suis reveillé ce matin il me semble que j'ai enseveli une part de moi-même dans les pages qui sont là devant mes yeux. Et cependant je suis content — un peu. — [42]

The first draft had been completed.

Conrad made important revisions in his story before he submitted it to a publisher. Apparently he had had a preliminary typescript made of the first ten chapters of the novel, which he showed Mme. Poradowska on a visit to Brussels in March, 1894.[43] When he completed the manuscript, he promised to send her "les deux chap*tres* [eleven and twelve] aussitot typés." [44] About the end of April he sent her the typescript of chapter eleven and declared:

"Moi je re-ecris le 4 premiers chapitres." [45] He did not find the revision easy. On May 2 he complained:

Je trouve le travail du remaniement de mes 3 premiers chapîtres non seulement désagréable mais absolument pénible. Et difficile avec cela! Et cependant il faut que cela se fasse!

Je vous enverrai bientôt le dernier Chap:. Il commence avec un *trio* Nina, Dain, Almayer, et il finit dans un long *solo* pour Almayer qui est presque aussi long que le Tristan-solo de Wagner. Enfin! Vous verrez! mais je crains fort que vous ne trouviez la chose fade.[46]

A comparison of the manuscript and the existing typescript in their entirety reveals how much work Conrad must have done on the whole intermediate typescript: the prose and especially the plot have been much altered.[47] Conrad must have been thinking of these alterations when in 1900 he remembered that he had practically rewritten *Almayer's Folly*.[48] About the middle of May he apologized for not yet having sent Mme. Poradowska chapter twelve, adding, "Le manuscrit entier est entre les mains d'un critique assez distingué: Edmund Gosse. Combien de temps le gardera-t-il je n'en sais rien." [49] The details of Gosse's connection with *Almayer's Folly* remain a mystery; he must have returned the typescript before summer was well along, for Conrad wrote Mme. Poradowska in late June or early July, "Je vous enverrai le chap XII et dernier, qui est pret." [50] But Mme. Poradowska had not seen the last chapter by September 8,[51] when the typescript had already been two months in Unwin's hands, nor is there any evidence that she read it before it appeared in book form.

On July 4 Conrad sent the typescript to T. Fisher Unwin.[52] He chose Unwin because of the Pseudonym Library, of which he had read a volume or two.[53] *Almayer's Folly* was intended for the Library: on the title page of the

Leeds typescript Conrad's name does not appear and the story is said to be by Kamudi. The word is Malay, is pronounced Kamondi and means rudder.[54] The anonymity emphasized the amateur spirit with which he viewed the whole venture.

At this point Conrad's first novel reached the most perilous period of its history. He seems to have expected rejection automatically. He told Mme. Poradowska on July 12, 1894:

J'ai envoyer mon manuscript a Fisher Unwin and C° qui publient une serie des romans anonymes. Pas de reponse encore. Elle viendra sans doute dans la forme de renvoi de ce chef d'oeuvre en vue de quoi j'ai envoyé les timbres-postes nécéssaires. —

A vous dire toute la verité je n'eprouve aucun interet au sort d' "Almayer's Folly." — C'est fini. Du reste dans tous les cas cela ne pouvait être qu'un épisode sans conséquence dans ma vie.[55]

His indifference was more than matched by Unwin's. For two months the publisher sent no reply, and the delay might have had a profound effect upon Conrad's literary career. Though he had already had ambitions for a French translation, Unwin's long silence apparently roused him to another scheme. He suggested to Mme. Poradowska:

Je n'ai pas de reponse de Fisher Unwin. Cela peut durer des mois et puis je ne pense [pas] que l'on acceptera. . . .

Si Vous n'aviez rien dit a la Revue nous aurions pu peut-être faire paraître Almayer pas comme traduction mais comme collaboration. Ai-je du toupet pour Vous parler comme ça chère Maitre? [56]

He may have hoped to profit by her connection with the *Revue des Deux Mondes* and her reputation as a novelist.[57] From Champel he elaborated his plans for a collaboration:

Puisque Vous êtes assez bonne pour Vous en occuper, parlons de cet imbécile d'Almayer. J'ai envoyé reclamer le renvoi du MS. et aussitôt mon retour en Angl: je le tiendrais a Votre disposition. Je desire garder mon nom de *Kamudi*. . . . Je ne veux pas des grandes lettres et tout ça. C'est tout-a fait comme Votre bonne amitié de penser a ces choses là! Avoir Votre beau langage pour exprimer mes pauvres pensées est un bonheur et un honneur. Ceci n'est pas politesse mais conviction sincère. Le nom de "Kamondi" en petites lettres quelque part suffira. Laissez votre nom paraitre en titre — une note explicative suffira pour dire que K. y a collaboré. Voulez Vous? Du reste il me semble tout drôle de Vous écrire tout cela. J'ai peine a croire a mon bonheur. — [58]

Back in London, Conrad continued to move toward collaboration. On September 8 he prodded Unwin to accept or to return the story:

On the 4th July 1894 there was delivered in your pubg offices of Paternoster Row a typewritten work.

Title: "Almayer's Folly"; it was enclosed in brown paper wrapper addressed to J. Conrad, 17 Gillingham St. S.W. and franked, for return by parcel post, by twelve 1d stamps. The brown paper package was put between two detached sheets of cardboard secured together by a string. One of the cardboard sheets bore your address. The boy messger produced the usual receipt slip, duly signed, but I do not remember the name or initials of the signature.

I venture now upon the liberty of asking you whether there is the slightest likelihood of the MS (Malay life, about 64,000 words) being read at some future time? If not, it would be — probably — no worse fate than it deserves, yet, in that case, I am sure you will not take it amiss if I remind you that, however worthless for the purpose of publication, it is very dear to me. A ridiculous feeling — no doubt — but not unprecedented I believe. In this instance it is intensified by the accident that I do not possess another copy, either written or typed.[59]

On the same day he wrote Mme. Poradowska:

> Je viens d'ecrire a Fisher Unwin quand au Almayer. Je leur demande une reponse ou le retour du MS. Quand je l'aurai je Vous enverrai le dernier Chap. que Vous n'avez pas encore lu. Si je pars on tiendra le MS a Votre disposition chez M.M. Barr, Moering. . . . Vous ecrirez que l'on Vous l'envoie quand Vous Vous sentirez l'envie de commencer.[60]

The proposal of collaboration involved so many possibilities that Conrad's fate as a novelist seemed to hang by a hair. The question of literary ethics may be put aside as too complex for discussion. If *Almayer's Folly* had appeared under these conditions and had not been a success in France, Conrad might never have fallen back upon literature when he could not find a job at sea. If it had been successful, he might have been encouraged, despite all his later protests,[61] to write in French. Joseph Conrad might have been a name not in English but in French literature. The possibility seemed even more likely on October 2, when he complained: "Je ne peux pas obtenir mon manuscript. J'ai réclamé deux fois et chaque foi j'ai eu la reponse que l'on s'en occupe. Je vais attendre quelque jours encore avant de demander le renvoi quand même." [62] On October 4, 1894, he heard that Unwin had accepted the novel.[63] Though Conrad made special efforts to retain the French copyright, Mme. Poradowska finally decided against making the French translation herself.[64] The novel was translated years later as *La Folie-Almayer* by Geneviève Seligmann-Lui.

Conrad's excitement over the acceptance was not caused by Unwin's terms. If it had not been for Edward Garnett, who as publisher's reader recommended the novel, *Almayer's Folly* might never have been accepted. Garnett said of his discovery: "W. H. Chesson, whose duty it was to take charge of the manuscripts, tells me that he called my particular attention to the manuscript." [65] The publisher made his new author two alternative offers. In the letter of acceptance he offered Conrad twenty pounds for all the rights to the novel. "J'ai ecrit que j'acceptais les conditions," Conrad told Mme. Poradowska. "J'ai pris ce que l'on m'offrait car vraiment le fait même de la publication est de grande importance. Chaque semaine des douzaines des romans paraissent – et il est bien difficile de se faire imprimer. – A presant il ne me manque qu'un navire pour être a peu près heureux." [66] In his first interview with Unwin on October 8 [67] the publisher made a second proposal. "Il m'a dit franchement," Conrad explained on October 10, "que si je voulais prendre une part dans le risque de la publication je pourrai participer au profits. Sinon on me donne 20£ et les droits français. J'ai choisi cette dernière alternative." [68]

Even Unwin must have thought the terms disappointing; he gave an elaborate excuse for them. Conrad reported the talk verbatim:

"Nous Vous payons très peu — a-t-il dit — mais considerez cher monsieur que Vous êtes un inconnu et que Votre livre appelle a un public très limité. Puis il y a la question du gout. Le Public le goutera-t-il? Nous risquons quelque chose aussi. Nous Vous fairons paraître en un beau volume a 6 shillings et Vous savez que ce qui paraît chez nous reçoit toujours des critique serieuses dans le journaux littéraires. Vous êtes sur d'une longue "notice" dans la "Saturday Review" et l' "Atheneum" sans parler de la presse en general. Voilà pourquoi nous pensons de ne Vous faire paraître que l'année prochaine en Avril pendant la saison. On va imprimer tout de suite pour que Vous puissiez corriger et nous enverrons les "proof sheets" a Mme Poradowska avant la Noël. Ecrivez quelque chose de plus court — même genre — pour notre Pseudonym Library et si la chose convient nous serons très heureux de pouvoir Vous donner un bien meilleur chèque." [69]

Unwin's plausibilities and promises were backed by the compliments of two of his readers who, according to Conrad, "m'ont reçu et m'on complimenté avec effusion (se sont-ils moqué de moi par hasard?)" [70] Because of its length Unwin decided against including *Almayer's Folly* in the Pseudonym Library.[71] If the author desired anonymity, he was satisfied with the protection of "Joseph Conrad."

He did not wait for the advance sheets before he began touching up the novel. He seems to have worked on the typescript at once while on a visit to friends in the country.[72] Unwin was not quick about printing the story, though Conrad expected the advance sheets by mid-November.[73] When they failed to appear, he spoke of the delay with indifference:

J'ai eu une longue entrevue avec monsieur T. Fisher Unwin. Decidement on ne mettra l'ouvrage en type que l'année prochaine en Fevrier. Cela m'est absolument égal. Je n'ai rien a corriger en fait de style ou composition et quand aux fautes d'imprimerie les correcteurs de la maison en prendront bon soin. — Moi j'espère de tout mon coeur et de toute mon âme que je ne serai plus a Londres a cette époque.[74]

He did not get to sea, however, and the proofs began to arrive, the first sixteen pages on Christmas Eve, 1894. "J'en ai eu horreur," he protested. "Absolument horreur de la chose imprimée qui a l'air si bête – pire – vide de sens." [75] The proofs were partly corrected on board the *Ildegonda*, a cutter which he shared with G. F. W. Hope.[76] Unwin set the first week of March for publication and later moved the date up to March 18.[77] As the spring wore on, Conrad became impatient.[78]

The novel did not appear serially and was brought out on April 29, 1895, in an edition of two thousand copies which sold at six shillings each.[79] Publication had been held up by the American edition. "Je ne suis pas encore publié," Conrad wrote on April 12, "mais c'est pour ce mois pour sur. On ne peut pas me donner la date definitive encore. La maison MacMillan de New York se charge de la publication en Amerique et a cause de la loi sur le Copyright il faut attendre qu'ils soient prêts la-bas." [80] He did not see the American edition of six hundred and fifty copies until 1919.[81] The novel is dedicated "To the Memory of T. B.," Tadeusz Bobrowski, who had died on January 29, 1894.[82] "Il me semble que tout est mort en moi," he told Mme. Poradowska at the time of Bobrowski's death. "Il semble emporter mon ame avec lui." [83] It was a dedication to Conrad's past life, for his uncle represented father, mother, and country to him. The Author's Note, unlike most of those in his novels, was written contemporaneously with the story: it is dated 1895.[84] Unwin did not print it in the first edition. When Conrad wanted the note for the Collected Edition, he had to ask John Quinn, who had bought the manuscript, to send a copy to Doubleday, Page and Company.[85]

Conrad's feeling for the story grew more paternal with the years. His "perpetual surprise" [86] at fathering a novel gave way to a period of reaction. A few months after publication he viewed the novel "with bitter disappointment" and dubbed it "a miserable failure." [87] By the time *A Personal Record* [88] was written he looked back on his transfiguration of Olmeijer with pride. He refused to allow hopeful dramatists to tamper with it: "Several people in England and America (amongst them a couple of recognized playwrights) attempted to dramatize this novel, but in no case could I approve the result of their work." [89]

The manuscript and typescript of the novel were sold to Quinn in 1912, according to the postmark on the wrapper, and the collector resold them at auction in New York in November, 1923, for $5300 and $650 respectively.[90] The entire Quinn collection of Conrad realized over a hundred thousand dollars. Conrad commented ironically on the sale to his American publisher, F. N. Doubleday:

> The reverberation in the press here was very great indeed; and the result is that lots of people, who never heard of me before, now know my name, and thousands of others, who could not have read through a page of mine without falling into convulsions, are proclaiming me a very great author. And there are a good many also whom nothing will persuade that the whole thing was not a put-up job and that I haven't got my share of the plunder.[91]

The only profit for the Conrads from the Quinn sale was a check from the *Daily Mail* for Mrs. Conrad's article on the preservation of the manuscripts.[92]

An Outcast of the Islands

Though Conrad did not feel that his second novel was worthy of a commentary like *A Personal Record*, *An Outcast of the Islands* was important in his life. It closely resembles the first novel in subject matter and in genesis. Its history also is complicated by Conrad's misstatements.

In the Author's Note to *An Outcast* he reconstructed his mood after the completion of *Almayer's Folly*. Though he still considered the sea his profession, writing had revealed a new way of life, contemplative instead of active. The vision was unsettling. "I was a victim of contrary stresses which produced a state of immobility," he recalled. "I gave myself up to indolence."[93] Yet he was separated from the sea not by writing but by his inability to get a job.[94] He was not so indolent as he supposed.

Conrad first mentioned his "second novel in the absolute sense of the word; second in conception, second in execution, second as it were in its essence" [95] about the middle of August, 1894. *Almayer's Folly* had not yet been accepted. At Champel he outlined the new story under the title of *Two Vagabonds*:

J'ai commencer d'ecrire — avant-hier seulement. Je veux faire cela tout court — Disons 20 a 25 pages comme celles de la Revue. J'apelle ça "Deux Vagabonds" (Two Vagabonds) et je veux decrire a grands traits — sans ombres ni details — deux epaves humaines comme on en rencotre dans les coins perdus du monde. Un homme blanc et un Malais. Vous voyez que les Malais me tiennent. Je suis voué au Borneo. Ce qui m'ennuie le plus ce que mes personnages sont si vrais. Je les connais si bien qu'ils m'entravent l'imagination. Le blanc c'est un ami d'Almayer le Malais c'est notre vieil ami Babalatchi avant qu'il soit arrivé a la dignité du Ier Ministre . . . du Rajah. Voilà. Mais une catastrophe dramatique me me manque. La tête est vide et même pour le commencement il y a du tirage! Je ne Vous dis que ça! J'ai envie de lacher tout déjà.[96]

Though he had been writing the story for only three days, he was already feeling the strain of composition. He showed more than one symptom of later difficulties. For *An Outcast* was originally intended as a short story,[97] but, like *Lord Jim*, was to grow into a novel. He had begun without any clear idea of the end of his story. The letter reveals also that he started his second novel as casually as his first. He was taking a cure and once more his Borneo associations "came nobly to the rescue." [98]

Conrad's dissatisfaction with the story made him put it aside entirely before September 8, when, back at 17 Gillingham Street, he admitted:

Les deux Vagabonds dorment. Je ne suis pas satisfait avec moi-même — du tout. Il me manque des idées. J'ai beaucoup brulé. Ce sera a recommencer! [99]

Apparently the story remained at a stand-still during the next month. The publisher's suggestion in writing, when he accepted *Almayer's Folly*, that Conrad also submit "quelque chose de plus court (25000 mots)," awakened no response. He confessed on October 4, "Les 2 Vagabonds chôment Je suit trop occupé a courir après les navires." [100]

Within the week he was stimulated by his first interview with Unwin. Conrad reported the conversation directly:

"Ecrivez quelque chose de plus court — même genre — pour notre Pseudonym Library et si la chose convient nous serons très heureux de pouvoir Vous donner un bien meilleur chèque."

Voilà. J'avance tout doucement avec un vagabond sous chaque bras dans l'espoir de les vendre a Fisher Unwin. Traite d'esclaves! [101]

Seeing Unwin personally and receiving a promise of larger pay encouraged Conrad to take up the story again. The length suggested was much what he had planned. Yet the encouragement did not provide him with the missing catastrophe nor turn him away from the sea. Not two weeks later he was complaining:

L'autre ouvrage va très doucement. Je suis très decouragé. Les idées ne viennent pas. Je ne *vois pas* ni les personnages ni les evenements. A vrai dire je suis preoccupé de mes plans pour partir et comme ils n'ont pas l'air de se realiser je suis dans un état d'irritation qui ne me permet pas de m'oublier dans mon récit — par consequent le travail ne vaut rien.[102]

"Contrary stresses" had again reduced him to "a state of immobility"; he was in need of stimulation.

Some stimulation came from his first contact with Edward Garnett, the reader who had recommended the publication of *Almayer's Folly*. When they were introduced by Unwin in November, 1894,[103] Garnett struck just the right note to reawaken Conrad's interest in the *Two Vagabonds.* "A phrase of Edward Garnett's is, as a matter of fact, responsible for this book," Conrad admitted in the Author's Note to the completed novel. "He pointed out that there was no need to determine my future absolutely. Then he added: 'You have the style, you have the temperament; why not write another?' . . . Had he said, 'Why not go on writing?' it is very probable he would have scared me away from pen and ink forever; but there was nothing either to frighten one or arouse one's antagonism in the mere suggestion to 'write another.' And thus a dead point in the revolution of my affairs was insidiously got over. The word 'another' did it. . . . On getting home I sat down and wrote about half a page of '*An Outcast of the Islands*' before I slept." [104] Apparently he did not admit to Garnett that he had already begun a second novel.[105]

When Conrad wrote the Author's Note in 1919, he was obviously mistaken if he thought that he began the novel the night he met Garnett.[106] He even overestimated the effect of Garnett's encouragement: contemporary evidence reveals his inactivity. About the first of November, 1894, he developed a new scheme for the story:

> Mme M. Wood m'a volé mon titre. Elle vient de publier un livre: "The Vagabonds" et me voilà joliment embêté. Non! Si vous saviez comme ça m'ennuie Vous auriez pitié de moi.—
>
> Quand a l'idée de cet ouvrage a presant sans titre. . . . Le motif d'abord c'est une vanité effrenée, feroce d'un homme ignorant qui a du succés mais n'a ni principes ni d'autre ligne de conduite que la satisfaction de sa vanité.—Aussi il n'est même pas fidèle a soi même. D'ou chute, degringolade subite jusqu'a l'esclavage physique de l'homme par une femme absolument sauvage. J'ai vu ça! La catastrophe sera amenèe par les intrigues d'un petit etat Malais, dont le dernier mot est: empoisonnement. Le denoument est: suicide par vanité encore.

Tout cela ne sera qu'esquissé car comme j'écris pour la "Pseudonym Library" je suis limité a 36000 mots pour faire un volume. Voilà. —[107]

At last he had a fitting catastrophe, and with it the whole plan of the novel changed. The length far outgrew the limitation of thirty-six thousand words.

In the same letter he confessed that, though he had written three chapters, he was again the victim of nervous sterility:

> Oui c'est vrai. On travaille le plus quand on ne fait rien. Voilà trois jours que je m'assois devant une page blanche — et la page est toujours blanche excépté pour un IV en tête. A vrai dire je suis mal parti. . . . Je ne ressens le moindre enthousiasme. C'est fatal, cela.

Despite the new plan and Garnett he was unproductive throughout November. He admitted shortly: "Le travail ne va pas, et la santé n'est plus aussi bonne. Si je reste plus longtemps a terre tout se gatera." [108] "Il y a quinze jours déjà que je n'ai ecrit un seul mot," he lamented to Mme. Poradowska toward the end of the month. "C'est bien fini il me semble. J'ai envie de bruler ce qui est là. C'est très mauvais! Trop mauvais! Ceci est ma profonde conviction et non pas un cri de stupide modestie. Je me suis débattu assez longtemps comme cela." [109]

His pace mended in December. To Mme. Poradowska's anxious inquiry he answered:

> Je n'ai rien brulé. On parle comme ça et puis le courage manque. Il y en a comme ça qui parlent du suicide! . . . Je travaille un peu. J'agonise la plume a la main. Six lignes en six jours.[110]

By December 27 he had a new title and had conquered his inability to write but not his anxiety about writing:

La chose est faite. J'ai changé mon titre. Ce sera: 'An Outcast of the Islands' Et la chose elle-même est changée. Tout est changé . . . excepté la peur de ces phantômes que l'on evoque soi même et qui si souvent refusent d'obeir la cervelle qui les a crées. —

Enfin. Voilà le chap.–VIII terminé. Encore quatre! Quatre siècles d'agonie — quatre minutes des délices et puis la fin — la tête vide — le decouragement et le doute eternel. — [111]

He had managed to produce five chapters in two months. The title, "Two Vagabonds," and the subtitle, "A Tale of the Islands," appear in the manuscript on "the opening page of each chapter until the eighth, which has 'An Outcast of the Islands' instead, and this is repeated in the following chapters." [112] The scale of the story had not yet been expanded. He was still expecting to complete in four chapters what took eighteen.

During the next two months Conrad added appreciably to the number of chapters. He had completed the tenth by the end of January, 1895:

Je viens d'écrire XI en tête d'une page blanche et blanche elle restera peut-être dix jours ou je ne me connais pas. — Vous voyez mon idée de travail. Drôle! n'est-ce pas? [113]

A few weeks later he announced that " 'The Outcast etc etc' fait son petit bonhomme de chemin au millieu des pleurs et des grincements des dents usuels." [114] On March 8 he sent for Garnett's criticism four chapters among which was twelve (in the published version chapter five of part two). He was feeling his way with experiments in style; he wrote Garnett: "In Chap. XII beginning with the words: 'and now they are . . .' are the two par[agraph]s. in the new style. Please say on the margin what you think. One word will do. I am very much in doubt myself about it." [115]

The change in style was marked by a transition from the past to the present tense in narrative. Garnett must have disapproved, for the new style was dropped after three paragraphs.

Conrad left little information about the further progress of the novel, and that little dealt mostly with the difficulty of composition. The nervous tension he felt in writing was to grow until it cast a shadow over his entire life. The first attack reached a climax in the spring of 1895, following a winter of intense concentration. After a spell in bed [116] he decided to try hydropathic treatment at Champel, where he had begun the novel. On May 1 he explained to Garnett: "Seriously, I find I can't work. Simply can't! I am going to try what mountain air combined with active fire-hose (twice a day) will do for divine inspiration. I shall try it for about 3 weeks and maybe the lenient gods will allow me to finish that infernal Manuscript. Sorry can't send you the 4 chaps. Just come from type – not corrected." [117] He was submitting the novel, four chapters at a time, to Garnett. Before leaving London, he wrote, while working on the seventeenth chapter, that he expected the novel to run to twenty or perhaps twenty-one chapters.[118]

At Champel he was able to write, though not fluently. After a week there he told Mme. Poradowska, "Je continue a ecrire et cela n'en finit pas. Je crains les longueurs mais je ne sais pas comment leur echapper." [119] He never learned. "I am working every day: – tolerably bad work," he informed Garnett on May 12. "Like poor Risler the Elder's cashier [in Alphonse Daudet's *Fromont jeune et Risler ainé*] 'I haf' no gonfidence'. . . . I dread the moment when you shall see my 'Outcast' as a whole. It seems frightful bosh. I never felt like that even in the first days of my 'Folly.'" [120] On May 20 he was still complaining: "Je travaille peu et mal – très mal." [121] Years later he told

Pinker that he had written one third of *An Outcast* at Champel. He returned to London on June 4, 1895.[122]

In July Conrad notified Garnett that the manuscript now numbered four hundred pages and that he expected to finish in another fifty pages.[123] Not completed for another two months, it finally reached five hundred and sixteen pages.[124] He dated the last page of the manuscript September 14, 1895, and repeated the date in a memorandum for Quinn.[125] But on September 17 he wrote a facetious letter to Garnett:

> It is my painful duty to inform you of the sad death of Mr. Peter Willems late of Rotterdam and Macassar who has been murdered on the 16th inst at 4 p.m. while the sun shone joyously and the barrel organ sang on the pavement the abominable Intermezzo of the ghastly Cavalleria. As soon as I recovered from the shock I busied myself in arranging the affairs of the two inconsolable widows of our late lamented friend and . . . everything was decently settled before midnight. You know what strong affection I had for the poor departed so you won't be surprised to hear that to me — since yesterday life seems a blank. . . .
>
> Almayer was the last to go. . . . I was glad to see him go, but — such is the inconsequence of the human heart — no sooner he went than I began to regret bitterly his absence. . . . The detailed relation of the heartrending occurrences of the last two days will be deposited tomorrow in Paternoster Bdgs for your perusal.[126]

The letter described comprehensively the last eight pages of the novel following the death of Willems, and stated specifically that the whole was completed before midnight of September 16. It further implied that Conrad was retouching the conclusion on September 17. The conflicting dates cannot be explained.

When Garnett read the end of the novel, he was not entirely satisfied. He gave his impressions:

On the delivery of the final installment . . . I criticized adversely the psychology of Willems' motives and behaviour just before his death at Aissa's hand; and Conrad agreed, with reservations, to my strictures and set to work to remodel various passages. I think now that my criticism was not so just as I imagined at the time.[127]

Conrad answered Garnett's comments on September 24.

I am glad you like the XXIII chapter. . . . As to the XXIV I feel convinced that the right course would be to destroy it. . . . The only question is: can I?

I am afraid I can't! I lack the courage to set before myself the task of rewriting the thing. . . . The whole conception seems to me wrong. I seem to have seen the wrong side of the situation. I was always afraid of it. — For months I have been afraid of that chapter — and now it is written — and the foreboding is realized in a dismal failure.

Nothing now can unmake my mistake. I shall try — but I shall try without faith. . . .[128]

A month later Conrad declared: "It took me a year to tear the *Outcast* out of myself and upon my word of honor, – I look on it (now it's finished) with bitter disappointment." [129] In 1900 he called it "a heap of sand." [130] Finally in the Author's Note, completed on January 29, 1919, he confessed: "The story itself was never very near my heart." [131]

Conrad was able to sell the novel on August 23, 1895, before he completed it; [132] he was beginning a business habit that later caused him much suffering. He wrote E. L. Sanderson, to whom the novel was dedicated, on August 24:

I have been extremely busy and half the time in Paris. I have crossed the Channel six times (three trips) in a fortnight. . . . As you may imagine Willems has been considerably neglected during that time and is not dead yet. . . .

Yesterday I sold him. I've sold him for about 12 1/2 per cent. royalty, and fifty pounds cash payable on the 1st of December. I have half serial and American rights. F[isher] U[nwin] wants to get the book accepted for a serial by some magazine or newspaper. I hate the idea but have given in to his arguments. My opinion is he shall not be able to place it. As a book it will be a 6/. — edition uniform with *Almayer*.[133]

He was right in his prediction; the novel was not published serially. Unwin fulfilled his promise of a "meilleur chèque": *An Outcast* brought two and a half times as much as *Almayer's Folly*.

Publication was attended by mishaps. Conrad complained on October 28, 1895: "I have finished correcting my proofs, a ghastly occupation. I come out in November 25th or 30th." [134] Before the novel appeared, "the printer's plates were destroyed by fire." [135] It was "passed for the press, Jan. 28, 1896," [136] presumably for the second time, and was issued on March 16. The impression was 3000 copies, the price six shillings a copy.[137] The first American edition was also published in 1896, and Conrad did not correct the proofs.[138]

He wrote in August, 1911, that he had sold the manuscript to John Quinn for £30 to help pay for an illness of Norman Douglas': "This will come extremely handy now, or else I wouldn't have sold it for the price." [139] Quinn resold it for $4100.[140]

The Sisters and *The Rescue*

The completion of *An Outcast of the Islands* marks an important change in the history of Conrad's career. Though his second novel caused him real difficulty, he had not yet faced a serious paralysis of creative impulse. The circumstances of his life now combined against him. His attempts to find a command in the winter of 1895–96 failed; his health was bad; and his responsibilities increased after his marriage on March 24, 1896.[141] He began to realize, as he admitted in a letter of March 10, that "only literature remains to me as a means of existence." [142] The realization seemed immediately to increase his trouble with composition. He started one novel, *The Sisters*, which he was soon to abandon and never to finish. His next, *The Rescue*, he did not complete for some twenty-three years.

Conrad said little about *The Sisters*. Most of the information came from his friends and was not specific. How soon he began the story after he completed *An Outcast* is not known. Edward Garnett remembered that Conrad rested for some time "and when he began again he found it impossible to make headway with *The Sisters*." [143] Garnett seems to have disapproved of the story from the start and to have advised Conrad to drop it.[144] About March 23, 1896, Conrad resolved to abandon what he called his "foolishness" and to begin *The Rescue*.[145] After some ten thousand words he had found it impossible to proceed. The memorandum for John Quinn, to whom he sold the manuscript, was inaccurate: he did not write it in 1896 and drop it in 1897 when the idea of *The Nigger* came to him.[146]

Ford advanced some interesting theories in his Introduction to the published fragment. Yet his recollections were too hazy to be trusted implicitly. He heard Conrad mention *The Sisters* with a sort of shame "perhaps half a dozen times in the course of ten years. And, in 1906, I should say, when desperately casting about for 'subjects' he contemplated finishing this story seriously enough to get out the manuscript and look it through though I do not remember to have seen it myself." [147] Ford surmised that *The Sisters* was to deal with incest. After sketching a possible plot, he declared that Conrad abandoned the novel because of the difficulty of differentiating his priest from Maupassant's in *Une Vie*.[148] Ford admitted his impressions to be "a sort of composite photograph." In the absence of any statement by Conrad it is safer to consider the development of *The Sisters* a mystery as yet unsolved.

Conrad dropped the story to write something with greater chance of financial success. The first mention of *The Rescuer*, as the new novel was originally called, was in the letter ascribed to March 23, 1896, which announced to Garnett that *The Sisters* had been given up:

> You have driven home the conviction and I *shall* write the sea-story — at once (12 months). It will be on the lines indicated to you. I surrender to the infamous spirit which you have awakened within me and . . . I am looking for a sensational title. . . . You have killed my cherished aspiration and now must come along and help to bury the corpse decently. I suggest
>
> THE RESCUER.
>
> A Tale of Narrow Waters.[149]

Garnett had urged a popular tale about the sea, and Conrad had relied heavily on his adviser's judgment. The desire to be popular may well have contributed to his difficulty in writing.

The day after he informed Garnett of his latest plans he married and left for Brittany.[150] In making arrangements for his honeymoon, he took his work into account: "It is there [Brittany] that I shall set about writing my third book since one must write to live."[151] Since *The Sisters* had been set aside before he left for the Continent, he pressed on with his new project. The exact day on which he began *The Rescuer* is unknown, though he must have started very soon after reaching Lannion on March 27. On April 6 he boasted of having written eleven pages.[152] The next day he and his wife moved to their first home, on Ile Grande, where they stayed until the end of August.[153] Despite the move he had written four pages more, fifteen in all, by April 9.[154] On the same day he sketched the novel for Unwin: "If the virtues of Lingard please most of the critics, they shall have more of them. The theme of it shall be the rescue of a yacht from some Malay vagabonds and there will be a gentleman and a lady cut out according to the regulation pattern." [155] On April 13 he sent the first chapter, twenty-four pages altogether, to Garnett for advice and as "a sample to show to the Mag. Editors." [156] He wanted encouragement: "I am so afraid of myself, of my likes and dislikes, of my thought and of my expression that I must fly to you for relief – or condemnation – for anything to kill doubt with." [157] Garnett gave him warm praise for the first chapter, especially for the description and the characterization of the crew, and suggested improvements in expression.[158] During the rest of April he added nearly fifty pages to the novel. The excellent pace at which he was working did not, unfortunately, continue.

In May Conrad experienced his first difficulties, brought about by gout. He informed Garnett on May 24: "I have been rather ill. Lots of pain, fever, etc. etc. The left hand is useless still. This month I have done nothing to the Rescuer. – but I have about 70 pages of the most rotten twaddle. In the intervals of squirming I wrote also a short story of Brittany ["The Idiots"]." [159] Like so many of his stories, "The Idiots" was undertaken during his acute difficulties with *The Rescuer*. Lack of inspiration began to prey on his mind. Acknowledging on June 2 Garnett's comments on the first chapter, he added, "And every day the Rescuer crawls a page forward – sometimes with cold despair – at times with hot hope. I have long fits of depression, that in a lunatic asylum would be called madness. I do not know what it is. It springs from nothing. . . . It lasts an hour or a day; and when it departs it leaves a fear." [160] Garnett begged him to fix a date for the completion of *The Rescuer*, perhaps to discipline his imagination, certainly to attract publishers to the novel.[161] Conrad could promise nothing. On June 6 he told Garnett: "As soon as part I of the stupid *Rescuer* is finished I shall send it straight to you. I am gnawing my fingers over the end of it now. If you knew how idiotic the whole thing seems to me you would pity me. . . . I feel as if could go and drown myself – in a cesspool at that – for twopence." [162] He was further demoralized by the illness mentioned in a letter of June 12: "I had an attack of rheumatism in my hand and foot. This attack not only kept me in bed for two weeks, but it has so shaken me that I still feel giddy. . . . Fortunately I was able to finish before I was taken ill the first part of my new novel." [163] He had been able to push the story ahead some thirty-three pages in three weeks.[164]

On June 10 he promised Garnett "all that there is of the Rescuer. It is the whole of the first part. You will see that I have given up dividing it into chapters – formally. I think I had better divide the thing into parts only. Say five. Then in places – where necessary and proper – a wider interval between the paragraphs will mark the subdivisions of the parts; this arrangement will give me more freedom I think.[165] I do not know what to think of the pages I am sending you. Mostly they fill me with dismay. . . . Here I have used up 103 pages of manuscript to relate the events of 12 hours. I have done it in pursuance of a plan. But is the plan utterly wrong? Is the writing utter bosh?" [166] Once again Garnett bolstered him by calling it the best work Conrad had ever done.[167]

Probably Conrad began *The Nigger of the "Narcissus"* around June 10. Though he did not record the exact day, he wrote in a memorandum for Quinn "begun in 1896 – June."[168] It seems logical that after completing the first part of *The Rescuer*, he should have sought a momentary relief in a new subject. According to Jean-Aubry he completed ten pages of *The Nigger* before he turned back to the Malay novel.[169]

The new division into parts did not give Conrad "more freedom" with *The Rescuer*. His real difficulties, which may be said to have started with part two, were all the greater for being psychological. On June 19 he confessed to Garnett:

> Since I sent you that part 1st (on the eleventh of the month) I have written one page. Just one page. I went about thinking and forgetting — sitting down before the blank page to find that I could not put one sentence together. To be able to think and unable to express is a fine torture. . . . Now I've got all my people together I don't know what to do with them. The progressive episodes of the story *will* not emerge from the chaos of my sensations. I feel nothing clearly. And I am frightened when I remember that I have to drag it all out of myself.[170]

At the beginning of part two he changed the title of the novel to *The Rescue: A Romance of Narrow Waters*,[171] though he did not refer to the new title in a letter until August 28, 1897.[172] In the manuscript the first title of part two was "Belarab," later altered to "The Shore of Refuge."[173]

His nervous tension increased during the summer. On July 10, 1896, he wrote Garnett a letter which showed his efforts to be accurate in his work: "If you have no further use for it please send the 1st part *Resc* to *G. F. W. Hope*. . . . I want him to look over the seamanship of my expressions. . . . I trust I will live long enough to finish that story but at the pace I am going now I am preparing for myself an interminable old age. I am now setting Beatrix, her husband and Linares (the Spanish gent) [174] on their feet. It's a hell of a job – as Carter [one of the characters] would say." [175]

Again Conrad had to seek relief from *The Rescue*. In July he was engaged on "An Outpost of Progress." [176] Soon after he completed it, he must have begun "The Lagoon," which he first mentioned on August 5: "In desperation I took up another short story. I must do something to live and meantime perhaps a ray of inspiration may come and light me along the labyrinth of incertitude where I am now lost." [177] Neither story cured him of his psychological ills.

The climax of Conrad's mental difficulties came in August. He reported to Garnett *The Rescue's* stagnation:

> There is 12 pages written and I sit before them every morning, day after day, for the last 2 months and cannot add a sentence, add a word! I am paralyzed by doubt and have just sense enough to feel the agony but am powerless to invent a way out of it. . . . I had bad moments with the Outcast but never anything so so ghastly nothing half so hopeless. When I face that fatal manuscript it seems to me that I have forgotten how to think — worse! how to write.

So unbalanced was his condition that Garnett's praise of part one unnerved him further:

> Your commendation of part I plunges me simply into despair — because part II *must* be very different in theme if not in treatment and I am afraid this will make the book a strange and repulsive hybrid, fit only to be stoned, jumped upon, defiled and then held up to ridicule as a proof of my ineptitude. You see I must justify — give a motive — to my yacht people. . . . Now the justification that had occurred to me is unfortunately of so subtle a nature that I despair of conveying it in

say 20 pages well enough to make it comprehensible. . . . Besides I begin to fear that supposing everything conveyed and made acceptable (which seems impossible) . . . I have not enough imagination . . . to make anything out of the situation; that I cannot invent an illuminating episode that would set in a clear light the persons and feelings. I am in desperation and I have practically given up the book.[178]

The inevitable conclusion was reached in another ten days. On August 14, 1896, Conrad showed that he had already "given up the book": "I wish I could tackle the *Rescuer* again. I simply *can't*! "[179] Thus ended his first attempt to write the novel.

Little more is known of his work on the story until September, 1897. Jean-Aubry stated that after Conrad returned to England in September, 1896, he "set aside *The Rescue* and devoted himself entirely to writing *The Nigger of the 'Narcissus.'* "[180] Conrad himself informed Garnett on February 7, 1897, that " the *Rescuer* sleeps yet the sleep like of death. Will there be a miracle and a resurrection? Quien sabe!"[181] According to Jean-Aubry, Conrad made another attempt at the story after he completed *The Nigger* in the winter of 1897,[182] though he did not refer to it in any published letter. In fact he declared on March 26, "I've done nothing since finishing the *Nigger*, but am at something now."[183] The "something" was "Karain," which was sent off to Unwin on April 14.[184] He immediately began "The Return,"[185] but, encountering many obstacles, he laid it aside. On June 2 he insisted, "I *must* go on now with the *Return*, – then shall jump upon the *Rescuer*"; yet on June 11 he was only "thinking of *Rescuer*; writing nothing."[186] "The Return" was not finished until September 24, 1897.[187] Consequently Conrad could have had no time to work on *The Rescue*.

About September 27 he submitted the uncompleted

novel to *Blackwood's Magazine*,[188] probably the stimulus towards writing again. He was soon experiencing his old psychological complications: "I don't think I will ever write anything more. That shall wear off, but meantime I can't write a word of the Rescue. . . . There are . . . whole pages of erasures with perhaps one solitary and surviving line hiding amongst the ranges of scored out words."[189] By October 11 his despair had deepened: "I can't get on with the *Rescue*. In all these days I haven't written a line, but there hadn't been a day when I did not wish myself dead. . . . I positively don't know what to do. Am I out to the end of my tether? Sometimes I think it must be so."[190] Within three days he became slightly optimistic: "I'm having a tussle with the *Rescue*. I've sent a long epitome to P[awling, of Wm. Heinemann, Ltd.]. The necessity to write it out has brought me to terms with myself. But it's most damnably hard – all the same."[191] A letter of October 26, by comparison, shows definite encouragement: "I feel cheerful and have at last made a start with the *Rescue*."[192]

Fluctuations in mood and progress are nowhere so well illustrated as in the history of *The Rescue*. On December 5 he was again hopeless: "I am trying to write the *Rescue* and all my ambition is to make it good enough for a magazine – readable in a word. I doubt whether I can. I struggle without pleasure like a man certain of defeat."[193] On December 23 he was almost ecstatic: "I am writing the *R*! I am writing! I am harassed with anxieties but the thing comes out!"[194] His hopefulness persisted a while, for on January 7, 1898, he was going to complete part two "by first week Febry."[195] Within a week he was able to announce that "about 30,000 out of 90,000 words are ready."[196]

Unfortunately Conrad's optimism about *The Rescue*

now declined. Financial pressure contributed to his nervous tension. The need of immediate cash drove him to make arrangements for publication before he had any expectation of completing the story, and these arrangements enormously increased his difficulties. As far back as August, 1897, he planned to give the novel to *Blackwood's Magazine*, at William Blackwood's request. He sent them specimen chapters around September 27 and was disappointed that he had not received an acceptance by October 8. Though in November he was still hopeful, negotiations had fallen through by January, 1898.[197] His prospects of selling the story to Frank Harris' *Fortnightly Review* in January and to *Scribner's Magazine* in February came to nothing.[198] In desperation he even thought of trying to borrow money from Pawling on the serial rights of the novel.[199] He was spared this embarrassment, since by March 5 he had sold his American serial rights to McClure: the terms were £250, another £50 "on accept. of book rights in the States (15% royalty)," and the novel was to be delivered "end July at the latest."[200] At this time it contained approximately forty-five thousand out of the proposed ninety thousand words.[201] Though the arrangement solved Conrad's immediate need, it involved him in the keenest worries he had ever encountered.

All winter the tension grew under financial pressure. On February 2, 1898, he spoke of "the slough of despond [of] that damned and muddy romance," and on March 21 he admitted, "I hate the thing with such great hatred that I don't want to look at it again."[202] Less than a month after he had sold the serial rights, writing under contract forced a full confession of his nervous condition: "I sit down religiously every morning, I sit down for eight hours every day – and the sitting down is all. In the course of that working day of 8 hours I write 3 sentences which I erase before leaving the table in despair . . . and time passes – and McClure waits. . . . My story is there in a fluid – in an evading shape. I can't get hold of it. . . . I would be thankful to be able to write anything, anything, any trash, any rotten thing – something to earn dishonestly and by false pretences the payment promised by a fool." [203] The strain persisted for months. In August Conrad told Garnett: "Looking back, I see how ill, mentally, I have been these last four months." [204] He had been able to accomplish little on *The Rescue.*

Probably to relieve tension he began *Lord Jim* in May, 1898.[205] On May 18 he confessed that only "a ridiculously small quantity of the *Rescue* has been done." [206] Though he had arranged not to begin serial publication until October, he admitted: "I don't feel a bit more hopeful about the writing of Rescue than before. It's like a curse. I can't *imagine* anything." [207] Yet he felt bound to the novel by moral obligation. "I intend to write nothing else. I am not even going to finish Jim now. . . . I shall not abandon it – even temporarily. I must get on with it, and it will destroy my reputation," he informed Garnett late in May. "In the matter of R. I have lost all sense of form and I can't see *images*," he complained. "But what to write I *know.* I have the action only the hand is paralysed when it comes to giving expression to that action." [208]

Creative paralysis made it impossible for Conrad to complete *The Rescue* before working on anything else. Again seeking relief, he began "Youth" at the end of May, wrote it in a few days, and finished it on June 3.[209] The change helped him with *The Rescue.* Soon he was able to send Garnett "a few pages of P[art] III." The contract with McClure still haunted him. "I am awfully behind," he lamented. "Here, I have already had a 100 pounds on acct/! And the end is not in sight." [210]

Though he was "much calmer and more hopeful" on July 12,[211] a week later he was urging Cunninghame Graham to get him a position at sea: "Now some shadow of possibility to go to sea has been thus presented to me I am almost frantic with the longing to get away." [212] Undoubtedly such an opportunity seemed the solution of his problems. Although he pulled all possible wires, he gave up hope by the middle of October: "I can't think of going away till I've liberated myself from the incubus of that horrid novel I am trying to write now." [213]

While searching for a berth, he had trouble with *The Rescue.* On August 3 he confessed: "I am writing hopelessly – but still I am writing. . . . Pages accumulate and the story stands still. I feel suicidal. . . . I am utterly out of touch with my work – and I can't get in touch." [214] Later in the month he was encouraged by Garnett's praise: "Unable to try for something better, higher, I did try for the visual effect. And I must trust to that for the effect of the whole story from which I cannot evolve any meaning. – and have given up trying. The book will be of 150,000 words. That's certain. I am able to write now." [215] In seven months he had broadened the scope of the novel from ninety thousand words to a hundred and fifty thousand.

His momentary confidence was soon exploded. "Shorter of the *Illustrated London News* who bought *Rescue* from McClure suddenly decided to put it into the last quarter of the *News*," he complained to Cunninghame Graham on August 26. "Begins in October. I thought I had months before me and am caught. The worst is I had advances from McClure. So I must write or burst. . . . Half the book is not written and I have only to 1st Nov. to finish it. . . . I am really in a deplorable state, mentally. . . . I haven't the courage to tackle my work." [216] Either Conrad had recently made a different arrangement or had forgotten the date of serial publication. He had been aware in May that the novel was to be published in magazine form in October. His procrastination is well illustrated by his writing on August 31 that he had until November 15 to complete *The Rescue*.[217]

The approach of serial publication and the exertions of finding a new home upset Conrad for some weeks. Though he wrote in the Author's Note that the novel was put "aside at the end of the summer of 1898," [218] he was working at it all the autumn. On October 12 he announced: "I've destroyed all I did write last month but my brain feels alive and my heart is not afraid now." [219] He moved to Pent Farm, near Hythe in Kent, on October 26, and found he was able to work: "I can write a little, a very little. A little is better than nothing, but it is so little that out of the present worries I look with terror into the future still." [220] He later mentioned that "it was not until November that I started to work." [221] By December 19 he was ready to begin part four, which in the manuscript was called "The point of honour and the point of passion," a title transferred in the published text to part five.[222] The full title of the novel had now been chosen. Conrad wrote at the beginning of part four, "The Rescue A Romance of the Shallows," [223] the title used in the published text. By this time April had been fixed as the date for the novel to begin in the *Illustrated London News*,[224] but the arrangement was later canceled.

Part four did not progress rapidly. In December, 1898, Conrad began again on *Lord Jim*,[225] though by the eighteenth he had abandoned it also for "Heart of Darkness": "Now I am at a short story for B'wood which I must get out for the sake of the shekels. Then again at the *R*." [226] On January 12, 1899, he was hurrying to finish "Heart of Darkness." Later in January he visited London.[227] He had an interview with Shorter who informed him that *The Rescue* was too long to appear in the *Illustrated London News* and who probably was using length as an excuse to rid himself of a hopelessly unpunctual author.[228] On his return to the Pent Conrad apparently did some work on the story, for on February 2 he expected to finish it "about end March unless it makes an end of me before." [229] By February 7 he had received a letter from Shorter which must have terminated their connection and Conrad's efforts with *The Rescue*.[230] Though he wrote in 1918 that he had laid *The Rescue* aside at the end of 1899,[231] there is no evidence that he worked on it after the first week in February. A letter of June 8, 1916, shows that he had progressed at least as far as twenty-four manuscript pages of part four when he stopped work in February, 1899.[232] The letters for the rest of 1899 indicate that he was working on *Lord Jim*.

Conrad left valuable information, somewhat confused by incorrect dates, about his mood when he abandoned the novel. In the Author's Note he declared it was

not laid aside in despair. Several reasons contributed to this abandonment and, no doubt, the first of them was the growing sense of general difficulty in the handling of the subject. The contents and the course of the story I had clearly in my mind. But as to the way of presenting the facts, and perhaps in a certain measure as to the nature of the facts themselves, I had many doubts. I mean the telling, representative facts, helpful to carry on the idea, and, at the same time, of such a nature as not to demand an elaborate creation of the atmosphere to the detriment of the action. I did not see how I could avoid becoming wearisome in the presentation of detail and in the pursuit of clearness. I saw the action plainly enough. What I had lost for the moment was the sense of the proper formula of expression, the only formula that would suit. This, of course, weakened my confidence in the intrinsic worth and in the possible interest of the story — that is in my invention. But I suspect that all the trouble was, in reality, the doubt of my prose, the doubt of its adequacy, of its power to master both the colours and the shades.[233]

Though according to the Author's Note Conrad laid *The Rescue* aside in the summer of 1898 to write *The Nigger*, in reality he did not stop work until February, 1899, and *The Nigger* had been completed by February 19, 1897.[234]

There were many references to *The Rescue* during the seventeen years before Conrad made his next attempt at the novel. On "Good Friday in sorrow and tribulation," 1899, he wrote that McClure was "trying to ram the *Rescue* into the Atlantic Monthly but the *R* is *not* finished yet – not yet – not yet." [235] He informed Algernon Methuen, the publisher, in a letter of May 25, 1899, which took stock of his literary obligations, that he was almost a year behind in his contract with Heinemann and McClure for *The Rescue:* "The thing simply *won't* come out as quick as I fondly hoped." [236] A letter to Garnett proves he was not working at it in the autumn of 1899: "Your question about the Rescue sent a shiver down my back. Jim's dragging his slow length along – *après nous verrons.*" [237]

The novel was not mentioned again until December, 1902, when Conrad intended to finish it in March.[238] That he began writing again is improbable. In a letter which Jean-Aubry placed early in 1903 Conrad mentioned his plans for a new novel, *Nostromo*.[239] He was then working with Ford on *Romance*.[240] By August, 1903, he had postponed *The Rescue* indefinitely. He intended to write a "Mediterranean story" after he completed *Nostromo:* "What will become of the *Rescue* then, devil only knows!" [241]

The postponement was more prolonged than even Conrad had expected: *The Rescue* was not mentioned for seven years. On August 27, 1910, he explained to Galsworthy how far away from the story he had grown:

> Of course I will do the *Rescue*. To tell you the truth, I've forgotten that stuff. I've a hazy recollection of something lightly inflated and verbose. But no doubt I can match it well enough out of the rubbish floating in my softened brain. . . .
>
> My only objection to the *Rescue* would be that it does not advance me very much, whereas *Chance*[242] would have been a long step. But on the other hand, as you say, the enterprise looks easier. . . . I shall ask him [J. B. Pinker] to forward me the typed copy of *Rescue*. It will take me a week to read and think myself into a proper frame of mind.[243]

His inclinations caused him to take up *Chance* again rather than *The Rescue*. For another six years the novel dropped out of the published correspondence.

In 1916 Conrad returned to *The Rescue* at Pinker's suggestion.[244] Though the time when he began cannot be established, work went well at first. On June 8, 1916, he informed his agent:

> I am sending you 135 pp. of Part IV consisting of old, (24 pp.) newly arranged, rewritten, and new stuff. . . .
>
> It will be an immensely long book. It can't be helped. And if that fact stands in the way of serial pub^on — why then it must stand. . . . It doesn't follow that it will be wearisome to read. Indeed I have never thought so well of it as now since I have devoted myself to it exclusively. I only wish I could absorb myself utterly, forget myself in it — but this is impossible. I have neither the power of detachment nor yet that intensity of belief in my work which perhaps would have made it possible. My health, however, has improved in the last fortnight in a marked way. . . . The mind perhaps will follow.[245]

In December, 1916, he was still working but with some difficulty. The novel, he told his publisher, was "not very far from its termination now. . . . You mustn't be angry with me for the delay. My psychology has been affected by the way of inability to concentrate. . . . It isn't so much the war itself, as the course it has taken which is the cause of that unsatisfactory state. I am more emotional, it appears, than I imagined myself to be." [246] His "psychology" must have been increasingly disturbed; he did not mention the story again for nearly two years. Exactly when he laid *The Rescue* aside has not been recorded, though he began *The Arrow of Gold* in September, 1917.[247] He had completed one hundred and ninety-five pages of part four.[248]

After finishing *The Arrow* on June 14, 1918,[249] Conrad began his final drive on *The Rescue.* The exact day on which he resumed work cannot be established. The first step was to read over and condense the manuscript. His memorandum for T. J. Wise, who bought the manuscript, described the condensation:

> This Ms dating from years 1896 to 1898 is absolutely the first state of the novel The Rescue *pubd* (finished on May 25 — 1919) as to two thirds. By successive diminutions and corrections these two thirds have been reduced to a little more than one half of the text as printed in the first edition.[250]

He reduced part one from 23,366 to 14,000 words, part two to 22,000, and part three to 37,000.[251] He must have begun work in August, 1918. He wrote on September 25 that he did not want any other work to take him "out of the mood for *The Rescue*, which I have been cultivating most earnestly for the last six weeks and have in a measure attained now. . . . I intend to stick to *The Rescue* exclusively. After all every page of that is money too." [252] The implications are that he had begun writing.

Conrad gave reasons for this renewed interest. In the Author's Note he stated:

> The years passed and the pages [of other stories] grew in number, and the long reveries of which they were the outcome stretched wide between me and the deserted 'Rescue' like the smooth hazy spaces of a dreamy sea. Yet I never actually lost sight of that dark speck in the misty distance. It had grown very small but it asserted itself with the appeal of old associations. It seemed to me that it would be a base thing for me to slip out of the world leaving it out there all alone, waiting for its fate — that would never come!
>
> Sentiment, pure sentiment as you see, prompted me in the last instance to face the pains and hazards of that return.[253]

He explained more personally in September, 1920: "It struck me then that my time was running out and I wanted the deck cleared before going below. As to leaving any loose ends hanging over the side, I couldn't bear the thought of it!" [254] Anticipation of death, still five years away, moved him to a successful attack on his most refractory novel.

Beyond doubt Conrad had begun writing by October 2, 1918, when he sent a letter about the fragmentary manuscript of the novel, six hundred and two pages long,[255] to T. J. Wise, who had just bought it: "Several typed copies have been taken of it, each introducing changes and alterations till this last (I believe the 4th) typed copy on which I am working now, and I intend to finish the tale by dictating. . . . There will be no further pen and ink pages. The first complete state of the novel will be a typed copy bearing pen and ink corrections and alterations." [256] Within a week he was again in difficulties. He complained to Curle that his "frontal attack upon *The Rescue*, which was indeed begun some time ago . . . has been pushed feebly and has died out for a time." [257]

Conrad did not refer to the novel again until, after completing part four, he mentioned the serial publication in a letter which Jean-Aubry dated towards the end of 1918: "Much as I would be pleased to appear in the *Cosmopolitan*, I am afraid I can do nothing in the way of a rush." [258] On December 21 he wrote more hopefully: "*The Rescue* is approaching completion and I believe that the last words will be written before the end of January." [259] The expectation was too optimistic by four months. Evidently he had been discussing the story with Garnett, to whom he wrote on December 22: "It was a great and comforting experience to have your ever trusted and uncompromising soul come forward again from the unforgotten past and look closely at my work with the old, old wonderful insight, with unimpaired wisdom and in unalterable friendship." [260] The end of the year found Conrad in health and at work, if not in high spirits. He told John Galsworthy on Christmas Eve: "I haven't had any gout for a long time. . . . I have been working, – or is it playing? – at a novel. But I am not unduly elated." [261]

The first month of 1919 brought a severe attack of gout that was to give him "a most awful time" [262] until he finished the novel. He was forced to lay his work aside: he declared on January 30 that he was about to "revise and correct the latest pages of *The Rescue*. . . . There is quite a batch of them – a good part of Part V all done before this beastly gout knocked me over. The production of further copy shall begin on Thursday morning next, I say – and there is no doubt whatever about it." [263] On May 29 he announced: "On the 25th May (Rogation Sunday) I wrote the last words of *The Rescue*, which I began about 22 years ago. On the 28th I finished revising the final chapter, and now I am done with the thing till proofs of book-form begin to come in – next year sometime." [264] Since the task had been long and arduous, his estimate of the time spent on *The Rescue* was understandably inaccurate. It was some twenty-three years and two months since he had written the first eleven pages of *The Rescuer* in Brittany.

The strain was increased by serial publication, begun in England four months before Conrad completed the story. *The Rescue* ran in *Land and Water* from January 30 through July 31, 1919, illustrated by Maurice Greiffenhagen, Dudley Hardy, H. L. Bacon, and Christopher Clark. F. N. Doubleday, his American publisher, arranged serialization in the United States; the story appeared in *Romance* from November, 1919, through May, 1920.[265] In a letter of April 17, 1919, Conrad thanked him "for all the trouble and also for the success of your efforts in serializing *The Rescue*. I feel that your remarks on the advantage of appearing in the columns of a newly started magazine are eminently just. . . . I am glad to say that the proprietors of *Land and Water* profess themselves very pleased by the reception given to the serial here, and by its good effect on the circulation of the paper." [266] The profit of the serial publication makes a startling contrast with the £20 Conrad received for his first novel: "*The Rescue* . . . earned nearly £3,000 serial rights." [267]

His difficulties with the novel were not over: he labored on the serial text before *The Rescue* was published in book form. Curle recorded that the serials of *The Rescue* and *Nostromo* differ more from the first editions than do any other of the stories.[268] As early as March 12, 1919, more than two months before the novel was completed, Conrad requested Garnett: "Pray *do* by all means jot your remarks and criticisms on the margin of the L and W text. . . . You know dear Edward that my first impulse (and also the last) was always to agree with your pronouncements. In this instance you give a voice to the vague uneasiness I always felt from the first while writing the Rescue." [269] In September he was gratefully profiting by Garnett's comments: "I have looked at once, here and there, at your marks and marginal notes in various numbers. I quite see. As it happened I came upon one par.[agraph] which you condemn in toto but which I can't take out as it bears on the story itself – the plot. But I shall try to put it into other words." [270]

Conrad had begun the revision by December 8, when he wrote Garnett: "My renewed thanks for your marginal notes and your letters about *The R.* I have started on the text now." [271] He found the work hard from the first. On December 12 he confessed: "My mind is a blank. I can't even look through the *R.* proofs." [272] He repeated the complaint in an undated letter which Curle placed in early January, 1920: "I can't even tackle the text of the *Resc.* My mental state is awful." [273] The difficulty was so great that he abandoned the work until January 17. On January 19 he was busily "engaged in correcting the text of *The Rescue*, which I promised the publishers in England and America would be ready end of Jany. As I have done nothing to it till the last three days Miss H.[allowes, Conrad's secretary] and I are slaving at it all the morning and often in the afternoon in order to get through somewhere near the promised date." [274] He kept his promise, though the strain made him ill. On January 24 he completed the revision in bed.[275] Writing about the novel to Garnett on July 11, he declared: "I tried to make the best of your advice in the general current of the last half; and, as to details, all your remarks and suggestions (in the margin of the *L. and W.* text) have been adopted and followed except in one instance amounting to about a line and a half." [276] But the long struggle with the novel was not quite finished.

The first edition of twenty-five thousand copies, at two dollars a copy, was issued on May 21, 1920, in the United States by Doubleday, Page and Company.[277] The English publication of *The Rescue* was delayed on account of "some muddle in the delivery of the paper." [278] The first English edition was not issued until June by J. M. Dent and Sons, Ltd., and consisted of only forty copies that were distributed to reviewers; the text, which was that of the uncorrected page proof, differed from the American and the regular English first editions.[279] Conrad had one copy especially bound in morocco for F. C. Penfield, who had helped him to leave Austria at the beginning of the Great War and to whom the novel was dedicated.[280] The first English published edition, consisting of 23,750 copies, at nine shillings a copy, was issued in August, 1920, by J. M. Dent and Sons, Ltd., in finally corrected form.[281] Nearly a quarter of a century from its inception he was through with *The Rescue* at last.

"The Idiots"

"The Idiots" was written during an early difficulty with *The Rescue*.[282] The short story is distinguished as Conrad's first. Though chronologically the lost 1886 "Black Mate" deserves consideration as the first, he excluded it from his official literary life. His contradictory and ambiguous statements about "The Idiots" require clarification. In the Author's Note for *Tales of Unrest* [283] he erroneously declared that of these stories "The Lagoon," completed around August 14, 1896,[284] was "the earliest in date." Though it is impossible to establish the exact days on which he began and finished "The Idiots," the story was written in May, 1896, and concluded before the twenty-fourth of the month. By then the manuscript had been typed and sent to London. On May 24 he informed Garnett: "This month I have done nothing to the Rescuer. . . . In the intervals of squirming I wrote . . . a short story of Brittany. Peasant life. . . . My wife typed it and it is in London now with a friend. I shall direct him to send it to you soon."[285] Shortly after, he described his mood to Unwin: "The Idiots" was "written in a state of exasperation caused by physical pain and more still by the helplessness that trammeled the work in hand (The Rescuer)."[286]

Conrad mistrusted "The Idiots." The influence of Brittany on the story brought it too close to the work of Maupassant. Conrad's inspiration had been "not mental but visual: the actual idiots," whom he had seen near Lannion.[287] He depended upon the critical judgment of Garnett, whom he asked on May 24 for an appraisal of the story. "I do not know whether it's worth anything," he confessed. "The worst of it is that the Patron [Unwin] knows of it. I don't know why I told him about it. I never know what to write to that man. He numbs me like an electric eel. I want to know . . . what you think of it."[288] On May 28, when he discussed possible markets with Unwin, who seems to have acted as agent on a commission, he insisted on consulting Garnett: "I am very glad you do not think much of the 'Savoy.' The personality (as disclosed in some verses) of A. S. [Arthur Symons] is *not* sympathetic to me. I would rather wait longer and fare better. I tell you frankly that I don't think the story would be good enough for the Cosmo[polis]. . . . I would consider it very friendly of you to have a look at it—yourself; and then to let Garnett . . . have also a try. He has a wonderful sense of what 'will do' and spares me not in his criticism which I consider most valuable."[289] The final decision on the merits of the story he left to Garnett: "I *would not* have it published unless you see and pass it as fit for the twilight of a popular magazine. I want to know what you think of it with an absurd intensity of longing that is ridiculous and painful." [290]

In the first week of June the *Cornhill Magazine*, because of Garnett's exertions,[291] asked Conrad for a story at their usual rate of a guinea for a page of 450 words. He was flattered by the request.[292] "I think the *Cornhill* is not a bad mag. to appear in," he wrote Unwin on June 7, " – and, if you have not placed the 'Idiots' yet, we might try there. But I am not in a hurry in the least, and in any case should like Garnett to have a look at the story before sending it off." [293] Conrad's finances were not yet so straitened as to make him jump at the offer. Perhaps he counted upon Unwin's or Garnett's finding a better market, and Unwin tried to force the story into *Cosmopolis*. When Conrad heard that *Cosmopolis* had twice refused it,[294] he was not appeased by the magazine's request for something different. On July 10 he informed his publisher:

> I am sorry the story was not judged worthy or convenient for the *Cosmopolis*. . . . I trust the *Cornhill* will take it but I doubt it — to tell you the truth.
>
> I would write with extreme pleasure a short story for the *Cosmopolis* if I only had an idea what they considered as suitable. I am rather taken up with the 'Rescuer' and would not care to get out of tune — so to speak — with my novel for the sake of a story which may turn out useless. I take it that no objection has been taken to the workmanship (the technique if you like) for the manner of work and my view of life I cannot alter.[295]

Apparently the *Cornhill* also turned down "The Idiots," as Conrad implied in a letter of July 22 to Unwin: "The acceptance of my story would have given me pleasure. But its refusal is not without its compensations, – for it is exactly what I did foresee. . . . I am not ashamed of it for all that. Bad or good I cannot be ashamed of what is produced in perfect single-mindedness – I cannot be ashamed of those things that are like fragments of my innermost being produced for the public gaze." [296]

Garnett liked "The Idiots" and arranged to have it published. When it appeared unsalable, he advised Conrad to try the *Savoy*. Arthur Symons had asked Garnett for a contribution "from the author of *An Outcast of the Islands*." [297] Despite his previous aversion to the magazine and his unwillingness to offend Unwin in his capacity as agent, Conrad sent the story to the *Savoy*, which offered a guinea more a page than the *Cornhill*.[298] Symons accepted it and must have paid him forty guineas.[299] Conrad declared mistakenly that it appeared "in the last published number." It was published, as T. J. Wise established, in number six of the *Savoy*, for October, 1896, and the magazine ended with the eighth number.[300] "The Idiots" was Conrad's first published short story as well as his first appearance in a magazine. He was especially pleased that the story was given the place of honor at the beginning of the magazine.[301] In 1898 it was published in book form as the second story in *Tales of Unrest*.

Tales of Unrest was Conrad's first collection of short stories. The order of the tales was arbitrary, for the chronological arrangement would have been "The Idiots" (placed second in the collection), "An Outpost of Progress" (placed third), "The Lagoon" (placed fifth), "Karain: A Memory" (placed first), and "The Return" (placed fourth). Yet Conrad made a point of arranging them unchronologically, perhaps for variety and interest.[302] "The Lagoon," "Karain," and "The Return" had not been written when he planned the collected volume, which Unwin was considering as early as July 22, 1896.[303] At first he had no title and asked his publisher to suggest one.[304] Conrad wished to dedicate the collection to Garnett, a natural expression of gratitude, and told him on August 14: "*All* ["The Idiots," "An Outpost of Progress," "The Lagoon"] the short stories (*ab initio*) were *meant alike* for a vol to be inscribed to *you*. . . . And then I thought that the story ["An Outpost"] would be a good title story – better than the *Idiots*. It would sound funny a title like this: *Idiots and other Stories*. While *Outpost of Progress and Other Stories sounds* nice and proper." [305]

The plans for the collection depended somewhat on the success of the yet unfinished *Nigger*, which Conrad tried to use as bait for Unwin's interest. In a letter of December 13 he sounded out his publisher:

> I think I have conquered Henley. He has practically accepted my story [*The Nigger*] for the N.R. [*New Review*] and it will appear some time next year. . . .
>
> It strikes me that – should that story prove more popular than my previous work — my other stories will become more valuable. . . . If my hopes are even partly realized it may become, perhaps, worth your while (in a year or so) to publish them — and in that case I should try by and by to write a couple more so as to form a vol. for which you shall give me what you think fit. This is only an idea and if it appears practicable to you so much the better. . . . Meantime I shall look upon the three stories as provisionally belonging to you.[306]

Though Conrad was as good as his word in writing "Karain" and "The Return," he did not agree with what Unwin thought fit payment.

Publication was delayed for nearly two years on account of the disagreement on terms. On October 16, 1896, Conrad informed Garnett that Unwin wanted "60,000 words for a 6/ volume," to be delivered in March, 1897, and to be published "within *six* months of delivery." He offered 90% of the serial rights, 10% royalty on the published price for the first 2,000 copies sold, 12% on the next

2,000, and "after *4,000 copies* the royalty is to be 15% on net proceeds of sales." [307] So far the terms satisfied Conrad, but he objected to Unwin's unwillingness to pay more than £50 in advance of royalties because this was no increase over the advances for *An Outcast.*

Again Conrad depended upon Garnett's advice, this time in a financial problem. He reported on October 25: "I've written to F U exactly in the terms suggested by you *that is. £100* in two payments. 12 1/2% [royalties] for the first 3000 copies. *15%* for every thing over 3000 c[opies]. *one half* American rights. *90%* of serial rights." [308] In a letter to Unwin written on October 19 he had remonstrated: "As to my demands, which you might think excessive, it's just this: I can't afford to work for less than ten pence per hour and must work in a way that will give me this magnificent income." To Unwin's contention that his work did not sell, Conrad had countered with a threat to give up writing and risk everything on going back to sea. "I don't like to give up anything I have taken hold of," he admitted, "and intend to stick to scribbling till I am fairly convinced of my wisdom or my folly. . . . After all my work has some value, but if people won't have any of it, I can do one or two other things less gentlemanly (save the mark) but not a whit less honorable or useful. But I have no time to lose and must look about quickly so as not be left standing between two stools occupied by better men." [309] Conrad's terms were refused outright by Unwin, who insisted on his original offer.[310]

Though negotiations were not reopened until after "The Return" was completed in September, 1897,[311] Conrad felt that he had promised the collection to Unwin. On September 27, he consulted Garnett about a new agreement and a new title: "The *Return* completes the Vol. of short stories promised to Unwin. The promise is mine and I would not go back on it. Together it'll be 63000 words. Five stories. I've been casting about for a title – for the whole. I've thought of: *Tales of Unrest.* What do you think? – When I parted with Unwin . . . his terms, roughly, were *£50* down, and 10% progressing to 15%. I shall propose: *£60* down. . . . Percentages as he likes. . . . Can I ask for these terms."[312]

Unwin's final terms have not been disclosed, but the new title was used. Conrad sent his publisher the signed contract on November 6, 1897.[313] Garnett finished correcting the proofs for Conrad by January 24, 1898.[314] *Tales of Unrest* was first published in America by Charles Scribner's Sons in an edition of 1250 copies on March 26.[315] Conrad did not read these proofs.[316] The English edition of 3000 copies at six shillings a copy was brought out by Unwin on April 4.[317]

Tales of Unrest was not dedicated to Edward Garnett, after all, but to Adolph P. Krieger, one of Conrad's first friends in England.[318] On the change of intention Conrad made no direct comment, but a letter of February 28, 1897, shows that he changed after March 1.[319] He may have been somewhat hurt by Garnett's dislike of "An Outpost of Progress." Probably he became too impatient to wait for *Tales of Unrest* but instead dedicated to Garnett *The Nigger of the "Narcissus,"* which was issued in England on December 2, 1897.[320] Conrad expressed a final dissatisfaction with the collection in August, 1910: "Mais, à parler franchement, le volume de '*Tales of Unrest*' est celui de toute mon oeuvre que j'aime le moins. Je m'y vois 'dérivatif' plus que de raison."[321]

The Author's Note was written in the spring or early summer of 1919; it was not dated. On April 17 he promised it to F. N. Doubleday. On August 14 he told Pinker that the note was ready.[322]

The *Academy* on January 14, 1899, awarded a prize of fifty guineas to *Tales of Unrest.*[323] Conrad must have been informed of the award a few days earlier, for on the thirteenth he wrote Garnett in a tone which, though ironically exaggerated, showed no real respect for this appreciation of his work: "I've lost the last ounce of respect for my art. I am lost – gone – gone – done for – for the consideration of 50 gs." [324]

Tales of Unrest had the distinction of being the first of Conrad's works to be translated: the Swedish version was published in Stockholm in 1903.[325]

The Nigger of the "Narcissus"

Conrad sought relief from *The Rescue* by beginning *The Nigger of the "Narcissus."* On the wrapper of the manuscript he noted for John Quinn: "Begun in 1896 – June." [326] It was probably about June 10. He had just finished the first part of *The Rescue* [327] and had reached a natural place for a change. He wrote ten pages of *The Nigger*, according to Jean-Aubry, before he left Brittany in September.[328] Probably he had written them by June 19, when apparently he resumed *The Rescue*,[329] at which he worked intermittently until he left for England. The time taken from *The Rescue* was devoted to "An Outpost of Progress" in July and "The Lagoon" in August.[330]

After his return to England, he again took up *The Nigger*. According to Jean-Aubry, "during the autumn of 1896 Conrad set aside *The Rescue* and devoted himself entirely to writing *The Nigger of the 'Narcissus.'* " [331] Conrad must have been thinking of this new effort when he stated erroneously that he began the novel in September, 1896.[332]

The Nigger, like *An Outcast*, *Lord Jim*, and *The Rover*, was planned as a short story. On October 25 Conrad sought

Garnett's opinion: "It will be about *30,000* words. I must enshrine my old chums in a decent edifice. Seriously, do you think it would be too long? There are so many touches necessary for such a picture!" [333] Conrad was not concerned at the length which *The Nigger* threatened to assume, since he wanted a story long enough to make up a fair-sized volume of four stories with "The Idiots," "An Outpost of Progress," and "The Lagoon." On November 1 he informed Garnett: "I am letting myself go with the *Nigger*. He grows and grows. I do not think it's wholly bad though. Moreover I must have about 55000 words (in all the 4 stories) to go to a Publisher with." [334]

The task of writing *The Nigger* was made no easier in 1896 by disagreements with Unwin about *Tales of Unrest*. The dispute, Conrad lamented, "interferes with my *Nigger* damnably." By October 27 he had written Unwin a "farewell letter," and he immediately took his four stories to another publisher.[335] Smith, Elder and Company, to whom Garnett introduced him in November, made him an equally unacceptable offer: they would give him "*at once* £50 for the right to put them away for a time. . . . Still it worries me to think that my 'nigger' would be locked up for a year or two. More likely two. I feel horribly unsettled. It takes the savour out of the work. And the 'N' is not yet quite finished." [336] By November 16 on the advice of Garnett he had rejected Smith, Elder's terms and suggested another arrangement, which apparently was refused.[337]

At once Garnett introduced Conrad to S. S. Pawling of William Heinemann, Limited. Pawling promised to show a sample of *The Nigger* to W. E. Henley, editor of the *New Review*, owned by Heinemann, and to consider the story for publication.[338] On November 21 Conrad wrote: "One of the short stories (a pretty long one too, – about half the length of *Almayer*) is now under Henley's consideration for serial publication in the *New Review*. If accepted by Henley, then Heinemann will publish it afterwards in a small volume. I want £100 for serial and book rights and of course some percentage on the sales." [339] His difficulties in placing *The Nigger* were now at an end. Henley remarked to Pawling, " 'Tell Conrad that if the rest is up to the sample it shall certainly come out in the *New Review*.' The most gratifying recollection of my writer's life," [340] Conrad declared.

After such encouragement he worked on *The Nigger* with redoubled vigor and nervous anxiety. "I am as you may imagine exceedingly pleased with what Pawling writes," he explained to Garnett on November 25, 1896. "My only fear is that I will droop with the end of the 'Narcissus.' I am horribly dissatisfied with the ideas yet unwritten. Nothing effective suggests itself. . . . I shall, end [of] by this week, send you on a good many pages – but the end is not yet. I think I could almost *pray* for inspiration if I only knew where to turn my face." [341] Inspiration came, for on November 29 he sent Garnett

> seventeen pages more — *65–82* of my Beloved Nigger. Send them on to Mr. Pawling, but first look at them yourself. I am ashamed to think how much of my work you have not seen. . . . I do not feel very safe. Of course nothing can alter the course of the 'Nigger.' Let it be unpopularity it *must* be. But it seems to me that the thing — precious as it is to me — is trivial enough on the surface to have some charm for the man in the street. As to lack of incident well — it's life. The incomplete joy, the incomplete sorrow, the incomplete rascality or heroism — the incomplete suffering. Events crowd and push and nothing happens. . . . The opportunities do not last long enough. Unless in a boy's book of adventures. . . . I am going on. Another 20 pages of type — or even less — will see the end, such as it is. . . . Till it's over there's no watch below for me. A sorry business this scribbling.[342]

The last twenty pages took more time and effort than Conrad anticipated. On December 2 he planned to meet Garnett in London to show him more manuscript. He wrote him on December 19: "Ever since I left you . . . I have been at work. I had some real bad days but since last Monday I am going on all right. I think the pages just written won't dishonour the book. Your book which you try to coax into bloom with such devotion and care. And the thing is dramatic enough. It will be done by the 7th Jan. Not before!" [343] The prophecy proved a little optimistic. Though he finished the death of Wait by January 7, the conclusion gave him trouble. On January 10, 1897, he announced: "Nigger died on the 7th at 6 p.m.; but the ship is not home yet. Expected to arrive tonight and be paid off tomorrow. And the end! I can't eat – I dream – nightmares – and scare my wife. I wish it was over! But I think it will do! It will do! – Mind I only think – not sure. But if I didn't think so I would jump overboard." [344] It is not entirely clear how much Conrad hoped to write on January 11, but the story was completed by January 17 at the latest. On January 19 he had already been ill in bed for two days – "a cheap price for finishing that story." [345]

Writing was always a strain for him, and his tension while he was finishing *The Nigger* was particularly acute. Edward Garnett surmised: "Those seven weeks were perhaps the most strenuous in the whole of his writing life. . . . And had Conrad failed to 'bring off' *The Nigger*, or had the novel missed fire, in the reviewers' eyes, as many a masterpiece has done, nothing more disheartening for Conrad and ominous for his future could be imagined." [346] Garnett did all he could to help the novel to success: some thirty pages of the manuscript bear his marginal comments.[347]

Conrad made the usual contradictory statements about

the date of completion of *The Nigger.* On the wrapper of the manuscript he noted for John Quinn, "Finished in 1897 – Febr 7," [348] but the note was made years later. The manuscript itself is dated at the end: "Stanford-le-Hope – 19 Febr. 1897." Jean-Aubry accepted February without a definite day in the official *Life and Letters.*[349] It is difficult to reconcile the discrepancy between the probable January 17, accepted by Edward Garnett,[350] and February 19. Perhaps the later date represents the completion of corrections on the manuscript.[351]

Conrad was kept in suspense by the *New Review.* "I had a letter from Pawling," he commented on February 4. "It appears from it that the final decision as to serial publication would be taken at some meeting (of directors I suppose) on Monday (yesterday). I haven't heard any more and am anxious." [352] Anxiety developed into stoical indifference. On March 12 he declared: "I don't exactly understand my position vis-a-vis of the *N.R.* Is it a question of 'to be or not to be' or the more gross question of time only? To tell you the truth, now Henley has accepted me I don't care much whether I appear or not in the *N.R.* Or at least care only for the additional cash it may bring. Otherwise I would like to appear at once in book form and be done with it." [353] The matter had not been decided by March 24, though the delay seems to have been only over the time of publication: "Pawling wrote a very friendly letter but nothing explicit. I have still no idea when I am likely to come out." [354] Conrad did not mention the serialization again until it had been finally arranged. On June 2 he told Garnett: "The Nigger is bought in the States by the Batchelor Syndicate for serial and by Appleton for book. I begin in the August Number of the New R. (26th July)." [355] Though the letter does not tell when the arrangements had been completed, it must have been quite recently: in a letter of May 26 to Garnett Conrad did not refer to them. Probably he received small payment from the Syndicate. In February, 1894, Irving Bacheller had bought Stephen Crane's *Red Badge of Courage* "for less than a hundred dollars." [356]

Crane did all he could to spur on the Bacheller Syndicate to serialize *The Nigger*. When Conrad sent him the proof sheets of the novel to read in the autumn, Crane wrote:

> The book is simply great. The simple treatment of the death of Waite is too good, too terrible. I wanted to forget it at once. It caught me very hard. I felt ill over that red thread lining from the corner of the man's mouth to his chin. It was frightful with the weight of a real and present death. By such small means does the real writer suddenly flash out in the sky above those who are always doing rather well. In the meantime I have written to Bacheller and told him to be valiant in the matter of 'The Nigger' — I have also written some other little notes to America.[357]

The novel first appeared from August through December, 1897, in the *New Review*, in which it opened all five numbers. In a letter of August 9, 1897, Conrad complained: "The installment plan ruins it." [358] The Bacheller Syndicate did not succeed in serializing the story. Apparently Conrad became dissatisfied with their efforts and tried to find a market through Heinemann, for he wrote on September 27 that S. S. Pawling had sent "a personal letter to Scribner offering the *N of the 'N.'* " [359] Nothing came of the offer. *The Nigger* was not issued serially in the United States.[360]

Conrad expected the novel to appear in England in book form by November, 1897,[361] but publication was delayed. On July 29 Heinemann issued, for copyright purposes, seven paper bound copies of *The Nigger of the "Narcissus": A Tale of the Forecastle*, "struck off from type set up for the *New Review.*" [362] Two months later Conrad inspected an advance copy of the regular first English edition of the book. He wrote Garnett on September 27: "The *Nigger* according to sample sent me by P.[awling] makes up to 288 pages.[363] The preface another five or six – if not more. I think it can come out at 6/–. (My royalties [15% and 20%] are on *Published price throughout.*) Ain't I a sordidly vile old man?" [364] By October 11 Conrad finished correcting the proofs for the regular first English edition, making certain changes demanded by Heinemann: "I've sent away the last batch of proofs today. Now the Nigger is cast adrift from me. The book strikes me as good; but I quite foresee it will have no sale." [365]

Though the proofs were ready by October 12, the English publication was delayed almost two months. On November 30, 1897, the American edition was issued by Dodd, Mead and Company under the title of *The Children of the Sea: A Tale of the Forecastle.*[366] The English edition of fifteen hundred copies, entitled *The Nigger of the "Narcissus": A Tale of the Sea* followed two days later.[367] The motto from Pepys on the title-page of the first English edition Conrad discovered while calling upon James.[368]

The various titles prove that Conrad decided upon the final title after the copyright and American editions had been printed. Some idea of his difficulties may be gathered from what he wrote John Galsworthy about the title of *The Island Pharisees:* "Why don't you let them [the publishers] try their hand themselves at a name, if they are so mighty difficult to please? There was some bother of that sort about the *Nigger of the N.* I remember." In a note on the letter Jean-Aubry asserted: "I remember the late William Heinemann showing me a letter by J. C. suggesting *thirteen different titles* for *The Nigger of the 'Narcissus.'* Unfortunately, that letter which was seen for the last time in 1920, has been mislaid and has evaded every search." [369] Despite the loss it is still possible to study the evolution of the full title: *The Nigger of the "Narcissus": A Tale of the Sea.*

Conrad had the final title of the novel in mind when he began to write. In the center of the top line of the first manuscript page appears "*The Nigger of the 'Narcissus,'*" and in the upper left hand corner of most of the other pages appears "The N of the 'N' [or N]." Generally he referred to the story as "the *Nigger*," occasionally as "the 'Narcissus.'" [370] After completing the novel, he asked Garnett's advice about the title: "I've sent him [Pawling] a suggestion for a title. What do you think of it? . . . THE FORECASTLE. A Tale of Ship and Men. . . . It's rather late to ask your opinion for I've already sent a slip to P." [371] Garnett's advice is unknown, but within a week Conrad referred to the novel as *The Nigger: A Tale of Ships and Men.*[372] By the time of serial publication he had evolved another subtitle from earlier suggestions. The novel ran in the *New Review* as *The Nigger of the "Narcissus": A Tale of the Forecastle.* The same full title was used for the copyright edition.[373]

Conrad had to choose an inoffensive title for the American edition. There is no evidence of how he arrived at the American title, *The Children of the Sea: A Tale of the Forecastle*, which he adopted "in deference to Am. prejudices." [374] Only the title was changed; the old subtitle was retained. Conrad had no use for the change: he called the new title "absurdly sweet." [375] He was delighted when Doubleday, Page and Company reissued the novel with its proper title in America in 1914.[376] Yet the edition, made up from remaindered sheets, had "The Children of the Sea" for headline on all pages but the first.[377] The old subtitle, *A Tale of the Forecastle*, was kept.

Conrad was not satisfied with the subtitle of the copyright edition. After it was issued he made a final change. In the copy which he presented to Edward Garnett's mother the original subtitle, *A Tale of the Forecastle*, has been "corrected in Conrad's own hand to 'A Tale of the Sea.'"[378] Thus he abandoned the tentative *A Tale of Ships and Men*, *A Tale of Ship and Men*, and *A Tale of the Forecastle* for the final subtitle which the novel bears officially today.[379]

As late as February 28, 1897, Conrad intended to dedicate *Tales of Unrest* to Edward Garnett. Then he decided that Garnett, who had been its literary godfather, would value *The Nigger* more highly. On May 26 he wrote what is obviously a reply to Garnett's thanks for the dedication: "I do not know how to thank you for your letter about the *Nigger*. It has made me happy and very proud. And I am glad that your name shall be inscribed on something you like."[380] The dedication did not appear either in the copyright edition or in the American *Children of the Sea*, but was included in the first English trade edition.[381] Conrad always associated the novel with Edward Garnett. On August 24, 1897, he wrote him: "The Nigger is *your* book."[382] Constance Garnett, praising the novel's "extraordinary reality and the great beauty of . . . style," which she compared to Turgenev's, added: "It gives me the greater pleasure that you should have dedicated your book to Edward, and I am sure that in sympathy you are never divided."[383] When the dedication was accidentally omitted from the limited edition, Conrad was much upset. On January 6, 1920, he made Garnett a long explanation of the mistake and of the steps he had taken: "I have arranged with Pawling that 780 pages with the dedication should be printed at once and inserted into those sets that are not gone out yet. Those subs[ers] who have already received their sets will have the dedication page sent to them with an explanatory letter." [384]

Of all the books *The Nigger* was probably his favorite. Once or twice he referred to it slightingly from modesty or irony. On December 6, 1897, he told Cunninghame Graham: "I am afraid the *Nigger* will bore you. *C'est vécu, – et c'est bête.* There are twenty years of life, six months of scribbling in that book, – and not a shadow of a story." [385] Three years later he called it "a splash of water." [386] Most of his references were affectionate and proud. He was flattered when Stephen Crane "appreciated my effort to present a group of men held together by a common loyalty, and a common perplexity in a struggle not with human enemies, but with the hostile conditions testing their faithfulness to the conditions of their own calling . . . – the crew of a merchant ship, brought to the test of . . . the moral problem of conduct." [387] Even after twenty years he was grateful to Heinemann for publishing it: "I have preserved a very vivid sense of that firm's friendly attitude towards my earlier work. They did everything that was possible to give a chance to the *Nigger of the 'Narcissus'* – a pretty hopeless book at that time." [388]

His seriousness was apparent in his letters. He admitted in January, 1897: "Candidly, I think it has certain qualities of art that make it a thing apart. I tried to get through the veil of details at the essence of life." [389] In May he declared: "God . . . knows the spirit in which I approached the undertaking to present faithfully some of His benighted and suffering creatures; the humble, the obscure, the sinful, the erring upon whom rests His Gaze of Ineffable Pity. My conscience is at peace in that matter." [390] In December, 1903, he wrote: "*Je me considère comme le dernier* des marins à voiles. *Personne en tout cas ne décrira plus cette ancienne vie maritime, – comme oeuvre d'imagination, le*

'Nègre' clot cette époque de la plus grande perfection en même temps que de la fin de la marine à voile."[391] Thrice Conrad repeated his final opinion of the novel. He told Quinn, to whom he sold the manuscript: "It is the story by which, as a creative artist, I stand or fall, and which, at any rate, no one else could have written. A landmark in literature, I can safely say, for nothing like it has ever been done before. I intended to keep it by me for the sake of old associations and then leave it to the Manuscript Department of the British Museum. They preserve many less significant manuscripts there."[392] In the note, "To My Readers in America," he again stressed the personal importance of the book: "It is the book by which, not as a novelist perhaps, but as an artist striving for the utmost sincerity of expression, I am willing to stand or fall. Its pages are the tribute of my unalterable and profound affection for the ships, the seamen, the winds and the great sea – the moulders of my youth, the companions of the best years of my life."[393] In Curle's copy he laconically reiterated: "By these pages I stand or fall."[394]

The Preface of *The Nigger* had an importance and history really separate from the novel. The creed of Conrad's literary faith, it was his acceptance of a new purpose in living. In the note, "To My Readers in America," he recorded his mood and the occasion on which he composed it: "After writing the last words of that book, in the revulsion of feeling before the accomplished task, I understood that I had done with the sea, and that henceforth I had to be a writer. And almost without laying down the pen I wrote a preface, trying to express the spirit in which I was entering on the task of my new life."[395] Though presumably it was written around January 17, 1897, it is impossible to tell how much time is covered by Conrad's "almost." The first mention of the Preface was in a letter of August 24 to Garnett:

"I send you . . . a short preface to the 'Nigger.' I want you not to be impatient with it and if you think it at all possible to give it a chance to get printed. That rests entirely with you. . . ." [396]

Only about the Preface did Conrad seriously question his friend's judgment. Possibly because he considered them too apologetic, Garnett recommended cutting the two following paragraphs just before the end:

if not downright

somewhat

It may seem strange *and even* suspicious that so much should

unimportant

of the sea *is sure*

be said in introduction to the tale which follows. *It may be*

It may also appear the height of *folly* conceit or folly

of the preface

to appear unwise since every word may be brought in judgment

against the work it is meant to introduce. But a preface — if

perfect

anything — is spoken in good faith, as one speaks to friends,

the [word illegible] unprovoked confidence

and in the hope that *it shall be heard* with scrupulous

shall be treated And, after all,

fairness. Everyone desires to be understood;

with mutual indulgence forgive give way to the pressing

[line of correction illegible]

we all *are condemn desirous of*

need of explaining ourselves the fool

explaining themselves — *all* the politician, the prophet,

they all

the bricklayer do it: and if so then why should not the writer of tales who is, as far as I know, no greater criminal than any of these. It is true that the disclosure of the aim otherwise than by the effective effort towards it is a confession of doubt and so far a confession of weakness. Yet it [in?] the region of art such an avowal is not so fatal as it would be

alone enterprises

elsewhere. For in art of all the *works* of men there is meaning in endeavour disassociated from success and merit — if any merit there be — is not wholly centered in achievement but may

discerned

be faintly *visible* in the aim.

and ideals

For, art is long and life is short, *very often too short*

very also

are practically unreachable except by the great who can command the sanction of *success* recognized success. To others

a worthy

the consciousness of *aim is the reward aim is everything; in*

dignity

it is conscience, honour, truth, honesty honour — and no man may for ever be kept from talking about his own virtues aim is everything; it is conscience dignity, truth, honour — the reward and the peace.[397]

The two paragraphs must have been for Conrad an expression more of faith than of failure. On August 28 he replied to Garnett's comments: "I do not care a fraction of a damn for the passage you have struck out – that is, the personal part. But I think that the eight lines at the end (of the paragraph struck out) conveying the opinion that in 'art alone there is a meaning in endeavour as apart from success' should be worked in somehow. And whether your wisdom lets me keep them in or not I tell you plainly – fangs or no fangs – that there is the saving truth – the truth that saves most of us from eternal damnation." [398] Despite the protest, and the opportunity to incorporate the idea into the last paragraphs, the note of apology is not found in the Preface.[399] He still trusted Garnett's judgment above his own.

In the letter of August 28 Conrad implied that he had considered publishing the Preface separately as a magazine article. "I shall promptly patch the hole you have made and show you the thing with the infamous taint out of it. – If then, there is the slightest chance of it doing some good to the Nigger it shall *not* go to the Saturday or any other Review. Hang the filthy lucre. I would do any mortal thing for Jimmy." [400] For a man in his financial position the sacrifice had real meaning. Not only Garnett but also W. E. Henley thought it would do "some good to the Nigger." It was first published immediately following the final installment in the *New Review* [401] for December, 1897. Conrad's pleasure was evident in a letter of December 5: "Henley printed the preface at the end as an Author's note. It does not shine very much, but I am glad to see it in type." [402]

When the novel was being prepared for book publication, Conrad decided not to include the Preface with it "on advice (which I now think was wrong). . . ." [403] It did not appear in the copyright, the first American, or English editions. He did not record who was able to persuade him against his own inclinations.

He was unwilling to leave the statement of his artistic ideals buried in the files of a magazine. In 1902 he arranged to have the Preface printed by J. Lovick of Hythe. Of the hundred copies printed for private distribution, about forty were " accidentally destroyed." [404] He told Quinn: "The little pamphlet I have distributed to a few friends." [405] He could not have given away more than 25 copies, for in April, 1916, he informed Curle: "I have 35 copies and [want] to get some New York dealer to make me an offer of £50 for them." [406]

Conrad believed when he sold the manuscript of the Preface to Quinn that it would "never be published now, unless perhaps in a complete edition of my work – when that comes to pass." [407] He overlooked the appearance of the Preface as "The Art of Fiction" in *Harper's Magazine* for May 13, 1905.[408] He even refused in 1914 to allow Richard Curle to reprint it in his *Joseph Conrad: A Study* for fear that critic and subject would seem to have collaborated.[409] Early in 1914, however, he wrote the note "To My Readers in America" for the reprint of the Preface brought out as *Joseph Conrad on the Art of Writing* in April, 1914, by Doubleday, Page and Company.[410] There must have been some question at the time of cutting the text still further. Conrad made a note on the copy of the Hythe reprint which he sent Alfred A. Knopf, who was then with Doubleday, Page: "You may, my dear Knopf, cut out either or both of the crossed paragraphs – or let them stand according to your judgment." [411] The fourth and eighth paragraphs were marked with large crosses, but they were allowed to stand in the republished text, which follows the Hythe version throughout. Again in 1914 "To My Readers in America," the Preface, and *The Nigger* were united in a single volume issued by Doubleday, Page and Company. At last the book was in the form Conrad desired.

"An Outpost of Progress"

Like most of the stories collected in *Tales of Unrest*, "An Outpost of Progress," the second short story of Conrad's official literary life, belonged to a moment of despair about *The Rescue*. The only definite fact is that it was written on Ile Grande in July, 1896. Though Conrad dated the manuscript "17th–21st of July 1896. Ile Grande," the date probably applies to the days on which he made the manuscript ready to send Garnett. The original title, "A

Victim of Progress," was changed at this time to "An Outpost of Progress." [412] Writing on July 22 when the story was completed and about to be mailed, Conrad declared:

> *Cosmo*[*polis*] asked for a story. I was then writing a story especially for you. I was polishing, perfecting, simplifying. It's finished. I send it to you first of all. It's yours. It shall be the first of a vol ded to you — but this story is *meant* for you. I am pleased with it. That's why you shall get it. I am sure you will understand the reason and meaning of every detail, the meaning of them reading novels and the meaning of *Carlier not* having been armed. The story is going by this post. After reading send please to *F*[*isher*]. *U*[*nwin*].[413]

Clearly he had begun "An Outpost" by July 10 when he discussed with Unwin the *Cosmopolis* request for a story.[414] He did not then divulge the fact, undoubtedly because of the "electric eel" effect of his publisher which had made him regret mentioning "The Idiots." As Mrs. Conrad remembered that he wrote "An Outpost" in "three weeks or so," [415] it was apparently begun about the first of July. All the time, according to his wife, Conrad was "in a somewhat savage mood. It was the one story he refused to allow me to begin to copy till he had written the last word. He then handed me the manuscript with a request that I should do it as quickly as possible, 'I want it out of the house!' " [416]

The day he sent the story off to Garnett he also described his mood to Unwin:

> You will soon receive a story for the *Cosmo*. I suspect they won't take it after all. I send it to Garnett for the reason that it refers (in its execution) to a certain discussion we had on matters of art and I should like to know whether I have succeeded in achieving my purpose — my artistic purpose. The effect produced on him will tell me that.
>
> It is a story of the Congo. There is no love interest in it

and no woman — only incidentally. The exact locality is not mentioned. All the bitterness of those days, all my puzzled wonder as to the meaning of all I saw — all my indignation at masquerading philanthropy have been with me again while I wrote. The story is simple — there is hardly any description. The most common incidents are related — the life in a lonely station on the Kassai. I have divested myself of everything but pity, — and some scorn — while putting down the insignificant events that bring on the catastrophe. Upon my word I think it is a good story — and not so gloomy — not fanciful — alas! I think it interesting — some may find it a bore! If the *Cosmo* won't take it (it is as long as the other) I shall put it by — a day may come for it.[417]

His haste to get the story out of the house at once assumes significance. The poison of his African days was still in his mind and his body: he had not yet penetrated to the heart of darkness. Perhaps the letter also explains some of his disagreements with Unwin. There was a defensive tone to his sketch of the story, as if his publisher had warned him against indefiniteness of locality, excessive description, and lack of love interest.

Conrad was doubly wrong in predicting the reception of the story. It was unsuccessful with Garnett but successful with *Cosmopolis*. Before he heard from his friend, he began to mistrust the story. "I made there an effort at conciseness – as far as in me lies – and just managed it short of 10,000 words," he protested on August 5. "Do you find it very bad? I can't bear to look at my MS of it." [418] By August 14 he had received Garnett's criticism, which dampened his enthusiasm. He hastened to disassociate his friend from "An Outpost": "I must explain that that particular story was no more meant for you than the *Idiots* – that is *all* the short stories (*ab initio*) were *meant alike* for a vol to be inscribed to *you*. Only then [when Conrad was writing "An Outpost"] I had not heard from you so long that you were naturally constantly in my thoughts." [419] Perhaps he was hurt; but more probably he was unwilling to offer his friend a story that did not please him.

Garnett found fault with the opening of the story. Conrad agreed at once:

> You are right in your criticism of *Outpost*. The construction is bad. It is bad because it was a matter of conscious decision, and I have no discrimination — in artistic sense. Things get themselves written — and you like them. . . . But when I want to write — when *I* do consciously try to write or try to construct then my ignorance has full play and . . . is disclosed to the scandalized gaze of my literary father. . . . I always told you I was a kind of inspired humbug. . . . Let me assure you that your remarks were a complete disclosure to me. . . . It's very evident that the first 3 pages kill all the interest. And I wrote them of set purpose!! I thought I was achieving artistic simplicity!!!!!! . . . Am I totally lost? Or do the last few pages save the thing from being utterly contemptible? You seem to think so — if I read your most kind and friendly letter aright.[420]

He disclosed a reliance upon instinct and distrust of intellect that may account for some of his difficulty with *The Rescue*. His letter showed shame for his own shortcomings rather than animosity towards Edward Garnett.

Despite the flaw in construction the story was sold to *Cosmopolis* for £50 by Unwin before August 14.[421] Conrad was much upset by the editors' request that he divide the story in two for serial publication. On November 21 he was wondering "where it could best be cut without spoiling the effect too much. It is too long for one number, they say. I told the unspeakable idiots that the thing halved would be as ineffective as a dead scorpion. There will be a part without sting, — and the part with the sting, — and being separated they will be both harmless and disgusting." [422] Though he expected the story to appear in March and April, 1897, it was not run until June and July.[423]

However Conrad felt about "An Outpost" in the end, it had fulfilled its primary purpose. It eased the stricture of the imagination which made him put aside *The Rescue* early in July, 1896. The short story provided a "very different atmosphere. . . . I found there a different moral attitude. I seemed able to capture new reactions, new suggestions, and even new rhythms for my paragraphs. For a moment I fancied myself a new man – a most exciting illusion. It clung to me for some time. . . . It was only later that I perceived that in common with the rest of men nothing could deliver me from my fatal consistency. We cannot escape from ourselves." [424] Yet even illusory ease lessened the strain of creation. And payment for the story relieved a strain no less severe and equally recurrent.

"An Outpost" was published in *Tales of Unrest* in 1898 as the third story, although it should have been the second chronologically. Conrad retained his fondness for it and allowed it to be reprinted as his favorite story, with a companion article, both of which appeared in the *Grand Magazine* as "My Best Story and Why I Think So." [425]

"The Lagoon"

Conrad left little information about his third short story, "The Lagoon," and that little was full of mistakes and contradictions. He did not record how he conceived or when he began writing it. It was written on Ile Grande during the same spell of despair about *The Rescue* in which he wrote "An Outpost of Progress," which it must have followed almost immediately. "An Outpost" was completed by July 21, 1896. On August 5 he told Garnett: "I wrote the *Outpost of Progress* with pleasure if with difficulty. The one I am writing now I hammer out of myself with difficulty but without pleasure. It is called *the Lagoon*, and is very much Malay indeed. I shall send it to the *Cornhill* straight or else through F. U[nwin]." [426] The story had been finished and dispatched by August 14, 1896, when he informed Garnett: "I've sent a short thing to the *Cornhill*. A malay tells a story to a white man who is spending the night at his hut. It's a tricky thing with the usual forests river – stars – wind sunrise, and so on – and lots of second hand Conradese in it. I would bet a penny they will take it. There is only 6000 words in it so it can't bring in many shekels. . . . Don't you think I am a lost soul?" [427] Though the dates of "The Lagoon" can be fixed only approximately between July 21 and August 14, 1896, Conrad was obviously mistaken when he declared in the Author's Note of *Tales of Unrest* [428] that it was "the first short story I ever wrote."

He sent the story straight to the *Cornhill*, and at once his scrupulous sense of fair-play began to trouble him. On August 14 he made Unwin an elaborate explanation:

> If I have done wrong by sending my short story direct to the *Cornhill* that belief [that Unwin was not in London] must be my excuse. As a matter of fact I have already written a short note to the Editor asking him to send the story to you after perusal — which note was dispatched together with the Ms. The first page of the Ms. has also the direction: J. Conrad c/o T. Fisher Unwin Esqre and your address so that they have no excuse if the story does not reach you in case of rejection.

Conrad's politeness forced him to add a denial of his dissatisfaction with Unwin, who had disappointed him as an agent:

I thank you very much for undertaking to place my stories on the terms you mention. It is I am convinced a most advantageous arrangement for me and I look upon it as further proof of your goodwill. Whatever you do in that matter will be — I am sure — the best that could be done.[429]

Though the *Cornhill* had apparently refused "The Idiots," they accepted "The Lagoon" on August 19 at their usual rate of a guinea a page.[430] Conrad received some twelve and a half guineas.[431]

His attitude towards the story was inconsistent. Some of his letters showed no fondness for it. Branding the story as "second hand Conradese," he disparaged the *Cornhill* for accepting it and let it go for less than its two predecessors. He had not found the story easy to write. Probably his contradictory letter of March 14, 1897, to Miss Watson, the fiancée of his friend E. L. Sanderson, was written more to please socially than to tell the truth: "I am right glad to know you like the 'Lagoon.' To be quite confidential I must tell you it is, of my short stories, the one I like the best myself. I did write it to please myself, – and I am truly delighted to find that I have also pleased you." [432] A more genuine statement of pleasure is found in the Author's Note of *Tales of Unrest*: [433] "I have lived long enough to see it guyed most agreeably by Mr. Max Beerbohm in a volume of parodies entitled *A Christmas Garland* [1912], where I found myself in very good company. I was immensely gratified. I began to believe in my public existence. I have much to thank 'The Lagoon' for."

An explanation for the implied dislike was provided by the Author's Note. " 'The Lagoon' . . . ," Conrad wrote, "marks, in a manner of speaking, the end of my first phase, the Malayan phase with its special subject and its verbal suggestions. Conceived in the same mood which produced 'Almayer's Folly' and 'An Outcast of the Islands,' it is told in the same breath . . . , seen with the same vision, rendered in the same method – if such a thing as method did exist then in my conscious relation to this new adventure of writing for print." [434] Perhaps he had already outgrown "the Malayan phase." The feeling would help to account for his finding *The Rescue* difficult. Yet the Author's Note, written in 1919, must be recognized as a *post facto* interpretation of an earlier mood. "Karain" and the latter part of *Lord Jim*, which were still to come, continued the "Malayan phase." Conrad himself warned the student: "One does one's work first and theorizes about it afterwards. It is a very amusing and egotistical occupation of no use whatever to any one and just as likely as not to lead to false conclusions." [435]

The story was printed in the *Cornhill Magazine* for January, 1897.[436] Conrad's belief that it was his "first appearance in a serial of any kind" [437] was incorrect: the distinction belonged to "The Idiots." "The Lagoon" was reprinted as the last story, though chronologically it should have been third, in *Tales of Unrest* in 1898.

"Karain"

In the period of comparative rest that followed the completion of *The Nigger of the "Narcissus,"* Conrad planned "Karain." He informed Garnett on February 7, 1897: "I am thinking of a short story. Something like the Lagoon but with less description. A Malay thing. It will be easy and may bring a few pence. I shall send it to Unwin; ask him to place it (on 10% com) and look upon it as a further contribution to the Vol. of short stories that is to come in the far future [*Tales of Unrest*]. The *Rescuer* sleeps yet the sleep like of death." [438] He was not so weary of his Malay material as he believed by the time he wrote the Author's Note for *Tales of Unrest*. But in the Author's

Note he maintained that he had been using the material with a difference: "I had not gone back to the Archipelago, I had only turned for another look at it. I admit that I was absorbed by the distant view, so absorbed that I didn't notice then that the *motif* of the story is almost identical with the *motif* of 'The Lagoon.' " [439] The theorizing, done twenty-three years later than the stories themselves, was not strictly trustworthy.

Conrad left one mysterious, arresting hint about the conception of "Karain." After completing it, he wrote E. L. Sanderson that a letter from Miss Helen Watson, Sanderson's fiancée, "had something to do with the shaping of that story." [440] Miss Watson's letter made a great impression on Conrad; he "laid [it] away with some of my very particular papers. It is so unaffectedly, so irresistibly charming, and profound too. One seems almost to touch the ideal conception of what's best in life." [441] When he received the letter cannot be established exactly. On March 14, 1897, he thanked her for it and apologized for a "delay. . . . I was finishing another story, a promised and belated story!" [442] Now *The Nigger*, promised to Heinemann, was finished about January 17 and corrected by February 19. Hence Miss Watson's letter must have arrived in time to influence the planning of "Karain" in February.

Much confusion exists about the time when Conrad actually began the story. The date cannot be referred to the manuscript, which on its way to Quinn went down on the *Titanic*.[443] Jean-Aubry believed that the "thirty pages of MS." which Conrad sent Garnett on February 13, 1897, were "very probably a part of his short story 'Karain.' " [444] In view of later statements of Conrad's the thirty pages must have been revisions of *The Nigger*. One statement which invalidates Jean-Aubry's conjecture is in itself open to question. In the Author's Note of *Tales of Unrest* [445]

Conrad declared that " 'Karain' was begun on a sudden impulse only three days after I wrote the last line of 'The Nigger.' " As he was planning "Karain" on February 7, he could not have begun it "on a sudden impulse." And it is impossible to know whether he meant January 17 or February 19 as the date on which he finished *The Nigger*. Probably he was thinking of February 19 when the revisions seem to have been completed. Hence the date for the beginning of "Karain" would be February 22. As the Author's Note was made in 1919, it is helpful to have a contemporary statement also. On February 19, 1897, Conrad told Garnett: "I shall try to begin that short story today. My heart is in my boots when I look at the white sheets." [446] "Karain" was apparently begun about February 19.[447]

Conrad left a good deal of information, some of it incorrect, about the progress of the story. On February 28 he gave Garnett as much as he had written, probably the first fifteen pages.[448] With the manuscript he sent a mock defiance suggesting the imaginative difficulties that made him dread revision: "Ecco là! I deliver my misguided soul into your hands. Be merciful. I want you, besides as much criticism as you have time and inclination for, to tell me whether the thing is printable. . . . And understand well this: If you say 'Burn!' I will burn – and won't hate you. But if you say: 'Correct – Alter!' I won't do it – but shall hate you henceforth and for ever!" [449]

Despite the ultimatum Garnett insisted that Conrad do just what he refused to do – and Conrad did it. Mrs. Conrad remembered the trouble the story caused: "Several attempts were made, only to be suddenly torn and flung in the wastepaper basket. Then for days the few pages that had survived would lie on the table, the corners of the paper turned up, ragged, and twisted." [450] By March 10 the painful revision had been completed. Conrad told Garnett:

I have been at Karain and have rewritten all you had seen. A painful task. Strangely, though I always recognized the justness of your criticism it is only this evening after I had finished the horrid job that the full comprehension of what you objected to came to me like a flash of light into a dark cavern. It came and went, but it left me informed with such knowledge as comes of a short vision. The best kind of knowledge because the most akin to revelation.[451]

In the early stage of authorship he depended largely for success on intuition – and the critical judgment of Edward Garnett.

Conrad took slightly more than a month to finish the story after he made the suggested improvements. He did not find the task easy and he was not sure of his work. On March 12 he informed Garnett: "I am going on with Karain – and going wrong no doubt!" [452] On March 24 he complained: "It's that infernal story. I can't shake myself free of it, though I don't like it – never shall! But I can get rid of it only by finishing it coûte-que-coûte." [453] He reiterated his dissatisfaction in a letter of March 26: "Lots of writing but not much else in it." [454] Within another three weeks he finished the story. He did not record anywhere the exact day on which it was completed, but by April 14 he had finished, revised, and dispatched "Karain" to his publisher. Then he wrote Garnett, upon whom he still depended even after the completion of the story:

Karain gone to Unwin today. In the letter I ask *U.* to give the story to you before sending out amongst editors. I ask you to read it specially because it is your advice that has reshaped it and made it what it is — in good. I have not got rid of *all* the bad (in the first 15 pages) but I am nevertheless grateful to you for putting me on the right track. I worked rather hard. Been seedy.[455]

He finally disparaged the story as "magazine'ish." [456]

Conrad left other information about the composition of "Karain" which though incorrect is interesting. In the Author's Note of *Tales of Unrest* [457] he declared that at the time he began "Karain" he also took up again "the unfinished 'Return,' . . . the only instance in my life when I made an attempt to write with both hands at once as it were." There is no evidence that he began "The Return" before "Karain" or worked on both together. There is even a definite statement to the contrary: "Immediately after Karain I wrote the Return." [458] Possibly Conrad was thinking of his trouble with *The Rescue* when he spoke of writing "with both hands at once."

Just as he had suggested the *Savoy* for "The Idiots," so Garnett suggested, when Unwin was unable to place "Karain," that Conrad send the story to *Blackwood's Magazine*. The author thanked him on April 20: "My dear fellow you keep me straight in my work and when it is done you still direct its destinies!" [459] Blackwood was the first publisher to give Conrad a feeling of self-confidence. He recalled about "Karain": "The story is mainly made memorable to me by the fact that it was my first contribution to *Blackwood's Magazine* and that it lead to my personal acquaintance with Mr. William Blackwood whose guarded appreciation I felt nevertheless to be genuine, and prized accordingly." [460]

From the facts of the acceptance it is remarkable that the acquaintance ever came into being. At first *Blackwood's* seems to have made an offer which Unwin urged Conrad to accept but with which Conrad was dissatisfied. In a letter of July 18 he explained to Garnett his reply to *Blackwood's*, which was foolhardy for an impecunious author:

My Private Devil got into me. This P.D. suggested the refusing of Blackwood's offer and argued with me all the morning. He ended by convincing me — as you might expect — so I wrote to the Patron [Unwin] that £40 was my price for Karain and nothing less would do. The truth is that my P.D. wanted to annoy the Patron who advised me to accept the Scotch offer. This is the secret of my P.D's activity.

Yesterday the Patron forwarded me a letter from B'wood's which says that they accept my terms on the understanding that I shall give them the refusal of any short story I may write. As soon as I recovered from the shock I wrote saying I would be most happy to agree if Messrs. Blackwood undertake to decide upon the MSS. within a fortnight from reception and in case of acceptance print within four months. This is a distinct good turn in my affairs — and like everything else good I owe it to you — for did you not advise to try Blackwood? [461]

William Blackwood's "guarded appreciation" must have been stronger than Conrad supposed, though the Scotsman hesitated over the terms. On July 19 Conrad explained the transactions to Sanderson and added: "They demurred at first at my price, but I stuck to it heroically (while I felt very vile all the time),– tho'– really, – £2.10. per thousand words of my painful prose is not extortionate." [462] Probably he referred to the period of demurring in a letter of August 11, 1900, where he affirmed that *Blackwood's* "were 3 weeks accepting 'Karain.' " [463]

"Karain" was to have been published in October, but *Blackwood's* postponed it to November, 1897.[464] It appeared as the first story in *Tales of Unrest* in 1898, though chronologically it should have been fourth, not third as Conrad declared in the Author's Note.[465]

"The Return"

"The Return," like *The Nigger of the "Narcissus"* and "Karain," was written largely during a long holiday from

The Rescue. Though he did not record the exact day on which he began the story, he left information sufficient to establish the approximate date. He informed Quinn, to whom he sold the manuscript: "The Nigger was finished in February 1897. Then I wrote Karain and immediately after Karain I wrote The Return." [466] He had completed "Karain" and sent it off to his publisher by April 14, 1897.[467] Hence "The Return" was begun soon after April 14; the supposition is strengthened by a letter of July 19 in which he said that he had been working on the story for ten weeks.[468]

Conrad had difficulties with "The Return" almost from the start. Before June, 1897, domestic troubles forced him to put it aside: "Of course I have not written much while Jess was in bed being busy nursing and so on. I *must* go on now with the *Return*." [469] He did not find the story easy, for he confessed on July 18: "I go on groping through the *Return*. I feel helpless. That thing has bewitched me. I can't leave it off." [470] The next day he gave Sanderson a despairing account of his difficulties literary and domestic:

> Alas! — I've been ten weeks trying to write a story of about 20 pages of print. I haven't finished yet! and what I've written seems to me too contemptible for words. Not in conception perhaps, — but in execution. This state of affairs spells Ruin, — and I can't help it, — I can't. . . . There is no other news, — unless the information that there is a prospect of some kind of descendant may be looked upon in the light of something new. I am not unduly elated. Johnson [the Conrad's doctor] says it may mend Jess's health permanently, — if it does not end her. . . . This attitude does not contribute to my peace of mind, — and now, when I think of it, there is nothing very shocking in my not being able to finish a short story in three months.[471]

The combination of worry about his work and worry about his wife interacted viciously to prevent his completing the story. On August 24 he complained to Garnett: "I've been a martyr to various worries and can't send you the *Return* yet." [472]

Conrad did not finish the story for exactly a month. The manuscript is "inscribed at the end '22,000. *Stanford-le-Hope. 24th Septer. 1897.*' " [473] It is characteristic that he should have immediately written Edward Garnett for criticism. A letter of September 24 asked: "The Return accomplished in about 23,000 steps. . . . Am I to send it to you? Are you at leisure and have you the disposition?" [474] Apparently Garnett consented to read it, for on September 27 Conrad explained to him: "The *Return* completes the Vol. of short stories promised to Unwin. . . . The work is vile – or else good. I don't know. I can't know. But I swear to you that I won't alter a line – a word – not a comma – for you. There! And this for the reason that I have a physical horror of that story. I simply won't look at it any more. It has embittered five months of my life. I hate it. . . . It is not quite typed yet. I shall send it off *to you first* either tomorrow . . . or Wednesday noon." [475]

Garnett's opinion of the story must have been far from favorable. Despite his own expressed dislike of "The Return" Conrad tried to shield it from his friend's attack. His first reaction to criticism on September 29 was almost defensive:

> I don't know whether to weep or to laugh at your letter. . . . I am hoist with my own petard. . . . I wanted to produce the effect of insincerity, of artificiality. Yes! I wanted the reader to *see him* [Alvan Hervey] *think* and then to hear him speak — and shudder. The whole point of the joke is there. . . . But if I have to explain that to you — to you! — then I've egregiously failed. I've tried with all my might to avoid just these

trivialities of rage and distraction which you judge necessary to the truth of the picture. I counted it a virtue, and lo and behold! You say it is sin. . . . It is evident that my fate is to be descriptive and descriptive only. There are things I *must* leave alone. . . . And the question presents itself: is it to be put away in an unhonoured grave or sent into the world? To tell you the truth I haven't the courage to alter it. It seems to me, if I do, it will become so utterly something else something I did not mean. . . .

Can it be placed as it is in some Mag? Perhaps before the book comes out I shall see the true daylight from somewhere and then — and then! . . . I do not want to defend it. I want only to thoroughly understand.[476]

Henceforth Conrad was disillusioned about "The Return." "The true daylight" began gradually to illuminate his opinions. On October 8 he voiced his bewilderment:

Yes. I begin to see — Just to see a glimmer. . . . I feel what you mean and I am utterly powerless to imagine anything else. It's like being bewitched; it's like being in a cataleptic trance. . . . I wish to goodness I could *not* believe you. But I can't. I *feel* all you say and all the same I remain in the dark as though you had spoken an impassioned discourse — in Chinese. I feel — and I can't understand. . . .

Perhaps in time — perhaps in time! Who knows? If you don't abandon me in disgust I may yet learn the truth of art. . . . Even now I have an imperfect apprehension — for that story has been a heavy trial to me while I was writing it. It has made me ill: I hated while I wrote.[477]

Every day increased his dissatisfaction with "The Return." He admitted in a letter of October 11:

But the more I think of the story the more I feel (I don't see yet) the justice of your pronouncement as to the unreality of the dialogue. Where we differ is there: You say: it is too logical

— I say: It is too crude; but I admit that the crudeness (proceeding from want of skill) produces that effect of logic — which is offensive. You see I wanted to give out the gospel of the beastly bourgeois — and wasn't clever enough to do it in a more natural way. Hence the logic which resembles the logic of a melodrama. The childishness of mind coming to the surface. All this I feel. I don't see; because if I did see it I would also see the other way the mature way — the way of art. I would work from conviction to conviction — through inevitable moments to the final situation. Instead of which I went on creating the moments for the illustration of the idea. Am I right in that view? If so the story is bad art. It is built on the same falsehood as a melodrama.[478]

Here particularly Conrad emphasized how much he depended upon intuition and how unsuccessful were his early efforts to understand his work consciously.

By January 24, 1898, he came to repudiate "The Return" entirely: "It is bad – and in sober truth I can't bear the sight of it any more." [479] Ford recalled how Conrad regarded the story "as something slightly obscene at which one could only peep in secret." [480] The Author's Note of *Tales of Unrest* [481] contained his final condemnation:

Indeed my innermost feeling, now, is that 'The Return' is a left-handed production. . . . Psychologically there were no doubt good reasons for my attempt; and it was worth while, if only to see of what excesses I was capable in that sort of virtuosity. In this connection I should like to confess my surprise on finding that notwithstanding all its apparatus of analysis the story consists for the most part of physical impressions. . . . I know how much the writing of that fantasy has cost me in sheer toil, in temper, and in disillusion.

Conrad's disillusion was three-fold. He and Garnett both disliked the story, and no magazine would accept it. Soon after completing it, he began to think of serial publication. On September 27, 1897, he asked Garnett: "Now, as to selling the odious thing. It has 23000 words – who would take it? It won't stand dividing – absolutely not. Shall I give it to Unwin to place? What Mag: would you advise? *Yellow Book* or Chapman – perhaps." [482]

Apparently he decided to try to place it himself, since Unwin's efforts with his other short stories had been unsuccessful. Though he wrote on October 8, "I'm sending it to Chapman today," [483] he did not think it would be accepted. Chapman and Hall did not refuse the story outright. Conrad gave an acount of the negotiations on October 11:

> I sent the story to Chap & Hall with a letter, subtle but full of assurance. I had an answer by *return of post* from Oswald Crawford. He said the story is too long for any single number of the Magazine. . . . He thinks it may be used in the Xmas Number . . . tho' it is somewhat too long even for that. He wants to know my price for serial rights Brit: and Am:
>
> I replied: Delighted he likes my work, follows a small lecture on art to prove that the story *cannot* be divided. (If so the *MORAL* effect lost.) A hint that the moral effect is nothing less than beautiful. . . . A declaration that I attach a great importance to the story. Then: my price for serial rights *Brit* & *Am* is *£50* and I point out that this is at a rate *less* than what Messrs Blackwood pay me for my story [Karain] to appear in their Nov^er^ number. — That is perfectly true. *£50* works out at about 43/ — per thou[sand words]: while Blackwood pays 45/–
>
> A week has elapsed since and I haven't heard. . . .[484]

He did not hear for more than two weeks. On October 26 he complained: "Chap and Hall (O. Crawford) rejected the Return which I fully expected. Only he need not have been three weeks about it." [485]

In desperation he turned once more to Unwin. In discussing *Tales of Unrest*, he informed his publisher on November 5:

> As to the 5th story *The Return* which has not appeared yet anywhere I shall send the Ms to you as soon as I myself can get hold of the infernal thing. It's knocking about somewhere. I've asked peremptorily for its return. . . .
>
> Would you like to have for the vol *The Return* as an entirely new story not published anywhere before? At any rate in this country. I think it much too good for any blamed magazine. If I send it to you at once perhaps you could place it *serially* in some *advanced* Am. Mag: Fossils won't care for it. Anyway if you think that it may be an advantage to the vol: I may drop my search for serial rights here. *Pearson's* have been asking me for some time to give them something. I think it much too good to be thrown away where the *right people* won't see it. Of course I am unwilling to lose what I may obtain from some periodical; and if you have nothing to propose I feel inclined to try here and there for another month or so.[486]

The pathetic attempt to puff the story did not impress Unwin. A month later Conrad was pleading again with a franker insistence on his need of money: "I trust you'll be able to place the *Return* as the loss of serial rights would be serious to me." [487]

Though Garnett declared that Conrad unsuccessfully "sent the story about to various editors," [488] there is no specific reference to a further attempt to sell it. It was never published serially.[489] Conrad's disgust with "The Return" seems to have become so great that he even contemplated not using it for *Tales of Unrest*. According to a letter of January 24, 1898, Garnett persuaded him to include it: "You are right in everything – even in the suggestion to let the story go as it is. It shall go – and be hanged to it. . . . No one will notice it particularly, and even if someone arose to solemnly curse it, the story and the curse would be forgotten before the end of the week." [490] "The Return" completed the collection, published some two months later. It appeared as the fourth story in *Tales of Unrest*, though chronologically it should have been the last. The greatest profit from it fell to Quinn, who sold the manuscript for sixteen hundred dollars.[491]

Lord Jim

During the spring of 1898 Conrad had special difficulty with *The Rescue.* On May 18 he confessed to Edward Garnett: "Things aren't well with me. . . . Writing is as difficult as ever. . . . A ridiculously small quantity of the *Rescue* has been done." [492] His next two letters to Garnett, who placed them later in May, showed that shortly after the eighteenth Conrad resorted to the well-tried expedient of beginning another story. The indefinite date of the letters causes uncertainty about the order of two of the three stories worked on during this particular holiday from *The Rescue.* Priority seems to belong to *Lord Jim.* In the first undated letter Conrad announced that he was planning a collection of short stories for McClure in America and possibly for Blackwood in England to contain "*Jim* (20,000) Youth (13,000) A seaman (5,000) Dynamite (5,000) and another story of say 15,000." [493] At first *Lord Jim* was to be an unusually long "short story, concerned only with the pilgrim ship episode; nothing more," [494] and to be done primarily for McClure. Of the other stories in the proposed volume "Youth" alone can be definitely identified.[495]

The evidence that *Lord Jim* was begun before "Youth" is entirely circumstantial: both were mentioned for the first time in connection with the proposed volume for McClure. Yet in the second undated letter which Garnett assigned to May, 1898, Conrad declared: "As to *Rescue* you are under a 'misapyrehension' as Shaw [Lingard's mate] would have said. I intend to write nothing else. I am not even going to finish Jim now. Not before Septer. The talk about short stories has been commenced by those men B[lackwood] and Mcl[McClure]. and seeing them willing to discuss the future I gave them an idea of what I would do." [496] The implications are that he wrote some of *Lord Jim* and put it aside before beginning any of the other stories. He did not go on with *The Rescue*, according to his promise, but began "Youth," which was written in a few days and completed by June 3, 1898.[497] The deduction is corroborated by the Author's Note in *Lord Jim*: [498] "After writing a few pages, however, I became for some reason discontented and I laid them aside for a time." Though Conrad estimated the "few pages" at seventeen, probably they were the twenty-seven in the Polish memory book in the Harvard University Library.[499] Before he went back to *Lord Jim*, he completed "Heart of Darkness," wrote more of *The Rescue*, and collaborated with Ford Madox Ford.[500]

When he took up *Lord Jim* again, he extended his conception of the story and rewrote what he had already done. In a letter ascribed to June, 1899, he asked for Garnett's criticism of an example of "the sort of rot I am writing now . . . the first part of a B'wood story in two parts." [501] William Blackwood had been so much impressed by "Youth" and "Heart of Darkness" that he had "suggested I should give something again to his magazine. It was only then that I perceived that the pilgrim ship episode" – already begun and discarded – "was a good starting-point for a free and wandering tale. . . . The few pages I had laid aside were not without their weight in the choice of subject. But the whole was re-written deliberately. When I sat down to it I knew it would be a long book, though I didn't foresee that it would spread itself over thirteen numbers of 'Maga.'" [502] Conrad's intended story in two parts must slowly have expanded as he saw the full possibilities of his "free and wandering tale." The novel grew as he decided "to cram as much character and episode into it as it could hold."[503] Consequently he was always miscalculating the time necessary to complete *Lord Jim* and he was frequently dispirited about the quality of his work.

Conrad looked forward time after time to an immediate completion of the story. At the beginning of September, 1899, he expected to finish it by the end of the month.[504] He was still trying to complete it on October 12. His worry was intensified by the beginning of serial publication in the October issue of *Blackwood's Magazine*. Though the serial did not have such a paralyzing effect as the premature sale of *The Rescue*, possibly because Conrad had now become a professional writer, it aggravated his usual difficulty with creation. "I am at it day after day," he lamented, "and I want all day, every minute of a day, to produce a beggarly tale of words or perhaps to produce nothing at all."[505] It is hard to tell how much was written when the novel began to appear in *Blackwood's*. On October 26 he noted: "The fifth (and last inst[allment]) is not written yet."[506] As *Lord Jim* was published serially in fourteen installments, he must have written ten more installments rather than one, for it took him nine months more to complete the story. On November 13 he reported, "Jim's dragging his slow length along."[507] After an illness in February, 1900, he confessed on March 26, "I am still at Jim. . . . I've been cutting and slashing whole parts out. . . . How bad oh! How BAD!"[508] He wrote Mme. Poradowska wearily in mid-April: "Il est fort tard. J'ai envoyé Jessie se coucher et je suis resté a travailler. Quel métier de chien."[509] He was working busily in the middle of May and in early June.[510] By June 10 he hoped to finish in two days.[511] Yet only on July 16 did he complete *Lord Jim* "with a steady drag of

21 hours."[512] He went immediately to Belgium to join Ford and at Knocke-sur-mer he finished correcting the typescript by August 6.[513]

Conrad suffered the usual disillusionment with his work. Half-facetiously in June, 1899, he referred to it as "rot."[514] "I *feel* it bad," he admitted on October 26, "and, unless I am hopelessly morbid, I cannot be altogether wrong."[515] When Cunninghame Graham[516] and Garnett reassured him, he persisted in his complaints. He wrote Garnett on January 20, 1900: "You see the work fragmentarily; and the blessed thing is so defective that even . . . (with all your penetration and sympathy) you cannot possibly know where I tend and how I shall conclude this most inconclusive attempt. You don't; and the truth is that it is not my depth but my shallowness which makes me so inscrutable(?)."[517] On November 12 he again insisted:

> You've put your finger on the plague spot. The division of the book into two parts. . . . I admit I stood for a great triumph and I have only succeeded in giving myself utterly away. . . . You have detected me falling back into my lump of clay I had been lugging up from the bottom of the pit, with the idea of breathing big life into it. And all I have done was to let it fall with a silly crash.
>
> For what is fundamentally wrong with the book — the cause and the effect — is want of power. I do not mean the 'power' of reviewers' jargon. I mean the want of illuminating imagination. I wanted to obtain a sort of lurid light out (of) the very events. . . . I haven't been strong enough to breathe the right sort of life into my clay — the *revealing* life. . . . *Jim* [is] a lump of clay.[518]

Conrad disliked the effect of serialization, which diminished the cumulative power of the novel. He wrote Garnett that he ought not to read the first installment until he had the second to read continuously with it, and that the second installment "would have been less shocking if it had included another chapter." [519] His comment in Curle's copy showed what he thought of the public's preference for *Lord Jim*: "When I began this story which some people think my best – personally I don't – I formed the resolve to cram as much character and episode into it as it could hold. This explains its great length which the tale itself does not justify." [520]

Lord Jim ran as a serial in *Blackwood's Magazine* from October, 1899, through November, 1900. On October 15, 1900, before the serialization was concluded, the book was issued by William Blackwood and Sons in an edition of 2893 copies, at six shillings a copy.[521] Though the number of copies surpassed that of *Almayer's Folly* (2000) and *The Nigger* (1500), it was slightly less than *An Outcast* (3000) and *Tales of Unrest* (3000). The first American edition was published after the English in 1900 by the Doubleday and McClure Company of New York.[522] Conrad said that the American edition was "neither revised nor in any other way corrected by me." [523] Of the two Conrad preferred the American because "c'est moins lourd, et le papier est blanc au lieu d'être jaune sale." [524] *Lord Jim* was dedicated to Mr. and Mrs. G. F. W. Hope, who were Conrad's friends before his literary days and who brought him and his future wife together.[525] The Author's Note appeared for the first time in the edition of 1917 brought out by J. M. Dent and Sons, Ltd., of London.[526] The fragment of the manuscript now in the collection of Dr. Rosenbach brought $3900 at the Quinn sale.[527]

The title of the novel changed almost as often as that of *The Nigger*. Conrad first intended, according to the Harvard manuscript, to call the story *Tuan Jim: A Sketch*. For the serial he translated the Malay to *Lord Jim: A Sketch*.[528] Since he always referred to the novel in his letters familiarly as *Jim*, it is impossible to know when he made the change. The first English edition kept the serial title, *Lord Jim*, and introduced a new subtitle, *A Tale*. The first American also kept the title but used a third subtitle, *A Romance*. Later English and American editions generally retained the difference. The signed, limited edition brought out by Heinemann was entitled *Lord Jim: A Tale*, and the Canterbury Edition, *Lord Jim: A Romance*.

"Youth"

The difficulty of determining the priority of *Lord Jim* or "Youth" has already been noticed. In a letter ascribed by Edward Garnett to a date in May, 1898, later than the eighteenth, they were both mentioned for the first time as proposed short stories in a collection for McClure.[529] Conrad soon announced that he was not going to write any of the proposed stories, "not even" *Lord Jim*, which accordingly must have been started, but was going on with *The Rescue*.[530] He did not abide by the resolution. On June 3 he completed "Youth," which had been written in a few uninterrupted days.[531] The story must have been begun almost at the end of May,[532] since it was a continuous and rapid piece of work. Though he deliberately put aside *Lord Jim* to return to *The Rescue*, the impulse to write "Youth" was so "genuine . . . and . . . strong"[533] that he was unable to resist it.

Inspiration came from the past, for Conrad called "Youth" "a feat of memory. It is a record of experience" – the experience of his first remarkable voyage to the East on the *Palestine* from September, 1881, to April, 1883.[534] The feat of memory explains the tentative title in the manuscript, "A Voyage," and his remark, "I cannot help thinking what a lucky day it was for me when in 1880 [actually 1881] I shipped in the *Palestine*."[535] The tentative title he abandoned, restoring the one originally selected for the story, "Youth." According to the plan of the volume for McClure, "Youth" was to contain 13,000 words, the approximate number of the completed version.

Though Conrad felt, on principle, that he should never be entirely satisfied with any of his work, a note of pride crept into his strictures of "Youth." On June 15, 1898, shortly after he completed the story, he described it as "a sort of sea narrative without head or tail." [536] Later his tone became more partial. By August "Youth" was "a bit of life, – nothing more, – not well done, – 'a small thing, – but mine own.'" [537] He even defended certain defects to Wells in a letter of September 6: "As to the flaws of 'Youth' their existence is indisputable. . . . The feeling however which induced me to write that story was genuine (for once) and so strong that it poked its way through the narrative (which it certainly defaces) in a good many places. I tell you this in the way of explanation simply. Otherwise the thing is unjustifiable." [538] There was satisfaction in Conrad's statement in the Author's Note of the collection called *Youth*,[539] "Even before appearing in book-form 'Youth' was very well received."

The story was immediately taken by *Blackwood's Magazine*. On June 15, 1898, Conrad announced that he had "written a species of short story for Blackwood. That pays pretty well." [540] The acceptance and the price can be traced back to the understanding which he had reached with *Blackwood's* in July, 1897, when he sold them "Karain." [541] They accepted the story within two weeks, as the dates show, and published it within four months, in the issue of September, 1898.[542]

Sometime thereafter Blackwood seems to have planned a collection of Conrad's short stories. On October 12, 1899, Conrad announced: "A book of mine . . . is to come out in March. Three stories in one volume. If only five thousand copies of that *could* be sold! If only! But why dream of the wealth of the Indies?"[543] The plans took a long time to mature. In mid-June, 1902, while he was working on "The End of the Tether," which with "Youth" and "Heart of Darkness" was to make up the collection, he looked forward optimistically to publication in "two three months."[544] About November 21, 1902, William Blackwood and Sons republished "Youth," with "Heart of Darkness" and "The End of the Tether," in the volume called *Youth: A Narrative and Two Other Stories*. The edition consisted of 3150 copies, 257 more than the same firm had printed of *Lord Jim*, and the largest Conrad edition to date; the price was six shillings a copy.[545] The collection was dedicated to Mrs. Conrad.[546] Conrad referred to the volume as the "three-headed monster in the green cover. I hate the sight of the thing."[547] *Youth* was brought out in America in 1903 by McClure, Phillips and Company, in an "edition printed from unrevised proofs. Probably much nearer the *Maga* text than the 1st Eng: Edition."[548] In 1920 J. M. Dent and Sons, Ltd., of London, brought out a volume which contained "Youth" and "Gaspar Ruiz," a special Author's Note, a "Conrad Catechism," and a "Bibliography."[549] The manuscript of "Youth" brought $2000 at the Quinn sale.[550]

"Heart of Darkness"

Little is known of the history of the last short story Conrad wrote before he completed *Lord Jim*. The idea was in his mind when he visited Garnett at the Cearne in the late summer of 1898.[551] He gave his host "in detail a very full synopsis of what he intended to write. To my surprise," Garnett remembered, "when I saw the printed version I found that about a third of the most striking incidents had been replaced by others of which he had said nothing at all. The effect of the written narrative was no less sombre than the spoken, and the end was more consummate; but I regretted the omission of various scenes, one of which described the hero lying sick to death in a native hut, tended by an old negress who brought him water from day to day, when he had been abandoned by all the Belgians." [552] The impetus for writing came under especially flattering circumstances. The Blackwoods were sufficiently impressed by "Karain" and "Youth" to request a contribution for the one thousand issue of *Maga* in February, 1899.[553]

Apparently he promised the story for November, 1898; on January 6, 1899, he mentioned that he was "fort occupé au milieu d'un travail qui attend et que l'on attend de moi avec impatience puisqu'il devait être fini en Novembre. . . ." [554] The story seems to have been finished around the middle of January for he wrote on January 12, "I am finishing in a frightful hurry a story for *B'wood* and it's an immense effort." [555] Richard Curle remembered "Conrad telling me that its 40,000 words occupied only about a month in writing." [556] All that can be said of the composition of "Heart of Darkness" is that it was probably written between the middle of December, 1898, and the middle of January, 1899.[557] This story and "An Outpost of Progress" were, according to the author, who neglected to mention his jungle fever, "all the spoil I brought out from the center of Africa, where, really, I had no sort of business." [558]

The story ran under the title of "The Heart of Darkness" in *Blackwood's Magazine* for February, March, and April, 1899, and was republished as "Heart of Darkness" in *Youth: A Narrative and Two Other Stories*.[559] When the first installment appeared, Conrad was delighted to hear from Cunninghame Graham that he liked it but cautioned his friend: "I am simply in the seventh heaven to find you like the 'H. of D.' so far. You bless me indeed. Mind you don't curse me by and bye for the very same thing. There are two more instalments in which the idea is so wrapped up in secondary notions that you, – even you! – may miss it." [560] His fear of the obscurity of the story reappeared years later when he thanked Garnett on December 22, 1902, for his review of the collection *Youth* in the *Academy:* "And your brave attempt to grapple with the foggishness of H of D, to explain what I myself tried to shape blindfold, as it were, has touched me profoundly." [561] Yet Conrad was well aware of the savage power of the story. He described it once as "histoire farouche d'un journaliste qui devient chef de station à l'intérieur et se fait adorer par une tribu de sauvages. Ainsi décrit le sujet a l'air rigolo, mais il ne l'est pas." [562]

Chapter VI

CONRAD AND THE PUBLIC

CONRAD'S relationship to the reader and the critic rounds out the study of his early development. Before the appearance of *'Twixt Land and Sea* in 1912 he had barely a succès d'estime. Though he exaggerated the misunderstanding of the press and the neglect of the public, his work was long unpopular. The reviews of his first books explain the public's disappointing indifference.

Conrad's interest in the reading public was strong. He published his first novel not to make money but primarily to attract an audience.[1] He looked upon the reader as an imaginative collaborator. "For one writes only half the book," he insisted to Cunninghame Graham in 1897; "the other half is with the reader."[2] The ideal reader "puts so much of his own high quality into a work he is reading, directly the writer has been lucky enough to awaken his sympathy!"[3] Despite later discouragement Conrad persisted in his "one invariable intention, . . . to capture the reader's attention, by securing his interest and enlisting his sympathies."[4] Even when the indifference of the public induced his desperate scorn, he clung to the hope of a large and varied audience. A succès d'estime did not appeal to him. "I am sufficient of a democrat to detest the idea of being a writer of any 'coterie' of some small self-appointed aristocracy in the vast domain of art or letters," he asserted as late as 1918. "As a matter of feeling – not as a matter of business – I want to be read by many eyes and by all kinds of them, at that."[5] For almost twenty years he was limited to a very small coterie indeed.

Conrad's reactions to the reviewer naturally resembled his attitude to the reader, for the critics were in his estimation only articulate readers. "The majority of writers of notices in newspapers are men of average tastes," [6] he told Knopf in 1913, and the writers for weeklies and monthlies were, generally, no more unusual. At the beginning of his career he looked to the reviews expectantly. He repeated to Mme. Poradowska Unwin's promise of "des critique serieuses dans le journaux littéraires . . . une longue 'notice' dans la 'Saturday Review' et l' 'Atheneum' sans parler de la presse en general." [7] Yet he estimated the critic's function and abilities too high: "It is the critic's affair to bring to its [the "final effect" of a story] contemplation his own honesty, his sensibility and intelligence. . . . If his conscience is busy with petty scruples and tramelled by superficial formulas then his judgment will be superficial and petty." [8] The predominance of "superficial formulas" in the criticism of his early work wounded and irritated him. He tried to disregard the reviewers. Though he insisted that he never looked at the notices,[9] he inadvertently showed that he watched them with jealous attention.[10]

The reviews [11] often exhibited the formulas with which Conrad so quickly lost patience; yet they were more sympathetic than his impatience would suggest. Those considered here deal specifically with the early volumes, *Almayer's Folly*, *An Outcast*, *The Nigger*, *Tales of Unrest*, *Lord Jim*, and *Youth*. The notices of *The Rescue*, based on his reputation and success in 1920, do not belong in this study. The other stories with which Conrad's were reviewed show the critic's problem in separating the wheat from the chaff, and the implicit comparison must have been a constant irritation to Conrad. Even before *Almayer's Folly* appeared, he scoffed, "Ici, dans ce pays, . . . il parait

4 romans par semaine (et quels romans bon Dieu!). . . ."[12] A few criticisms were general studies. On this mass of critical material he made an occasional comment that sometimes reflected pleasure but more often annoyance and disappointment.

Almayer's Folly had a varied reception. In England it was given an enthusiastic review by T. P. O'Connor in his own paper, the *Weekly Sun*.[13] Other newspapers – the *Birmingham Post*, the *British Weekly*, the *Daily Chronicle*, the *Guardian*, and the *Manchester Courier* – found much to praise.[14] Only a little less commendatory than the *Weekly Sun* were the notices in the *Athenaeum*,[15] the *Saturday Review*,[16] the *Sketch*,[17] the *Speaker*,[18] and the *Spectator*.[19] The *Academy* [20] and the *National Observer* [21] considered the story indifferent, and the *World* [22] definitely poor. In the United States it ran the same gamut. The *Bookman* [23] gave it a highly complimentary notice, signed by James MacArthur, which was reprinted in the *Literary News*,[24] and so did the *Critic* [25] in its London Letter by Arthur Waugh. In two other notices the *Critic* [26] found the novel somewhat disappointing. The *Book Buyer* [27] and the *Literary World* [28] condemned it, and the *Nation* [29] treated it with real hostility. In France it received high praise from André Bellessort in the *Revue Politique et Littéraire* (*Revue Bleue*).[30]

The critics seem to have read the novel with attention. The *Book Buyer*,[31] it is true, called it "an Australian story." Macmillan and Company, the American publishers, with unbelievable ignorance, in an article over their name in the *Critic* [32] referred to Almayer as a Dutch-Englishman and to Nina's going to school in England. Yet many reviewers read carefully enough to find resemblances between *Almayer's Folly* and other stories. T. P. O'Connor in the *Weekly Sun* [33] likened it to Turgenev's *Lear of the Steppes* and Balzac's *Père Goriot.* The *Athenaeum*[34] compared Conrad with two such dissimilar writers as Louis Becke and Zola, and the *Bookman*[35] with Swettenham. Both the *Bookman* and the *Spectator*[36] coupled him with Kipling, a comparison that did heavy service as the years went by.

One aspect of *Almayer's Folly* which the critics were quick to seize was its local color. "The 'parochial' spirit in fiction," Arthur Waugh pointed out in the *Critic*,[37] "has extended to Borneo, a tract hitherto untouched by the novelist, but now annexed by Mr. Joseph Conrad, a new writer." As the fashion for exoticism was still strong with both critic and reader, Conrad's Sambir met almost unanimous praise. The *Nation*[38] was nearly alone in its complaint: "We have become inured to tiresome fiction supposed to be descriptive of outlandish places, but a feeling of resentment smoulders. 'Almayer's Folly' offers a good opportunity for protest. Borneo is a fine field for the study of monkeys, not of men. The only interesting native of Borneo got away and was long ago introduced to an astonished civilization as

'The old man from Borneo
Who's just come to town.' "

Most of the journals, like the *Academy*,[39] found the local color "just sufficient." The critics agreed that the novel was "written with manifest knowledge of the life which it portrays";[40] even the Malays were accepted as unquestionably authentic,[41] though later Hugh Clifford, an authority on Malaya, declared them spurious.[42] The *Spectator*[43] even hoped that Conrad "might become the Kipling of the Malay Archipelago."

Conrad's exotic description received considerable attention, most of it favorable. The *National Observer*[44] expressed the general opinion in declaring: "The descriptions of native life and scenery are vigorous and interesting, and bear witness to careful observation." The *Weekly Sun*[45] stressed the importance of the setting to the meaning of the story. A dissenting voice was raised by the *Sketch*,[46] which suggested that "the author is just a little careless whether or not he is wearying his readers while he is himself absorbed in the fascinations of Malay landscape." Yet even the *Sketch*, like its fellows, admitted that the "poetic" quality of Conrad's work came largely from "his power of revealing natural beauty." The style of the description was on the whole praised. The *Athenaeum*[47] might find it "suffers from exuberance, so that at times one feels all but stifled by its convolutions." Other critics, and the French in particular, commended the style – "chaud, fermé, imagé, créé de toutes pièces."[48]

The excellence of the characterization was less generally acknowledged. The *Athenaeum*[49] thought Almayer "a pitiable creature . . . whose nerveless doings arouse but little interest." Though the *Academy*[50] liked Almayer, it censured the other figures for "a certain indistinctness." Agreeing that the characters were "well drawn,"[51] most reviewers disagreed on which was the psychological center of the story. Some, like the *Speaker*[52] and the *World*,[53] awarded the place to Almayer. A greater number considered Nina the "central conception."[54] She was seen as a symbol of the tragedy, the struggle between East and West.[55]

The critics were almost unanimous in condemning Conrad's handling of the action. Though the *Critic*[56] and the *Weekly Sun*[57] praised the narrative technique, the majority attacked it as clumsy. The *Spectator*[58] declared that "the plot is not so well compacted as it might have been." The *Sketch*[59] accused Conrad of a "terrible offence – he forces his readers too often to turn back and re-read something of importance to the narrative. . . ." The *National Observer* [60] blasted the whole story because "its artistic possibilities are constantly thrown aside and sacrificed to a laboured and muddle-headed involution. The sequence of events is at times very hard to follow, and now and then the reader becomes bored and bewildered."

On the tragic tone of the story the reviews were entirely in accord. The *World* [61] thought it "unrelieved by one . . . gleam of humour," though the *Saturday Review* [62] considered Babalatchi comic relief. The *Literary World* [63] found it "dull and dreary," and the *Book Buyer* [64] "sordid and common." The *Sketch* [65] voiced what must have been a general and crucial "disappointment that what promises to be a tale of sturdy adventure in an unfamiliar and picturesque world, should turn into a long-drawn story of despair." Yet the most disappointed could not deny the force of the novel, and *power* appeared in most of the reviews.[66] As the *Academy* [67] reluctantly put it, "Still, the book somehow leaves an impression of grasp and power."

However they might resent a tragic conception of life, the reviewers were on the whole favorably disposed to Conrad. Many of them commented on the general critical acclaim which the novel had won.[68] Though T. P. O'Connor dared to hail the arrival of a "writer of genius," [69] the majority of critics were more cautious. The *Sketch* [70] prophesied unpopularity for *Almayer's Folly* but looked forward, like many other magazines, to Conrad's next story. Unwilling for the most part to commit themselves irrevocably on his first achievement, the critics compromised by emphasizing his promise. The *Academy* [71] was wary: "*Almayer's Folly* is not a book which it is easy to appraise with confidence, because it is so much more of a promise than a performance, and it is difficult even to say what the promise amounts to." The *Athenaeum* [72] committed itself to an unforunate suggestion as to what the next story should contain: "Why should he not give his readers, if he can, a sketch of the Straits Settlements, whose petition for fairer treatment, in respect of their military contribution, at the hands of the Government at home has brought them into temporary prominence?" The *Speaker* [73] gave the happiest expression to the general opinion: "If Mr. Conrad can give us another story as striking and life-like as this, his place in our literature ought to be an assured one."

Conrad was keenly interested in the reviews of *Almayer's Folly*. Before the novel appeared, he was trying in March, 1895, to arrange through Mme. Poradowska "a short appreciation" in the *Revue des Deux Mondes*.[74] The book had been out only three days when he wrote Mme. Poradowska: "Les journaux ecossais (quotidiens) ont commencé les critiques de ma 'Folie'. C'est court, journalistique mais très louangeur! Surtout le 'Scotsman' grand journal d'Edinburg est presque enthusiasmé. Le 'Glasgow-Herald' parle avec une bienveillance plus contenue. A present nous attendons les Quotidiens de Londres et *surtout* les revues hebdomadaires non politiques." [75] While the more important notices were appearing, he seems to have subscribed to a clipping agency. Unwin, who was as good as his word in obtaining reviews from the *Athenaeum* and the *Saturday Review*, also sent them on to him. Writing to his publisher from Champel on May 18, 1895, Conrad commented:

Thanks very much for the cuttings which have been sent to me from your office. . . .

I have since received many cuttings from the agency. The provincial press is very good to me so far. The "Realm" so-so, but with evident good will. But the poor old "World" kicks at me (in 15 lines) like a vicious donkey. It is severe blame (perhaps deserved) but, I think, no criticism in the true sense of the word.[76]

When he told Mme. Poradowska about his press, he was highly pleased:

> Toute la presse de province a parlé avec bienveillance — d'aucuns avec enthusiasme — de ma "Folie" — Un grand journal de Londres a parlé aussi tout ce qu'il y a de plus gentil. Vous verrez ça. J'ai les coupures. Du reste les critiques se font attendre. Il y a evidement qui hesitent a se prononcer mais les plumes jetées au vent flottent dans la direction voulue.[77]

Possibly the "grand journal de Londres" was the *Weekly Sun*, for Conrad was most excited at receiving seven and a half columns from T. P. O'Connor.[78] He was far from dissatisfied with the critical reception of his first novel despite the trash with which it had been reviewed. In October, 1895, he even confessed to Edward Noble: "Every critic (but two or three) overrated the book." [79]

An Outcast of the Islands met with much the same reception as its predecessor. The English daily press [80] treated it well: it was greeted with high praise by the *Citizen*,[81] the *Daily Chronicle*,[82] the *Glasgow Record*,[83] the *Guardian*,[84] and with praise only less high by the *Daily Telegraph*.[85] The English periodicals showed more variety. This time the *Academy* [86] was enthusiastic. The *Athenaeum* [87] and the *Saturday Review*,[88] in an article which, Conrad later discovered, was by Wells, were laudatory. Though the *Speaker*,[89] *Spectator*,[90] and *Illustrated London News*,[91] in a review by James Payn, gave tolerable notices, the *World* [92] found much to berate. The *National Observer* [93] was hostile. In America too the novel met a varied reception. The *Literary News* [94] praised it warmly; the *Book Buyer* [95] liked it. The *Bookman* [96] admitted its power but shrank from it, and the *Nation* [97] disapproved.

The reviewers made the usual number of careless mistakes. The *Book Buyer* [98] identified the scene as "the Celebes group of the Indian Ocean." The *Daily Chronicle* [99] referred to the hero as Petro. In a fury with the entire story the *Nation* [100] damned the Malays, Babalatchi and Lakamba, as "negro potentates." Once more the critics were interested in comparisons. The *Bookman* [101] likened the story to Harold Frederic's *Damnation of Theron Ware* (1896). The *Daily Chronicle* [102] found Conrad's description comparable to Melville's. Though the *Citizen* [103] thought Conrad superior to Crocket, Besant, and Corelli, the *National Observer* [104] considered him inferior to Stevenson and not to be mentioned with Kipling. The *Illustrated London News* [105] called him a disciple of Victor Hugo's.

By formula, local color was again singled out for emphasis and praise in almost all the reviews. True, the *Nation* [106] again centered its attack on the novel around exoticism. "There is no reason to suppose that he is by nature irrational or vain," it concluded about Conrad, "or that he would have mistaken his vocation had he clung to centres of civilization. But the accident of residence in Borneo, Celebes, and circumambient isles has tempted him to write novels, and has therefore made him appear a person of little discernment and poor judgment. The climate and the vegetation of the East Indies instigated a book." The *World* [107] complained that Conrad had not sufficiently identified the setting. Yet most of the critics acclaimed the background.[108] Conrad's knowledge of his subject was everywhere admitted; even the Malay characters went unquestioned.[109]

The descriptive power of the novel was widely applauded. The *Daily Chronicle* [110] declared, "Excepting in Melville, perhaps, we know nothing to match [Conrad's] scenic descriptions of tropical islands." Grasping the interplay of environment and characterization, the *Book Buyer* [111] felt that "the rich and fatal splendor of the tropics seems to determine the moral life of its enchanted prisoners. . . ." The *Literary News*[112] thought the characterization less impressive than the description: "The background of barbaric life and customs before which these figures move is so marvellously drawn and colored that it is not likely to be forgotten, though the figures themselves may, perhaps, fade. . . ."

The characterization in itself met with almost universal favor, though the *Nation*[113] took exception on social grounds: "Society, black and white, of a sort which no reputable person would meet at home, commanded a novel." The *Illustrated London News*[114] and the *World*[115] complained of the characters' morals. The *Academy*[116] devoted most of its review to praise of the "remarkably clever psychological study." The *Literary News*[117] used Willems as a text for an attack on imperialism and its emissaries. Some of the critics found Conrad's psychological power too strong for them. "It is a terrible psychology," complained the *Bookman*,[118] "realised with as awful an imagination as we can remember in present fiction excepting Stevenson." The comparison, inept by modern standards, shows the tender susceptibilities of the 1890's. The tone of the *Saturday Review*[119] has now a truer ring:

It is hard to understand how the respectable young gentlemen from the Universities who are engaged in cutting out cheaper imitations of the work of Mr. Stanley Weyman and Mr. Anthony Hope can read a book like this and continue in that industry. Think of the respectable young gentleman from the University, arrayed in his sister's hat, fichu, rationals, and cycling gauntlets, flourishing her hat-pin, and pretending, in deference to the supposed requirements of Mr. Mudie's public, to be the deuce and all of a taverning mediaeval blade, and compare him with Willems the Outcast. . . .

The narrative technique received severe criticism. Though the *Academy* [120] praised it, the *Saturday Review* [121] complained that the "story is not so much told as seen intermittently through a haze of sentences." Taking up the accusation of wordiness, the *National Observer* [122] delivered the most damaging condemnation:

> Mr. Conrad . . . is diffuse. He spreads his story over a wilderness of chapters and pages. Instead of the few vivid touches with which Mr. Kipling paints a scene, his narrative wanders aimlessly through seas of trivial detail. . . . When he resists his besetting sin of wordiness, he can be extremely effective. . . . But . . . he seems to lose grip of his subject. The story melts away among a desert of words, and the desert alas is dry. . . . The action is not quick enough, a serious charge to make against a book of adventure. Even schoolboys will probably have some difficulty in getting through it and we fear adults will find it impossible.

The charge of verboseness was leveled frequently against Conrad's style. The *Saturday Review* [123] prefaced its high praise of his work with a detailed indictment of his prolixity. After a long, censorious column it concluded: "He has still to learn the great half of his art, the art of leaving things unwritten." [124] Many of the other reviewers found the style well adapted to the subject matter – as the *Glasgow Record* [125] put it, "that masterly creation of an atmosphere appropriate to the scene of the action which is the outstanding feature of Mr. Conrad's style." The *Academy* [126] allowed itself the unfelicitous pronouncement: "His diction is round and picturesque; we can best describe his style by calling it mellow."

The critics agreed in disliking the tone of the novel. The newspapers warned their subscribers that the story was "darkly pessimistic." [127] The *Spectator* [128] was of the austere opinion that "genius will not win forgiveness for the repulsive cynicism of the dialogue between Almayer and the Professor in the last chapter." The *Athenaeum* [129] dared to call "the moral atmosphere . . . magnificently sordid." Like the *Athenaeum*, most of the disapproving notices were willing to admit the power and originality of the tale. Yet the *Bookman* [130] summed up outraged proprieties: "This is power: but it is perhaps the literary weakness of such a book as *An Outcast of the Islands* that its strain is too intense, too prolonged, too unmitigated for artistic harmony or truth to life."

In estimating the chances of the novel for popularity the reviewers were more charitable than their moral condemnations imply. Only the *National Observer* [131] called it a bore: "*An Outcast of the Islands* is undeniably dull. It is like one of Mr. Stevenson's South Sea stories, grown miraculously long and miraculously tedious." The same magazine denied emphatically that Conrad had become the prophesied "Kipling of the Malay Archipelago." Other magazines, more kindly, suggested that the second novel might disappoint because it was no improvement on the first.[132] Yet the majority of reviewers endorsed the opinion of the *Athenaeum* [133] that the promise of *Almayer's Folly* was "fully maintained" in *An Outcast*. Though the *Literary News* [134] felt it was not a novel "for which ordinary readers will care much," H. G. Wells in the *Saturday Review* [135] "deliberately" applied to it the word "greatness."

The discovery that Wells had written the notice in the *Saturday Review* excited Conrad more than all the rest of the press of *An Outcast*. On May 24, 1896, he told Garnett:

I was puzzled by it. . . . Something brings the impression [of the novel] off — makes its effect. What? It can be nothing but the expression — the arrangement of words, the style — Ergo: the style is not dishonourable. I wrote to the reviewer. I did! And he wrote to me. He did!! And who do you think it is? — He lives in Woking. Guess. Can't tell? I will tell you. It is H. G. Wells. May I be cremated alive like a miserable moth if I suspected it! Anyway he descended from his 'Time-Machine' to be kind as he knew how. It explains the review. He dedicates his books to W. Henley — you know.[136]

When Conrad had written to thank the anonymous reviewer of the *Saturday Review*, Wells had replied:

I really don't see why you should think gratitude necessary when a reviewer gives you your deserts.

Since you don't make the slightest concessions to the reading young woman who makes or mars the fortunes of authors, it is the manifest duty of a reviewer to differentiate between you and the kind of people we thrust into the 'Fiction' at the end, the Maples and Shoolbreds of literature.

Where the irony of an author thanking an anonymous reviewer comes in, is in the fact that the latter is almost invariably an unknown man and quite incapable of the workmanship the traditions of journalism require him to discuss in such an authoritative manner. I, for instance, could no more write your 'Outcast' than I could fly. But, unlike the huge majority of reviewers, I do happen to have written an (unsuccessful) book or so and to have learnt something from my failures of the method of the art.

If I have indeed put my finger on a weak point in your armour of technique, so that you may be able to strengthen it against your next occasion, I shall have done the best a reviewer can do. You have everything for the making of a splendid novelist except dexterity, and that is attainable by drill.[137]

Perhaps Conrad's pride was more hurt than the correspondence with Wells suggests. Defiance is certainly apparent in a letter of May 28 to Unwin:

My critic in Sat: Rev: is *H. G. Wells.* I wrote to him and he was good enough to reply. It (the notice) is valuable — but it is fallacious on the critic's own showing. I do not defend my performance. There is nothing respectable there but the endeavour. I grant, the achievement is wretched — but not in the way the critic says — at least not altogether. But enough of this. My style may be atrocious — but it produces its effect — is as unalterable as — say — the size of my feet — and I will never disguise it in boots of Wells' (or anybody else's) making. It would be utter folly. I shall make my own boots or perish.[138]

Though he wanted to vindicate himself to his adviser, Garnett, and his publisher, Unwin, he took the "valuable" part of the criticism to heart. In September, 1898, he admitted the lesson to Wells:

For the last two years (since your review of the *Outcast* in *Saturday Review* compelled me to think seriously of many things till then unseen) I have lived on terms of close intimacy with you, referring to you many a page of my work, scrutinizing many sentences by the light of your criticism. You are responsible for many sheets torn up and also for those that remained untorn and presently meeting your eye have given me the reward of your generous appreciation.[139]

The painful attention to style that left its traces on the manuscript of *The Nigger of the "Narcissus"* may have owed much to Wells.

In comparison with the *Saturday Review* the other criticisms were unimportant. "They struck me all of a heap so to speak," Conrad commented jocosely. "Ought I to wish myself dead? Or only insane?"[140] Though the reviews in general treated *An Outcast* less kindly than *Almayer's Folly*, he was not disturbed. On April 6, 1896, he remarked:

I had a few reviews. Nothing remarkable. The *Illustrated London News* says I am a disciple of Victor Hugo, and is complimentary! Very! So are the Irish papers, — the *White-*

hall Review and the *World*. But there is plenty of criticism also. They find it too long, too much description, — and so on. Upon the whole I am satisfied.[141]

When criticisms like the *Nation* and the *National Observer* appeared later in April, he was less satisfied. He referred scathingly in October to "snipes of enlightened criticism reaching me across the pond." [142]

The Nigger of the "Narcissus" was acclaimed by almost all the reviews. The English newspapers [143] greeted it with warm praise. Greatest enthusiasm was shown by the *Army and Navy Gazette*,[144] *Books and News Gazette*,[145] the *Daily News*,[146] and the *Literary World*.[147] The *Birmingham Gazette*,[148] the *Bradford Observer*,[149] the *Christian World*,[150] the *Daily Chronicle*,[151] the *Glasgow Evening News* [152] in two notices, the *Irish Independent*,[153] the *Liverpool Daily Courier*,[154] the *Morning Leader*,[155] the *News Agent*,[156] the *Star*,[157] and the *Sunday Times* [158] all commended the novel highly. *Country Life*,[159] the *Court* [?] *Journal*,[160] the *Daily Telegraph*,[161] the *Glasgow Herald*,[162] the *Manchester Courier*,[163] and the *Standard* [164] recommended it with only a few reservations. The English magazines did not endorse the novel quite so unanimously. Changing abruptly, the *Academy* [165] was hostile, and in the earlier of its two notices the *Illustrated London News* [166] was decidedly cool. In a later article signed by James Payn the *Illustrated London News* [167] was laudatory, as was *Pearson's Weekly*.[168] Though he did not sign it, Harold Frederic wrote the notice in the always favorable *Saturday Review*.[169] A. T. Quiller-Couch recommended the story warmly in the *Pall Mall Magazine*,[170] and the *Speaker* [171] and the *Spectator* [172] praised it highly. In the United States the novel was given critical acclaim almost everywhere. The *New York Tribune* [173] among the newspapers approved of it. Among the periodicals only the *Literary World* [174] treated it indifferently, though the *Literary News*[175] merely résuméd the story without comment. T. R. Sullivan recommended it in the *Book Buyer*,[176] and the *Nation*[177] reversed its formerly hostile comments. The *Bookman*[178] gave it splendid notices when it appeared as *The Children of the Sea* and in 1914 under its proper title. Probably the most enthusiastic American review appeared in *Literature*.[179] In France Henri-D. Davray praised it earnestly in the *Mercure de France*[180] when it first came out and later gave it a second laudatory notice in the same magazine.

The critics of *The Nigger* made their most amusing mistakes about Conrad himself. The *Liverpool Daily Courier*[181] referred to him as John Conrad. In comparing him to Loti, the *Nation*[182] based its distinction on Conrad's being an Englishman and emphasized "all the difference in race." The *Mercure de France*,[183] on the contrary, denied any English spirit in *The Nigger*: "C'est une oeuvre fort peu anglaise et qui n'a en somme d'anglais que la langue dans laquelle elle fut écrite et quelques-uns des personnages." In their comparisons the critics roamed widely through English, American, and French literature. Conrad was likened repeatedly to Becke,[184] Blackmore, Coleridge,[185] Carlyle,[186] Defoe,[187] Kipling,[188] Marryat,[189] Meredith,[190] Morley Roberts,[191] Clark Russell,[192] Michael Scott,[193] Smollett,[194] Stevenson;[195] to James Fenimore Cooper,[196] Stephen Crane,[197] Dana,[198] Harte,[199] and Melville;[200] to Hugo, Zola,[201] and Loti.[202] Not only did comparisons used with the earlier novels survive, but the field was enormously broadened. The reviewers made an occasional reference to the Preface,[203] printed in the *New Review* but omitted from the first edition.

On both sides of the Atlantic the title was attacked. The *Daily Telegraph*[204] called *The Nigger of the "Narcissus"* "the ugliest conceivable title." The *New York Tribune*[205] preferred the English title to the American *Children of the Sea.* The originality of the novel itself was generally praised.[206] Conrad's knowledge of his subject, different as it was from his Eastern tales, was everywhere admitted.[207] Just as he had been commended for bringing a new region into the fiction of local color with *Almayer's Folly* and *An Outcast*, he was now hailed for opening a new vista in the novel of the sea. The *Army and Navy Gazette*[208] called *The Nigger* "virtually a new departure in modern fiction." In the *Illustrated London News*[209] James Payn voiced the highest contemporary praise: "Mr. Conrad has in this book introduced us to the British merchant seaman, as Rudyard Kipling introduced us to the British soldier." The opinion of the *Books and News Gazette*[210] bears closer scrutiny today: "He has given us the most artistic and natural picture of sea-life that has yet appeared in literature." Conrad had convinced the critics that he was more than an exotic writer.

The critics agreed that *The Nigger* differed from all earlier sea novels in its material. As the *Spectator*[211] put it, "There is no heroine . . . , no love interest, and practically no hero." A few reviewers resented the unconventionality. The *Academy*,[212] missing the familiar themes of love and fortune, grumbled that Conrad's "material is barely enough for half the number of pages, and he has not invented any *motif* that will lead the reader on from page to page." The majority were relieved that the stock "warfare, piracy, mutiny, romantic adventure, individual intrigue, shipwreck, and above all . . . sweethearting and . . . strenuous love, tragic or fortunate,"[213] were lacking. "In discarding all time-honored material, and in confining himself to the delineation of character and its development under circumstances of physical discomfort closely allied to privation," declared the *Book Buyer*,[214] "the author shows the courage of great skill, which is justified by the result."

The characterization occasioned much dispute. Some reviewers patronized or disliked the crew of the *Narcissus*. "The common sailors . . . are generally worthless personages," thought the *Illustrated London News*;[215] Captain Allistoun was "honest and sturdy but unattractive, his officers loyal but without much distinction as to character." The Nigger himself, according to the *Saturday Review*,[216] "wearies the reader from the outset, as one feels he bored and fatigued the writer." He "merely annoys" the critic of *Country Life*,[217] and the *Speaker*[218] would have omitted him altogether. On the whole the characterization was enthusiastically admired by Quiller-Couch[219] and lesser critics. The *Spectator*[220] averred, "As a picture of rough seafaring life, . . . illustrating with singular force the collective instincts of a ship's crew, as well as the strange and unlikely alliances that spring up on shipboard, this book is of extraordinary merit." In the *Mercure de France*[221] Davray insisted that he knew "rien de plus tragique que ce *nigger* du *Narcissus*. . . ."

The form of the novel was another source of disagreement. The *Daily Telegraph*[222] objected that Conrad did not "care for his story so much as for his technique." The *Academy*[223] attacked the length as proper neither to the novel nor the short story; it found badly inconsistent the point of view of the common seaman who told the tale and the language in which the tale was told. Yet the *Literary World*[224] found *The Nigger* "a wonderful and fascinating piece of workmanship," and the *Nation*[225] felt that "the narrative makes an indelible impression, because the narrator appears to be a seaman who knows all about the sea and a ship and sailors of every complexion, and because he has got the poet's trick of heightening and deepening, modifying and exaggerating, producing a harmony of untruth which is a powerful representation of truth." Five years later the *Bookman* [226] remarked, à propos of Conrad's work, "How largely the length of a story is dependent upon . . . individual temperament."

Conrad's description aroused almost unqualified enthusiasm. The hostile *Academy* [227] was forced to admit that "the sea-pictures are beyond praise." The *Speaker* [228] compared *The Nigger* to *The Red Badge of Courage* as "a worthy pendant" and joined Conrad and Crane to "a whole school of descriptive writers of a new class, who aspire to make visible . . . the inside of great scenes." The *Speaker* found the storm, which was extolled by all critics, to be "inside painting"; "its vivid colouring bites into the mind." The poetry of the novel, emphasized by many reviewers, was largely attributed to Conrad's "happy gift of painting her [the sea's] changing moods in words that glow with true poetic fire." [229]

Some reviewers detected flaws in the description on points of style. Though they agreed that "the style is original, strong, and impressively direct," [230] many deplored its excesses. The *Illustrated London News* [231] thought the storm was developed "at too great length, and in language too technical." Conrad was condemned for aping Meredith in such phrases as " 'rolled bloodshot eyes.' " [232] He was blamed for following Crane in building up his scenes "piece by piece, never by one large and comprehensive sentence, but through a mass of commas, semi-colons, and full-stops, especially when it is his business to depict character or narrate incidents." [233] He was accused of verbosity: "Instead of patiently seeking the one word," complained the *Nation*,[234] "he takes the half-dozen that offer themselves." The *Academy* [235] attacked his over-emphatic vocabulary as "what Martin Scriblerus called the 'art of sinking in poetry.' " Yet critics admitted in general that under Conrad's guidance "words . . . get a sharper edge on, and cut deep down into the heart of things." [236]

A few reviewers objected to the moral tone of the novel. Conrad's use of *bloody* moved the *Literary World* [237] to call the story "strong, brutal, and in many places absolutely repellent by reason of the robustness of the adjectives employed." The *Illustrated London News* [238] complained that "the school of fiction-brutality to which he belongs is not given to idealising fact." Most notices lauded his very robustness. "We do not know that this novel will please all readers," admitted the *News Agent*,[239] "but those who have seen something of life on board ship – but not in the cabin – will realise the strong character-drawing which the book contains." *Strong* was frequently used to convey the effect of the story.[240] Though it was more than once called "grim," [241] though it was found "at times almost unbearably depressing," [242] its power and truth could not be denied. Galsworthy gave the tone of the novel a final definition which earlier critics [243] had tried to phrase: *The Nigger of the "Narcissus"* was the "real epic of the sea." [244]

In estimating the chances of *The Nigger* for success, the critics again disagreed. The *Academy*,[245] frankly admitting that "in dealing with such a book . . . a reviewer is apt to come to grief," decided that Conrad lacked "tact and discrimination" and that the story was dull. Up in arms, the *Glasgow Evening News* [246] declared the *Academy* review "fudge, written obviously by someone incapable of recognising a good thing when he sees it"; Conrad had been done "rank injustice." Though the *Standard* [247] found the story "futile," the *Birmingham Gazette* [248] thought it more "human" and more successful than his earlier work. Many reviewers recommended it for its humor, a quality they had found noticeably lacking before.[249] They looked forward to Conrad's next publication; [250] they commented on the current success of *The Nigger* with other critics;[251] but they also sounded a note of warning. The *Books and News Gazette*[252] suspected that the novel was too good to "receive the appreciation it deserves at the hands of the public." The *Academy*[253] believed its "very cleverness and novelty may stand in the way" of popular success. The *Spectator*[254] came pessimistically closer to the truth when it declared: "Mr. Conrad is a writer of genius; but his choice of themes, and the uncompromising nature of his methods, debar him from attaining a wide popularity."

One passing comment on *The Nigger* definitely disturbed Conrad. In a review of an English translation of *The Triumph of Death* Arthur Symons praised d'Annunzio at the expense of Kipling and Conrad:

> We have a surprising number of popular story-writers, some of them very entertaining, some of them with great ability of the narrative kind. Look only at the last year, and take only two books: Mr. Kipling's "Captains Courageous" and Mr. Conrad's "Nigger of the 'Narcissus.'" In one of these what an admirable mastery of a single bit of objective reality, of the adventure of a trade, of what is external in the figures who are active about it! In the other there is an almost endless description of the whole movement, noise, order, and distraction of a ship and a ship's company during a storm, which brings to one's memory a sense of every discomfort one has ever endured upon the sea. But what more is there? Where is the idea of which such things as these should be but servants? Ah, there has been an oversight; everything else is there, but that, these brilliant writers have forgotten to put in. Now d'Annunzio, whether you like his idea or not, never forgets to put it in.[255]

Conrad questioned his work without finding a satisfactory answer at first. Two days after the review appeared, he unburdened himself to Cunninghame Graham: "Symons . . . went out of his way to damn Kipling and me with the same generous praise. He says that *Captains Courageous* and the *Nigger* have no idea behind them. I don't know. Do you think the remark is just? Now straight!" [256] His doubts were not assuaged. Inevitably he turned to Garnett. Sending him the disquieting clipping, he demanded: "Frankly – is the remark true?" [257] Within the week Conrad's introspection drove him to write an article for the *Outlook* – "chatter about Kipling provoked by a silly criticism," he told Sanderson. "It's called, – 'Concerning a certain criticism.' " [258] The article did not appear in the *Outlook*; if it ever saw publication, it was not reprinted in *Notes on Life and Letters* or *Last Essays*.

Conrad was more pleased by Quiller-Couch's notice in the *Pall Mall Magazine* than by all the rest. In December, 1897, Quiller-Couch wrote him of his intention to review the novel:

> Will you let me congratulate you on your "Nigger of the Narcissus," or, at any rate, thank you for the pleasure it gave me?
>
> I tried it promptly upon an expert seaman of my acquaintance, and we agree that it *is* a book. And I have tried to say this in a causerie I've been scribbling for the Pall Mall Magazine: though that doesn't amount to much, and won't appear before the middle of Feb.
>
> It is perhaps a pity that so good a yarn did not come out in book form earlier in the Autumn, and so give people a better chance of making its acquaintance before Christmas. But it *must* succeed anyway. Singleton and the skipper are splendid.
>
> No man, to my knowledge, has written of the merchant seaman so truthfully or so heroically.[259]

Conrad was delighted with the letter. He informed Garnett of Quiller-Couch's trying the story with success "on an old salt. . . . I am pleased with that appreciation." [260] "The clearest gain so far from the *Nigger*," he told Sanderson, "was the other day a letter from Q. The excellent man, – may his star ever be propitious, – writes enthusiastically a message short but packed full of sweetness. . . . In this way I am paid for the life and the writing that went up to the making of the book, the 'like of which' (the *D. Chronicle* says) 'we have never read before.' Apart from that I am afraid that Mr. Conrad 'who is in fact unique' (*Pall Mall Gaz.*) will not gain much from the book. Yet in a sense it is enough." [261] He followed the other reviewers carefully. "I had 23 reviews," he told Garnett early in January, 1898. "One indifferent (The Standard) and *one bad* (*the Academy*). Two or three of a hesitating kind in prov. papers. The rest unexpectedly appreciative." [262] A few days later he sent Garnett all his press clippings. He was flattered by letters from Chesson of Unwin's, Stephen Crane, Constance Garnett, Cunninghame Graham, and by Galsworthy's information that the novel was in much demand at the Junior Carlton Club.[263] E. V. Lucas wrote him, "It should kill the pasteboard ocean for ever." [264] The reception of *The Nigger* did not seriously displease or greatly gratify him.

Tales of Unrest had a better reception in England and France than in the United States. Most of the English reviewers liked it. Though the *World* [265] was hostile, the collection received good notices from the *Academy* [266] (now consistently favorable), the *Athenaeum*,[267] the *Saturday Review*,[268] and the *Spectator*.[269] The next year in a most enthusiastic criticism the *Academy* [270] awarded the volume a prize of fifty guineas. In France the *Mercure de France* [271] contained a laudatory notice by Davray. The American critics treated the short stories with less friendliness than any previous book of Conrad's. The *Book Buyer*,[272] the *Critic*,[273] and *Public Opinion* [274] praised it warmly, but the *Nation* [275] did not like it, the *New York*

Tribune[276] thought it inferior to its predecessors, and the *Literary News*[277] merely listed the titles of the individual stories. The *Chautauquan*,[278] *Literature*,[279] and the *Literary World*[280] were thoroughly inimical.

The critics judged *Tales of Unrest* by the usual formulas. Similarities were seen between Conrad and Turgenev.[281] "The Idiots" specifically was compared to Maupassant,[282] "An Outpost of Progress" to Stevenson,[283] and "The Return" to Hawthorne,[284] James,[285] and Marriott Watson.[286] Local color was once more emphasized, especially by the French.[287] The *Spectator*,[288] noting that Conrad had laid stories in Europe for the first time, decided that "the experiment . . . is necessarily interesting, but by no means satisfactory." Though the *Saturday Review*[289] considered his exoticism "a 'speciality,'" the *Book Buyer*[290] commended "his preference for themes as far removed from commonplaces as one may hope to find upon our planet."

The critics commended the other aspects of Conrad's story-telling. Although the *Spectator*[291] disliked the way in which his orientals morally outshone his occidentals, the characterization received general praise.[292] His description was everywhere extolled; he was compared to "the great landscape artists" and to the portraitists.[293] His exacting technique was admired.[294] While his prose was occasionally condemned as overloaded with detail, even his detractors conceded him to be "a careful student of style."[295]

Opinions differed drastically on the merits of the individual stories. "Karain" was hailed by the *Spectator*[296] for showing "really marvellous insight" and condemned by the *New York Tribune*[297] for having "less inspiration and more cleverness." Though "The Idiots" was praised by the *Nation*[298] for its "air of imperturbable veracity," and "An Outpost of Progress" was called by the *Saturday Review*[299] "distinctly superior" to *Almayer's Folly* and *An Outcast*, both short stories were condemned by *Literature* [300] as too "gruesome." The *Athenaeum* [301] found "The Return" "perhaps the best," but *Public Opinion* [302] "labored and tedious." "The Lagoon" was generally admired.[303]

The critics agreed that they disliked the tone of the collection as a whole. The *Academy* [304] protested in vain that Conrad had "seen strange things in strange lands, and he can describe what he has seen impersonally, incuriously, without sentimentality, and without wailing. He is not eloquent, and hysteria is unknown to him." The realism of the collection was too much for most reviewers. In an elaborate parable comparing Henry Harland's *Comedies and Errors* and *Tales of Unrest*, *Literature* [305] pictured a sunny room, full of comfortable chairs, flowers, and cheerful pictures, in which Mr. Harland's muse dwelled. Then it pictured a most gloomy apartment:

> On the walls prints depicting the failures and the tragedies of the world, haggard debauchees and their drunken wives, murders, suicides, and the living horrors of grinding, loveless poverty. Bookshelves filled with vast tomes of psychology leading nowhere and teaching nothing. Hard chairs and a large, plain deal table littered with medicine bottles and anatomical specimens. In every corner a close, stuffy, unhealthy smell. . . . [Here] we are told art has made its home, and on those hard chairs are seated its true votaries. The artist must devote himself to the truth and to nothing but the truth — but not to the whole truth. He must shut his eyes . . . to the tempting voices of love and happiness . . . until at last by due abstinence from the pleasures of the world, by a rapt contemplation of misery and sin, he may attain to the true aesthetic life.

After this unflattering description of the abode of Conrad's muse, the critic took himself off to "Mr. Harland's easy chairs." *Tales of Unrest* was damned to unpopularity. Despite its acknowledged power the collection was stamped as "a disagreeable book,"[306] "unbearably sinister,"[307] "grim beyond endurance,"[308] and "all very tragic, in one way or another quite horrible."[309] It was not surprising that the *New York Tribune*[310] found the tales "an anti-climax" after *The Nigger* and that the *Academy*[311] believed Conrad's "full achievement" was "still in the making."

When the *Academy* award was made, Conrad protested in mock-despair to Garnett. He pretended that such journalistic recognition established his failure as an artist:

> Have you seen *it*! *It*! The Academy. When I opened the letter I thought it was a mistake. But it was too true, alas. I've lost the last ounce of respect for my art. I am lost — gone — gone — done for — for the consideration of 50 gs.
>
> I suppose Lucas worked like a horse to get this awful, awful job through. I suppose you worked too — or no — I won't suppose. Where do you chaps expect to go to when you die?
>
> Ah if I could only write! If I could write, write, write! But I cannot. No 50 gs will help me to that. . . .[312]

Lord Jim received a more friendly press than its predecessor. In England, though the *Athenaeum*[313] qualified its praises, the *Academy*[314] and the *Speaker*[315] lauded the novel. The *Spectator*,[316] always friendly, showed the greatest enthusiasm. In the United States the *Book Buyer*[317] and the *Bookman*[318] were tepid in their comments, but the *Critic*,[319] *Current Literature*,[320] the *Outlook*,[321] and the *New York Tribune*[322] were decidedly warm. In France Davray gave the novel his usual appreciative review in the *Mercure de France*.[323]

Some of the criticisms of *Lord Jim* betrayed careless reading. The *Book Buyer*[324] called Marlow "a member of the court of Enquiry," and the *New York Tribune*[325] asserted that "on a night of tropic calm the rotten craft goes to the bottom like a shot, with all hands save a few members of the crew." The familiar comparisons with Becke, Stevenson, especially in *Ebb Tide*,[326] James,[327] Meredith,[328] and Turgenev[329] were made. In addition *Lord Jim* was likened to Zack's *On Trial*[330] and, some years later, Arthur Symons found Jim to bear a resemblance to Don Quixote and Marlow to Sancho Panza.[331]

The reviewers again stressed the importance of local color to Conrad's work. The *Academy*[332] struck a jingoistic note in praising Jim as one of the "men who are engaged in relating the East to the West; those strange links with the two civilizations; voluntary exiles from this country, denationalising themselves that the British flag shall find trade wherever it penetrates." More acutely the *Outlook*[333] saw that *Lord Jim* united the appeal of *Almayer's Folly* and *The Nigger:* "a wonderfully fascinating air of romance of the sea and of the mystery of the Orient."

The characterization aroused dispute. The *Academy*[334] was enthusiastic over the portrayal of all the characters, though it could not accept the suicide of Brierley. The *Bookman*[335] struck a peculiar moral attitude. Suggesting that Conrad was "wrongly devoted to analyzing the soul" in Jim, it inquired: "Is it well for us to be reminded that such persons may be as infinitely complicated, as civilisedly degenerate as any dweller in refined and sophisticated circles? We do not know. Mr. Conrad may have written an unwise . . . book." Reviewers expressed opposite opinions about Jim's courage. Though the *Bookman* was confident that Jim was a coward, the *Academy*[336] thought the novel "a searching study – prosecuted with patience and understanding – of the cowardice of a man who was not a coward."

The narrative technique was a source of critical disagreement. The *Academy* disapproved of Conrad's turning the story over to Marlow because such a long after-dinner conversation was an unacceptable convention and because Marlow's monologue was obviously written and not spoken. In a later article in the *North American Review* [337] Hugh Clifford also felt the monologue to be "an illusion which it is impossible to sustain." The *Athenaeum* [338] found the illusion more successful in serial form. The *Bookman* [339] thought the story much too long and believed "half of it should have been mercilessly sacrificed." The complex structure was defended by the *Critic* [340] in an elaborate figure:

> Imagine a fat, furry spider with green head and shining points for eyes, busily at work . . . on a marvellous web, and you have the plot of "Lord Jim." It spins itself away, out of nothing, with side tracks leading, apparently, nowhere, and cross tracks that start back and begin anew and end once more — sometimes on the verge of nowhere, and sometimes in the centre of the plot itself. . . .
>
> The completed web is a marvel of workmanship.

Though it knew the book had been first planned as a short story, the *New York Tribune* [341] believed the "unpremeditated expansion to the form of a full fledged novel has done nothing to spoil the simplicity and balance of the design"; it preferred the book to the serial form. With far more penetration the *Speaker* [342] pointed out that Marlow and the apparent artlessness of the narrative prevented the reader's becoming so absorbed in the action that he did not get the meaning of the tale. The style met with general approval. Though the *Speaker* accused Conrad "of the tricks of those who try to express more than they mean," most reviewers agreed with Davray, "Vous pouvez prendre n'importe quelle phrase . . . et cette phrase est *écrite*." [343]

The critics on the whole admired the final impression left by the novel. The *Bookman* [344] found it "more than usually serious, more than usually depressing, and to such as are not psychological students . . . very tedious," but the *Academy* [345] praised its "poetical, romantic, half-wistful air . . . its application to life, to all of us." It was hailed by the *Spectator* [346] as "at once superlatively artistic in treatment and entirely original in its subject." The power of the treatment was felt everywhere.[347] The book fulfilled the prophecies made for Conrad by those who read his earlier work.[348] *Lord Jim* was even called his "greatest." [349]

Despite the generous acknowledgment of its excellence many of the critics prophesied unpopularity for the novel. The *Spectator* [350] attributed Conrad's lack of success to his subjects:

> Mr. Conrad's matter is too detached from "actuality" to please the great and influential section of readers who like their fiction to be spiced with topical allusions, political personalities, or the mondanities of Mayfair, — just now the swing of the pendulum is entirely away from the slums, and almost altogether in the direction of sumptuous interiors. Mr. Conrad, in a word, takes no heed of the vagaries of fashion or of pseudo-culture — he only once mentions an author and only once makes a quotation — he eschews epigrams, avoids politics and keeps aloof from great cities. His scenes are laid in unfamiliar regions, amid outlandish surroundings.

The *Outlook* [351] ascribed his unpopularity to his subtlety: *Lord Jim's* "qualities are of a peculiarly refined and half-elusive kind which may well prove unattractive to the multitude." The *Critic* [352] put the blame squarely on the technique: "If he keeps on writing the same sort, he may arrive at the unique distinction of having few readers in his own generation, and a fair chance of several in the next." Whatever caused it, the unpopularity of *Lord Jim* was certain.

Like *Tales of Unrest*, *Youth* had some unexpectedly cool reviews. The English critics held divided opinions. John Masefield damned the volume wholeheartedly in the *Speaker* [353] (hitherto always favorable), and the London *Times Literary Supplement* [354] was unfriendly. Yet the *Academy and Literature*,[355] the *Athenaeum*,[356] and the *Spectator*,[357] in a review signed by Hugh Clifford, were warmly enthusiastic. In the United States the *Critic* [358] was guarded in its comments, but the *Nation* [359] was laudatory. The volume was well received by Davray in the *Mercure de France*.[360]

The criticisms of *Youth* contained the usual errors. Forgivable ignorance made the *Nation* [361] praise Conrad's "Anglo-Saxon sanity." Only the most careless reading could have led the *Bookman* [362] to call "Heart of Darkness" "The Heart of Blackness" and to define it as a "symbolic picture of the inborn antagonisms of two races, the white and the black." In the literary comparisons the familiar names recurred: Kipling, Loti,[363] and Stevenson.[364] Many new ones were added, called forth particularly by "Heart of Darkness": Grant Allen,[365] Dostoevski,[366] Flaubert,[367] and Poe.[368]

The separate stories in the collection, of which "Youth" and "Heart of Darkness" fall within the scope of this study, received separate attention in most reviews. "Youth" was praised for bringing out "the colour, the atmosphere of the East." [369] Though the same critic characterized the philosophy of the story as "barren and not very pretty," most found it heroic. To Davray the tale gave "la lutte de l'homme contre la nature, . . . et le drame est par instants d'une grandeur démesurée." [370] The poetry of the conception was emphasized by the *Nation*,[371] which called the story "a lyrical expression of the hope and courage and joy of youth." The *Academy and Literature* [372] summed up the spirit of the tale by calling it "a modern English epic of the Sea." Some critics thought it the best story in the collection;[373] a few considered it the best thing Conrad had yet done.[374] Writing as editor of *Smart Set*, George Jean Nathan declared: "If Joseph Conrad's *Youth* were yet unpublished, and if Conrad offered it to us to-morrow, we'd mortgage our salaries to buy it, and stop the presses to get it into the next number."[375]

"Heart of Darkness" created similar excitement. The story impressed the critics as drawn from life,[376] though after Conrad's death an unsuccessful attempt was made to discredit his picture of the Belgian colonizers in the Congo.[377] The *Speaker*[378] believed that the characterization failed, but the *Academy and Literature*[379] recognized it as "the acutest analysis of the deterioration of the white man's *morale*, when he is let loose from European restraint, and planted down in the tropics as an 'emissary of light' armed to the teeth, to make trade profits out of the 'subject races.'" The moral tone of the story was praised by the *Spectator*,[380] though the London *Times Literary Supplement*[381] called it "quite extravagant according to the canons of art." The *Spectator*, like other magazines,[382] thought it the strongest story Conrad had ever written. Yet even where it was awarded the highest praise, and perhaps because it was, the critics were confident that it would be unpopular.[383]

The reviewers disputed Conrad's ability as a short story writer. The *Athenaeum*[384] declared it "not unreasonable" to doubt his mastery of the short story form: "His short stories are not short stories at all," it complained, "but rather concentrated novels." In the *Speaker*[385] John Masefield declared that Conrad's narrative was "not vigorous, direct, effective" like Kipling's, nor "clear and fresh" like Stevenson's, nor "simple, delicate and beautiful" like

Yeats'. Yet the London *Times Literary Supplement*[386] praised Conrad for "telling tales, just spinning yarns." The *Nation*[387] vindicated him as an accomplished narrator by once more attacking the whole school of local-colorists:

> At the time when Mr. Joseph Conrad began to write tales of adventure in the Southern Pacific, novelists were much concerned about getting local color into their work. . . . There was little then in Mr. Conrad's work to indicate that he had any profounder reason for writing fiction than that suggested by the chance of first-hand acquaintance with scenes lying out of the beaten path of travel and people born or banished beyond the reach of social or moral law. Gradually, however, he has shown himself to be one of nature's licensed story-tellers. . . .

Conrad's ability to describe a character or a scene was questioned. The London *Times Literary Supplement*[388] found his style "a little precious; one notes a tasting of the quality of phrases and an occasional indulgence in poetic rhetoric." In his hostile notice John Masefield attacked Conrad's style in some of the worst writing of his own career: "His manner, indeed, shows a tendency towards the 'precious,' towards the making of fine phrases and polishing of perfect lines. He has filled his missal-marge with flowerets."[389] But the *Athenaeum*[390] lauded Conrad for his "true worker's eye, the true artist's pitilessness, in the detection and elimination of the redundant word, the idle thought, the insincere idiom." The *Academy and Literature*[391] believed that "his special individual gift, as an artist, is of so placing a whole scene before the reader that the air, the landscape, the moving people, the houses on the quays, the ships in the harbour, the sounds, the scents, the voices in the air, all fuse in the perfect and dream-like illusion of an unforgettable reality."

In estimating the popular appeal of the collection, the

critics were faced with a recurrent problem. On the whole they gave the stories a high place. Conrad was praised for his detachment, his lack of "prejudice." [392] Though the *Critic* [393] detected in *Youth* "the obscure and bizarre situation, beloved of Henry James," the *Athenaeum* [394] praised Conrad's artistry in creating an "atmosphere" by which "his other more incisive and purely intellectual message is translated for the proper understanding of simpler minds and plainer men." It was frequently felt that *Youth* was a distinct advance upon his earlier work.[395] Yet even the friendliest critic warned the public that the stories might be "too strong meat for the ordinary reader." [396] The enthusiastic Hugh Clifford in the *Spectator* [397] was forced to admit that Conrad was considered "stiff reading," and to prophesy that *Youth* would be no more popular than the earlier volumes because it too was "stiff reading."

Conrad was not displeased by the reviews of *Youth*. Of the notice in the *Spectator* he said: "As to Clifford, I think his reservations (and they are too few, in all conscience) are perfectly just and proper, as far as they go. As to his commendations, I am not sure; the personal element enters into that; we are on very friendly terms and he is very human." [398] The same self-deprecation entered his thanks to Edward Garnett for the review in the *Academy*:

With my usual brutality I've neglected to express my feelings very much awakened by your review of Youth.

How nice they are I renounce to tell. My dearest fellow you quite overcome me. And your brave attempt to grapple with the foggishness of H of D, to explain what I myself tried to shape blindfold, as it were, has touched me profoundly. You are the Seer of the Figures in the Carpet. . . .

The ruck takes its tone from you. You know how to serve a friend! I notice the reviews as they come in since your article. Youth is an epic; that's settled. And the H of D is this and that and the other thing — they aren't so positive because in this case they aren't intelligent enough to catch on to your indications. But anyhow it's a high water mark. If it hadn't been for you it would have been, dreary bosh — an incoherent bogie tale. Yes. That note too was sounded only you came just in time. . . .

However the *Manchester Guardian* was fairly intelligent — and, I suppose, you have seen the thawing of great snows on the hoary summits of the Athenaeum? I am still shaking at the august phenomenon.

J. Bl'wood sent me word that the thing sells decently and that if the Christmas does not kill it or if. . . .[399]

He wrote to Ernest Dawson when he discovered that the *Athenaeum* review had been written by his brother: "No review of any of my work has pleased me better. Fact is — I suppose — that I like to be taken seriously. And when the seriousness is of a laudative kind the effect upon my feelings is simply lovely." [400] Despite his contempt for the body of the press Conrad was not dissatisfied. He wrote in one of Curle's copies of *Youth*: " ' "Youth" and "Heart of Darkness" are the first short stories of mine which attracted attention to my work in a wider sphere.' " [401]

Here the reception of Conrad's early work by the critics reaches the limit set for this study. Though some of the reviews were hostile, more were genuinely enthusiastic. The tone of the press between the extremes was friendly. There were even two enthusiastic general criticisms in these early days: one by B.-H. Gausseron in the *Revue Encyclopédique* [402] for February 13, 1897, and one by Edward Garnett in the *Academy* [403] for October 15, 1898, which enormously gratified Conrad.[404] Garnett in particular discussed Conrad's moral and esthetic functions more fully than any reviewer could hope to. The very praises of the notices may have done Conrad unintentional harm with the public.

He was hailed for things that would scare away the common reader. He was compared with writers of a high order. His artistry was stressed, and the powerful tone of his books emphasized even when they were not outrightly called grim. After the subsiding of the craze for local-color stories, which gave him his first success, the critics still considered his material specialized. He was called "stiff reading": he was described as a writer's writer and not, it was carefully stipulated, a writer for the ordinary reader. The insistence on his inevitable unpopularity must have done him far more harm than all the inimical reviews put together. As Henry James expressed it to Edmund Gosse in 1902, "His production . . . has all been fine, rare and valid, of the sort greeted more by the expert and the critic than . . . by the man in the street." [405] The other novels with which his were noticed are excellent indications of the public taste of the time. Almost all forgotten for half a century, they show why fame and popularity came to Conrad so slowly. It was not condemnation from the critics but indifference from the public that kept him in poverty for more than half of his writing life.

As the years passed, Conrad grew more and more discouraged and irritated by critical misunderstanding. Probably he attributed to the reviews – somewhat unfairly – his lack of commercial success. In fulminating about the notices of *Kipps* by H. G. Wells, he was really defending himself:

The worst of our criticism is that it is so barren. Most of our reviewers seem absolutely unable to understand in a book anything but facts and the most elementary qualities of rendering. Thus Wells gets reviewed on the same plane with X.Y.Z. and a hundred others; whereas the whole point is that H. G. Wells is unique in the way he approaches his facts and absolutely distinctive in the way he leaves them.[406]

He disliked the literary comparisons to which he had been subjected. "I know how the minds of the professional critics work," he declared. "They live on comparisons, because that is the easiest method of appreciation. Whereas I hate them, even if made in my favour." [407] He vigorously denied Galsworthy's fatalistic belief that adverse criticism was valuable. "It is neither good nor bad," [408] he insisted. He attempted to develop an indifference to all criticism. Yet his comment on the success of *Chance*, though it attempted to maintain a stoical lack of interest, really showed what his earlier disappointments had cost him:

> *Chance* had a tremendous press. How I would have felt about it ten or eight years ago I can't say. Now I can't even pretend I am elated. If I had *Nostromo*, *The Nigger*, *Lord Jim*, in my desk or only in my head, I would feel differently no doubt.[409]

To what he considered critical misuse he never allowed himself any public reply. He had learned from seafaring not to answer back. As he explained in *A Personal Record*,[410] "Fifteen years of unbroken silence before praise or blame testify sufficiently to my respect for criticism, that fine flower of personal expression in the garden of letters."

When book after book was disregarded by readers, Conrad lost faith in his imaginative collaborators. In moments of self-defense he denied any interest at all in popularity. "J'ai quelque réputation, – littéraire," he declared in 1897, when *Almayer's Folly* and *An Outcast* were failing to bring him royalties,

> mais l'avenir est rien moins que certain, car je ne suis pas un auteur *populaire* et probablement je ne le serai jamais. Cela ne me désole point, car je n'ai jamais eu l'ambition d'écrire pour la toute-puissante populace. Je n'ai pas le goût de la démocratie, — et la démocratie n'a pas de goût pour moi. J'ai obtenu

l'appréciation de quelques esprits d'élite et je ne doute pas que je pourrai me créer un public, — restraint il est vrai, — mais qui me permettra de gagner mon pain. Je ne rêve pas de fortune, du reste ce n'est pas dans un encrier qu'on la trouve. Mais je vous avouerais que je rève la paix, un peu de renommée et une fin de vie vouée au service de l'Art et libre des soucis matériels.[411]

As his unsuccess continued, his condemnation became more bitter. "I despair of the current intelligence which nothing seems capable of stirring," he lamented in 1901. "It is like a viscous pool." [412] In 1910 he gave a frenzied diagnosis of the public to Galsworthy, who had to be reassured that his correspondent was not " 'wholly serious' ":

Le public introuvable is only *introuvable* simply because it is all humanity. And no artist can give it what it wants because humanity doesn't know what it wants. But it will swallow everything. It will swallow Hall Caine and John Galsworthy, Victor Hugo and Martin Tupper. It is an ostrich, a clown, a giant, a bottomless sack. It is sublime. It has apparently no eyes and no entrails, like a slug, and yet it can weep and suffer. It has swallowed Christianity, Buddhism, Mahomedanism and the Gospel of Mrs. Eddy. And it is perfectly capable, from the height of its secular stability, of looking down upon the artist as a mere windlestraw! [413]

Even after his success he still complained that books were "victims of that 'uncomprehension' which is the characteristic of the bulk of reading mankind." [414]

As his disillusionment with the imagination of the common reader increased, he looked scornfully and anxiously upon the public as only a financial supporter. He deplored popular taste but kept a worried eye on popular appeal. In advising Norman Douglas on technique, he warned:

You may not like a full close — but the ordinary reader expects it. And the ordinary reader also wants the nail hit on the head before his eyes very simply in order that he should *see* the nail. Later on you will realize the inconceivable stupidity of the common reader — the man who forks out the half crown.[415]

Perhaps the melodramatic conclusions of so many of Conrad's stories spring from a desire to pull the half crown out of the pocket. He could not forget the financial demands of his family. The pressure of material necessity on his work appears in a confession that certain stories had "no other merit but that of procuring bread and butter for 3 harmless persons for whom alone my work is intended really. The public is a mere circumstance." [416]

Since the press disappointed him, since the general public did not buy his books, Conrad compensated himself with the idea of an audience of friends who would appreciate his every intention. The group may have been slowly selected from "quelques esprits d'élite" he mentioned in October, 1897. Two months later he defined the personal audience – though he could not entirely keep his thoughts away from the great reading and buying public:

When writing one thinks of half a dozen (at least I do) men or so, — and if these are satisfied and take the trouble to say it in so many words, then no writer deserves a more splendid recompense. On the other hand there is the problem of the daily bread which cannot be solved by praise, public or private.[417]

The importance of the little group grew with his disappointments. He asserted to William Rothenstein, " 'It takes me a year of agony to make something like a book – generally longer. . . . When it is done there are not more than twenty people who understand *pourquoi on se tue pour écrire quelques phrases pas trop mauvaises.*' " [418] The number of friends fluctuated, – sometimes it was fixed at twenty, more often at a discriminating six – but the idea of writing for a sympathetic circle was essential. From time to time he would elect some friend to the group and let him know in a flattering allusion that he was of special importance. As he told Bennett, "One writes for a chosen little group – in my case a bare half-dozen men, of whom for the last fifteen years, you have been one. The public comes in or stays away – and really it does not matter." [419] In this circle with which Conrad protected himself from public indifference were specifically included Garnett, Wells, Sanderson, Symons, Colvin, Cunninghame Graham, Swinnerton, and Curle.[420]

Of these incomparably the most important, perhaps the only one with a direct influence, was Edward Garnett. Garnett actually supervised some pages of the stories, and when occasionally he did not read the earlier manuscripts, Conrad felt as if he had "broken with my conscience, quarreled with the inward voice." [421] Garnett suggested editors and publishers. In 1897 Conrad told him, "You keep me straight in my work and when it is done you still direct its destinies! And it seems to me that if you ceased to do either life itself would cease. For me you are the reality outside, the expressed thought, the living voice! And without you I would think myself alone in an empty universe." [422] The dependence was not merely the fulsomeness of the novice. A year before he died Conrad showed that his gratitude had lasted through his life: "How much you have done to pull me together intellectually only the Gods that brought us together know. For I myself don't. All I had [in 1895] . . . was some little creative gift – but not even one single piece of 'cultural' luggage." [423] Though Garnett's influence exceeded the others', the members of the group were one and all necessary to Conrad's confidence during the lean years. "As years go by and the number of pages grows," he admitted in *A Personal Record*,[424] "the feeling grows upon one too that one can write only for friends."

Conrad's self-reliance suffered a serious reverse when book after book failed to make him popular. In 1896, at the outset of his professional literary life and of his domestic responsibilities, he believed he could make a financial as well as an artistic success of writing.[425] Eighteen months later he was still hopeful.[426] By the turn of the century his hopes had wilted. *Almayer's Folly* did not reach a third impression for seven years; *An Outcast* and *Tales of Unrest* reached a second after eleven; *The Nigger* reached a third impression after seventeen years; and though *Lord Jim* needed only four years to reach a third, *Youth* took seven.[427] The *Critic* [428] blamed the public's indifference upon Conrad's distaste for advertising. With satirical intent it advised him to give interviews, publicize his personality, and issue photographs. Whatever the cause of the unpopularity, the prospect was discouraging. By 1907 he did not believe in the "probability of success." [429]

Yet he never quite lost faith in the possibility of success. He cherished confidence in his assets:

> When it comes to popularity I stand much nearer the public mind than Stevenson, who was super-literary, a conscious virtuoso of style; whereas the average mind does not care much for virtuosity. My point of view, which is purely human, my subjects, which are not too specialized as to the class of people or kind of events, my style, which may be clumsy here and there, but is perfectly straightforward and tending towards the colloquial, cannot possibly stand in the way of a large public.[430]

Conrad's self-confidence was finally justified. He reached astounding popularity before his death, and after his death the books which had taken so many years to appeal to the public retained their success. The figures for America alone are imposing. His publishers have stated:

Since August 1923, the following Conrad titles have sold the quantities shown:

ALMAYER'S FOLLY	12,669
THE NIGGER OF THE NARCISSUS	35,800
TALES OF UNREST	9,025
LORD JIM	109,300
YOUTH	59,150
OUTCAST OF THE ISLANDS	7,580

These figures represent total sales of the regular trade editions; they do not include sales of the titles in sets. During the same period subscription sets have sold approximately 1,157,401 volumes, containing, of course, many copies of the books above listed.[431]

The unhelpful press, the long indifference of the public, his own discouragement could not destroy the fundamental appeal of the books. Conrad's belief in himself and in the imaginative collaboration and financial support of the reader was finally justified.

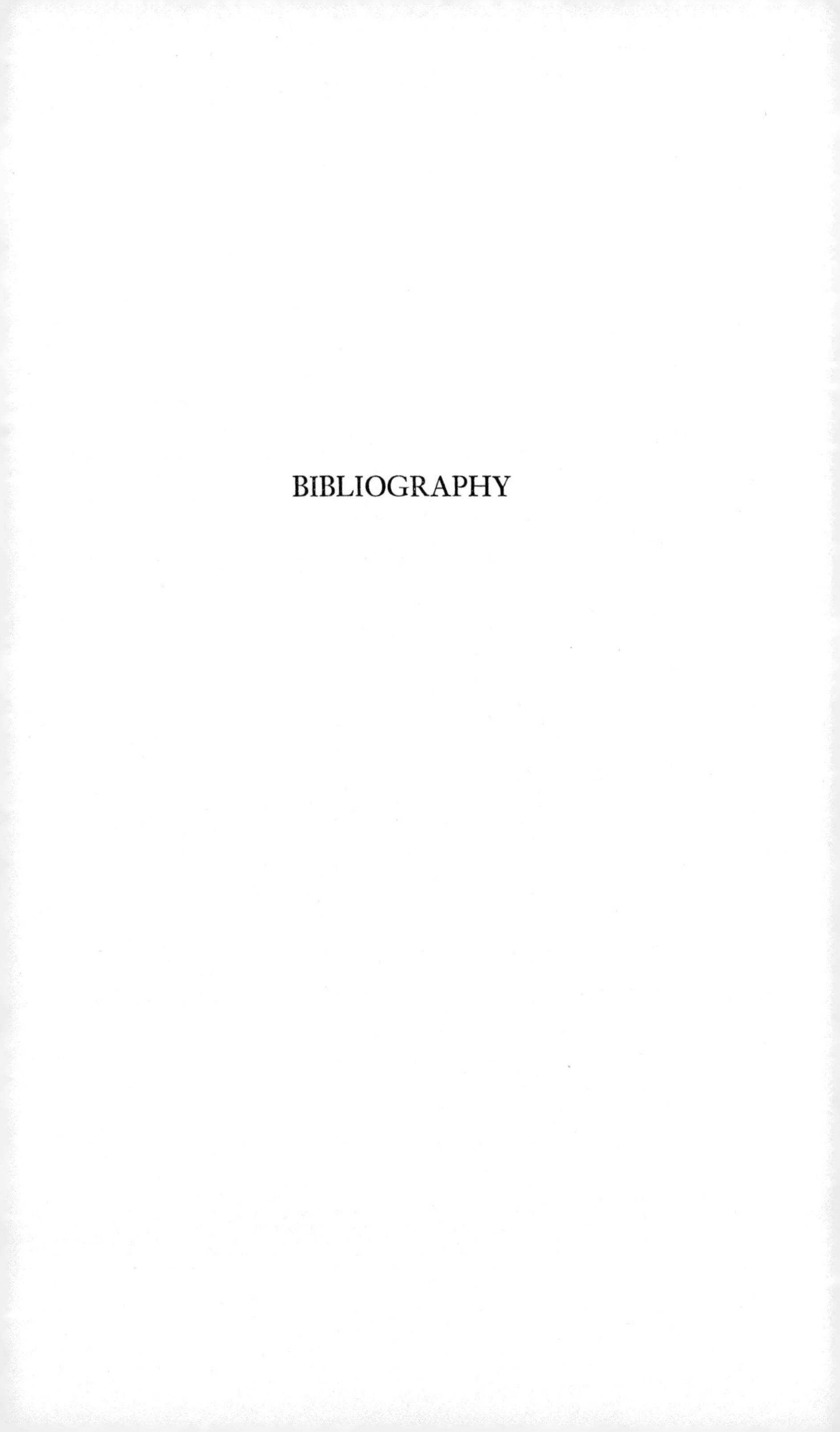

BIBLIOGRAPHY

GENERAL BIBLIOGRAPHY

I. WORKS BY JOSEPH CONRAD

A. Manuscripts

Almayer's Folly MS. Collection of Dr. A. S. W. Rosenbach.

Almayer's Folly TS. Collection of W. B. Leeds.

Congo Diary MS. Harvard University Library.

"Heart of Darkness" MS. Keating Collection, Yale University Library.

The Laugh MS. Keating Collection, Yale University Library.

Lord Jim [*Tuan Jim: A Sketch*] MS. Harvard University Library.

Lord Jim MS. Collection of Dr. A. S. W. Rosenbach.

Lord Jim: A Sketch. Blackwood's Magazine, CLXVIII (September, 1900), 358–383. Corrected in Conrad's hand. Collection of Barnet J. Beyer.

The Nigger of the "Narcissus" MS. Collection of Dr. A. S. W. Rosenbach.

The Nigger of the "Narcissus": A Tale of the Sea. Popular Edition; London: William Heinemann, 1910. Corrected in Conrad's hand. Keating Collection, Yale University Library.

The Nigger of the "Narcissus" Preface MS. Collection of Dr. A. S. W. Rosenbach.

The Rescue MS. British Museum: Ashley 4787.

The Shadow Line MS. Keating Collection, Yale University Library.

B. Published Works

Almayer's Folly: A Story of an Eastern River. London: T. Fisher Unwin, 1895.

Almayer's Folly: A Story of an Eastern River. Limited Edition; London: William Heinemann, Ltd., 1921.

Almayer's Folly. Canterbury Edition; Garden City, New York: Doubleday, Page and Company, 1924.

Almayer's Folly: A Story of an Eastern River. Memorial Edition; Garden City, New York: Doubleday, Page and Company, 1925.

The Arrow of Gold: A Story between Two Notes. Canterbury Edition; Garden City, New York: Doubleday, Page and Company, 1924.

Chance: A Tale in Two Parts. Canterbury Edition; Garden City, New York: Doubleday, Page and Company, 1924.

The Children of the Sea: A Tale of the Forecastle. New York: Dodd, Mead and Company, 1897.

"The Idiots." *Savoy*, no. 6 (October, 1896), 11–30.

"The Lagoon." *Cornhill Magazine*, New Series, II (1897), 59–71.

Last Essays. London and Toronto: J. M. Dent and Sons Ltd., 1926.

Lord Jim: A Sketch. *Blackwood's Magazine*,
CLXVI (1899), 441–459, 644–657, 807–828.
CLXVII (1900), 60–73, 234–246, 406–419, 511–526, 666–687, 803–817.
CLXVIII (1900), 88–106, 251–263, 358–383, 547–572, 688–710.

Lord Jim: A Tale. Edinburgh and London: William Blackwood and Sons, 1900.

Lord Jim: A Romance. New York: Doubleday, McClure and Co., 1900.

Lord Jim: A Tale. Limited Edition; London: William Heinemann, Ltd., 1921.

Lord Jim: A Romance. Canterbury Edition; Garden City, New York: Doubleday, Page and Company, 1924.

Lord Jim: A Tale. Memorial Edition; Garden City, New York: Doubleday, Page and Company, 1925.

The Mirror of the Sea. Canterbury Edition; Garden City, New York: Doubleday, Page and Company, 1924.

The Nigger of the "Narcissus": A Tale of the Forecastle. New Review, XVII (1897), 125–150, 241–264, 361–381, 485–510, 605–628.

The Nigger of the "Narcissus": A Tale of the Forecastle. London: William Heinemann, 1897.

The Nigger of the "Narcissus": A Tale of the Sea. London: William Heinemann, 1898.

The Nigger of the 'Narcissus': A Tale of the Sea. Limited Edition; London: William Heinemann, Ltd., 1921.

The Nigger of the Narcissus: A Tale of the Forecastle. Canterbury Edition; Garden City, New York: Doubleday, Page and Company, 1924.

The Nigger of the "Narcissus" Preface.
New Review, XVII (1897), 628–631.
Privately Printed, Hythe, n.d.
"The Art of Fiction," *Harper's Weekly*, XLIX (1905), 690.
"Joseph Conrad on the Art of Writing." Garden City, New York: Doubleday, Page and Company [1914].

Nostromo: A Tale of the Seaboard. Canterbury Edition; Garden City, New York: Doubleday, Page and Company, 1924.

Notes on Life and Letters. Canterbury Edition; Garden City, New York: Doubleday, Page and Company, 1924.

An Outcast of the Islands. Limited Edition; London: William Heinemann, Ltd., 1921.
Canterbury Edition; Garden City, New York: Doubleday, Page and Company, 1924.

A Personal Record. Canterbury Edition; Garden City, New York: Doubleday, Page and Company, 1924.

The Rescue: A Romance of the Shallows. Canterbury Edition; Garden City, New York: Doubleday, Page and Company, 1924.

Memorial Edition; Garden City, New York: Doubleday, Page and Company, 1925.

The Secret Agent: A Simple Tale. Canterbury Edition; Garden City, New York: Doubleday, Page and Company, 1924.

A Set of Six. Canterbury Edition; Garden City, New York: Doubleday, Page and Company, 1924.

The Shadow Line: A Confession. Canterbury Edition; Garden City, New York: Doubleday, Page and Company, 1924.

The Sisters. New York: Crosby Gaige, 1928.

Tales of Hearsay. Concord Edition; Garden City, New York: Doubleday, Page and Company, 1926.

Tales of Unrest. Limited Edition; London: William Heinemann, Ltd., 1921.

Canterbury Edition; Garden City, New York: Doubleday, Page and Company, 1924.

'Twixt Land and Sea. Canterbury Edition; Garden City, New York: Doubleday, Page and Company, 1924.

Typhoon: and Other Stories. Canterbury Edition; Garden City, New York: Doubleday, Page and Company, 1924.

Under Western Eyes: A Novel. Canterbury Edition; Garden City, New York: Doubleday, Page and Company, 1924.

Victory. Canterbury Edition; Garden City, New York: Doubleday, Page and Company, 1924.

Within the Tides: Tales. Canterbury Edition; Garden City, New York: Doubleday, Page and Company, 1924.

Youth and Gaspar Ruiz. London and Toronto: J. M. Dent and Sons, Ltd. [1920].

Youth: A Narrative and Two Other Stories. Limited Edition, London: William Heinemann, Ltd., 1921.

Youth: and Two Other Stories. Canterbury Edition; Garden City, New York: Doubleday, Page and Company, 1924.

II. BIOGRAPHY

A. Unpublished Letters and Documents

Letters from Joseph Conrad to
Miss M. Harriet Mary Capes. Keating Collection, Yale University Library.
Ernest Dawson. Keating Collection, Yale University Library.
Perceval Gibbon. Barnet J. Beyer Collection.
Mme. Marguerite Poradowska. Keating Collection, Yale University Library.
T. Fisher Unwin.
Barnet J. Beyer Collection.
Brick Row Book Shop.
Keating Collection, Yale University Library.
Unidentified Correspondents. Keating Collection, Yale University Library.

Curle, Richard, *Joseph Conrad: The History of His Books* MS. Barnet J. Beyer Collection.

B. Published Letters, Biography, and Reminiscence

Adams, Elbridge L., *Joseph Conrad: The Man*, and Zelie, John Sheridan, *A Burial in Kent*. New York: W. E. Rudge, 1925.

Anonymous, *Joseph Conrad: A Sketch with a Bibliography*. Garden City, New York: Doubleday, Page and Company [1924].

Beer, Thomas, *Stephen Crane: A Study in American Letters, with an Introduction by Joseph Conrad*. The Star Series; Garden City, New York: Garden City Publishing Company, Inc., 1927.

Bennett, Arnold, *Journal*. Garden City, New York: The Garden City Publishing Company, Inc., n.d.

Letters to the Colvins. Sale catalogue. New York: The Anderson Galleries, 1928.

Conrad, Jessie, *Joseph Conrad as I Knew Him*. Garden City, New York: Doubleday, Page and Company, 1926.

Joseph Conrad and His Circle. New York: E. P. Dutton and Co. [1935].
"Conrad's Skill as an Artist," *Saturday Review of Literature*, II (1925–26), 700–701.
Personal Recollections of Joseph Conrad. London: Privately Printed, 1924.

Joseph Conrad: A Record. A scrapbook. Keating Collection, Yale University Library.

Curle, Richard, "The History of Mr. Conrad's Books," London *Times Literary Supplement*, no. 1,128 (August 30, 1923), 570.
Joseph Conrad: The History of His Books. London: J. M. Dent and Sons, Ltd., n.d.
"Conrad in the East," *Yale Review*, New Series, XII, Part II (1923), 497–508.
Conrad to a Friend. Garden City, New York: Doubleday, Doran and Company, Inc., 1928.
The Last Twelve Years of Joseph Conrad. Garden City, New York: Doubleday, Doran and Company, Inc., 1928.

Douglas, Norman, *Looking Back: An Autobiographical Excursion.* New York: Harcourt, Brace and Company, 1933.

Ford (Hueffer), Ford Madox, *Ancient Lights and Certain New Reflections.* London: Chapman and Hall, Ltd., 1911.
It Was the Nightingale. Philadelphia and London: J. B. Lippincott Company, 1933.
Joseph Conrad: A Personal Remembrance. Boston: Little, Brown, and Company, 1925.
Portraits from Life. Boston and New York: Houghton Mifflin Company, 1937.
Return to Yesterday. London: Victor Gollancz Ltd., 1931.

Garnett, Edward, ed., *Letters from Joseph Conrad: 1895–1924.* Indianapolis: The Bobbs-Merrill Company, 1928.

Gissing, A. and E., edd., *Letters of George Gissing to Members of His Family.* London: Constable and Company, Ltd., 1927.

Graham, R. B. Cunninghame, *Inveni Portam.* Cleveland: The Rowfant Club, 1924.

Huneker, Josephine, ed., *Letters of James Gibbons Huneker.* New York: Charles Scribner's Sons, 1922.

Jean-Aubry, G., *Joseph Conrad in the Congo.* London: "The Bookman's Journal" Office, 1926.

Joseph Conrad: Life and Letters. Garden City, New York: Doubleday, Page and Company, 1927. 2 vols.

Jean-Aubry, G., ed., *Joseph Conrad: Lettres Françaises.* Paris: Librarie Gallimard, Nouvelle Revue Française [1929].

Twenty Letters to Joseph Conrad. London: The First Edition Club, 1926. 8 pamphlets.

Lubbock, Percy, ed., *The Letters of Henry James.* New York: Charles Scribner's Sons, 1920. 2 vols.

Marrot, H. V., *The Life and Letters of John Galsworthy.* New York: Charles Scribner's Sons, 1936.

Morf, Gustav, *The Polish Heritage of Joseph Conrad.* London: Sampson Low, Marston and Company, Ltd., n. d.

Noble, Edward, ed., *Five Letters by Joseph Conrad Written to Edward Noble in 1895.* London: Privately Printed, 1925.

Rothenstein, William, *Men and Memories.* New York: Coward-McCann, Inc., 1931 and 1932. 2 vols.

Saturday Review of Literature, X (1933–34), 55.

A Sketch of Joseph Conrad's Life: Written by Himself in 1900. n. p.: Privately Printed, 1939.

Sinjohn, John [John Galsworthy], *From the Four Winds.* London: T. Fisher Unwin, 1897.

Sutherland, J. G., *At Sea with Joseph Conrad.* Boston and New York: Houghton Mifflin Company, 1922.

Swinnerton, Frank, *Swinnerton: An Autobiography.* Garden City, New York: Doubleday, Doran and Company, Inc., 1936.

Whyte, Frederic, *William Heinemann: A Memoir.* London: Jonathan Cape [1928].

III. BIBLIOGRAPHY

Book Buyer, XVI (1898), 350–352.

Curle, Richard, ed., *Notes by Joseph Conrad: Written in a Set of his First Edition.* London: Privately Printed, 1925.

The Richard Curle Conrad Collection. New York: American Art Association, 1927.

Eno, Sara Wooster, "Joseph Conrad: A Contribution toward a Bibliography," *Bulletin of Bibliography*, IX (1917), 137–139.

The Historic Edward Garnett Conrad-Hudson Collection. New York: American Art Association, 1928.

Gee, John Archer, "The Conrad Memorial Library of Mr. George T. Keating," *Yale University Library Gazette*, XIII (July, 1938), 16–28.

Good Reading About Many Books Mostly by Their Authors. London: T. Fisher Unwin, 1895–1896.

Illustrated London News, CVII (1896), 662.

Keating, George T., ed., *A Conrad Memorial Library.* Garden City, New York: Doubleday, Doran and Company, Inc., 1929.

"A Check List of Additions to *A Conrad Memorial Library*: 1929–1938." Compiled by James T. Babb. *Yale University Library Gazette*, XIII (July, 1938), 30–40.

Millet, Fred B., *Contemporary British Literature: A Critical Survey and 232 Author-bibliographies.* New York: Harcourt, Brace and Company, 1935.

Complete Catalogue of the Library of John Quinn. New York: The Anderson Galleries, 1924. Vol. I.

The Sea: Books and Manuscripts. Philadelphia and New York: The Rosenbach Company, 1938.

Wise, Thomas J., *The Ashley Library.* London: Printed for Private Circulation Only, 1936. Vol. XI.

A Bibliography of the Writings of Joseph Conrad (1895–1921). 2nd ed.; London: Printed for Private Circulation Only, 1921.

A Conrad Library: A Catalogue of Printed Books, Manuscripts and Autograph Letters. London: Printed for Private Circulation Only, 1928.

IV. MATERIAL RELATING TO CONRAD'S SOURCES

Bills of Lading of S. S. *Vidar*
12 August, 1887.
30 September, 1887.
4 December, 1887.
Keating Collection, Yale University Library.

Boldrewood, Rolf, *A Modern Buccaneer.* New York and London: Macmillan and Company, 1894.

Clemens, Florence, "Conrad's Favorite Bedside Book," *South Atlantic Quarterly*, XXXVIII (1939), 305–315.

Ferguson, J. DeLancey, "The Plot of Conrad's *The Duel*," *Modern Language Notes*, L (1935), 385–390.

Gordan, John D., "The Rajah Brooke and Joseph Conrad," *Studies in Philology*, XXXV (October, 1938), 613–634.

Jacob, Gertrude L., *The Raja of Sarawak: An Account of Sir James Brooke, K.C.B., LL.D., Given Chiefly through Letters and Journals.* London: Macmillan and Company, 1876. 2 vols.

Keppel, Captain the Hon. Henry, *The Expedition to Borneo of H. M. S. Dido for the Suppression of Piracy: With Extracts from the Journal of James Brooke, Esq., of Sarawak (Now Agent for the British Government in Borneo).* New York: Harper and Brothers, 1846.

A Visit to the Indian Archipelago in H. M. Ship Maeander, with Portions of the Private Journal of Sir James Brooke, K. C. B. London: Richard Bentley, 1853. 2 vols.

Lubbock, Basil, *Bully Hayes: South Sea Pirate.* Boston: Charles E. Lauriat Company, 1931.

Melville, Herman, *Redburn: His First Voyage.* Pequod Edition; New York: A. and C. Boni, 1924.

Mundy, Captain Rodney, *Narrative of Events in Borneo and Celebes, down to the Occupation of Labuan: From the*

Journals of James Brooke, Esq., Rajah of Sarawak, and Governor of Labuan. Together with a Narrative of the Operations of H. M. S. Iris. London: John Murray, 1848. 2 vols.

Stevenson, R. L., and Osbourne, Lloyd, *The Ebb Tide: A Trio and Quartette.* New York: Charles Scribner's Sons, 1901.

Templer, John C., ed., *The Private Letters of Sir James Brooke, K. C. B., Rajah of Sarawak, Narrating the Events of his Life, from 1838 to the Present Time.* London: Richard Bentley, 1853. 3 vols.

London *Times Literary Supplement*,
no. 1, 129 (September 6, 1923), 588.
no. 1, 134 (October 11, 1923), 670.
no. 1, 258 (February 25, 1926), 142.

Wallace, Alfred Russel, *The Malay Archipelago: The Land of the Orang-Utan and the Bird of Paradise; a Narrative of Travel with Studies of Man and Nature.* London and New York: Macmillan and Company, 1890.

Wood, Miriam Hathaway, "A Source of Conrad's *Suspense*," *Modern Language Notes*, L (1935), 390–394.

V. REVIEWS

Academy,
XLVII (1895), 501–502.
XLIX (1896), 525.
LIII (1898), 1–2 of Fiction Supplement, 417–418.
LVI (1899), 66–67.
LIX (1900), 443.

Academy and Literature, LXIII (1902), 606–607. [By Edward Garnett.]

Army and Navy Gazette, February 19, 1898.

Athenaeum,
no. 3,526 (May 25, 1895), 671.
no. 3,586 (July 18, 1896), 91.
no. 3,679 (April 30, 1898), 564.

no. 3,810 (November 3, 1900), 576.
no. 3,921 (December 20, 1902), 824.

Birmingham Gazette, December 27, 1897.

Book Buyer,
XII (1895), 353.
XIII (1896), 537–538.
XVI (1898), 350–352. Signed by T. R. Sullivan.
XXII (1901), 63.

Bookman,
II (1895), 39–41. Signed by James MacArthur.
IV (1896), 166.
VIII (1898), 91.
XIII (1901), 187.
XVIII (1903), 311.
XXXIX (1914), 563–565.

Books and News Gazette, December 11, 1897.

Bradford Observer, January 3, 1898.

Chautauquan, XXVII (1898), 428.

Christian World, January 27, 1898.

Citizen, May 2, 1896.

Country Life, January 1, 1898.

Court [?] *Journal*, December 11, 1897.

Critic,
New Series, XXIII (1895), 349, 481. Both signed by Arthur Waugh.
New Series, XXV (1896), 335. Signed by Macmillan and Company.
New Series, XXIX (1898), 328.
XXXVIII (1901), 437–438. Signed by J. B. P.

Current Literature, XXX (1901), 222.

Daily Chronicle,
May 16, 1896.
December 22, 1897.

Daily News, January 7, 1898.

Daily Telegraph,
May 15, 1896.
December 8, 1897.

Glasgow Evening News,
December 16, 1897.
January 13, 1898.

Glasgow Herald, December 9, 1897.

Glasgow Record, May 2, 1896.

Guardian, June 10, 1896.

Illustrated London News,
CVIII (1896), 418. Signed by James Payn.
CXII (January 8, 1898), 50.
CXII (February 5, 1898), 172. Signed by James Payn.

Irish Independent, December 18, 1897.

Literary News,
New Series, XVI (1895), 268–269. Signed by James MacArthur.
New Series, XVII (1896), 307.
New Series, XIX (1898), 152.
New Series, XXIV (1903), 106–107.

Literary World, January 2 [?], 1898. [English newspaper.]

Literary World [American Magazine],
XXVI (1895), 155.
XXIX (1898), 187, 204.

Literature,
(April 6 [March 26], 1898), 354.
(May 11 [April 30], 1898), 507–508.

Liverpool Daily Courier, December 30, 1897.

London Mercury, XXII (1930), 40–43, 261–263, 350.

Manchester Courier, December 22, 1897.

Mercure de France,
Série Moderne, XXXI (1899), 265–266. Signed by Henri-D. Davray.

Série Moderne, XXXVIII (1901), 262–263. Signed by Henri-D. Davray.
Série Moderne, XLV (1903), 830–831. Signed by Henri-D. Davray.

Morning Leader [date unknown].

Nation,
LXI (1895), 278.
LXIV (1897), 287.
LXVII (1898), 54.
LXXVI (1903), 478.

National Observer,
XIV (1895), 513–514.
XV (1896), 680.

News Agent, December 11, 1897.

New York Tribune,
April 3, 1898.
November 3, 1900.

Outlook, LXVI, Part II (1900), 711.

Pall Mall Magazine, XIV (1898), 425. Signed by A. T. Quiller-Couch.

Pearson's Weekly, January 15, 1898.

Public Opinion, XXIV (1898), 665–666.

Reader, May, 1903 [quoted in *Saturday Review of Literature*, IV (1927–28), 519].

Revue Politique et Littéraire (Revue Bleue), LVIII (1920), 599–603. Signed by André Bellessort.

Saturday Review,
LXXIX (1895), 797.
LXXXI (1896), 509–510. [By H. G. Wells.]
LXXXV (1898), 145–146, 211 [by Harold Frederic].

Sketch, XI (1895), 314.

Speaker,
XI (1895), 722–723.
XIII (1896), 376.
XVII (1898), 83–84.

New Series, III (1900), 215–216. Signed L. R. F. O.
New Series, VII (1903), 442. Signed by John Masefield.

Spectator,
LXXV (1895), 530.
LXXVI (1896), 778.
LXXIX (1897), 940.
LXXXI (1898), 219.
LXXXV (1900), 753.
LXXXIX (1902), 827–828. Signed by Hugh Clifford.

Standard, December 24, 1897.

Star, December 16, 1897.

Sunday Times, December 19, 1897.

London *Times Literary Supplement*, no. 48 (December 12, 1902), 372.

Weekly Sun [quoted in an advertising pamphlet for *The Rover* entitled *Joseph Conrad* (London: T. Fisher Unwin Ltd., n.d.), pp. 4–8]. Signed by T. P. O'Connor.

World,
no. 1,089 (May 15, 1895), 31.
no. 1,135 (April 1, 1896), 31.
no. 1,245 (May 11, 1898), 33–34.

VI. CRITICAL STUDIES

Anonymous, "Literary Miscellany," *Literary News*, XXIII (1902), 156.

Bancroft, W. M., *Joseph Conrad: His Philosophy of Life*. Boston: The Stratford Company, 1933.

Beach, Joseph Warren, *The Twentieth Century Novel: Studies in Technique*. New York and London: D. Appleton-Century Company, 1932.

Bennewitz, Hildegard, *Die Charaktere in den Romanen Joseph Conrads*. Greifswald: Hans Dallmeyer, 1933.

Burkhardt, Johanna, *Das Erlebnis der Wirklichkeit und seine Kunstlerische Gestaltung in Joseph Conrads Werk*. Marburg: H. Bauer, 1935.

Clifford, Hugh, "The Genius of Mr. Joseph Conrad," *North American Review*, CLXXVIII, Part II (1904), 842–852.
"A Sketch of Joseph Conrad," *Harper's Weekly*, XLIX, Part I (1905), 59.

Conrad, Jessie, *Did Joseph Conrad Return as a Spirit?* Webster Groves, Missouri: International Mark Twain Society, 1932.

Crankshaw, Edward, *Joseph Conrad: Some Aspects of the Art of the Novel.* London: John Lane, 1936.

Cross, Wilbur Lucius, *Four Contemporary Novelists.* New York: The Macmillan Company, 1934.
"The Illusions of Joseph Conrad," *Yale Review*, New Series, XVII (1928), 464–482.

Curle, Richard, *Joseph Conrad: A Study.* Garden City, New York: Doubleday, Page and Company, 1914.
"Joseph Conrad: Ten Years Later," *Virginia Quarterly Review*, X (1934), 420–435.

David, Maurice, *Joseph Conrad: L'Homme et l'Oeuvre.* Paris: Nouvelle Revue Critique, n.d.

Davray, Henri-D., "Lettres anglaises," *Mercure de France*, Série Moderne, XXXIX, Part III (1901), 249.
"Lettres anglaises," *Mercure de France*, Série Moderne, XLIII, Part III (1902), 542.

Follett, Wilson, *Joseph Conrad: A Short Study of His Intellectual and Emotional Attitude toward His Work and of the Chief Characteristics of His Novels.* Garden City, New York: Doubleday, Page and Company, 1915.

Follett, Wilson and Helen T., "Contemporary Novelists: Joseph Conrad," *Atlantic Monthly*, CXIX (1917), 233–243.

Ford (Hueffer), Ford Madox, "Joseph Conrad," *English Review*, X (1911), 68–83.
"On Conrad's Vocabulary," *Bookman*, LXVII, Part II (1928), 405–408.

Forster, E. M., *Abinger Harvest.* New York: Harcourt, Brace and Company, 1936.

Freeman, John, *The Moderns: Essays in Literary Criticism.* New York: Thomas Y. Crowell Company, 1917.

Galsworthy, John, *Castles in Spain and Other Screeds.* New York: Charles Scribner's Sons, 1927.

"Joseph Conrad: A Disquisition," *Living Age*, Seventh Series, XXXIX (1908), 416–420.

Two Essays on Conrad. Freelands: Privately Printed, 1930.

Garnett, Edward, *Friday Nights: Literary Criticisms and Appreciations, First Series.* The Travellers' Library; London: Jonathan Cape, 1929.

"Introductory Essay" in *Conrad's Prefaces to His Works.* London: J. M. Dent and Sons, Ltd., 1937.

"Joseph Conrad," *Century Magazine*, CXV (1928), 385–395, 593–600.

Gausseron, B.-H., "Le Mouvement Littéraire en Angleterre: Les Prosateurs," *Revue Encyclopédique* (February 13, 1897), 126.

Hicks, Granville, "Conrad after Five Years," *New Republic*, LXI (1930), 192–194.

"Homage à Joseph Conrad," *Nouvelle Revue Française*, Nouvelle Série, CXXXV (1924), 649–806.

Huneker, James, "The Genius of Joseph Conrad," *North American Review*, CC, Part I (1914), 270–279.

Ivory Apes and Peacocks. New York: Charles Scribner's Sons, 1915.

Huxley, Aldous, ed., *The Letters of D. H. Lawrence.* New York: The Viking Press, 1932.

Jackson, Holbrook, *The Eighteen Nineties: A Review of Art and Ideas at the Close of the Nineteenth Century.* New York: Alfred A. Knopf, 1923.

James, Henry, *Notes on Novelists: With Some Other Notes.* New York: Charles Scribner's Sons, 1914.

Leslie, Shane, *The Passing Chapter.* New York: Charles Scribner's Sons, 1934.

Lillard, R. G., "Irony in Hardy and Conrad," *PMLA*, L (1935), 316–322.

Lovett, Robert Morss, "The Realm of Conrad," *Asia*, XXIII (1923), 325–327, 377–378.

Lucas, Edward Verrall, *Reading, Writing, and Remembering: A Literary Record.* London: Methuen and Company, Ltd., 1932.

Lynd, Robert, *Books and Authors.* London: Richard Cobden-Sanderson [1922].

Mandl, Elly Veto, *Die Frau bei Joseph Conrad.* Budapest: Drückerei der Pester Lloyd-Gesellschaft, 1934.

Mann, Thomas, *Past Masters and Other Papers.* New York: Alfred A. Knopf [1933].

Maurois, André, *Prophets and Poets.* New York and London: Harper and Brothers, 1935.

McFee, William, "Conrad After Fourteen Years," *Yale University Library Gazette*, XIII (July, 1938), 3–15.

"Rolling Home," *Saturday Review of Literature*, I (1924–25), 89–90.

"The Sea — and Conrad" *Bookman*, LIII (1921), 102–108.

Swallowing the Anchor: Being a Revised and Enlarged Collection of Notes Made by an Engineer in the Merchant Service Who Secured Leave of Absence from his Ship to Investigate and Report upon the Alleged Superiority of Life Ashore. Garden City, New York: Doubleday, Page and Company, 1925.

Mégroz, R. L., *Joseph Conrad's Mind and Method.* London: Faber and Faber Limited [1931].

A Talk with Joseph Conrad: And a Criticism of His Mind and Method. London: Elkins Mathews, Ltd., 1926.

Mencken, H. L., *A Book of Prefaces.* The Star Series; Garden City, New York: Garden City Publishing Company, Inc., 1927.

Mille, Pierre, "Why Conrad Didn't Write French," *Living Age*, Eighth Series, CCCXXIV (1925), 622–623.

Moffat, Donald, *The Prejudices of Mr. Pennyfeather*. Boston: Little, Brown and Company, 1938.

Moore, Edward, "A Note on Mr. Conrad," *New Statesman*, XIII (1919), 590–592.

Morf, Gustav, "Conrad and Cowardice," *Living Age*, Eighth Series, CCCXL (1931), 571–576.

Morley, Christopher, "Conrad and Stevenson," *Catholic World*, CXXXV (1932), 472–473.

"A Note on Conrad," *Saturday Review of Literature*, IV (1927–28), 519.

Shandygaff: A Number of Most Agreeable Inquirendoes upon Life and Letters, Interspersed with Short Stories and Skitts, the Whole Most Diverting to the Reader; Accompanied also by some Notes for Teachers Whereby the Booke may be Made Usefull in Class-room or for Private Improvement. Garden City, New York: Doubleday, Page and Company, 1926.

Nathan, G. J., in "Why are Manuscripts Rejected?" *Bookman*, XLIII (1916), 281.

O'Flaherty, Liam, *Joseph Conrad: An Appreciation*. London: E. Lahr [1930].

Phelps, William Lyon, "The Advance of the English Novel: Part VIII," *Bookman*, XLIII (1916), 297–304.

Robertson, J. M., "The Novels of Joseph Conrad," *North American Review*, CCVIII (1918), 439–453.

Shannon, Homer S., "Joseph Conrad and Ford Madox Ford," *Bookman*, LXVIII, Part I (1928), 216–217.

Smet, Joseph de, "Joseph Conrad," *Mercure de France*, Série Moderne, XCVII (1912), 51–75.

Stauffer, Ruth, *Joseph Conrad: His Romantic Realism*. Boston: The Four Seas Company, 1922.

Swinnerton, Frank, *The Georgian Scene: A Literary Panorama*. New York: Farrar and Rinehart [1934].

Symons, Arthur, "Conrad," *Forum*, LIII, Part II (1915), 579–593.

Notes on Joseph Conrad: With some Unpublished Letters. London: Myers and Company, 1925.

Tomlinson, H. M., "Joseph Conrad," *Saturday Review of Literature*, IV (1927–28), 191–192.

Voisins, Gilbert de, "Joseph Conrad," *Revue de Paris* (March 1, 1918), 5–16.

Vorse, M. H., "A Writer Who Knows the Sea," *Critic*, XLIII (1903), 280.

Walpole, Hugh, *Joseph Conrad.* London: Nisbet and Company, Ltd. [1916].

Waugh, Arthur, *Tradition and Change: Studies in Contemporary Literature.* London: Chapman and Hall, Ltd., 1919.

Wells, H. G., *Experiment in Autobiography: Discoveries and Conclusions of a Very Ordinary Brain (Since 1866).* New York: The Macmillan Company, 1934.

Whiting, G. W., "Conrad's Revisions of Six of His Short Stories," *PMLA*, XLVIII (1933), 552–557.

"Conrad's Revision of 'The Lighthouse' in *Nostromo*," *PMLA*, LII (1937), 1183–1190.

Woolf, Leonard, "The World of Books: Joseph Conrad," *Nation and Athenaeum*, XXXV (1924), 595.

Woolf, Virginia, *The Common Reader.* New Edition; London: The Hogarth Press, 1929.

Mr. Bennet and Mrs. Brown. 2nd impression; London: The Hogarth Press, 1928.

"Mr. Conrad: A Conversation," *Nation and Athenaeum*, XXXIII (1923), 681–682.

NOTES

NOTES

Unless otherwise designated, all references to Conrad's works are to the Canterbury Edition.

INTRODUCTION

1. *Almayer's Folly: A Story of an Eastern River* (Memorial Edition; Garden City, New York: Doubleday, Page and Company, 1925), p. vii.
2. G. Jean-Aubry, *Joseph Conrad: Life and Letters* (Garden City, New York: Doubleday, Page and Company, 1927), I, 196.
3. *The Rescue: A Romance of the Shallows*, p. xi.
4. *Nostromo: A Tale of the Seaboard*, p. vii.

CHAPTER I

1. *Mr. Bennett and Mrs. Brown* (2nd impression; London: The Hogarth Press, 1928), p. 11.
2. *Personal Record*, p. v.
3. *Ibid.*, p. 119. His name seems to have been Komorowski (Jessie Conrad, *Joseph Conrad and His Circle* [New York: E. P. Dutton and Company [1935], p. 46]).
4. *Life and Letters*, I, 4, n. 2, 291, II, 64.
5. Gustav Morf, *The Polish Heritage of Joseph Conrad* (London: Sampson Low, Marston and Co., Ltd., n.d.), pp. 1–22. Also *Life and Letters*, I, 290–292, and *Personal Record*, pp. 31–34, 46–64.
6. *Polish Heritage*, p. 4, n. This statement was based on Tadeusz Bobrowski's *Memoirs* and hence is probably more accurate than Conrad's belief that Stefan Bobrowski "died assassinated soon after the Polish outbreak of 1863" (*Life and Letters*, I, 291).
7. *Life and Letters*, I, 6, 8. If Robert was fifty when he died, he was born in 1813. Apollo was born in 1820 (*ibid.*, I, 2, n. 1).
8. *Ibid.*, II, 175, n. 2. *Polish Heritage* (p. 9) quotes T. Bobrowski's *Memoirs* which say that Hilary was "arrested before the rising."
9. *Life and Letters*, I, 6–7.
10. *Ibid.*, I, 12, 20.
11. *Notes on Life and Letters*, p. 169, and *Life and Letters*, I, 23.
12. *Life and Letters*, I, 21–22, and *Personal Record*, pp. 22–23. See also Tadeusz Bobrowski's first letter to Conrad in *Polish Heritage*, pp. 50–52.
13. *Personal Record*, pp. 41–42. Conrad fixed the time as the year he traveled abroad with his tutor, Mr. Pulman. Jean-Aubry gave 1872 and said Conrad had been thinking of the sea "for two or three years" (*Life and Letters*, I, 23), but he advanced no evidence.

14. Quoted in *Polish Heritage*, pp. 7–9. The probability of this being Bobrowski's attitude was first suggested by Jean-Aubry in *Life and Letters*, I, 23.

15. *Personal Record*, p. 42.

16. *Loc. cit.*

17. *Ibid.*, pp. 35, 110.

18. *Ibid.*, p. 121.

19. *Ibid.*, p. 35.

20. *Ibid.*, p. 36.

21. *Ibid.*, pp. 70–71.

22. *Notes on Life and Letters*, p. 168.

23. *Personal Record*, p. 72.

24. It has also been suggested that he was influenced by the stories of Louis-Ambroise Garneray (*Polish Heritage*, p. 60). Morf gave no reference for his statement, and no direct evidence for the belief seems to exist.

25. *Notes on Life and Letters*, p. 53.

26. Edward Garnett, ed., *Letters from Joseph Conrad: 1895–1924* (Indianapolis: The Bobbs-Merrill Company, 1928), pp. 185–186.

27. *Notes on Life and Letters*, p. 56.

28. *Chance: A Tale in Two Parts*, p. 288.

In Lord Jim's case, too, "after a course of light holiday literature his vocation for the sea had declared itself" (*Lord Jim: A Romance*, p. 5).

29. *Last Essays* (London and Toronto: J. M. Dent and Sons Ltd., 1926), p. 17.

30. *Ibid.*, p. 20.

31. *Ibid.*, p. 23.

Mrs. Conrad informed the author in September, 1936, that Barth's *Travels* remained one of Conrad's favorite books all his life.

32. *Ibid.*, p. 22.

33. *Personal Record*, p. 13. Conrad said he was "nine years old or thereabouts"; he was actually eleven. *A Personal Record* was completed by June, 1909 (Thomas J. Wise, *A Bibliography of the Writings of Joseph Conrad (1895–1921)* [2nd ed.; London: Printed for Private Circulation Only, 1921], p. 48). Conrad first repeated the incident in "Heart of Darkness" (*Youth*, p. 52), completed in 1899 (*Life and Letters*, I, 265), in which he said he used to finger the map for other such unexplored spots, including the North Pole – about which his earliest geographical reading was done. He later used the same incident in "Geography and Some Explorers" (*Last Essays*, p. 24).

34. *Life and Letters*, I, 24–26.

35. *Polish Heritage*, pp. 71–78.

36. *Life and Letters*, I, 25. "The year before in the late summer of his last school holiday" would have been 1873, for he left Poland for France in October, 1874 (*ibid.*, I, 27).

37. *Under Western Eyes: A Novel*, pp. 65, 71, 83, 89.
38. *Ibid.*, p. 84.
39. *Ibid.*, pp. 70–71.
40. *Ibid.*, p. 77.
41. *Personal Record*, p. 121.
42. *Ibid.*, p. 42.
43. *Life and Letters*, I, 23–24.
44. *Personal Record*, pp. 40–44.
45. *Life and Letters*, I, 27.
46. *Mirror of the Sea*, p. 149.
47. *Personal Record*, pp. 122–138.
48. *Life and Letters*, I, 31–32.
49. *Mirror of the Sea*, p. 153.
50. *Life and Letters*, I, 34.
51. *Ibid.*, I, 40.
52. *Mirror of the Sea*, p. 156.
53. *Personal Record*, p. 126.
54. *Life and Letters*, I, 35, 37.
55. *Mirror of the Sea*, pp. 157–183.
56. Her identity has never been established. Conrad wrote about these Marseilles adventures in "The 'Tremolino'" in *The Mirror of the Sea* and at greater length in *The Arrow of Gold*.
57. *Life and Letters*, I, 43–47. The affair, according to Jean-Aubry, is hard to date but probably took place in the latter part of 1877 and the early part of 1878.

The *New York Times* for Sunday, August 15, 1937, mentioned the discovery of a letter from Tadeusz Bobrowski to Stefan Buszczynski in which the uncle told of an attempt by Conrad to kill himself at Marseilles. "Prompted by the hunger of adventure and youthful imprudence," said the *New York Times*, "he allowed himself to be mixed up in a smuggling affair. When he also lost heavily at Monte Carlo Casino, he could see no other issue than to take his life." Bobrowski hurried to Marseilles on February 27, 1878. Conrad recovered and soon after went to England.

Clearly this is another version of the concluding events in Conrad's life at Marseilles. Conrad himself vouched for the truth of the story of his love for Doña Rita (*Life and Letters*, II, 224, 229). Perhaps the uncle wished to conceal this part of the story and hence substituted suicide for a duel. Perhaps the letter was misinterpreted by the *Kurier Warszawski* from which the *New York Times*, without reprinting the letter, took its information.

58. *Life and Letters*, I, 48.
59. *Ibid.*, I, 47.
60. *Personal Record*, p. 119. Conrad remembered making this statement at his examination for a master's certificate in 1886.

61. *Notes on Life and Letters*, p. 155. Also *ibid.*, p. 150, and *Life and Letters*, I, 50.

62. *Life and Letters*, I, 50–52.

63. *Notes on Life and Letters*, p. 151.

64. *Life and Letters*, I, 54, 56, 87.

65. *Ibid.*, I, 83.

66. *Ibid.*, I, 57, 74, 88. For accounts of these examinations see *A Personal Record*, pp. 112–120.

67. *Personal Record*, p. 120.

68. *Ibid.*, pp. 68, 70. Also G. Jean-Aubry, ed., *Joseph Conrad: Lettres Françaises* (Paris: Librairie Gallimard, Nouvelle Revue Française [1929]), p. 57.

69. *A Sketch of Joseph Conrad's Life: Written by Himself in 1900* (n.p.: Privately Printed, 1939), p. 1. Now and hereafter the pagination refers to the facsimile of the manuscript. Excerpts from the sketch were first published in *The Historic Edward Garnett Conrad-Hudson Collection* (New York: American Art Association, Inc., 1928), p. 12.

70. *Polish Heritage*, pp. 191–192, 220.

71. *Life and Letters*, II, 235.

72. *Ibid.*, I, 291, 292.

73. *Polish Heritage*, p. 6.

74. *Personal Record*, pp. 72–73. Also Richard Curle, *The Last Twelve Years of Joseph Conrad* (Garden City, New York: Doubleday, Doran and Company, Inc., 1928), p. 103.

75. R. L. Mégroz, *Joseph Conrad's Mind and Method* (London: Faber and Faber Limited, 1931), p. 28. Mégroz took the conversation down in shorthand (*ibid.*, p. 7).

76. *Life and Letters*, I, 27, n. 1.

77. *Lettres Françaises*, p. 60. Also *Mirror of the Sea*, pp. 155–156.

78. *Personal Record*, p. 68.

79. *Life and Letters*, I, 93–95, 98.

Jean-Aubry was strangely inconsistent on this subject. He stated: "It is not likely that he took more notes of what he heard and saw during this period than he did at any other." Then two sentences later he declared: "He could not resist those secret stirrings toward authorship. . . . It may be said that, on board the *Vidar*, Captain Joseph Conrad Korzeniowski served in his spare moments his apprenticeship as a writer" (*ibid.*, I, 98).

80. *Last Essays*, p. 136. Though there is no proof of a Borneo diary, it could well have existed and have been destroyed, for Mrs. Conrad twice saved the Congo diary from the waste-paper basket (*ibid.*, p. 235). Conrad also kept the log-book of the *Torrens* (*Personal Record*, p. 17) in the early 1890's (*Life and Letters*, I, 149–150). The Congo diary was reprinted in *Last Essays*, pp. 231–253.

81. *Life and Letters*, I, 64–65, 89.

82. See the recollections of Galsworthy (*Life and Letters*, I, 153),

Garnett (*Letters from Joseph Conrad*, p. 5), and Ford (*Joseph Conrad: A Personal Remembrance* [Boston: Little, Brown, and Company, 1924], pp. 25, 28–29).

83. *Mirror of the Sea*, p. 122.

84. For instance *ibid.*, pp. 30, 38, 90, 153.

85. *Personal Record*, p. 68. Also *ibid.*, pp. 9–10, 91.

86. *Life and Letters*, I, 103–116. Conrad was not on the *Otago* for two years and a quarter, as he said in *The Mirror of the Sea* (p. 19).

87. *Personal Record*, pp. xvi–xvii.

88. Page 183.

89. *Life and Letters*, I, 117–147.

90. Letter to Mme. Poradowska dated February 17, 1891 (Yale), and *Life and Letters*, I, 144.

91. (Yale).

92. Apparently he intended to begin work in July and was prevented by "une attaque de malaria sous forme de dyspepsie. . . . Je suis comme abasourdi par ce nouveau desastre – car c'en est un pour moi dans les circonstances" (letter to Mme. Poradowska dated July 30, 1891 [Yale]). In quotations from the Yale French letters the errors in language are Conrad's.

93. (Yale).

94. "Le soir – de retour chez moi – je me sens si paresseux que je regarde les plumes avec horreur, et quand a l'encrier je l'ai banni de ma chambre depuis longtemps" (letter to Mme. Poradowska dated August 26, 1891 [Yale]).

95. "Tous mes projets ont manqué et je crois qu'il me faudra rester a Londres pour de bon" (letter to Mme. Poradowska dated July 22, 1891 [Yale]).

96. Conrad's dislike of the job is plain in the letter to Mme. Poradowska dated August 26, 1891 (Yale): "Après tout je ne suis pas aussi heureux de travailler comme Vous semblez le penser. Il n'y a rien de bien rejouissant a faire un travail qui déplaît."

97. *Life and Letters*, I, 149–153. In September, 1891, he had hopeful plans of getting a berth for Australia (letter to Mme. Poradowska dated September 30, 1891 [Yale]). He was offered the *Torrens* position, November 13, and accepted, November 14 (letter to Mme. Poradowska dated November 14, 1891 [Yale]). He signed on, November 20, and sailed, November 25 (*Life and Letters*, I, 149). When Conrad said he severed his connection with the *Torrens* on October 15, 1893 (*Last Essays*, p. 40), he probably referred to being a nominal member of the crew (*Life and Letters*, I, 153–154).

98. *Personal Record*, pp. 15–18.

99. *Life and Letters*, II, 235.

100. *Last Essays*, p. 40.

101. "Je suis en ce moment sans occupation et depuis mon retour de

Pologne j'ai passé les journées dans une désésperante oisivété" (letter to Mme. Poradowska dated November 5, 1893 [Yale]). Conrad had returned "to London early in October" (*Life and Letters*, I, 153).

102. *Life and Letters*, I, 154–155.

103. Letter to Mme. Poradowska dated January 20, 1894 (Yale).

104. Letter to Mme. Poradowska dated December 18, 1893 (Yale).

105. Letters to Mme. Poradowska dated March 2, 1894, and December 20, 1893 (Yale).

106. *The Richard Curle Conrad Collection* (New York: American Art Association, Inc., 1927), item 19.

107. See pp. 181–182, above.

108. *Life and Letters*, I, 158–159, and *Personal Record*, pp. 7–8.

109. (Yale).

110. Letter to Mme. Poradowska written from La Roserai, Champel, Geneva, dated "Samedi" and assigned by Dr. Gee to Saturday, August 18, 1894 (Yale).

The visit to Champel in 1894 escaped the attention of Jean-Aubry, who mentioned the treatments of 1891 and 1895 (*Life and Letters*, I, 145, 162–163).

111. Still searching for "une occupation convenable," he made arrangements for the manuscript to be held at Barr, Moering and Company should he have left London when it was returned (letter to Mme. Poradowska dated September 8, 1894 [Yale]).

112. See p. 185, above.

113. Letter to Mme Poradowska (Yale).

114. Letter to Mme. Poradowska dated October 23, 1894 (Yale).

115. Letter to Mme. Poradowska dated, "Mercredi, 94," and assigned by Dr. Gee to Wednesday, November 14 or 21, 1894 (Yale).

116. *Outcast of the Islands*, p. vii.

117. *Letters from Joseph Conrad*, pp. 2–5.

118. *Outcast*, p. viii. It is to be noticed that Conrad left another account of the incident contradicting the above version: "Before beginning this book I hesitated whether I would go on writing or not. Edward Garnett's remark 'You have the temperament, you have the style – why not write?' tipped the scale" (*Richard Curle Conrad Collection*, item 22).

119. Letter to Mme. Poradowska dated "Lundi matin" and assigned by Dr. Gee to Monday, October 29 or November 5, 1894 (Yale).

120. Letter to Mme. Poradowska dated "Samedi" and assigned by Dr. Gee to Saturday, February 23, 1895 (Yale).

121. *Bibliography*, p. 9.

122. *Letters from Joseph Conrad*, pp. 16–17. Garnett testified to Conrad's anxiety to get to sea during the years 1894–1896 (George T. Keating, ed., *A Conrad Memorial Library* [Garden City, New York: Doubleday, Doran and Company, Inc., 1929], p. 50).

123. *Joseph Conrad and His Circle*, pp. 18–19.

124. Jessie Conrad, *Joseph Conrad as I Knew Him* (Garden City, New York: Doubleday, Page and Company, 1926), pp. 25, 103.
125. See pp. 199–200, above.
126. *Life and Letters*, I, 185.
127. *Personal Record*, pp. 18–19.
128. *Life and Letters*, I, 191.
129. *Ibid.*, I, 223. Also *Letters from Joseph Conrad*, p. 127.
130. *Joseph Conrad as I Knew Him*, p. 124.
131. *Life and Letters*, I, 227.
132. *Ibid.*, I, 241.
133. See pp. 222–225, above.
134. *Letters from Joseph Conrad*, pp. 142–143.
135. *Life and Letters*, I, 251, 253.
136. *Ibid.*, I, 167.
137. *Joseph Conrad and His Circle*, p. 59.
138. *Life and Letters*, I, 251.
139. *Ibid.*, I, 266.
140. *Joseph Conrad as I Knew Him*, p. 124. "Borys was then nearly old enough to go to school," said Mrs. Conrad. In *Joseph Conrad and His Circle* (p. 104) she said, "It was after our return from our Italian holiday that the small boy embarked seriously on the steep path of learning." The Conrads returned from Capri on May 24, 1905 (*Life and Letters*, II, 2).
141. Mégroz was inclined to underestimate the importance of Conrad's attempts to remain at sea and the accidental elements of his adopting a literary career (*Joseph Conrad's Mind and Method*, pp. 76, 79–80, 90–91).
142. *Life and Letters*, I, 244.
143. *Sketch of Joseph Conrad's Life*, p. 1.
144. *Mirror of the Sea*, p. 148. The incident must have occurred during his French days, for he did not cross the Atlantic in the English days, and the rescue of "the crew of a Danish brig homeward bound from the West Indies" took place "in mid-Atlantic" (*ibid.*, p. 137).
145. Page 136. See also pp. 119–120, 128–136.
146. *Life and Letters*, I, 234.
147. *Ibid.*, I, 91–93. In the autobiographical sketch there are emendations that apparently bear on the accident. Conrad wrote first that before the Congo he had not had "a day *of ill* of indisposition since the age of sixteen," and then altered it to "simple indisposition" (*Sketch of Joseph Conrad's Life*, p. 2).
148. *Mirror of the Sea*, pp. 54–55.
149. *Life and Letters*, I, 93–95. Also *Personal Record*, p. 85.
150. He arrived at Matadi on June 12 and was taken sick about July 8 (*Life and Letters*, I, 127, 131).

151. Letter to Mme. Poradowska written at Kinchassa and dated September 26, 1890 (Yale).

152. Quoted in *London Mercury*, XXII (1930), 41.

153. *Youth*, pp. 150–152, and *Personal Record*, p. 14.

Mrs. Conrad, too, heard "from several of his friends how nearly he had died from dysentery while being carried to the coast when he left the Congo" (*Joseph Conrad and His Circle*, p. 13).

154. *Life and Letters*, I, 144–145. Also letters to Mme. Poradowska dated February 27 and March 12, 1891 (Yale).

155. *Life and Letters*, I, 147–148. See Jean-Aubry's analysis (*ibid.*, I, 141–143).

156. *Last Essays*, p. 36.

157. *Ibid.*, pp. 40–41. Mrs. Conrad said Conrad's ill-health was fundamentally responsible for his not going to sea (*Joseph Conrad and His Circle*, p. 59).

158. Letter to Mme. Poradowska written from Port Adelaide and dated February 3, 1893 (Yale).

159. *Sketch of Joseph Conrad's Life*, p. 2. See also his refusal of a Newcastle ship in 1891 on account of his health (letter to Mme. Poradowska dated March 30, 1891 [Yale]).

160. *Outcast*, p. vii.

161. *Personal Record*, p. 69.

162. *Life and Letters*, I, 185. Also *Joseph Conrad: A Personal Remembrance*, pp. 130–131.

163. *Richard Curle Conrad Collection*, item 26.

164. *The Nigger of the Narcissus: A Tale of the Forecastle*, pp. ix–x.

165. *Personal Record*, p. 18.

CHAPTER II

1. *Nigger*, p. xii. Also Edward Noble, ed., *Five Letters by Joseph Conrad Written to Edward Noble in 1895* (London: Privately Printed, 1925), p. 11.

2. *The Shadow Line: A Confession*, p. viii. He called Scevola, in *The Rover*, "to be frank about it, a pathological case" (*Life and Letters*, II, 326).

3. *Life and Letters*, II, 78.

4. *Nostromo*, p. vii.

5. Page xi.

6. Page vii.

7. *Life and Letters*, II, 116. Writing about his work to Doubleday, Page and Company in 1913, he commented somewhat acrimoniously: "Is it interesting? Well, I have been and am being translated into all the European languages, except Spanish and Italian. They would hardly do that for a bore" (*ibid.*, II, 147).

8. *Rescue*, p. x.

9. *Life and Letters*, II, 68.

10. *Ibid.*, II, 139. Similar statements appear in *Tales of Unrest* (p. ix): "The sustained invention of a really telling lie demands a talent which I do not possess"; and in *The Arrow of Gold: A Story between Two Notes* (p. ix): "In the case of this book I was unable to supplement these deficiencies by the exercise of my inventive faculty. It was never very strong; and on this occasion its use would have seemed exceptionally dishonest."

11. *Set of Six*, pp. ix–x.

12. *Personal Record*, p. xvii.

He communicated the same information to Curle (*Last Twelve Years*, p. 36) and Mégroz (*Joseph Conrad's Mind and Method*, p. 41).

13. *Youth and Gaspar Ruiz* (London and Toronto: J. M. Dent and Sons, Ltd. [1920]), p. 167.

14. Letter to Mme. Poradowska dated "Samedi" and assigned by Dr. Gee to Saturday, August 18, 1894 (Yale).

15. *Personal Record*, p. xvii, and *Nigger*, p. xiv.

16. *Letters from Joseph Conrad*, p. 59.

17. *Life and Letters*, II, 14.

18. *Personal Record*, pp. xv–xvi.

19. *Last Essays*, p. 80. Also *Arrow of Gold*, p. ix.

20. "But if I had not got to know Almayer pretty well it is almost certain there would never have been a line of mine in print" (*Personal Record*, p. 87).

21. *Nigger*, p. xiv.

22. *Personal Record*, pp. 87–89, *Nigger*, pp. 172–173, and *Youth*, pp. 41–42.

23. *Life and Letters*, II, 147.

24. *Shadow Line*, p. ix.

25. See Conrad on the relative importance of subject and treatment (*Letters from Joseph Conrad*, pp. 292–293, and *Life and Letters*, II, 54).

26. "Conrad After Fourteen Years," *Yale University Library Gazette*, XIII (July, 1938), 6.

27. *Life and Letters*, II, 316.

28. *Within the Tides: Tales*, p. viii.

29. Richard Curle, ed., *Conrad to a Friend* (Garden City, New York: Doubleday, Doran and Company, Inc., 1928), p. 153. The suggestion was taken: see the almost verbatim use of this sentence and other parts of the letter in Curle's "History of Mr. Conrad's Books" (London *Times Literary Supplement*, no. 1,128 [August 30, 1923], 570).

30. *The Sea: Books and Manuscripts* (Philadelphia and New York City: The Rosenbach Company, 1938), p. 40.

31. *Conrad to a Friend*, p. 153.

32. *Shadow Line*, p. ix.

33. *Arrow of Gold*, p. viii.

34. *Life and Letters*, II, 213.

35. *Ibid.*, I, 77.

36. *Youth*, p. xi.

37. *Life and Letters*, II, 195.

38. *Ibid.*, II, 20, and *Mirror of the Sea*, p. 143.

39. *Mirror of the Sea*, p. 137. The rescue may well have taken place in 1875 or 1876 when Conrad made his only recorded voyage to the West Indies (*Life and Letters*, I, 33–38). It seems unlikely that on any voyage around the Cape Conrad would have been in mid-Atlantic.

40. *Mirror of the Sea*, p. 146. Almayer, who was Dutch, also used English to speak to the hallucination of Nina, who was half Dutch and half Malay (*Almayer's Folly*, p. 202).

41. *Life and Letters*, I, 47.

42. Conrad showed how complex the chemistry of his subjects could be: "Il Conde (misspelt by-the-by) is an almost verbatim transcript of the tale told me by a very charming old gentleman whom I met in Italy. I don't mean to say it is only that. Anybody can see that it is something more than a verbatim report, but where he left off and where I began must be left to the acute discrimination of the reader who may be interested in the problem. I don't mean to say that the problem is worth the trouble. What I am certain of, however, is that it is not to be solved, for I am not at all clear about it myself by this time" (*Set of Six*, p. vii). Conrad also forgot the exact origins of *The Nigger*.

43. *Personal Record*, pp. xvii–xviii. "Writing about them [his subjects], he is only writing about himself" (*ibid.*, p. xv).

44. *Within the Tides*, p. vii. See also *Last Essays* (p. 211) in which Conrad admitted that "my past had, by the very force of my work, become one of the sources of what I may call, for want of a better word, my inspiration – of the inner force which sets the pen in motion."

45. *Last Essays*, p. 216. The quotations are taken from the preface of *The Shorter Tales of Joseph Conrad*, in which the stories mentioned are included.

46. *Life and Letters*, II, 68.

47. For instance *ibid.*, II, 13, 41, 240, *Set of Six*, p. viii, and *Nostromo*, p. viii.

48. *Typhoon*, p. ix. Cf. *Last Essays*, p. 216.

49. *Personal Record*, p. 87.

50. *Life and Letters*, I, 95.

51. *Ibid.*, I, 93. Jean-Aubry referred to Captain Craig under the disguise of Captain C––, as Conrad did in *A Personal Record*, but a reference in one of Conrad's letters discloses the full name (*ibid.*, II, 103).

52. *Ibid.*, I, 96.

53. *Ibid.*, I, 94.

54. *Almayer's Folly* MS., chap. II, p. 6, and chap. III, p. 1 (Rosenbach), and TS., pp. 27, 41 (Leeds).

55. *Almayer's Folly* MS., chap. III, p. 14 (Rosenbach), and TS., p. 51 (Leeds), and (Canterbury Edition), p. 42.

56. Letter dated May 2, 1894 (Yale).

57. *Life and Letters*, I, 136.

58. "Heart of Darkness" MS., p. 55 numbered in black pencil (Yale).

59. *Shadow Line* MS., p. 145 (Yale). See *Shadow Line*, p. 62. Born was the actual name (holograph letter from Henry Simpson and Sons to Joseph Conrad, dated April 5, 1888 [Yale]; misquoted as Burns in *Life and Letters*, I, 106).

60. *Life and Letters*, I, 96. Jean-Aubry did not make it clear whether Captain Craig was referring to the portrait of Almayer in *A Personal Record* or in *Almayer's Folly* and *An Outcast*. Other Bornean friends of Conrad's also recognized the source of his creations (*ibid.*, II, 103).

61. Pages 75, 76.

62. *Almayer's Folly*, pp. 35, 103, 205. At first the beard was merely "grey" (*Almayer's Folly* MS., chap. XII, p. 31 [Rosenbach]), but the change of color added years to his appearance.

63. *Personal Record*, p. 74, and *Almayer's Folly*, p. 35.

64. *Personal Record*, p. 76, and *Almayer's Folly*, p. 23.

65. Pages 76–77, 84. Almayer was suspicious of the visiting Dutch naval officers (*Almayer's Folly*, pp. 122–126) and even of his friend Dain Maroola (*ibid.*, pp. 14, 73–74). He suspected Willems of trying to supplant him in Lingard's favor (*Outcast*, pp. 62–64).

66. *Personal Record*, p. 76.

67. *Almayer's Folly*, p. 3.

68. *Personal Record*, p. 86.

69. *Ibid.*, pp. 75–76.

70. *Almayer's Folly*, pp. 35, 121.

71. *Personal Record*, pp. 85, 86.

72. *Almayer's Folly*, pp. 122, 203.

73. *Life and Letters*, I, 102, n. 1.

74. *Almayer's Folly*, pp. 4, 36–37.

75. *Personal Record*, p. 88. Also notice Almayer's complaint that even death as a "way of escape from inclement fortune was closed to him" (*ibid.*, p. 78).

76. *Almayer's Folly*, pp. 3, 18.

77. Pages 77, 88.

78. *Almayer's Folly*, pp. 191–192, 196–207.

79. *Personal Record*, p. 85.

80. Page 9.

81. *Almayer's Folly*, p. 206.

82. *Almayer's Folly* MS., chap. I, p. 8 (Rosenbach). See *Almayer's Folly*, p. 7.

83. *Almayer's Folly* MS., chap. III, p. 13, and chap. II, p. 2 (Rosenbach). See *Almayer's Folly*, pp. 41, 22.

84. *Almayer's Folly*, pp. 7, 21–23. In the manuscript (chap. II, p. 2 [Rosenbach]) Conrad gave Mrs. Almayer's age first as fourteen, then as fifteen, once more as fourteen. Finally he removed it altogether from the printed text (Canterbury Edition, p. 21).

85. *Almayer's Folly*, pp. 7, 9, 10, 22, 41. The location was further complicated by the marriage of the Almayers, which did not take place in Samarang (or Sourabaya) as would be expected but in Batavia (*ibid.*, p. 23). In the manuscript (chap. II, p. 4 [Rosenbach]), the marriage was performed in Singapore, but the change to Batavia was made in the typescript (p. 26 [Leeds]), doubtless because Nina, as a child, was sent to Singapore to be educated (*Almayer's Folly*, pp. 26–27).

86. *Personal Record*, p. 88.

87. *Life and Letters*, II, 183.

88. *Ibid.*, I, 97.

89. *Ibid.*, II, 103.

90. *Ibid.*, I, 97.

91. See *Mirror of the Sea*, pp. 162–183, *Arrow of Gold*, p. viii, and *Nostromo*, p. xii.

92. John D. Gordan, "The Rajah Brooke and Joseph Conrad," *Studies in Philology*, XXXV (1938), 619–625.

93. *Life and Letters*, I, 92–93.

94. Page 51.

95. *Almayer's Folly*, p. 6.

96. Conrad had first: " 'Welcome Capitan! Ver' you come vrom– . . . I want ponies' "; he changed it: " 'Welgome Capitan! Ver' you gome vrom? . . . I vant bonies' " (*Almayer's Folly* MS., chap. I, p. 6 [Rosenbach]). In the typescript (p. 5 [Leeds]) he was still breaking Hudig's English. In *Almayer's Folly* (p. 6) *Capitan* was altered to *Gapitan*: the *w* in *welcome* remained inconsistent.

97. Pages 18–19, for instance.

98. *Life and Letters*, I, 94, and *Almayer's Folly*, p. 29.

99. Pages 75 ff.

100. *Life and Letters*, I, 94 ff., and II, 103.

It is to be noted that Lingard referred to a friend of his named Craig (*Outcast*, pp. 189, 190).

101. *Life and Letters*, I, 94. A bill of lading preserved in the Yale University Library shows that the name was also spelled Syed Mohsin Bin S. Al Jaffree. In the records of the Master Attendant at Singapore it was spelled Syed Moshin bin Salley Ali Jeoffree. Conrad mentioned this Arab, though not by name, as being the owner of the ship, flying the British flag, on which he had been before he received his first command (*Shadow Line*, pp. 4–5). The ship was, of course, the *Vidar*, and it is characteristic of Conrad's use of details from his past that, according to

Jean-Aubry, she flew not the British but the Dutch flag (*Life and Letters*, I, 95).

102. *Life and Letters*, I, 98.

103. *Almayer's Folly*, pp. 15, 43–44.

104. Chap. II, p. 8 (Rosenbach).

105. *Almayer's Folly*, pp. 25, 29.

106. Page 109.

107. Page 82. Also *Outcast*, p. x.

108. *Shadow Line*, pp. 4–5. The scene was "an Eastern port." Singapore was the homeport of the *Vidar* (*Life and Letters*, I, 95).

109. Page 110. Also *Life and Letters*, I, 98.

110. Bill of lading dated August 12, 1887 (Yale).

111. Bill of lading dated September 30, 1887 (Yale). The Mahmat of Mahmat Banjer may have been taken from one of the sailors on the *Vidar* (*Life and Letters*, I, 95).

112. *Almayer's Folly*, p. 24, *Outcast*, pp. 50–51, and *Life and Letters*, I, 95.

113. *Personal Record*, p. 75.

114. *Life and Letters*, I, 98. Captain Craig's memory failed him again when he said that Babalatchi lived at Berouw. A bill of lading dated August 12, 1887 (Yale) shows Babalatchie shipping goods from Dongala. It is not unreasonable to suppose that Lakamba lived at Dongala, too, since Mr. Cools stated that no one at Berouw had knowledge of either man.

115. *Almayer's Folly*, pp. 24–25, 38.

116. *Ibid.*, pp. 27, 38, 53.

117. Chap. III, p. 8 (Rosenbach). See *Almayer's Folly*, p. 38.

118. Though Conrad most of the time referred to the character as Dain, Dain is not a name but a title given by Malays to the children of men of pure blood by the daughters of freemen (Rodney Mundy, *Narrative of Events in Borneo and Celebes*, etc. [London: John Murray, 1848], I, 73–74).

119. *Almayer's Folly* MS., chap. IV, p. 19 (Rosenbach), and TS., p. 71 (Leeds).

120. *Almayer's Folly*, p. 130.

121. *Almayer's Folly* MS., chap. XI, pp. 16–17 (Rosenbach), and (Canterbury Edition), p. 174.

122. *Life and Letters*, I, 95. Also *Personal Record*, p. 75. The spelling of Malay place-names varies with each map and commentator.

123. "Conrad in the East," *Yale Review*, New Series, 12, Part II (1923), 500.

124. *Conrad to a Friend*, pp. 113–114. For the paragraph in question see *Youth*, pp. 37–38.

125. *Almayer's Folly*, p. 5. In the manuscript (chap. I, p. 3 [Rosen-

bach]) Borneo was mentioned in the fifth paragraph and then omitted from the text.

126. *Almayer's Folly* MS., chap. II, p. 6, chap. III, p. 1 (Rosenbach), and TS., pp. 27, 41 (Leeds).

127. *Almayer's Folly* MS., chap. III, p. 14 (Rosenbach), and TS., p. 51 (Leeds), and (Canterbury Edition), p. 42.

128. *Almayer's Folly* MS., chap. III, p. 4 (Rosenbach), and TS., p. 44 (Leeds). In *An Outcast* (p. 277) which dealt with Sambir, too, the settlement was inconsistently put some fifty-five miles from the sea.

129. *Personal Record*, p. 74.

130. *Almayer's Folly*, pp. 91, 14.

131. *Ibid*., p. 93.

132. *Almayer's Folly* MS., chap. II, p. 16, and chap. III, p. 15 (Rosenbach).

133. *Almayer's Folly: A Story of An Eastern River* (London: T. Fisher Unwin, 1895), pp. 43, 58, and (Canterbury Edition), p. 30. The second phrase was omitted from the Canterbury Edition (p. 42).

134. *Almayer's Folly*, p. 6. Conrad gave him a wife at this time in *An Outcast* (p. 10).

135. *Almayer's Folly*, pp. 26, 27.

136. Letter to Mme. Poradowska dated "Lundi matin" and assigned by Dr. Gee to Monday, October 29 or November 5, 1894 (Yale).

137. *Almayer's Folly* MS., chap. II, p. 12 (Rosenbach), and TS., p. 32 (Leeds), and (1895), p. 39.

138. *Almayer's Folly* (Canterbury Edition), p. 27.

139. *Ibid*., pp. 27, 88.

140. *Outcast*, pp. ix-x, and *Life and Letters*, I, 97.

141. Letter to Mme. Poradowska dated "Lundi matin" and assigned by Dr. Gee to Monday, October 29 or November 5, 1894 (Yale).

142. In his preface to *The Sisters* ([New York: Crosby Gaige, 1928], pp. 1–16) Ford Madox Ford failed to notice the similarity, and his omission was pointed out in the *Bookman* (LXVIII [1928], 216–217) by Homer S. Shannon, who made a partial comparison of the two stories. A fuller comparison reveals many similarities. The heroine was named Rita (*Sisters*, p. 55; *Arrow of Gold*, p. 5) and came from the Basque country (*Sisters*, pp. 50–52; *Arrow of Gold*, p. 36). She had a sister who was devoutly religious (*Sisters*, p. 55; *Arrow of Gold*, pp. 141, 335). In the Pyrenees she had been brought up by her uncle, a priest (*Sisters*, p. 52; *Arrow of Gold*, p. 36). Then she was sent to Paris to live with another uncle and his wife, orange merchants (*Sisters*, pp. 50–56; *Arrow of Gold*, pp. 35–36). The family was Carlist (*Sisters*, pp. 51–52; *Arrow of Gold*, pp. 47–48, 57). In a pavilion behind the uncle's house in Passy (*Sisters*, pp. 46–50; *Arrow of Gold*, p. 22) lived an enormously rich painter (*Sisters*, pp. 19, 24; *Arrow of Gold*, p. 22) of humble origin (*Sisters*, p. 24; *Arrow of Gold*, p. 47). Other less important details also

connect the two stories. Some of the material Conrad used a third time in *The Mirror of the Sea* (pp. 160–161).

143. *Life and Letters*, II, 224, and Richard Curle, ed., *Notes by Joseph Conrad: Written in a Set of His First Editions* (London: Privately Printed, 1925), p. 33.

144. *Joseph Conrad and His Circle*, pp. 37, 40.

145. *Joseph Conrad as I Knew Him*, p. 118.

146. Page xiv. Also Ford Madox Ford, *Return to Yesterday* (London: Victor Gollancz Ltd., 1931), p. 111, and *Joseph Conrad and His Circle*, p. 196.

147. *Joseph Conrad as I Knew Him*, p. 142.

148. *Life and Letters*, I, 108.

149. *Ibid.*, I, 54, n. 1, II, 171.

150. Pages x–xvii.

151. Page ix.

152. *Tales of Hearsay* (Concord Edition; Garden City, New York: Doubleday, Page and Company, 1926), pp. 33–35. All further references are to the Concord Edition. Conrad declared the whole story to be true (*Life and Letters*, I, 17, II, 181).

153. *Nigger*, p. 36. There is a reference to "our nigger" (*ibid.*, p. 34); but this *our* could be understood as a sort of general possessive that included the reader.

154. *Life and Letters*, I, 77. The fictional *Narcissus* had a first mate, Mr. Baker, and a second, Mr. Creighton, neither of whom bore Conrad any resemblance.

155. *Nigger*, pp. 64, 65.

156. *Ibid.*, pp. 170–173.

157. *Ibid.*, pp. ix–x.

158. "The History of Mr. Conrad's Books," London *Times Literary Supplement*, no. 1,128 (August 30, 1923), 570. The comments and corrections Conrad made on the manuscript (Beyer) show that the article was semi-official. It appeared in pamphlet form as *Joseph Conrad: The History of his Books* (London: J. M. Dent and Sons, Ltd., n.d.).

159. *Life and Letters*, I, 76–77.

160. Unpublished letter to an unknown correspondent dated February 25, 1912 (Yale).

161. Page 50, for instance.

162. See the photograph of Conrad's certificate of dismissal (*Life and Letters*, I, facing p. 82). Jean-Aubry put the day of arrival on October 17 (*ibid.*, I, 77).

163. *Nigger*, pp. 103, 145. The ship was four months out when Jimmy died; his funeral was the day after Flores was sighted, and a week later the *Narcissus* entered the Channel (*ibid.*, pp. 156, 161). Time must be allowed for the ship to get to London.

164. *Life and Letters*, I, 78.

165. *Ibid.*, I, 77, and *Nigger*, p. 113.
166. *Life and Letters*, I, 77–78, and *Nigger*, p. 155.
167. *Life and Letters*, I, 77, 78, and *Nigger*, pp. 167–173.
168. Pages 102–108.
169. *Life and Letters*, I, 77.
170. *Loc. cit.* Also *Joseph Conrad as I Knew Him*, p. xvi.

No real connection can be traced between *The Nigger* and Herman Melville's *Redburn*, in which appeared a religious Negro cook and a malingering white sailor, Jackson. Jackson had some unnamed malady (perhaps tuberculosis, perhaps syphilis) on account of which he shirked his work; he bullied the crew; and he died of a hemorrhage while aloft and fell into the sea. The similarities seem to be only coincidental.

171. It is not altogether impossible that the impression made upon Conrad by the actual Sullivan was strengthened by his memories of an old pilot at Marseilles, him of the incredible age, the extensive recollections, and the respected position among the younger men (*Personal Record*, pp. 131–133).

172. Though a Captain John Anderson has recently been suggested as "the original captain" of the *Narcissus* and "the original of the captain" (*Sea*, p. 41), Arch. Duncan was beyond question the captain of the *Narcissus* (*Life and Letters*, I, facing p. 82).

173. *Life and Letters*, I, 77.
174. *Nigger*, p. ix.
175. *Life and Letters*, I, 77, and *Nigger*, pp. 147–154.
176. *Life and Letters*, I, 77.

177. *Nigger*, pp. 17–18. Conrad at times seems to have confused the events of the *Sutherland* voyage and of the *Narcissus* voyage: in "To My Readers in America" he spoke of "that evening when James Wait joined the ship – late for the muster of the crew . . ." (*ibid.*, p. ix).

178. *Life and Letters*, I, 65–73, 117–143. Also G. Jean-Aubry, *Joseph Conrad in the Congo* (London: "The Bookman's Journal" Office, 1926).

179. *Youth*, p. xii. During his days on the *Vidar* Conrad was afraid of losing his eyesight (*Life and Letters*, I, 100).

180. *Life and Letters*, I, 104–109. Also *Notes by Joseph Conrad*, p. 23.

181. London *Times Literary Supplement*, no. 1,128 (August 30, 1923), 570. Also *Life and Letters*, I, 113, and *Joseph Conrad as I Knew Him*, p. 139.

182. London *Times Literary Supplement*, no. 1,128 (August 30, 1923), 570. Also *Shadow Line*, p. ix.

183. Pages viii, ix.
184. *Life and Letters*, II, 195.
185. *Ibid.*, I, 97.
186. *Lord Jim*, pp. 202 ff.
187. *Life and Letters*, I, 97.
188. *Loc. cit.*

189. *Lord Jim*, p. ix.
190. *Ibid*., p. 40.
191. *Life and Letters*, I, 91–95.
192. *Lord Jim*, pp. 11–13.
193. *Life and Letters*, I, 65–73, and *Personal Record*, p. 72.
194. *Lord Jim*, p. 237.
195. *Saturday Review of Literature*, II (1925–26), 700.
196. *Lord Jim*, pp. 251, 253–254.
197. *Ibid*., p. viii. See a letter to Garnett in May, 1898, in which he referred to a proposed story "*Jim* (20,000)" (*Letters from Joseph Conrad*, p. 138).
198. London *Times Literary Supplement*, no. 1,134 (October 11, 1923), 670.
199. *Life and Letters*, I, 52, 154.
200. London *Times Literary Supplement*, no. 1,129 (September 6, 1923), 588, and no. 1,134 (October 11, 1923), 670.
201. *Lord Jim*, p. 13. Perhaps the name was taken from some ship Conrad encountered during his life at sea. Patna seems to have derived from "a city, district, and division of British India, in the Behar province of Bengal" (*Encyclopaedia Britannica* [11th ed.], XX, 929).
202. Pages 17 (Harvard) and 154 (Rosenbach). For a description of the divided condition of the manuscript of *Lord Jim* see pp. 150–152, above.
203. *Lord Jim*, pp. 11–15.
204. Page 22 (Harvard).
205. London *Times Literary Supplement*, no. 1,129 (September 6, 1923), 588, and no. 1,134 (October 11, 1923), 670.
206. *Lord Jim*, pp. 14, 20, 101, 97.
Perhaps the insurance scheme influenced "The End of the Tether."
207. London *Times Literary Supplement*, no. 1,129 (September 6, 1923), 588, and no. 1,134 (October 11, 1923), 670.
208. *Lord Jim*, pp. 134, 136–137. Clearly Conrad did not know one of the most dramatic details of the rescue, recounted by Sir Frank Swettenham: "When the pilgrims found they had been abandoned . . . , and when they realized their desperate situation, they all left the decks for a while and then reappeared clothed in their winding sheets" (London *Times Literary Supplement*, no. 1,129 [September 6, 1923], 588).
209. *Lord Jim*, p. 57.
210. Page 9.
211. *Lord Jim*, p. 133.
212. Marlow attended the inquiry, after seeing the deserters when they first arrived (*ibid*., pp. 28, 34, 36). There was no indication of Marlow's or the deserters' going to another city for the inquiry.
213. London *Times Literary Supplement*, no. 1,129 (September 6, 1923), 588.
214. *Lord Jim*, p. 134.

215. Jim had been imagining the voices of the drowning pilgrims "'day after day'" before he reached the Eastern port (*loc. cit.*).

216. *Life and Letters*, I, 76–77.

217. *Lord Jim*, p. 163. In the port of investigation Marlow met Chester, a native of Western Australia, who had come "'over six thousand miles'" to get capital for his guano island scheme because his attempts to raise money in Auckland and Brisbane had failed (*ibid.*, pp. 164–165).

218. *Ibid.*, pp. 37–39, 42.

219. *Ibid.*, pp. 40, 47.

220. *Webster's Collegiate Dictionary* (5th ed.), pp. 420, 1019.

221. *Lord Jim*, pp. 161, 87, 68, 158, 32. Conrad included what seems to have been a personal reminiscence: during the investigation Jim stayed in the Sailors' Home (*ibid.*, p. 134), where Conrad himself stayed during his visit to Bombay (*Life and Letters*, I, 76).

222. *Lord Jim*, p. 5. Following the statement about the retreat "towards the rising sun," Conrad declared: "Thus in the course of years he was known successively in Bombay, in Calcutta, in Rangoon, in Penang, in Batavia – and in each of these halting-places was just Jim the water-clerk." Though the list of places might cast some doubt on Bombay as the scene of the inquiry, Conrad clearly was not following the sequence. Jim's first job after the inquiry was in a rice mill in Rangoon (*ibid.*, pp. 187, 152).

223. London *Times Literary Supplement*, no. 1,134 (October 11, 1923), 670, and no. 1,129 (September 6, 1923), 588.

224. *Ibid.*, no. 1,129 (September 6, 1923), 588.

225. *Lord Jim*, pp. 13, 36–48.

226. London *Times Literary Supplement*, no. 1,134 (October 11, 1923), 670.

227. *Ibid.*, no. 1,129 (September 6, 1923), 588, and *Lord Jim*, p. 47.

228. *Lord Jim*, pp. 5, 79.

229. "As for the story itself it is true enough in its essentials. The sustained invention of a really telling lie demands a talent which I do not possess" (*Tales of Unrest*, p. ix). Jean-Aubry believed that Conrad was told the story in Africa: the names of the protagonists, Kayerts and Carlier, he took from two actual men, "an agent and a captain, whom he met in the Congo" (*Life and Letters*, I, 128, n. 2; also *ibid.*, I, 140, n. 1).

230. *Typhoon*, p. vii.

231. *Conrad Memorial Library*, p. 115. Also *Mirror of the Sea*, pp. 63–66.

232. *Joseph Conrad as I Knew Him*, p. 118.

233. Page vii.

234. Page ix.

235. *Set of Six*, p. ix.

236. *Notes by Joseph Conrad*, p. 28.

237. *Set of Six*, p. vii. Also *Life and Letters*, II, 2.

238. *'Twixt Land and Sea*, p. viii.

239. *Life and Letters*, II, 133. Conrad apparently forgot that he had worked the same incident into *The Rescue* (p. 101) as a passing allusion in dialogue.

240. *Tales of Hearsay*, p. xii. Also *Conrad Memorial Library*, p. 365.

241. *Last Essays*, pp. 167, 172.

242. *Tales of Hearsay*, p. xiii.

243. Because of the acknowledged similarity in theme (*Tales of Unrest*, p. ix), "The Lagoon" and "Karain" probably grew from one anecdote which Conrad heard while he was in Borneo.

244. *Lord Jim*, p. viii.

245. *Letters from Joseph Conrad*, p. 171.

246. See my article, "The Rajah Brooke and Joseph Conrad," *Studies in Philology*, XXXV (1938), 615–618.

247. *Ibid.*, pp. 613–615.

248. The aggregation of details, based on internal evidence, in my first article (*ibid.*, pp. 618–633) is reinforced by a piece of external evidence, advanced in a recent article (*ibid.*, XXXVII (1940), 130–132).

249. Speaking with Conrad's authority in "The History of Mr. Conrad's Books," Curle put Patusan "on the south coast of north-west Sumatra. . ." (London *Times Literary Supplement*, no. 1,128 [August 30, 1923], 570).

250. The actual Patusan was "nearly seventy miles" upstream (Henry Keppel, *Expedition to Borneo*, etc. [New York: Harper and Brothers, 1846], p. 269), and the fictional only thirty or "about forty" (*Lord Jim*, pp. 226, 220). Here Conrad apparently tempered his reading with his recollection of Berouw, which was "forty miles up, more or less, a Bornean river" (*Personal Record*, p. 74).

251. Another incident in Brooke's career seems to have been refurbished for the novel. There was a tale in Sarawak that even the gentle Muda Hassim had had a young man "chained without covering, and exposed to sun and rain at the entrance of the Balei or Hall" (Henry Keppel, *A Visit to the Indian Archipelago*, etc. [London: Richard Bentley, 1853], II, 104). In the novel one of Stein's captains on a visit to Patusan had been " 'tied up by the neck with a rattan halter to a post planted in the middle of a mud-hole before the Rajah's house' " (*Lord Jim*, p. 240).

252. The fortifications of Brooke's house, from which he dominated his capital, seem to have supplied Conrad with the plans for Jim's. Brooke's was "surrounded by palisades and a ditch," forming a square, and it contained a mess-room "with every description of firearms . . . ready for use (Keppel, *Expedition to Borneo*, p. 222). Jim's had " 'a deep ditch, an earth wall topped by a palisade, and at the angles guns mounted on platforms to sweep each side of the square' " (*Lord Jim*, p. 340). Both houses were really forts.

253. Conrad did not rely, apparently, upon any of the obvious sources for the character of Gentleman Brown. He compared the character to "'his contemporary brother ruffians, like Bully Hayes or the mellifluous Pease, or that perfumed, Dundreary-whiskered, dandified scoundrel known as Dirty Dick. . .'" (*Lord Jim*, p. 352). Though Dirty Dick could not be identified, a search for parallels in the careers of Gentleman Brown and Bully Hayes or Ben Pease produced nothing really convincing (see Basil Lubbock, *Bully Hayes: South Sea Pirate* [Boston: Charles E. Lauriat Company, 1931]) and Rolf Boldrewood, *A Modern Buccaneer* [New York and London: Macmillan and Company, 1894]). The closest resemblance was the theft of a schooner from the Spanish by Brown (*Lord Jim*, pp. 354–355) and Pease's "seizing a Spanish revenue vessel under the very guns of a fort" (*Modern Buccaneer*, p. 73). Conrad may have picked up the facts he gave in the story of Gentleman Brown from anecdotes never recorded in print.

254. When Brooke's friend Budrudeen was driven to suicide by the enemies of British interests in Brunei, he sent the Englishman his ring and a message of farewell by his faithful retainer, Jaffer (Mundy, *Borneo and Celebes*, II, 129–134).

255. Pages 98, 473.

256. The portrait of Rajah Allang in *Lord Jim* may have been rounded off with a few touches borrowed from the Sultan of Sulu. The latter was accustomed to "the too free use of opium" (Keppel, *Indian Archipelago*, I, 66), like Rajah Allang (*Lord Jim*, p. 228). The Sultan of Sulu also had a suite "dressed with . . . gaudiness, in bright silks" (Keppel, *Indian Archipelago*, I, 67), just like Rajah Allang's "'youths in gay silks'" (*Lord Jim*, p. 228).

The character of Rajah Allang seems to contain details taken from reading other than in the Brookiana. In *Last Essays* (pp. 131–132) Conrad mentioned "the Sultan of Perak, or perhaps his brother-ruler next door in Selangor, [who] having listened attentively to a lecture from a British admiral on the heinousness of a certain notable case of piracy, turned round quickly to his attending chiefs and to the silent throng of his Malay subjects, exclaiming, 'Hear now, my people! Don't let us have any more of this little game.'" The anecdote apparently reappeared in *Lord Jim* (p. 250) in the scene in which Jim upbraided Rajah Allang before his court for some of his thefts: "'When Jim had done there was a great stillness. Nobody seemed to breathe even; no one made a sound till the old Rajah sighed faintly, and looking up, with a toss of his head, said quickly, "You hear, my people! No more of these little games."'"

257. It is to be noted that divorce played a prominent part in the legal operations of both Brooke (Keppel, *Indian Archipelago*, II, 19–21) and Jim (*Lord Jim*, p. 269).

258. "The Rajah Brooke and Joseph Conrad," *Studies in Philology*, XXXV (1938), 626–633. Footnotes 249–258, above, are supplementary to

the footnotes to be found with the article in *Studies in Philology*. Slight verbal emendations have been made.

259. *Ibid.*, pp. 619–625.

260. Pages 20–22.

261. (Macmillan's Colonial Library; London and New York: Macmillan and Company, 1890), pp. 133–134.

In an interesting article, "Conrad's Favorite Bedside Book," in the *South Atlantic Quarterly* (XXXVIII [1939], 305–315), Miss Florence Clemens collected further evidence, tangible and intangible, of Wallace's influence on Conrad.

Though we did not know each other's conclusions until after they had been reached, Miss Clemens and I, working entirely separately, both noticed the importance of Brooke and Wallace as sources of Conrad's material.

262. Richard Curle, "Joseph Conrad: Ten Years Later," *Virginia Quarterly Review*, X (1934), 431.

263. Page viii.

264. Page xi.

265. *Joseph Conrad as I Knew Him*, p. 118.

266. *Set of Six*, pp. viii-ix. Also *Life and Letters*, II, 299. See also Conrad's preface to *Youth and Gaspar Ruiz*, pp. 167–168.

267. *Set of Six*, p. x. Also J. DeLancey Ferguson, "The Plot of Conrad's *The Duel*," *Modern Language Notes*, L (1935), 385–390.

268. *Life and Letters*, II, 13, 41, 240, and *Conrad Memorial Library*, p. 327.

269. *Letters to the Colvins* (New York: The Anderson Galleries, 1928), p. 31.

270. No. 1,258 (February 25, 1926), 142. Also Miriam Hatheway Wood, "A Source of Conrad's *Suspense*," *Modern Language Notes*, L (1935), 390–394; Miss Wood made no mention of Miss Atkinson's previous investigation.

271. *Conrad Memorial Library*, p. 340.

272. London *Times Literary Supplement*, no. 1,128 (August 30, 1923), 570.

CHAPTER III

1. The Conrads were engaged for six weeks (*Joseph Conrad and His Circle*, p. 16) before they were married on March 24 (*Joseph Conrad as I Knew Him*, pp. 25, 103).

2. *Life and Letters*, I, 157, n. 1, 164. In his *Memoirs* Tadeusz Bobrowski complained that the Korzeniowski family had "a passion for speculation" (*Polish Heritage*, p. 9). Also *Life and Letters*, I, 65.

3. *Joseph Conrad and His Circle*, p. 27. The faint hope that Conrad had of regaining a little from the investment was lost when the director,

who might have been able to save something, was drowned in the disaster of the *Drummond Castle* that same summer (*ibid.*, p. 31).

4. *Sketch of Joseph Conrad's Life*, p. 3.

5. *Life and Letters*, I, 185.

6. *Letters from Joseph Conrad*, p. 9.

7. *Joseph Conrad: A Personal Remembrance*, pp. 130–131.

8. *Life and Letters*, I, 82–83, 87.

9. *Joseph Conrad: A Personal Remembrance*, pp. 53–54.

10. *Letters from Joseph Conrad*, pp. 99–109, and *Life and Letters*, I, 206, II, 146–149.

11. Conrad did not have a financial success with the public until *'Twixt Land and Sea* (1912) and *Chance* (1913) were published (*Last Twelve Years of Joseph Conrad*, pp. 136–137). When Conrad himself dated his success from 1913 (*Life and Letters*, II, 284), he was probably reckoning from the time the royalties came in.

Mrs. Conrad confessed: "There were many years too lean not [sic] to be without grave anxiety" (*Joseph Conrad as I Knew Him*, p. 1). Ford, who knew him best in his leanest years, emphasized Conrad's "bitter poverty" (*Return to Yesterday*, pp. 25, 53, 288); he went so far in 1909 as to describe him as indigent to Arnold Bennett (Bennett, *Journal* [Garden City, New York: The Garden City Publishing Company, Inc., n.d.], p. 354).

12. *Conrad Memorial Library*, p. 42.

13. *Ibid.*, p. 62.

14. Unpublished letter to Unwin dated June 7, 1896, and unpublished letter to Conrad from the *Cornhill Magazine* dated August 19, [1896] (Yale).

15. *Letters from Joseph Conrad*, p. 67.

16. *Life and Letters*, I, 230, and *Letters from Joseph Conrad*, pp. 139–140.

17. *Letters from Joseph Conrad*, pp. 24, 99, 112. Conrad told Sanderson that *Blackwood's* paid him fifty shillings a thousand words (*Life and Letters*, I, 206).

18. Letters to Mme. Poradowska dated October 4 and 10, 1894 (Yale). Curle was out by £5 too much in his estimation (*Notes by Joseph Conrad*, p. 15, n. 1).

19. *Letters from Joseph Conrad*, p. 69.

20. *Life and Letters*, I, 230.

21. *Letters from Joseph Conrad*, p. 26. Conrad probably received £50 (*ibid.*, p. 105).

22. *Ibid.*, p. 69.

23. *Almayer's Folly: A Story of an Eastern River* (Limited Edition; London: William Heinemann, Ltd., 1921), p. vi. The first edition remained unsold on the booksellers' shelves until it became a joke in the

trade (*Letters from Joseph Conrad*, p. 16, and *Conrad Memorial Library*, p. 6).

24. *An Outcast of the Islands* (Limited Edition; London: William Heinemann, Ltd., 1921), p. vi.

25. *The Nigger of the 'Narcissus': A Tale of the Sea* (Limited Edition; London: William Heinemann, Ltd., 1921), p. vi.

26. *Tales of Unrest* (Limited Edition; London: William Heinemann, Ltd., 1921), p. iv.

27. *Lord Jim: A Tale* (Limited Edition; London: William Heinemann, Ltd., 1921), p. vi.

28. *Youth: A Narrative and Two Other Stories* (Limited Edition; London: William Heinemann, Ltd., 1921), p. vi.

29. Letter to Mme. Poradowska dated "Lundi matin" and assigned by Dr. Gee to Monday, October 29 or November 5, 1894 (Yale).

30. *Letters from Joseph Conrad*, p. 102.

31. *Life and Letters*, I, 280. Also *ibid.*, I, 219, 246, 283. All of these outcries were made before the completion of *Lord Jim.*

How apprehensively he faced the food bills was brought out by the bitter humor of a letter ascribed to February, 1898: "Everybody here is in rude health at which I am sorry because of the enormous appetites which is so expensive" (*Letters from Joseph Conrad*, p. 132).

32. *Life and Letters*, I, 272. Also *ibid.*, II, 99.

33. *Joseph Conrad and His Circle*, pp. 51–52, and *Life and Letters*, I, 207, 218. His own incessant anxiety made him want "to make a bargeman of [his son]: strong, knowing his business and thinking of nothing. That is *the* life . . . thinking of nothing! O! bliss" (*Letters from Joseph Conrad*, p. 136).

34. *Life and Letters*, I, 280. Also *ibid.*, I, 235.

35. *Joseph Conrad and His Circle*, pp. 47, 89, and *Life and Letters*, II, 1, 17. Curle also commented on Conrad's worrying about Mrs. Conrad (*Joseph Conrad as I Knew Him*, p. vii).

36. Unpublished letter of December 27, 1908, from Henri Davray to Mme. Poradowska (Yale), and *Letters to the Colvins*, p. 33. Mrs. Conrad almost had a nervous breakdown a year after the accident (*ibid.*, p. 20).

37. *Life and Letters*, II, 35–36.

38. *Ibid.*, II, 42–47. Borys' illness was later diagnosed as pleurisy (*Joseph Conrad as I Knew Him*, p. 55).

39. *Joseph Conrad: A Personal Remembrance*, p. 161.

40. *Ibid.*, pp. 159, 181.

41. *Ibid.*, p. 18.

42. In an unpublished letter to Perceval Gibbon (Beyer). The letter was not dated, but it seems to belong to a series of letters of which one was dated July 19, 1909, and it mentioned a visit from Captain Marris,

to which Conrad referred in a published letter of October, 1909 (*Life and Letters*, II, 103).

43. *Letters from Joseph Conrad*, pp. 69–71, 77. Garnett remarked that it was financially impossible for Conrad to accept the lower terms and for Unwin to give the higher because "the sales of Conrad's three early books showed a loss, in the publisher's ledger, for many years" (*ibid.*, p. 21).

44. *Conrad Memorial Library*, p. 42. The story was *The Nigger* (*ibid.*, p. 43, and *Letters from Joseph Conrad*, p. 72).

45. *Letters from Joseph Conrad*, pp. 70–79.

46. *Ibid.*, pp. 88, 116.

47. *Ibid.*, pp. 92, 95.

48. "I beg to acknowledge receipt of two bills of £25 each at 3 at 6 months" (unpublished letter to Unwin dated November 5, 1897 [Yale]).

49. *Letters from Joseph Conrad*, pp. 125–127.

50. *Ibid.*, p. 105, and *Bibliography*, p. 14.

51. *Bibliography*, pp. 16–19, 22–23.

52. *Life and Letters*, I, 278.

As far back as October, 1896, Conrad considered taking A. P. Watt as a literary agent, for "it would be a great relief to have someone to do one's 'dirty work'" (*Letters from Joseph Conrad*, p. 73).

For a somewhat bitter picture of Pinker as Ford saw him, see *Return to Yesterday*, pp. 58–60.

53. *Last Twelve Years*, p. 139.

54. *Life and Letters*, I, 326. Also *Lettres Françaises*, p. 65. Ford said that he lent Conrad the money to pay this fairly substantial overdraft (*Joseph Conrad: A Personal Remembrance*, pp. 159–160).

55. *Life and Letters*, II, 66. See also Conrad's warm defense of Pinker in 1904 against the charges that "'Pinker deals harshly with Conrad'" (*ibid.*, I, 331–332).

56. Letter to Mme. Poradowska dated February 5, 1908 (Yale).

57. Unpublished letter to Perceval Gibbon dated July 19, 1909 (Beyer).

58. Unpublished letter to Perceval Gibbon dated only "19 Dec." (Beyer). From the list of what Conrad had been working on (*Razumov*, "The Black Mate," and *Reminiscences* and a story written in ten days – "Il Conde" [*Life and Letters*, II, 74]), the letter can be assigned to 1908.

59. *Life and Letters*, II, 94.

60. *Last Twelve Years*, p. 139.

61. Mrs. Conrad declared that the incident occurred after the novel was completed (*Joseph Conrad and His Circle*, p. 140). It may have occurred somewhat earlier, for Conrad wrote to Perceval Gibbon, when the novel was still incomplete: "I was exasperated beyond endurance by a side-episode in this affair. . . . At the time I really felt as if could snatch all that pile of pages and fling it in the fire . . ." (undated letter

[Beyer]. The letter seems to belong at the end of the Beyer series, for it was the most intimate and it dealt with the affair in a final tone).

62. *Joseph Conrad and His Circle*, pp. 141–142.

About a year later Conrad quarreled violently over payment with the *Daily Mail* (*ibid.*, pp. 152–153).

63. Unpublished letter dated July 19, 1909 (Beyer).

64. *Life and Letters*, II, 102.

65. *Ibid.*, II, 154.

66. *Ibid.*, II, 266.

67. *Last Twelve Years*, p. 140. Also William Rothenstein, *Men and Memories* (New York: Coward-McCann, Inc., 1931 and 1932), II, 44.

68. *Life and Letters*, II, 55.

69. *Ibid.*, I, 34.

70. Unpublished letter to Perceval Gibbon dated "Wednesday" and probably written late in 1909 (Beyer), and *Life and Letters*, II, 66.

71. *The Rescue: A Romance of the Shallows* (Memorial Edition; Garden City, New York: Doubleday, Page and Company, 1925), pp. vii–viii. Perhaps the allowance was connected with the advance of £250 promised by McClure, who first bought *The Rescue* (*Life and Letters*, I, 230).

72. *Men and Memories*, II, 61.

73. *Life and Letters*, II, 2, 14–15, 130.

74. *Ibid.*, II, 219.

75. *Conrad to a Friend*, p. 132, and *Last Twelve Years*, pp. 136–151.

76. *Life and Letters*, I, 170, n. 1.

77. *Ibid.*, II, 65.

78. *Joseph Conrad: A Personal Remembrance*, p. 181.

79. *Life and Letters*, I, 321.

80. *Joseph Conrad and His Circle*, p. 26. Also *Life and Letters*, I, 293.

81. Letters dated February 27, March 12, May 1, July 30, and August 5, 1891 (Yale). Also letter to Mme. Poradowska dated August 26, 1891 (Yale).

82. *Life and Letters*, I, 144.

83. *Ibid.*, I, 145, 162–163. The second treatment escaped the attention of Jean-Aubry: see chapter I, n. 110.

84. *Letters from Joseph Conrad*, p. 243, and *Life and Letters*, I, 256.

85. *Letters from Joseph Conrad*, p. 301.

86. *Last Twelve Years*, p. 195. Also *Letters from Joseph Conrad*, p. 247.

87. *Life and Letters*, I, 293.

88. Letter to Mme. Poradowska written from Kinchassa and dated September 26, 1890 (Yale).

89. *Last Essays*, p. 36. Conrad was writing of his first voyage on the *Torrens* (*ibid.*, p. 35), on which he sailed on November 25, 1891 (*Life and Letters*, I, 149).

90. Letter to Mme. Poradowska dated May 10, 1891 (Yale). A recurrent expression in his letters revealed a chronic depression: "Je vois tout en noir" (letter to Mme. Poradowska dated April 14, 1891 [Yale]).

91. *Life and Letters*, II, 69.

92. Letter to Mme. Poradowska dated "Mercredi" and assigned by Dr. Gee to Wednesday, July 25, 1894 (Yale).

93. *Joseph Conrad and His Circle*, p. 67.

94. *Letters from Joseph Conrad*, p. 153.

95. *Life and Letters*, II, 72.

96. *Letters from Joseph Conrad*, p. 58.

97. *Lettres Françaises*, p. 101.

98. *Life and Letters*, II, 104.

99. *Ibid.*, II, 6.

100. See, for example, the letters in which he spoke of being ill and unable to write in 1896 in February, May (*Letters from Joseph Conrad*, pp. 44, 53), June (*Life and Letters*, I, 191), July, August, and December (*Letters from Joseph Conrad*, pp. 60, 64, 82). Letters in the other years before the publication of *Lord Jim* reveal similar interruptions. In fact the correspondence up to the time of Conrad's death was full of such complaints. More could undoubtedly be found if all the correspondence were published (*Life and Letters*, I, v).

101. *Letters from Joseph Conrad*, pp. 48, 98.

102. See, for instance, his distracted condition during the almost fatal illnesses of Borys and John at Montpellier and Geneva in the winter and spring of 1907 (*Life and Letters*, II, 42 ff.).

103. *Ibid.*, II, 11.

104. *Ibid.*, I, 282–283.

105. An unpublished letter written to Gibbon at the end of December, probably of 1908, gave a good picture of Conrad's life: "Practically from July last year till August this, I've been either actually laid up or recovering, or sickening for gout. Hard fact. That is either disabled utterly or hindered. Add to this a crushing load of anxiety" (Beyer).

106. *Life and Letters*, II, 5.

107. *Conrad to a Friend*, pp. 172–173.

108. Letter to Mme. Poradowska dated August 26, 1891 (Yale).

109. Letter to Mme. Poradowska dated November 5, 1893 (Yale).

110. Letter to Mme. Poradowska dated September 8, 1894 (Yale).

111. *Letters from Joseph Conrad*, p. 35.

112. Conrad wrote Garnett from Champel that he was doing "tolerably bad work" but that he "never felt like that even in the first days of my 'Folly'" (*ibid.*, pp. 36–37).

113. *Ibid.*, p. 44.

114. *Ibid.*, p. 59.

115. "Voilà trois jours que je m'assois devant une page blanche – et la page est toujours blanche excépté pour un IV en tête" (letter to Mme.

Poradowska dated "Lundi matin" and assigned by Dr. Gee to Monday, October 29 or November 5, 1894 [Yale]).

116. *Letters from Joseph Conrad*, pp. 63–65.

117. *Ibid.*, pp. 134–135. For similar outbursts scattered through the years see *Life and Letters*, I, 246, 252, 265, 275, II, 48.

118. *Life and Letters*, II, 100.

In an unpublished letter to Colvin written in August, 1910, Conrad applied to himself the desperate motto of the *Judea* in "Youth": "I have been doing uncommonly badly since April last. A most beggarly tale of pages! And just now I feel out of sorts – devil only knows why. However one must go on. Do or die" (*Letters to the Colvins*, p. 23). Also *Men and Memories*, II, 278.

119. *Life and Letters*, II, 129, 141, 166, 193.

120. *Ibid.*, II, 14.

121. *Letters from Joseph Conrad*, p. 268.

122. *Joseph Conrad as I Knew Him*, p. 110.

123. *Joseph Conrad: A Personal Remembrance*, p. 255.

See also Edward Garnett's comment on "the extraordinary nervous strain and agony which composition imposed on Conrad, in those early years" (*Letters from Joseph Conrad*, p. 18).

124. *Life and Letters*, II, 180. Also *Men and Memories*, II, 159.

125. *Life and Letters*, I, 278. Earlier in 1899 he had written approximately the same thing to Methuen (*ibid.*, I, 268).

126. *Conrad to a Friend*, p. 137. Also *Life and Letters*, II, 11, and *Letters from Joseph Conrad*, p. 189.

127. *Letters from Joseph Conrad*, p. 147.

128. *Personal Record*, pp. 98, 100.

129. *Life and Letters*, II, 114. Also *'Twixt Land and Sea*, p. viii.

130. *Letters from Joseph Conrad*, p. 156.

131. *Ibid.*, p. 85. Also *Life and Letters*, I, 271, 334.

132. *Lettres Françaises*, p. 117.

133. *Life and Letters*, II, 339.

134. *Letters from Joseph Conrad*, p. 188.

135. *Personal Record*, pp. 73–74.

136. *Life and Letters*, II, 332.

137. *Ibid.*, I, 244, and *Letters from Joseph Conrad*, p. 189.

138. *Lettres Françaises*, p. 84.

Mrs. Conrad declared that though Conrad "was at all times mentally active, physically he was extremely indolent" (*Joseph Conrad as I Knew Him*, p. 13).

139. *Letters from Joseph Conrad*, p. 142.

140. *Life and Letters*, I, 252. Also *Last Twelve Years*, p. 71.

141. *Life and Letters*, II, 29–30.

142. *Ibid.*, II, 104.

143. *Letters from Joseph Conrad*, pp. 139–140. Also *Joseph Conrad: A Personal Remembrance*, p. 181.
144. *Letters from Joseph Conrad*, p. 153.
145. *Life and Letters*, I, 282. Also *ibid.*, II, 65.
146. *Ibid.*, I, 199.
147. *Lettres Françaises*, p. 62.
148. *Joseph Conrad: A Personal Remembrance*, p. 275.
149. *Life and Letters*, II, 105.
150. Pages 98–99.
151. *Life and Letters*, II, 6.
Mrs. Conrad also deplored the isolation which came with poverty and the exactions of writing (*Joseph Conrad and His Circle*, p. 50).
152. Letter to Mme. Poradowska dated September 27, 1910 (Yale).

CHAPTER IV

1. *Letters from Joseph Conrad*, p. 5.
2. *Ibid.*, p. 46.
3. *Joseph Conrad as I Knew Him*, pp. 29–30.
4. *Joseph Conrad and His Circle*, p. 22.
5. *Ibid.*, p. 41.
6. *Life and Letters*, I, 268.
7. *Last Twelve Years*, p. 123. The references which Mrs. Conrad made to a study in their first house at Stanford-le-Hope do not distinguish it from the general living room of the house (*Joseph Conrad and His Circle*, p. 44).
8. *Life and Letters*, II, 11, 109. Also *Joseph Conrad and His Circle*, p. 155.
9. *Joseph Conrad as I Knew Him*, p. 154, and *Complete Catalogue of the Library of John Quinn* (New York: The Anderson Galleries, 1924), I, 176. Also *Joseph Conrad's Mind and Method*, p. 38; Mégroz implied his information came from Mrs. Conrad rather than Conrad himself.
10. *Letters from Joseph Conrad*, p. 68. Mrs. Conrad said they did not move in until "late October" (*Joseph Conrad and His Circle*, p. 44) but she was writing years afterward.
11. *Joseph Conrad and His Circle*, pp. 42, 44.
12. On March 12, 1897, Conrad wrote Garnett, "We shift camp at 7 a.m. tomorrow" (*Letters from Joseph Conrad*, p. 94).
13. *Joseph Conrad and His Circle*, pp. 45, 50.
14. *Life and Letters*, I, 261.
15. *Letters from Joseph Conrad*, p. 144.
16. *Life and Letters*, I, 251. Because of the definite statement, "We are leaving Stanford-le-Hope on the 26th Oct.," in this letter, which was dated October 16, it seems impossible to accept Jean-Aubry's belief that the move took place at the end of September (*ibid.*, I, 167). Further-

more as Conrad wrote Galsworthy from the Pent on October 28 that "the first letter in my new home was from you" (*ibid.*, I, 253), it is all the more likely that he moved on October 26. See also the letter to Garnett of September 29 in which Conrad spoke of negotiations for the house (*Letters from Joseph Conrad*, p. 144), and a letter of November 7 in which he said he had been at the Pent "over a week now" (*ibid.*, p. 148). When Conrad wrote Wells on September 11 that he was moving to the Pent "on the 26th of this month" (*Life and Letters*, I, 250), in the light of the evidence above he must have confused September and October.

17. *Joseph Conrad: A Personal Remembrance*, p. 35.

18. *Life and Letters*, I, 251.

19. *Joseph Conrad and His Circle*, p. 66.

20. *Letters from Joseph Conrad*, p. 148.

21. *Life and Letters*, II, 55.

22. *Joseph Conrad: A Personal Remembrance*, pp. 163–166.

23. *Personal Record*, p. 99.

24. *Joseph Conrad: A Personal Remembrance*, p. 166.

25. Unpublished letter dated August 20, 1907 (Yale). J. B. Pinker was one of the friends. Conrad dedicated *A Set of Six* (1908) to Miss Capes.

26. *Life and Letters*, II, 70. Though the house was larger, it was noisy (*Joseph Conrad and His Circle*, pp. 130–131). Also *Joseph Conrad as I Knew Him*, pp. 57–58.

27. *Life and Letters*, II, 96, and *Joseph Conrad and His Circle*, p. 137. The cramped quarters were the particular drawback. Conrad complained to Rothenstein that the four members of the family and servants were "crowded into four tiny rooms in half of a cottage" (*Men and Memories*, II, 158).

28. *Life and Letters*, II, 5, 109.

29. *Men and Memories*, II, 159.

30. *Life and Letters*, II, 111, 115. Mrs. Conrad mentioned his grumbling about Capel House too (*Joseph Conrad and His Circle*, p. 154).

31. *Life and Letters*, II, 219–230.

32. *Last Twelve Years*, p. 199.

33. *Ibid.*, pp. 3, 123.

34. *Life and Letters*, I, 330, II, 11, 208. The only undertaking he was able to carry on successfully away from his usual surroundings was apparently *The Mirror of the Sea* (*Joseph Conrad as I Knew Him*, p. 120).

35. *Letters from Joseph Conrad*, p. 284.

36. *Life and Letters*, II, 25.

37. *Ibid.*, I, 321.

38. *Joseph Conrad and His Circle*, p. 46.

39. *Life and Letters*, II, 92.

40. Letter to Mme. Poradowska dated "Jeudi" and assigned by Dr. Gee to Thursday, March 29 or April 5, 1894 (Yale).

41. *Letters from Joseph Conrad*, p. 64. In 1906, while awaiting the birth of his second son in Galsworthy's house in London, Conrad was sitting "religiously for 3½ hours every morning with sheets of paper before me and an American fountain pen in my hand," but not "writing much" (*Life and Letters*, II, 35).

42. *Letters from Joseph Conrad*, p. 134.

43. *Last Twelve Years*, p. 64. Conrad put it to Mégroz thus: "At one time I used to be an after-dinner man, or an anything man" (*Joseph Conrad's Mind and Method*, p. 38).

44. *Joseph Conrad as I Knew Him*, p. 22, and *Joseph Conrad and His Circle*, p. 66.

45. Rothenstein emphasized the strain under which Conrad wrote (*Men and Memories*, II, 43).

46. Unpublished letter to Perceval Gibbon dated "19 Dec." (Beyer). It seems to belong to the end of 1908. The story to which Conrad alluded was apparently "Il Conde," of which he wrote on August 18, 1908, that it had been written in ten days (*Life and Letters*, II, 74).

47. *Joseph Conrad's Mind and Method*, pp. 38–39, and *Life and Letters*, II, 102. The letter in which he mentioned the article brought out how much his indebtedness to Pinker put him on the defensive.

48. *Life and Letters*, I, 295.

49. *Ibid.*, I, 334, and *Joseph Conrad as I Knew Him*, pp. 115, 143–144.

50. *Joseph Conrad: A Personal Remembrance*, p. 185.

51. *Life and Letters*, II, 33. This was also the account he gave Mégroz (*Joseph Conrad's Mind and Method*, p. 40).

52. *Letters from Joseph Conrad*, p. 59.

53. *Last Essays*, p. 206.

54. Pages viii, ix. Also *Within the Tides*, p. viii.

55. *Personal Record*, p. 68.

56. *Last Essays*, p. 235.

57. "*Jim* (20,000) Youth (13,000) A seaman (5,000) Dynamite (5,000)" (*Letters from Joseph Conrad*, p. 138).

58. Conrad jotted down Corduroys, The Pilgrimage, Runagate, and after them the name Lucas; Belcolor, The Codger, Pavement Witch, Outcast, and after them the name Pawling. The words suggest the titles of prospective stories to be sent to E. V. Lucas and S. S. Pawling.

59. *Conrad Memorial Library*, pp. 131–133.

60. *Letters from Joseph Conrad*, p. 115.

61. Curle (*Last Twelve Years*, p. 67) and Mégroz (*Joseph Conrad's Mind and Method*, p. 41) both declared on Conrad's authority that he did not work from notes.

62. *Personal Record*, pp. 9, 74–89.

63. *Joseph Conrad: A Personal Remembrance*, p. 183.

64. *Joseph Conrad's Mind and Method*, p. 41.
65. Pages vii–xv.
66. Pages xii–xv.
67. Letter to Mme. Poradowska dated "Samedi" and assigned by Dr. Gee to Saturday, August 18, 1894 (Yale).
68. "Il me manque des idées" (letter to Mme. Poradowska dated September 8, 1894 [Yale]).
69. Letter to Mme. Poradowska dated October 23, 1894 (Yale).
70. Letter to Mme. Poradowska dated "Lundi matin" and assigned by Dr. Gee to Monday, October 29 or November 5, 1894 (Yale).
71. He seems to have had it by December 27, 1894, when he had written eight chapters and had changed his ideas (letter to Mme. Poradowska [Yale]).
72. Garnett remembered that when Conrad first talked the novel over with him, "the plot had already taken shape in Conrad's mind, but most of the action was still in a state of flux" (*Letters from Joseph Conrad*, p. 7).
73. Letter to Mme. Poradowska dated April 30, 1895 (Yale).
74. *Joseph Conrad as I Knew Him*, pp. 106, 134, 145.
75. Pages xix–xx.
76. *Life and Letters*, I, 183. Conrad's comment on *An Outcast of the Islands* (p. xi) disclosed the important part his emotions played in creation: "The story itself was never very near my heart. It engaged my imagination much more than my affection."
77. (Harvard).
78. *Saturday Review of Literature*, II (1925–26), 701.
79. Preface, p. 2 verso (Rosenbach).
80. *Joseph Conrad and His Circle*, p. 165. At the Curle sale Mrs. Conrad offered ten sketches by her husband, though none of them was of any scene in his work (*Richard Curle Conrad Collection*, items 225–234). Also *Conrad Memorial Library*, pp. 279–281, and Mrs. Conrad, "Conrad's Skill as an Artist," *Saturday Review of Literature*, II (1925–26), 700–701.
81. Page 49 verso (Yale).
82. *Conrad Memorial Library*, pp. [279], 342. Also *Saturday Review of Literature*, II (1925–26), 700–701.
83. Unpublished letter to Unwin dated July 10, 1896 (Beyer).
84. Letter dated "Jeudi" and assigned by Dr. Gee to Thursday, March 29 or April 5, 1894 (Yale).
85. Letter to Mme. Poradowska dated "Lundi matin" and assigned by Dr. Gee to Monday, October 29 or November 5, 1894 (Yale).
86. *Life and Letters*, II, 115.
87. *Ibid.*, II, 208.
88. Letter to Mme. Poradowska dated January 5, 1907 (Yale).
89. *Joseph Conrad as I Knew Him*, p. 141.

90. *Letters from Joseph Conrad*, p. 59. Also *ibid.*, pp. 63–64. For similar difficulties see *Chance*, p. ix.

91. *Letters from Joseph Conrad*, p. 138.

92. Letter to Mme. Poradowska dated February 2, 1894 (Yale).

93. Though Conrad feared and disliked the story, Ford thought he should have finished it and written more in the same vein (*Sisters*, pp. 1–5).

94. *Life and Letters*, II, 249. Also *Rescue*, p. xii.

95. *Life and Letters*, I, 326–327. Curle stated somewhat ambiguously that Conrad "had first, I believe, tried dictating when he was writing *Nostromo*" (*Last Twelve Years*, p. 62); Mégroz followed him in the belief (*Joseph Conrad's Mind and Method*, p. 97). Though the implications of Curle's remark are that Conrad began by dictating *Nostromo*, the implications of the letter to Wells are clearly that he wrote *Nostromo* in long hand and dictated *The Mirror*. Mrs. Conrad corroborated the latter assumption by declaring that parts of *The Mirror* were dictated to Ford (*Joseph Conrad as I Knew Him*, p. 120).

96. *Library of John Quinn*, I, 181.

97. *Joseph Conrad's Mind and Method*, p. 97, and *Life and Letters*, II, 209.

98. *Last Twelve Years*, p. 63.

99. *Notes on Life and Letters*, p. 26.

100. *Within the Tides*, p. viii.

101. *Last Essays*, p. 62. Also, *ibid.*, p. 65.

102. *Life and Letters*, II, 67 ff.

103. *Ibid.*, I, 279 ff.

104. *Ibid.*, II, 76 ff.

105. *Joseph Conrad: A Personal Remembrance*, pp. 111, 112.

106. *Conrad Memorial Library*, p. 62.

107. *Life and Letters*, I, 276.

108. *Personal Record*, p. xiv.

109. *Letters from Joseph Conrad*, p. 135.

110. *Ibid.*, p. 58. Because of his difficulty in finding the right expression at once, Conrad denied in a conversation with Mégroz that he was "'a literary man at all'" (*Joseph Conrad's Mind and Method*, p. 39).

111. For instance *Letters from Joseph Conrad*, p. 43.

112. *Life and Letters*, II, 47.

113. For instance *Letters from Joseph Conrad*, pp. 41, 270, and *Life and Letters*, II, 38, 87.

114. *Conrad Memorial Library*, pp. 133–134.

115. *Last Twelve Years*, p. 64.

116. Conrad's punctuation in both the manuscript and typescript was so eccentric and confusing that it was generally corrected in the published text. The corrections must have been made by the publishers them-

selves. It would be entirely unprofitable to enumerate here or elsewhere the variations in punctuation.

117. *Almayer's Folly* MS., chap. V, p. 5 (Rosenbach).

118. *Almayer's Folly* (1895), p. 85, and (Canterbury Edition), p. 62.

119. *Almayer's Folly* MS., chap. I, pp. 19–20 (Rosenbach).

120. *Almayer's Folly* (1895), pp. 21–22, and (Canterbury Edition), p. 14.

121. See pp. 181–182, above.

122. *Almayer's Folly* MS., chap. I, p. 13 (Rosenbach).

123. *Almayer's Folly* TS., p. 10 (Leeds).

124. *Almayer's Folly* MS., chap. II, p. 6 (Rosenbach).

125. *Almayer's Folly* TS., p. 28 (Leeds).

126. *Sketch of Joseph Conrad's Life*, p. 3.

127. *Almayer's Folly* MS., chap. XI, p. 14 (Rosenbach).

128. *Almayer's Folly* TS., p. 231 (Leeds).

129. See pp. 125–129, above.

130. The title page bears the word Kamudi, the nom de plume Conrad had adopted for the Pseudonym Library. The pages are covered also with compositors' marks.

131. *Almayer's Folly* TS., p. 206 (Leeds). Compare *Almayer's Folly* MS., chap. X, p. 11 (Rosenbach), with *Almayer's Folly* (1895), p. 201, and (Canterbury Edition), p. 153.

132. See p. 384, n. 72, below.

133. *Almayer's Folly* TS., p. 19 (Leeds).

134. *Almayer's Folly* (1895), p. 25, and (Canterbury Edition), p. 17.

135. *Almayer's Folly* TS., p. 232 (Leeds).

136. *Almayer's Folly* (1895), p. 227, and (Canterbury Edition), p. 173.

137. See p. 186, above. No trace of the proof sheets can be found even at Ernest Benn, Ltd., which recently bought out Unwin.

138. *Notes by Joseph Conrad*, p. 15, and Sotheby, Wilkinson and Hodge, Sale Catalogue (James B. Pinker), December 15, 1924, p. 73.

139. *Almayer's Folly* (1895), p. 26.

140. *Almayer's Folly* (Canterbury Edition), p. 17.

141. *Almayer's Folly* (1895), p. 24.

142. *Almayer's Folly* (Canterbury Edition), p. 16.

143. *Almayer's Folly* (1895), p. 31.

144. *Almayer's Folly* (Canterbury Edition), pp. 21–22.

145. *Joseph Conrad as I Knew Him*, p. 141.

146. *Almayer's Folly* MS., chap. II, p. 17 (Rosenbach).

147. *Ibid.*, chap. I, p. 26 (Rosenbach), for example.

148. *Ibid.*, chap. X, p. 18 (Rosenbach).

149. *Ibid.*, chap. I, p. 27 (Rosenbach), for example.

150. On September 8, 1894, writing about *An Outcast* to Mme. Poradowska, Conrad declared, "J'ai beaucoup brulé" (Yale).

151. Conrad sent this page as a specimen of his manuscript to Mme.

Poradowska (letter dated "Jeudi" and assigned by Dr. Gee to Thursday, March 29 or April 5, 1894 [Yale]).

152. *Almayer's Folly* MS., chap. X, p. 11 (Rosenbach).

153. *Almayer's Folly* MS., chap. VII, p. 1 (Rosenbach).

154. *Almayer's Folly* TS., p. 62 (Leeds).

155. *Almayer's Folly* (1895), p. 58.

156. *Almayer's Folly* (1895), pp. 42–43, and (Canterbury Edition), pp. 30–31, 42.

157. *Almayer's Folly* MS., chap. XI, p. 1a (Rosenbach).

158. *Ibid.*, chap. XI, pp. 2–3 (Rosenbach).

159. *Almayer's Folly* TS., p. 222 (Leeds), and (1895), p. 217.

160. *Almayer's Folly* (Canterbury Edition), p. 166.

161. Mrs. Conrad called attention to this trait indirectly in *Joseph Conrad as I Knew Him*, p. 160.

162. *Almayer's Folly* MS., chap. VIII, p. 10 (Rosenbach).

163. *Almayer's Folly* TS., p. 145 (Leeds), and (1895), p. 148, and (Canterbury Edition), p. 113.

164. *Almayer's Folly* MS., chap. X, p. 16 (Rosenbach).

165. Page 211 (Leeds).

166. *Almayer's Folly* (1895), p. 206, and (Canterbury Edition), p. 157.

167. *Almayer's Folly* MS., chap. X, p. 18 (Rosenbach).

168. *Almayer's Folly* (1895), p. 208, and (Canterbury Edition), pp. 158–159. The typescript (p. 213 [Leeds]) is exactly like the printed text.

169. *Almayer's Folly* MS., chap. I, pp. 1–2 (Rosenbach).

170. *Almayer's Folly* TS., pp. 1–2 (Leeds), and (1895), p. 8, and (Canterbury Edition), pp. 3–4.

Except for minor corrections in phrasing and choice of words the typescript is like the printed text.

171. *Almayer's Folly* MS., chap. I, pp. 1–2 (Rosenbach), and TS., pp. 1–2 (Leeds), and (1895), pp. 7–8, and (Canterbury Edition), pp. 3–4.

172. The Leeds typescript (pp. 19–21) clearly follows the lost state of the story: the typescript is not at all like the Rosenbach manuscript (chap. I, pp. 25–26) and, except for a few minor differences in phraseology, reads like the first edition (pp. 25–27). A comparison of the first edition with the Canterbury (pp. 17–18) reveals a few changes in wording that show Conrad's constant care for his texts.

173. For instance the analysis of Almayer's pathetic desire to visit Nina when she was a child in Singapore and his unwillingness to visit her in his unsuccessful condition ([Canterbury Edition], p. 29) is entirely lacking in the original manuscript (chap. II, pp. 14–15 [Rosenbach]).

174. *Almayer's Folly* MS., chap. I, p. 23 (Rosenbach).

175. *Almayer's Folly* (1895), p. 24, and (Canterbury Edition), p. 16.

176. *Almayer's Folly* MS., chap. I, pp. 17–18 (Rosenbach).

The implications of the manuscript are that Dain may have been more friendly with Lakamba, Almayer's enemy, than with the Dutchman himself. When Dain insisted on his visit to Lakamba on the opening night of the novel, he added suspiciously that he would talk to Almayer "'To morrow. I like to see the face of my friend when I am talking with him. As to Lakamba it does not matter'" (*Almayer's Folly* MS., chap. I, p. 18 [Rosenbach]).

Such an interpretation is borne out by a passage found in the manuscript (chap. IV, pp. 2–3 [Rosenbach]): "Lakamba had certain projects where the aid of Almayer and of Almayer's newly found friend Dain Maroola seemed to him indispensable." All reference to these projects was cut in the typescript (p. 60 [Leeds]) and the published text ([1895], p. 67, and [Canterbury Edition], p. 49).

177. *Almayer's Folly* TS., pp. 13, 14 (Leeds), and (1895), p. 21, and (Canterbury Edition), p. 13.

178. Chap. I, pp. 17–18 (Rosenbach).

179. Chap. I, p. 19 (Rosenbach).

180. Page 14 (Leeds). See *Almayer's Folly* (1895), pp. 20, 21, and (Canterbury Edition), pp. 13, 14.

181. *Almayer's Folly* TS., p. 101 (Leeds), and (1895), p. 107, and (Canterbury Edition), p. 79. In the typescript there is a further correction connected with the episode. In telling Lakamba of his fight with the Dutch, Dain first said that they had "'killed all my men,'" and this was changed to "'many of my men.'" Conrad found it hard either to make up his mind exactly or to be consistent.

182. *Almayer's Folly* MS., chap. I, p. 9 (Rosenbach).

183. Conrad had no idea at the time how important the secrecy of the Pantai River would be as the foundation of *An Outcast of the Islands.*

184. *Almayer's Folly* MS., chap. II, p. 7 (Rosenbach). The order of composition in this sentence presents difficulties. Did the sentence stand as it does now before *white competition* was canceled? If it did, the parenthesis would apply to the canceled phrase and would refer to the crowd whom "the Dutch merchants called those . . . English pedlars" (*Almayer's Folly* [Canterbury Edition], p. 7). If the parenthesis was written after the cancelation, it would apply, of course, to the Arabs. Perhaps it was written before the cancelation, and Conrad decided it would stand for the English or the Arabs.

185. "'I spoke to him but he would not come here tonight. Will come tomorrow, he said.' –

"'You asked him Father? said Nina.

"'I did. What could I do? There is nobody here I can trust to help me, and help I must have. Can I live here for ever, *and die in this swamp? No* and with the means of getting away almost within my reach die miserably in this swamp. Dain must help me! And I must at last trust a Malay!" (*Almayer's Folly* MS., chap. I, pp. 25–26 [Rosenbach]).

The conversation was entirely reworked in the lost typescript (*Al-*

mayer's Folly TS., pp. 19–20 [Leeds], and [Canterbury Edition], pp. 17–18).

Some hundred words later than the end of the two men's conversation appears the seed from which the mature conception of the gold hunt may have grown. In the paragraph beginning, "Almayer stepped homeward," there appears in the manuscript (chap. I, p. 19 [Rosenbach]) the following sentence: "Was Dain also going to play him false" (in the Leeds typescript [p. 15] changed to, "Surely Dain was not thinking of playing him false"). Perhaps Conrad meant that Almayer had already approached Dain with his project, though their conversation does not substantiate it. Probably Almayer was about to approach Dain and was wondering whether the Malay would be false.

186. *Almayer's Folly* TS., p. 20 (Leeds), and (1895), pp. 26–27, and (Canterbury Edition), p. 18.

187. *Almayer's Folly* MS., chap. V, p. 5 (Rosenbach). It was Lingard who discovered the resources of the interior and left his notebooks for Almayer.

188. *Almayer's Folly* TS., p. 77 (Leeds). See *Almayer's Folly* (1895), p. 85, and (Canterbury Edition), p. 62.

189. *Almayer's Folly* TS., p. 111 (Leeds).

190. *Almayer's Folly* MS., chap. V, p. 11 (Rosenbach), and TS., p. 82 (Leeds), and (1895), p. 89, and (Canterbury Edition), p. 65.

191. *Almayer's Folly* MS., chap. II, p. 13 (Rosenbach).

192. *Ibid.*, chap. I, p. 19 (Rosenbach).

193. *Almayer's Folly* TS., p. 33 (Leeds).

194. Chap. I, pp. 17–18 (Rosenbach).

195. *Almayer's Folly* TS., p. 13 (Leeds). See *Almayer's Folly* (1895), p. 20, and (Canterbury Edition), p. 13.

196. *Almayer's Folly* MS., chap. I, pp. 25–27 (Rosenbach), and TS., pp. 19–21 (Leeds), and (1895), pp. 26–28, and (Canterbury Edition), pp. 17–19.

197. ". . . solitude of his fear. Heavy breathings stirred the darkness. The sea gurgled . . ." (*New Review*, XVII [1897], 496, and *The Nigger of the "Narcissus": A Tale of the Sea* [London: William Heinemann, 1898], p. 176); ". . . solitude of his fear. The sea gurgled . . ." (*Nigger* [Canterbury Edition], p. 119).

198. *Nigger* MS., pp. 1–2 (Rosenbach).

199. *New Review*, XVII (1897), 125.

200. *Conrad Memorial Library*, p. 31. The American edition appeared on November 30, 1897, and the English on December 2, though its title-page is postdated 1898 (*ibid.*, pp. 38, 41). In the following analysis, unless otherwise designated, the English edition is the one described as the first edition and also as the edition of 1898.

201. *New Review*, XVII (1897), 148.

202. *Nigger* (1898), p. 53, and *The Children of the Sea: A Tale of the Forecastle* (New York: Dodd, Mead and Company, 1897), p. 44.

203. *Nigger* (1898), pp. 168–169, and *Children of the Sea*, p. 142.

204. *Nigger* (Canterbury Edition), p. 114.

205. For instance pp. 8–9, 23, 31, 34, 51, 58–60, 77, 80–81, 86, 92–97, 105–114, 128–129, 135–140, 142, 145–147, 157, 160–170, 172, 174–175, 178–179, 182–183, 185, 189, 193–194 (Rosenbach).

206. The first and definitive editions have their five chapter divisions in the same places. The serial, however, has seven chapters; in the *New Review* (XVII [1897], 241, 361, 485) chapters three, four, and six occur at places where there are no divisions in the book publication (*Nigger* [Canterbury Edition], pp. 40, 73, 103), because of the requirements of magazine publication. The manuscript is divided inconsistently: there is no division, for instance, for chapter five (*Nigger* MS., p. 152 [Rosenbach]).

207. Conrad later revised them thoroughly, for they are strikingly different from the text of the *New Review*.

208. For another page with a slip pasted over an abandoned passage see *Nigger* MS., p. 105 (Rosenbach).

209. For instance *ibid*., p. 79 (Rosenbach).

210. *Ibid*., pp. 57–58 (Rosenbach). For the final version see *Nigger* (Canterbury Edition), pp. 54–55.

211. *Lettres Françaises*, p. 128.

212. *Nigger* MS., p. 30 (Rosenbach). The *New Review* (XVII [1897], 144) kept *blue eyes;* the first edition (p. 43) and the Canterbury Edition (p. 30) emended *blue* to *grey*, thus adding the final touch of coldness to the impression.

213. *Loom* is "a seaman's term for the indistinct and exaggerated appearance of land on the horizon, an object seen through mist or darkness, etc." (*Oxford Universal English Dictionary* [n.p.: Doubleday, Doran and Company, Inc., 1937], V, 1166).

214. *Nigger* MS., p. 173 (Rosenbach). The corrected reading was kept in the *New Review*, XVII [1897], 615, the first edition (p. 229), and the Canterbury Edition (p. 154).

215. *Nigger* MS., p. 73 (Rosenbach). *Whispered* was kept in the *New Review* (XVII [1897], 261), the first edition (p. 101), and the Canterbury Edition (p. 69).

216. *Nigger* MS., p. 179 (Rosenbach). The emendation was kept in the *New Review* (XVII [1897], 619), in the first edition (p. 238), and the Canterbury Edition (p. 160).

217. *Nigger* MS., p. 91 (Rosenbach). The wording was kept in the *New Review* (XVII [1897], 369–370), in the first edition (p. 127), and in the Canterbury Edition (p. 86).

218. *Nigger* MS., p. 107 (Rosenbach). The corrected version was also

used in the *New Review* (XVII [1897], 379), the first edition (p. 147), and the Canterbury Edition (p. 100).

219. *Nigger* MS., p. 183 (Rosenbach). The corrections were followed in the *New Review* (XVII [1897], 621), the first edition (p. 243), and the Canterbury Edition (p. 163).

For another use of the same material see *Mirror of the Sea*, pp. 103–108.

220. *Nigger* MS., p. 1 (Rosenbach).

221. *Loc. cit.* See the *New Review* (XVII [1897], 125), the first edition (p. 1), and the Canterbury Edition (p. 3) in which the wording is the same as the expanded version, except for the removal of *the* before *mate*, though the punctuation has been corrected.

222. *Nigger* (Canterbury Edition), p. xiv.

223. *Nigger* MS., p. 69 (Rosenbach). The addition was kept in the *New Review* (XVII [1897], 258), the first edition (p. 95), and the Canterbury Edition (p. 65).

224. *Nigger* MS., p. 2 (Rosenbach). The *New Review* (XVII [1897], 125–126) did not improve matters a great deal by altering *pellucid* to *limpid*, and it was followed by the first edition (p. 2) and the Canterbury Edition (p. 4).

225. *Nigger* MS., p. 159 (Rosenbach). The emendation stood in the *New Review* (XVII [1897], 607), the first edition (p. 212), and the Canterbury Edition (p. 143).

226. *Nigger* MS., p. 76 (Rosenbach). The addition stood in the *New Review* (XVII [1897], 263), the first edition (pp. 105–106), and the Canterbury Edition (p. 72).

227. XVII (1897), 252.

228. *Nigger* (1898), p. 81, and (Canterbury Edition), p. 56.

229. XVII (1897), 509.

230. *Nigger* (1898), p. 204, and (Canterbury Edition), p. 138.

231. XVII (1897), 254.

232. *Nigger* (1898), pp. 85–86, and (Canterbury Edition), p. 59.

233. *New Review*, XVII (1897), 502, and *Nigger* (1898), p. 189, and (Canterbury Edition), p. 128.

234. *New Review*, XVII (1897), 619, and *Nigger* (1898), p. 239, and (Canterbury Edition), p. 160.

Undoubtedly the influence of French, a little freely employed, is found here.

235. Conrad wrote Garnett ironically on October 11, 1897: "Heinemann objects to the *bloody's* in the book. That Israelite is afraid of women. I didn't trust myself to say much in Pawling's room. Moreover Pawling is a good fellow whom I like more every time I see him; and it seemed to me he wanted me to give way. So I struck 3 or 4 *bloody's* out. I am sure there is a couple left yet but, damn it, I am not going to hunt 'em up" (*Letters from Joseph Conrad*, p. 113).

236. *New Review*, XVII (1897), 258, and *Nigger* (1898), p. 95, and (Canterbury Edition), p. 65. See *Nigger* MS., p. 69 (Rosenbach).

237. *New Review*, XVII (1897), 613, and *Nigger* (1898), p. 226, and (Canterbury Edition), p. 152. See *Nigger* MS., p. 171 (Rosenbach).

238. Sotheby, Wilkinson and Hodge, Sale Catalogue (James B. Pinker), p. 74, and *Life and Letters*, II, 221. The copy is now part of the Keating Collection (*Conrad Memorial Library*, pp. 47–48) in the Yale University Library.

239. *The Nigger of the "Narcissus": A Tale of the Sea* (Popular Edition; London: William Heinemann, 1910), p. 74, and (Canterbury Edition), p. 51.

240. *Nigger* (1910), p. 41, and (Canterbury Edition), p. 29.

241. *Nigger* (1910), p. 207, and (Canterbury Edition), p. 140.

242. *Nigger* (1898), p. 224, and (Canterbury Edition), p. 151.

243. *Nigger* (1898), p. 171, and (Canterbury Edition), p. 116.

244. *Nigger* (1898), p. 163. In the Rosenbach manuscript (p. 118) Conrad spelled *blooming* without the *g*, and tried *ymposishun* before settling on *himposyshun*. In the *New Review* (XVII [1897], 490) the *g* was still truncated from *blooming*, and *tyke* was spelled *take*. Obviously Conrad spent much time and thought on the phonetics of Donkin's speech from the beginning.

245. *Nigger* (Canterbury Edition), p. 110.

246. *Nigger* (1898), p. 32, and (Canterbury Edition), p. 23.

247. *Nigger* (1898), p. 16, and (Canterbury Edition), p. 13.

248. *Nigger* (Canterbury Edition), p. 112. The *you's* and *yer's*, *your's* and *yer's* were identical in the first edition (pp. 165–166). The use of *h* in the first edition, which followed the *New Review* (XVII [1897], 491), shows how thoroughly inconsistent Conrad could be with the aspirates, too:

"I've been a-hairing ov yer clothes. . . . Giv' us the key of your chest, I'll put 'em away for yer. . . . You can do it, hunless you *hare* sick. . . . If yer can look hafter yer clothes, yer can look hafter yerself."

There seems to be no consistency between *hafter* and *away*, and certainly *it* was an oversight.

249. *Life and Letters*, II, 247.

250. *Ibid.*, II, 248. In the definitive edition *minyt* and *hymposed* were not corrected (*Nigger* [Canterbury Edition], pp. 121, 132).

251. *Nigger* (1898), p. 144.

252. *Nigger* (Canterbury Edition), p. 98.

253. *Nigger* (1898), p. 132.

254. *Nigger* (Canterbury Edition), p. 90.

255. *New Review*, XVII (1897), 496.

256. *Nigger* (1898), pp. 175–176, and (Canterbury Edition), p. 119.

257. XVII (1897), 608.

258. *Nigger* (1898), p. 215.

259. *Nigger* (Canterbury Edition), p. 145.

260. *Nigger* MS., p. 175 (Rosenbach).

261. Conrad wrote in his memorandum for John Quinn: "The pencil notes in the margin are by Edward Garnett" (*Library of John Quinn*, I, 170).

262. *New Review*, XVII (1897), 615–616.

263. *Nigger* (1898), p. 231, and (Canterbury Edition), p. 155.

264. *Nigger* MS., p. 140 (Rosenbach). See *Nigger* (Canterbury Edition), p. 128.

265. *New Review*, XVII (1897), 502. The manuscript (p. 141 [Rosenbach]) had originally "a peaked face" and changed it to "a peaked nose." See *Nigger* (1898), p. 190, and (Canterbury Edition), p. 128.

266. *Nigger* MS., p. 2 (Rosenbach). Though not corrected in the manuscript, the statement did not stand in print (*New Review*, XVII [1897], 126, and *Nigger* [1898], p. 2, and [Canterbury Edition], p. 4).

267. *Nigger* MS., p. 10 (Rosenbach), and *New Review*, XVII (1897), 131, and *Nigger* (1898), p. 14, and (Canterbury Edition), pp. 11–12.

268. *Nigger* MS., p. 109 (Rosenbach).

269. *New Review*, XVII (1897), 380, and *Nigger* (1898), p. 150, and (Canterbury Edition), p. 102.

270. *Nigger* MS., pp. 163–164 (Rosenbach).

271. *Ibid*., p. 112 (Rosenbach).

272. *Ibid*., p. 163 (Rosenbach).

273. *Ibid*., pp. 112–113 (Rosenbach). The final manuscript reading was followed in the *New Review*, XVII (1897), 486, and *Nigger* (1898), pp. 155–156, and (Canterbury Edition), p. 105.

274. Laid in with *Nigger* MS. (Rosenbach). See *Nigger* (Canterbury Edition), pp. ix–x.

275. *Nigger* MS., pp. 119, 120 (Rosenbach).

276. *Ibid*., p. 138 (Rosenbach).

277. *Ibid*., p. 167 (Rosenbach). See *Nigger* (Canterbury Edition), p. 149.

278. The comment in *The Library of John Quinn* (I, 172) mentions ambiguously "a typed copy of pages 308–318": this refers to the pagination of the manuscript.

The manuscript carries Conrad's note: "Where MS illegible leave blank space. Mistakes – repetitions and imperfect sentences to be typed *exactly* as written."

279. The little brown leather book, inlaid with metal and mother-of-pearl, had belonged to Conrad's mother's sister (*Life and Letters*, I, 1). None of the pages is numbered. The book contains twenty-five pages of Polish poetry, of which the last poem is by Josef Korzeniowski, perhaps the novelist, not related to Conrad (*ibid*., I, 290). Next follow twenty-eight pages of the manuscript of *Lord Jim*, half a page of the

manuscript of *The Rescue*, half a page of notes, and a seven page sketch of a play.

280. *Lord Jim* MS., pp. 10–11 (Harvard). Now and hereafter the pagination refers to those pages of the Harvard notebook which contain the text of *Lord Jim*.

281. *Blackwood's Magazine*, CLXVI (1899), 446, and *Lord Jim: A Tale* (Edinburgh and London: William Blackwood and Sons, 1900), p. 10, and (Canterbury Edition), p. 11.

282. The extant pages are numbered 46–81, 90–108, 120–173 (one page is numbered both 168 and 169), A222–240 (page 222 is missing; there is an additional page, A225), 308–439 (313 and 369 are missing; one page is marked both 349 and 350), 470–523 (493 is missing), 574–589, 611–640. The numbering of the pages as given in *The Library of John Quinn* (I, 172) does not mention the two pages numbered doubly or the additional page, nor does the sum of the page numbers add up to the 362 pages given as a total. Perhaps 362 was reached by the addition of the pages as given in the catalogue, which gives 357, by the subtraction of the two pages doubly numbered, which gives 355, and by the addition of the seven pages of typescript, which gives 362. The additional page, A225, is still not accounted for.

283. *Lord Jim* MS., pp. 52–53 (Rosenbach).

284. *Blackwood's*, CLXVI (1899), 648, and *Lord Jim* (1900), p. 41, and (Canterbury Edition), p. 40.

285. *Letters from Joseph Conrad*, p. 169.

286. *Life and Letters*, I, 296. Since the story began to run serially in *Blackwood's Magazine* in October, 1899, there must have been a separate typescript of each instalment as it was sent to the publishers.

287. *Lord Jim* TS., p. 3 (Rosenbach). It exactly followed the manuscript (pp. 311–312 [Rosenbach]). Except for minor changes in punctuation, etc., it was followed in *Blackwood's*, CLXVII (1900), 512, and *Lord Jim* (1900), p. 168, and (Canterbury Edition), p. 158.

288. *Lord Jim* TS., p. 3 (Rosenbach). Except for a mistake in typography it followed the manuscript (p. 311 [Rosenbach]).

289. *Blackwood's*, CLXVII (1900), 512, and *Lord Jim* (1900), pp. 167–168, and (Canterbury Edition), p. 157.

290. *Lord Jim* TS., pp. 4–5 (Rosenbach).

291. *Blackwood's*, CLXVII (1900), 512, and *Lord Jim* (1900), pp. 168–169, and (Canterbury Edition), p. 158.

292. *Blackwood's*, CLXVIII (1900), 383.

293. *Lord Jim* (1900), p. 361, and (Canterbury Edition), p. 335.

294. *Blackwood's*, CLXVI (1899), 808.

295. *Lord Jim* (1900), p. 60, and (Canterbury Edition), p. 57.

296. *Richard Curle Conrad Collection*, item 36.

The differences of text are very inconsistent. Sometimes the first American edition is like the uncorrected text of *Blackwood's*:

"He talked feverishly, with a gleeful ferocity and a savage, unforgiving contempt for poor Jim; . . ." (*Lord Jim: A Romance* [New York: Doubleday, McClure and Co., 1900], p. 323, and *Blackwood's*, CLXVIII [1900], 552).

"He talked feverishly, . . ." (*Lord Jim* [London, 1900], p. 372).

Sometimes it is like the English first edition which was corrected from the serial reading:

. . . the attentive eyes whose glance stabbed, and those questions that stretched his soul on the rack. The face of the presiding magistrate . . . (*Blackwood's*, CLXVI [1899], 456).

. . . the attentive eyes whose glance stabbed. The face of the presiding magistrate . . . (*Lord Jim* [New York, 1900], p. 24, and [London, 1900], p. 28).

297. *Blackwood's*, CLXVIII (1900), 371 (Beyer).

298. *Lord Jim* (1900), p. 340, and (Canterbury Edition), p. 316.

299. *Blackwood's*, CLXVIII (1900), 369 (Beyer).

300. *Lord Jim* (1900), p. 336, and (Canterbury Edition), p. 313.

301. *Blackwood's*, CLXVIII (1900), 376 (Beyer).

302. *Lord Jim* (1900), p. 348, and (Canterbury Edition), p. 324.

303. *Blackwood's*, CLXVIII (1900), 383 (Beyer). The corrections were accepted in the first edition with one alteration: Conrad returned to *great blaze*, though he kept *one*, and cut *luminous* (*Lord Jim*) [1900], p. 361, and [Canterbury Edition], pp. 335–336).

304. For instance the first edition (p. 253) has "'". . . sail at four?"'" and the Canterbury Edition (p. 237) has "'"sail at four!"'"

305. For instance the first edition (p. 243), like *Blackwood's* (CLXVII [1900], 809), has "'a short sketch of life and character of each,'" while the Canterbury Edition (p. 227) has *the* before *life*.

306. For instance the first edition (p. 184) reads, "'As to an inaccessible guano deposit,'" and the Canterbury Edition (p. 173) changes *an* to *the*.

307. For instance *Lord Jim* MS., p. 425 (Rosenbach).

308. *Ibid.*, pp. 435–436, 489–490, 612, 626–631 (Rosenbach), and *ibid.*, pp. 7–11 (Harvard).

309. *Ibid.*, pp. 148–158, 226–228, 236–238, 340–345, 351–352, 358–360, 366–367, 383, 387–394, 406–410, 412–417, 470–472, 474–475, 501–502, 513–518, 585–586, 634 (Rosenbach).

310. The *Lord Jim* MS. (p. 233 verso [Rosenbach]), like that of *Almayer's Folly*, even contains a little drawing of mountains which may have some bearing upon the topography of Patusan.

311. *Lord Jim* MS., pp. 239, 240, both of which were attempts to write p. 238 (Rosenbach).

312. *Lord Jim* (Canterbury Edition), pp. 4, 5.

313. These pages are, approximately, in the Canterbury Edition, pp. 116–117.

314. For instance *Lord Jim* MS., p. 71 (Rosenbach).
315. *Ibid.*, pp. 168, 169, 349, 350 (Rosenbach).
316. *Ibid.*, p. 3 (Harvard), and p. 376 (Rosenbach).
317. *Ibid.*, pp. 336, 410 (Rosenbach).
318. *Ibid.*, pp. 129, 589 (Rosenbach).
319. *Ibid.*, p. 482 (Rosenbach).
320. See letter about the chapter divisions in *The Rescue* (*Letters from Joseph Conrad*, p. 57).
321. *Lord Jim* MS., p. 107 (Rosenbach).
322. "Heart of Darkness" MS., pp. 40–43 numbered in black pencil (Yale).
323. *Life and Letters*, II, 327.
324. For instance *Lord Jim* MS., p. 3 (Harvard).
325. *Ibid.*, p. 20 (Harvard). In *Blackwood's* (CLXVI [1899], 448), the first edition (p. 14), and the Canterbury Edition (p. 15), there is a further expansion: "the *Patna* cast off and backed away from the wharf."
326. *Lord Jim* MS., p. 575 (Rosenbach). See *Blackwood's*, CLXVIII (1900), 259, and *Lord Jim* (1900), p. 307, and (Canterbury Edition), p. 286.
327. *Lord Jim* MS., p. 226 (Rosenbach). *Blackwood's* (CLXVII [1900], 237) and the book form (*Lord Jim* [1900], 124, and [Canterbury Edition], p. 117) cut the sentence beginning "He never" and alter the wording of the third sentence.
328. *Blackwood's*, CLXVII (1900), 70.
329. *Lord Jim* (1900), p. 112, and (Canterbury Edition), p. 105.
330. One paragraph of one hundred and fifty words was cut (*Blackwood's*, CLXVI [1899], 826, and *Lord Jim* [1900], p. 90, and [Canterbury Edition], p. 85).
331. *Lord Jim* MS., p. 8 (Harvard).
332. *Loc. cit.*
333. *Ibid.*, p. 9 (Harvard).
334. *Ibid.*, pp. 9–10 (Harvard).
335. *Ibid.*, p. 10 (Harvard).
336. *Blackwood's*, CLXVI (1899), 446.
337. *Lord Jim* (1900), p. 10, and (Canterbury Edition), p. 11.
338. *Lord Jim* MS., pp. 124–125 (Rosenbach). See the rest of the paragraph for Conrad's use of the discarded sentences.
339. *Blackwood's*, CLXVI (1899), 819.
340. *Lord Jim* (1900), p. 79, and (Canterbury Edition), pp. 74–75.
341. *Lord Jim* MS., pp. 629–630 (Rosenbach). See the rest of the paragraph for Conrad's use of the discarded material.
342. *Blackwood's*, CLXVIII (1900), 369.
343. *Lord Jim* (1900), p. 336, and (Canterbury Edition), p. 313.
344. *Lord Jim* MS., p. 340 (Rosenbach).
345. *Lord Jim* (Canterbury Edition), p. 172.

346. *Lord Jim* MS., p. 162 (Rosenbach).

347. *Blackwood's*, CLXVII (1900), 61, and *Lord Jim* (1900), p. 95, and (Canterbury Edition), p. 90.

348. *Lord Jim* MS., pp. 162–163 (Rosenbach), and *Lord Jim* (Canterbury Edition), p. 90.

The idea of a murderous struggle taking place on a ship in distress was worked out with most ironic and dramatic effect in *Typhoon*.

349. *Lord Jim* (Canterbury Edition), pp. 136–137. An abbreviated version of the information was introduced two pages earlier: "'The *Patna* . . . French gunboat . . . towed successfully to Aden . . .'" (*ibid*., p. 134).

350. *Lord Jim* MS., p. 470 (Rosenbach). In the printed text only the opening sentence of the analysis was used: "Strange, this fatality that would cast the complexion of a flight upon all his acts, of impulsive unreflecting desertion – of a jump into the unknown" (Canterbury Edition, p. 229).

351. *Lord Jim* MS., p. 471 (Rosenbach).

352. *Blackwood's* CLXVII (1900), 810, and *Lord Jim* (1900), p. 245, and (Canterbury Edition), p. 229, 261.

353. *Lord Jim* MS., p. 471 (Rosenbach), and *Blackwood's*, CLXVII (1900), 810, and *Lord Jim* (1900), p. 245, and (Canterbury Edition), pp. 229, 275.

354. *Lord Jim* MS., pp. 391–392 (Rosenbach). For the final version see *Lord Jim* (Canterbury Edition), p. 195.

355. *Lord Jim* MS., pp. 393–394 (Rosenbach). For the final version see *Lord Jim* (Canterbury Edition), p. 196.

356. *Blackwood's*, CLXVII (1900), 810, and *Lord Jim* (1900), p. 245, and (Canterbury Edition), p. 229.

357. *Blackwood's*, CLXVI (1899), 442–443, and *Lord Jim* (1900), pp. 3–4, and (Canterbury Edition), p. 5.

358. *Lord Jim* MS., p. 308 (Rosenbach), and *Blackwood's*, CLXVII (1900), 419, and *Lord Jim* (1900), p. 165, and (Canterbury Edition), p. 155.

359. *Lord Jim* MS., p. 1 (Harvard).

360. *Blackwood's*, CLXVI (1899), 441, and *Lord Jim* (1900), p. 1, and (Canterbury Edition), p. 3.

361. *Lord Jim* MS., pp. 351–352 (Rosenbach).

362. *Blackwood's*, CLXVII (1900), 523, and *Lord Jim* (1900), p. 187, and (Canterbury Edition), p. 175.

363. *Lord Jim* MS., p. 16 (Harvard).

364. *Blackwood's*, CLXVI (1899), 447–448, and *Lord Jim* (900), pp. 12–13, and (Canterbury Edition), p. 13.

365. *Lord Jim* MS., pp. 26–27 (Harvard). Compare *Blackwood's*, CLXVI (1899), 449, and *Lord Jim* (1900), pp. 15–16, and (Canterbury Edition), p. 16.

366. *Lord Jim* MS., pp. 403–404 (Rosenbach).
367. *Blackwood's*, CLXVII (1900), 677, and *Lord Jim* (1900), p. 214, and (Canterbury Edition), p. 201.
368. *Lord Jim* MS., p. 487 (Rosenbach).
369. See for a cut and certain slight changes *Blackwood's*, CLXVII (1900), 815, and *Lord Jim* (1900), p. 254, and (Canterbury Edition), p. 238.
370. *Blackwood's*, CLXVIII (1900), 254. The manuscript lacks pages 524–573 in which the passage would appear.
371. *Lord Jim* (1900), p. 298, and (Canterbury Edition), p. 278.
372. *Lord Jim* MS., p. 613 (Rosenbach). For a few unimportant changes in the final version see *Lord Jim* (Canterbury Edition), p. 306.
373. *Tales of Unrest*, p. vii.
374. *Lettres Françaises*, p. 62.

CHAPTER V

1. His inaccurate memory was proverbial in his circle (*Joseph Conrad as I Knew Him*, p. 18, and *Last Twelve Years*, p. 33).
2. *Life and Letters*, II, 264.
3. *Richard Curle Conrad Collection*, item 134. The privately printed edition of "The Black Mate," in a copy of which the note was written, appeared in February, 1922 (T. J. Wise, *A Conrad Library: A Catalogue of Printed Books, Manuscripts and Autograph Letters* [London: Printed for Private Circulation Only, 1928], p. 44). Hence the statement was made after January 19, 1922.
4. I, 89. Though Jean-Aubry stated that Conrad wrote the story in 1885, he corrected himself three sentences later by saying that "the existing version is no indication of Conrad's command of English in 1886. . . ."
Cunninghame Graham, who wrote the introduction to the posthumous volume of collected tales in which the story was printed, increased the complication by guessing: " 'The Black Mate' . . . must have been written about 1884, as a friend of Conrad's tells me" (*Tales of Hearsay*, pp. viii–ix). He did not identify the source of his information.
5. *Conrad Memorial Library*, p. 365. Mrs. Conrad expanded the anecdote for R. L. Mégroz: " 'I can remember giving Conrad material for "The Black Mate." But on one of his naughty days he said that "The Black Mate" was his first work, and when I said, "No, *Almayer's Folly* was the first thing you ever did," he burst out: "If I like to say 'The Black Mate' was my first work, I shall say so" ' " (*Joseph Conrad's Mind and Method*, p. 88).
6. Pages viii–ix.
7. *Notes by Joseph Conrad*, p. 37, n. 2.
8. *Life and Letters*, I, 89.
9. *Bibliography*, p. 115.

10. *Life and Letters*, II, 264, and *Conrad to a Friend*, p. 64, n. 1.
11. *Life and Letters*, II, 264.
12. *Conrad Library*, p. 44.
13. *Richard Curle Conrad Collection*, item 134.
14. *Notes by Joseph Conrad*, p. 37, n. 1.
15. *Library of John Quinn*, I, 166.

The misleading statements are worth noticing:

In *A Sketch of Joseph Conrad's Life* (p. 1) Conrad gave 1890 as the year.

In a note which he wrote in Richard Curle's copy of the first edition Conrad recorded that he began the novel "in the spring of the year 1889" (*Richard Curle Conrad Collection*, item 19). The time of year was incorrect.

The latter inaccuracy proved dangerous, for it was apparently followed by Thomas J. Wise in his *Bibliography* (p. 5): "Mr. Conrad has stated that the novel was commenced in the spring of 1889."

16. Page 73.
17. *Life and Letters*, I, 91–119.
18. A good example of the sort of misinformation about the circumstances under which Conrad began to write can be found in Arnold Bennett's *Journal* (pp. 403–404): "F. M. Hueffer [Ford] . . . told us Conrad had first idea of writing through seeing a 'Pseudonym' [Library] at the bookstall at Vevey Station. He chose English in preference to French because, whereas there were plenty of stylists in French, there were none in English." Conrad may well have been the original source of such statements.
19. *Personal Record*, p. 9. With characteristic inaccuracy Conrad fixed the number of years at four (*ibid.*, p. 74), whereas it was actually two.
20. *Ibid.*, p. 69. The statement casts much doubt upon Ford's recollection that "the first words of Conrad's first book were pencilled on the flyleaves and margins of 'Madame Bovary' " (*Joseph Conrad: A Personal Remembrance*, p. 7). Ford himself somewhat discredited his anecdote by later adding *L'Education Sentimentale* to *Madame Bovary* (*Return to Yesterday*, p. 246). As colorful as the information is, it is too open to question to be accepted as trustworthy.

Conrad denied that he read Flaubert until after he had completed *Almayer's Folly* (*Life and Letters*, II, 206). Yet he said in a letter to Mme. Poradowska dated April 6, 1892 (Yale): "Je viens de relire Mme Bovary."

21. *Sketch of Joseph Conrad's Life*, pp. 1–2.

In view of the greater specificness of these statements the generalization Conrad made in the memorandum for John Quinn does not stand: "Laid aside during voyages to Congo and Australia. Taken up again in 1893" (*Library of John Quinn*, I, 166).

22. *Life and Letters*, I, 123.

In renumbering the chapters Conrad later changed the pagination to chapter four, page one. He seems to have altered the chapter numbers after completing six pages of the original chapter seven, when he combined the original chapters one and two and hence renumbered the original chapter seven as chapter six. Except for occasional misnumberings he followed the new order.

23. *Personal Record*, p. 14, and *Life and Letters*, I, 141.

24. *Life and Letters*, I, 145.

25. In renumbering the chapters and pages Conrad later changed the pagination to chapter five, page twenty-five.

26. In renumbering the chapters and pages Conrad later changed the pagination to chapter six, page four.

27. The arrangement of the computations suggests that Conrad cast up his accounts at the end of the second week. The evidence discredits his statement, "Geneva, or more precisely the hydropathic establishment of Champel, is rendered forever famous by the termination of the eighth chapter in the history of Almayer's decline and fall" (*Personal Record*, p. 14).

28. *Personal Record*, p. 14.

29. Information taken from the addresses on several letters to Mme. Poradowska (Yale).

30. "Me voilà malade encore – juste comme j'allais commencer a travailler" (letter to Mme. Poradowska dated July 30, 1891 [Yale]). In a letter to Mme. Poradowska dated August 5, 1891 (Yale), he announced that he began working on the fourth.

31. *Joseph Conrad as I Knew Him*, p. 101.

32. Letter to Mme. Poradowska dated September 15, 1891 (Yale).

33. *Life and Letters*, I, 149. Ill-health, work in the warehouse, trips to Brussels to see Mme. Poradowska and general depression may well have prevented a fast rate of work (*ibid.*, I, 146–147).

34. *Ibid.*, I, 150, and *Personal Record*, pp. 15–18.

One of the longest-lived apocryphal Conrad stories was that Conrad showed the manuscript to Galsworthy when they first met as mate and passenger on the *Torrens* (*Life and Letters*, I, 152–153). In 1931 Ford was still giving it circulation in *Return to Yesterday* (pp. 246–247).

35. The not altogether trustworthy memorandum for Quinn asserted that the novel was laid aside during the Australian voyages (*Library of John Quinn*, I, 166).

36. *Personal Record*, p. 19. In describing the cold and the sleigh ride (*ibid.*, pp. 20–21) Conrad was confusing his visit in February, March, and April, 1890, with the visit in August, September, and October, 1893 (*Life and Letters*, I, 123, 153). Obviously he had not reached the ninth chapter of *Almayer's Folly* in February, 1890.

37. *Sketch of Joseph Conrad's Life*, p. 2, and *Joseph Conrad as I Knew Him*, p. 62.

38. Letters to Mme. Poradowska dated November 5 and 26, 1893 (Yale).

39. *Life and Letters*, I, 154–155, and letter to Mme. Poradowska dated January 9, 1894 (Yale). Also *Personal Record*, pp. 1–5.

40. Letter to Mme. Poradowska dated "Jeudi" and assigned by Dr. Gee to Thursday, March 29 or April 5, 1894 (Yale).

41. Letter to Mme. Poradowska dated April 16, 1894 (Yale). Conrad remarked in the same letter that he was leaving on April 20, and in a letter to Mme. Poradowska dated May 2, 1894 (Yale), said that he had stayed ten days with Sanderson. He had met Sanderson and Galsworthy when they were passengers on the *Torrens* in 1893 (*Life and Letters*, I, 152–153).

42. Letter to Mme. Poradowska dated April 24, 1894 (Yale). There is no heading on the letter: hence it was not written from Elstree but under the circumstances described therein most probably from London. In *A Sketch of Joseph Conrad's Life* (pp. 2–3) Conrad declared it was "while staying with some friends in the country and uncertain as to his future that he finished at last 'Almayers Folly' practically rewriting it." Obviously he had forgotten the order of events by 1900 and was merging several distinct stages into one.

It is interesting to compare with this letter of April 24 one to Garnett written immediately after *An Outcast of the Islands* was completed in which Conrad took leave of the characters in much the same way (*Letters from Joseph Conrad*, pp. 39–40).

The question of the exact date on which Conrad completed *Almayer's Folly* is thus cleared up. He dated the last page of the manuscript April, 1894, but the memorandum for Quinn declared that it was finished on May 22, 1894 (*Library of John Quinn*, I, 165–166). It was characteristic of Conrad's memory that he should first have written 1893 and then, on second thoughts, superimposed a four on the three. Jean-Aubry was right in his guess that the novel was completed "toward the end of April and the following month was taken up in correcting" (*Life and Letters*, I, 158, n. 1).

Conrad's habitual inaccuracy is seen in the letter he wrote Galsworthy on June 6, 1907: "To-day completes the round dozen of years since I finished *Almayer's Folly*" (*ibid.*, II, 52).

43. Conrad first mentioned *Almayer's Folly* to Mme. Poradowska in a letter dated "Dimanche" and assigned by Dr. Gee to January 7, 1894 (Yale). In a letter dated March 2, 1894 (Yale), he promised to visit her in Brussels if possible. In a letter dated "Jeudi" and assigned by Dr. Gee to Thursday, March 29 or April 5, 1894 (Yale), he sent her "la première page – (dont j'ai pris copie) pour Vous donner une idée de l'apparence de mon manuscrit. Cela vous est du puisque j'ai vu le Votre." Since he was to send her the final chapters in typescript, and since she had not seen his manuscript, she must have seen the first ten chapters in type-

script. On an undated scrap of paper, assigned by Dr. Gee to late April, 1894 (Yale), he mentioned rewriting the first four chapters of *Almayer's Folly* and spoke of her novel *Marylka* as if they had had a conversation about it. In a letter dated "Mercredi" and assigned by Dr. Gee to June, 1894 (Yale), he declared himself "ni plus ni moins bête qu'a Bruxelles quand j'ai eu le bonheur de m'infliger sur Vous." In a letter dated July 12, 1894 (Yale), he regretted, "Oui! Il serait bon de se revoir – mais!" All the evidence points to his having paid Mme. Poradowska a visit in Brussels, carrying with him a typescript of the first ten chapters of *Almayer's Folly*, and to his having seen and talked over her work with her.

44. Letter to Mme. Poradowska dated April 24, 1894 (Yale).

45. On an undated scrap of paper (Yale) which Dr. Gee assigned to late April, 1894, and believed accompanied the typescript of chapter eleven.

In a letter to Mme. Poradowska dated May 2, 1894 (Yale), he promised to send chapter twelve soon, implying that he had already despatched chapter eleven.

46. Letter to Mme. Poradowska dated May 2, 1894 (Yale). Dr. Gee believed the general reference to rewriting the first four chapters preceded the more specific reference to revising the first three chapters.

47. See pp. 113–115, 125–129, above.

48. *Sketch of Joseph Conrad's Life*, p. 3.

49. Letter to Mme. Poradowska dated "Jeudi" and assigned by Dr. Gee to Thursday, May 17, 1894 (Yale).

50. Letter to Mme. Poradowska dated "Mercredi" and placed by Dr. Gee in June, 1894, or certainly before a letter to Mme. Poradowska dated July 12, 1894 (Yale).

51. Letter to Mme. Poradowska dated September 8, 1894 (Yale).

52. See letter to Unwin dated September 8, 1894, first published in *Saturday Review of Literature*, X (1933), 55. Conrad later told Quinn incorrectly that he submitted the story on June 2, 1894 (*Library of John Quinn*, I, 165), the date followed by Jean-Aubry (*Life and Letters*, I, 159).

53. Letter to Mme. Poradowska dated July 12, 1894 (Yale), and *Life and Letters*, I, 159.

It may well be that the story Ford told Bennett of Conrad's having been inspired to write by seeing the Pseudonym Library at Vevey applied to his choice of publisher.

The books in the Library were, as the title implied, published under pseudonyms. Number eight, for instance, was *Some Emotion and a Moral* by John Oliver Hobbes, in reality Mrs. Pearl Mary Theresa (Richards) Craigie, and number ten was *John Sherman and Dhoya* by Ganconagh, in reality William Butler Yeats.

54. Letter to Mme. Poradowska dated "Samedi" and assigned by Dr. Gee to Saturday, August 18, 1894 (Yale).

55. (Yale).

56. Letter dated "Lundi" and assigned by Dr. Gee to Monday, July 30, 1894 (Yale).

57. *Life and Letters*, I, 120.

58. Letter dated "Samedi" and assigned by Dr. Gee to Saturday, August 18, 1894 (Yale).

59. *Saturday Review of Literature*, X (1933–34), 55. Conrad's statement that he possessed no copy of *Almayer's Folly* was palpably an excuse: he certainly had the first draft still and perhaps a first typescript.

60. Letter dated September 8, 1894 (Yale).

61. *Personal Record*, pp. v–viii, and *Life and Letters*, II, 206.

62. Letter to Mme. Poradowska (Yale). See letters to Mme. Poradowska dated "Samedi" (August 18 [?]) and September 8, 1894 (Yale).

63. Letter to Mme. Poradowska (Yale). The novel was not accepted in August, as Conrad declared in his memorandum for John Quinn (*Library of John Quinn*, I, 166).

64. Letters to Mme. Poradowska dated October 10, 1894, and "Lundi matin," assigned by Dr. Gee to Monday, October 29 or November 5, 1894 (Yale). Also *Conrad Memorial Library*, p. 8.

Mme. Poradowska later translated "An Outpost of Progress" (unpublished letter from Conrad to Unwin dated April 26, 1911 [Brick Row Book Shop]).

65. *Letters from Joseph Conrad*, p. 2.

Ford told an interesting story of Garnett's showing him the manuscript of *Almayer's Folly* down in the country (*Ancient Lights and Certain New Reflections* [London: Chapman and Hall, Ltd., 1911], pp. 226–227). The anecdote, however, was put seriously in question by his repeating it twenty years later with *An Outcast of the Islands* substituted for *Almayer's Folly* (*Return to Yesterday*, pp. 50–51).

66. Letter to Mme. Poradowska dated October 4, 1894 (Yale).

67. In writing to Unwin on October 8, Conrad referred to their conversation of "this morning" (unpublished letter [Beyer]).

68. Letter to Mme. Poradowska (Yale). Curle put the price £5 too high (*Notes by Joseph Conrad*, p. 15, n. 1).

69. Letter to Mme. Poradowska dated October 10, 1894 (Yale).

70. *Loc. cit.* It is tempting to identify the two readers as W. H. Chesson and Edward Garnett. Though there is no evidence to disprove that one may have been Chesson, Garnett specifically described first meeting Conrad on quite a different occasion (*Letters from Joseph Conrad*, pp. 2–3).

71. *Life and Letters*, I, 159.

72. Conrad wrote Unwin on October 8: "It was understood this morning that I should have the ms of 'Almayer's Folly' for a couple of days.

. . . I am going out of town this afternoon and would like to take it with me for a final revision" (unpublished letter [Beyer]).

73. Letter to Mme. Poradowska dated October 23, 1894 (Yale).

74. Letter to Mme. Poradowska dated "Mercredi, 94," and assigned by Dr. Gee to Wednesday, November 14 or 21, 1894 (Yale). Conrad worked on the proofs more than he expected.

75. Letter to Mme. Poradowska dated December 27, 1894 (Yale).

76. *Life and Letters*, I, 160, and II, 143.

77. Letter to Mme. Poradowska dated "Samedi" and assigned by Dr. Gee to Saturday, February 23, 1895 (Yale), and *Conrad Memorial Library*, p. 9.

78. *Conrad Memorial Library*, p. 11.

79. *Bibliography*, pp. 5–6. Conrad stated incorrectly in his memorandum for John Quinn that it was published in May (*Library of John Quinn*, I, 166).

80. Letter dated "Vendredi saint" and assigned by Dr. Gee to April 12, 1895 (Yale).

81. *Richard Curle Conrad Collection*, item 20.

82. *Life and Letters*, I, 160, n. 2, 157.

83. Letter dated February 18, 1894 (Yale).

84. *Almayer's Folly*, p. x.

85. *Life and Letters*, II, 221.

86. *Richard Curle Conrad Collection*, item 19.

87. *Life and Letters*, I, 183.

88. Pages 87–88.

89. *Conrad Library*, p. 1.

90. *Library of John Quinn*, I, 164 of priced copy.

91. *Life and Letters*, II, 324.

92. *Loc. cit.*

93. *Outcast*, p. vii.

94. See pp. 18–22, above.

95. *Outcast*, p. vii.

96. Letter to Mme. Poradowska dated "Samedi" and assigned by Dr. Gee to Saturday, August 18, 1894 (Yale). Conrad's memory played him completely false when he wrote in T. J. Wise's copy: "My second book, begun five weeks before Almayer's Folly was published, the actual writing occupying eleven months" (*Conrad Library*, p. 2).

97. Samplings from the *Revue des Deux Mondes* (123 [1894], 31, 131, 231, 331, 431, 531) reveal an average of 430 words to a page. Conrad, then, intended his story to be between 8,000 and 11,000 words.

98. *Personal Record*, p. 9.

99. Letter to Mme. Poradowska (Yale).

100. Letter to Mme. Poradowska dated October 4, 1894 (Yale).

101. Letter to Mme. Poradowska dated October 10, 1894 (Yale).

102. Letter to Mme. Poradowska dated October 23, 1894 (Yale).

103. *Letters from Joseph Conrad*, p. 2. Garnett declared that his encouraging words were spoken at the first meeting (*ibid.*, pp. 2–5). Though Conrad, whose memory was notoriously inaccurate, spoke as if the encouragement had been given at a later meeting (*Outcast*, p. viii), it seems safer to trust Garnett. See *Letters from Joseph Conrad* (p. 4, n. 1) for Garnett's comment on Conrad's inaccurate dating of the episode.

104. *Outcast*, pp. vii–viii.

105. Garnett heard nothing of *An Outcast* until his second meeting with Conrad some weeks later (*Letters from Joseph Conrad*, pp. 5–8).

106. Conrad was also mistaken in the memorandum for Quinn stating that he began the novel on November 18, 1894 (*Library of John Quinn*, I, 168), though the date may have some connection with his early conversations with Garnett.

107. Letter to Mme. Poradowska dated "Lundi matin" and assigned by Dr. Gee to Monday, October 29 or November 5, 1894 (Yale).

Mrs. Margaret Louise (Bradley) Woods, author of "The Vagabonds," was the daughter of the Dean of Westminster and was married to the Rev. H. G. Woods, President of Trinity College, Oxford (*Illustrated London News*, CVII [1896], 662).

By ironic coincidence Macmillan and Company advertised *The Vagabonds* in the first American edition of *Almayer's Folly*. A quotation from a review in the *Congregationalist* described Mrs. Woods' novel thus: "Life and love in an English circus company are its themes, and no little skill is shown in representing them. We will not betray the plot; indeed there is not much of a plot to be betrayed."

108. Letter to Mme. Poradowska dated "Mercredi, 94," and assigned by Dr. Gee to Wednesday, November 14 or 21, 1894 (Yale).

109. Letter dated "Lundi" and assigned by Dr. Gee to Monday, November 26 or December 3, 1894 (Yale).

110. Letter to Mme. Poradowska dated "Jeudi" and assigned by Dr. Gee to Thursday, December 6 or 13, 1894 (Yale).

111. Letter to Mme. Poradowska (Yale).

112. *Library of John Quinn*, I, 168. The change in title occurred in what became, with the redivision of chapters before publication, chapter one of part two.

113. Letter to Mme. Poradowska dated "Mercredi" and assigned by Dr. Gee to Wednesday, January 30 or February 6, 1895 (Yale). It is not impossible that the letter applied to *Almayer's Folly* and belonged to the winter of 1894.

114. Letter to Mme. Poradowska dated "Samedi" and assigned by Dr. Gee to Saturday, February 23, 1895 (Yale).

115. *Life and Letters*, I, 173. In his note on this letter in which he implied that the two paragraphs were untraceable, Jean-Aubry showed that he misread the sentence: he ascribed "beginning" to "chap." instead of "pars." The two paragraphs are easily found (*Outcast*, p. 135).

116. Letter to Mme. Poradowska dated April 30, 1895 (Yale).

117. *Letters from Joseph Conrad*, p. 35.

118. Letter to Mme. Poradowska dated only "Vendredi saint" and assigned by Dr. Gee to Friday, April 12, 1895 (Yale).

119. Letter dated May 6, 1895 (Yale).

120. *Letters from Joseph Conrad*, pp. 36–37.

121. Letter to Mme. Poradowska (Yale). Also *Conrad Memorial Library*, p. 12.

122. *Life and Letters*, I, 162, n. 3. Also *ibid.*, II, 46.

123. *Letters from Joseph Conrad*, p. 39.

124. *Library of John Quinn*, I, 168.

125. This was the date accepted by Jean-Aubry, for obviously September 4 in the *Life and Letters* (I, 162) is a misprint for September 14.

126. *Letters from Joseph Conrad*, pp. 39–40.

127. *Ibid.*, pp. 8–9.

128. *Ibid.*, pp. 41–42. See the entire letter for Conrad's explanation of his intentions (*ibid.*, pp. 41–43).

When the novel was rearranged for publication, chapter twenty-three probably became chapter one of part five and chapter twenty-four became chapter two.

129. *Life and Letters*, I, 183.

130. *Ibid.*, I, 299.

131. *Ibid.*, II, 218, and *Outcast*, p. ix.

132. Ford told an interesting story of the acceptance of the novel: Garnett, who emphasized the anti-imperialist connotations of the story, told Ford that Unwin was undecided about publishing a novel which might lose money; Ford was so impressed by the literary merits of the story that he offered to pay any loss the publisher might incur (*Return to Yesterday*, pp. 50–51). The anecdote is put seriously in question by the fact that twenty years before Ford ascribed much of the story to his first acquaintance with *Almayer's Folly* (*Ancient Lights*, pp. 226–227).

133. *Life and Letters*, I, 177.

134. *Ibid.*, I, 184. The novel was listed among the "Autumn Publications" (p. 8) in *Good Reading about Many Books Mostly by Their Authors* (London: T. Fisher Unwin, 1895–96). The Harvard University copy of Unwin's advertisement was received on January 21, 1896.

135. *Garnett Collection*, p. 2. Also *Joseph Conrad as I Knew Him*, p. 103.

136. *Library of John Quinn*, I, 168.

137. *Bibliography*, p. 9. Though Conrad declared that the novel was issued on March 4 (*Library of John Quinn*, I, 168), and Jean-Aubry adopted his date (*Life and Letters*, I, 163), Wise was corroborated by the advertisement of the book under "Publications Today" in the London *Times* for March 16, 1896.

For a more complete bibliographical report see *Bibliography* (pp.

6–9) and the catalogue of *Richard Curle Conrad Collection* (items 22, 23 and 24) for points not mentioned by Wise.

138. *Notes by Joseph Conrad*, p. 16.

139. *Life and Letters*, II, 134.

140. *Library of John Quinn*, I, 168 of priced copy. The manuscript is now priced at $4500 (*The Sea: Books and Manuscripts*, p. 41).

141. See pp. 20–21, above.

142. *Life and Letters*, I, 185.

143. *Letters from Joseph Conrad*, p. 16.

144. *Ibid*., p. 48, n. 2. See the adverse comment in the manuscript mentioned in *Sisters*, p. 13.

145. *Letters from Joseph Conrad*, p. 46.

146. *Sisters*, p. 16. Ford apparently accepted Conrad's statement.

147. *Ibid*., p. 7.

148. *Ibid*., pp. 7–9.

149. *Letters from Joseph Conrad*, p. 46.

150. *Life and Letters*, I, 163. The Conrads were married on March 24, crossed to St. Malo the night of March 25, spent the night of March 26 at St. Malo, and arrived at Lannion late on March 27 (*Joseph Conrad and His Circle*, pp. 19–23).

151. *Life and Letters*, I, 185.

152. *Ibid*., I, 188. Mrs. Conrad was mistaken in believing that the novel was not begun until "just three weeks after we were married, in our little peasant house on Ile Grande" (*Joseph Conrad as I Knew Him*, p. 106).

153. *Life and Letters*, I, 163.

154. *Letters from Joseph Conrad*, p. 49.

155. *Life and Letters*, I, 164, n. 1.

156. *Ibid*., I, 188.

157. *Letters from Joseph Conrad*, p. 49.

158. G. Jean-Aubry, ed., *Twenty Letters to Joseph Conrad* (London: The First Edition Club, 1926). The letters from each correspondent are in a separate pamphlet.

159. *Letters from Joseph Conrad*, pp. 53–54.

160. *Ibid*., pp. 55–56.

161. *Twenty Letters to Joseph Conrad*.

162. *Letters from Joseph Conrad*, pp. 56–57.

163. *Life and Letters*, I, 191.

164. On May 24 he had completed "about 70 pages" (*Letters from Joseph Conrad*, p. 54) and on June 10 he told Garnett he had completed the first part, 103 pages in all (*ibid*., pp. 57–58).

165. In the published version, *The Rescue*, Conrad divided each of the six parts into chapters.

166. *Letters from Joseph Conrad*, p. 57. On the last page (103) of the manuscript of part one Conrad wrote: "Sent off to London on the 11th

June 1896. Lannion pp. 103. Words 23366 page of type 43" (British Museum: Ashley 4787).

It was apparently this typescript which Mrs. Conrad rediscovered in 1926 (*Joseph Conrad as I Knew Him*, p. 148).

167. *Twenty Letters to Joseph Conrad.*
168. *Library of John Quinn*, I, 170.
169. *Life and Letters*, I, 164.
170. *Letters from Joseph Conrad*, p. 59.
171. (British Museum: Ashley 4787).
172. *Letters from Joseph Conrad*, p. 103.
173. *Rescue*, p. 63.
174. Later these names were changed to Edith and d'Alcacer.
175. *Letters from Joseph Conrad*, p. 61.
176. *Ibid.*, p. 62, n. 1.
177. *Ibid.*, p. 64.
178. *Ibid.*, pp. 63–64.
179. *Ibid.*, p. 68.

Mrs. Conrad was ambiguous when she declared that on Ile Grande Conrad wrote only "a good many pages of what may be called the introduction to 'The Rescue' – pages that were to precede the beginning of the dramatic action. Very, very little of all that is left in the published book" (*Joseph Conrad as I Knew Him*, p. 38). As a matter of fact he completed well over a hundred pages, and in the manuscript the descriptive introduction which he later reworked covers only two and a third pages (British Museum: Ashley 4787).

180. *Life and Letters*, I, 164.
181. *Letters from Joseph Conrad*, pp. 88–89.
182. *Life and Letters*, I, 165.
183. *Ibid.*, I, 204.
184. *Letters from Joseph Conrad*, p. 95.
185. *Library of John Quinn*, I, 172.
186. *Letters from Joseph Conrad*, p. 98.
187. *Library of John Quinn*, I, 172.
188. *Letters from Joseph Conrad*, p. 104.
189. *Ibid.*, pp. 109–110.
190. *Ibid.*, pp. 112–113.
191. *Ibid.*, p. 115.
192. *Loc. cit.*
193. *Ibid.*, p. 120; also *ibid.*, p. 110.
194. *Ibid.*, p. 123.
195. *Ibid.*, p. 125.
196. *Life and Letters*, I, 221.
197. *Letters from Joseph Conrad*, pp. 102–104, 109, 115, 126.
198. *Life and Letters*, I, 221, and *Letters from Joseph Conrad*, p. 132.
199. *Letters from Joseph Conrad*, pp. 125, 131.

200. *Life and Letters*, I, 230–231.
201. *Letters from Joseph Conrad*, p. 132.
202. *Ibid.*, pp. 130, 133–134.
203. *Ibid.*, pp. 134–136.
204. *Ibid.*, p. 142.
205. *Life and Letters*, I, 166.
206. *Letters from Joseph Conrad*, p. 137.
207. *Ibid.*, p. 138. Though no exact date was given for this letter, Garnett placed it after a letter dated May 18.
208. *Ibid.*, p. 139. The letter was not dated exactly, but Garnett placed it two beyond a letter of May 18, and it was the last letter placed in May, 1898.
209. *Life and Letters*, I, 166, 238.
210. *Letters from Joseph Conrad*, pp. 139–140.
211. *Ibid.*, p. 140.
212. *Life and Letters*, I, 241.
213. *Ibid.*, I, 251.
214. *Letters from Joseph Conrad*, p. 141.
215. *Ibid.*, pp. 141–142. 15,000 is obviously a misprint for 150,000. See *Garnett Collection*, p. 34.
216. *Life and Letters*, I, 245.
217. *Ibid.*, I, 247.
218. *Rescue*, p. ix. This is the earliest of many contradictory dates.
219. *Letters from Joseph Conrad*, p. 147.
220. *Life and Letters*, I, 251, 253.
221. *Ibid.*, I, 265.
222. (British Museum: Ashley 4787) and *Rescue*, p. 263. In the manuscript the beginning of part four is dated "19/12/98" and bears a canceled subtitle, "*d'Alcacer*."
223. (British Museum: Ashley 4787).
224. *Life and Letters*, I, 255.
225. *Ibid.*, I, 274.
226. *Letters from Joseph Conrad*, p. 149.
227. *Life and Letters*, I, 265, 266.
228. *Letters from Joseph Conrad*, pp. 151–152.
229. *Life and Letters*, I, 266.
230. *Ibid.*, I, 267–268.
231. *Ibid.*, II, 209.
232. *Ibid.*, II, 172. It is impossible to tell just when the "newly arranged, rewritten" work was originally done.
233. *Rescue*, pp. x–xi.
234. See pp. 229–230, above.
235. *Letters from Joseph Conrad*, p. 152.
236. *Life and Letters*, I, 277.
237. *Letters from Joseph Conrad*, p. 159.

238. *Life and Letters*, I, 308.
239. *Loc. cit.*
240. *Ibid.*, I, 312–314.
241. *Ibid.*, I, 316. Jean-Aubry suggested that the "Mediterranean story" was "The Tremolino" in *The Mirror of the Sea.*
242. *Chance* was begun in 1906 (*Library of John Quinn*, I, 190) and abandoned in May, 1907 (*Life and Letters*, II, 49).
243. *Life and Letters*, II, 114–115.
244. *Ibid.*, II, 165. Jean-Aubry's assertion that Conrad had put the novel "aside twenty years before" disregards all the intermediate attempts.
245. *Ibid.*, II, 172.
246. *Ibid.*, II, 180.
247. *Ibid.*, II, 165.
248. The last page of the manuscript is Part IV, p. 195 (British Museum: Ashley 4787). When he took the novel up again in 1918, he dictated to a typist (see note for Wise at end of manuscript and *Life and Letters*, II, 209, 243).
249. *Life and Letters*, II, 165.
250. (British Museum: Ashley 4787, blank page 2). In reality Conrad's work on the manuscript seems to have extended into 1917.
251. Conrad computed the number of words on the past page of parts one and three (British Museum: Ashley 4787).
252. *Life and Letters*, II, 208.
253. *Rescue*, p. xii.
254. *Life and Letters*, II, 249. Also *Letters from Joseph Conrad*, p. 263.
255. *Life and Letters*, II, 243.
256. *Ibid.*, II, 209.

After describing for Wise how the manuscript, by condensation, had been "reduced to a very little more than one half of the text as printed in the first edition," Conrad continued: "The second half of the text (as printed) is contained in the First Draft Typescript scored, corrected and interlined in pen and ink by my own hand" (British Museum: Ashley 4787, blank page 2).

257. *Conrad to a Friend*, p. 51.
258. *Life and Letters*, II, 212.
259. *Ibid.*, II, 215.
260. *Letters from Joseph Conrad*, pp. 259–260.
261. *Life and Letters*, II, 216.
262. *Conrad to a Friend*, p. 53.
263. *Life and Letters*, II, 219.
264. *Ibid.*, II, 222.
265. *Bibliography*, p. 103.
266. *Life and Letters*, II, 221.
267. *Conrad to a Friend*, p. 133.
268. *Notes by Joseph Conrad*, p. 34, n. 2.

269. *Letters from Joseph Conrad*, p. 262.
270. *Ibid.*, p. 264.
271. *Ibid.*, p. 267.
272. *Conrad to a Friend*, p. 66.
273. *Ibid.*, p. 69. See also unpublished letter to Colvin, described in *Letters to the Colvins*, pp. 42–43.
274. *Conrad to a Friend*, p. 70.
275. *Ibid.*, p. 71.
276. *Letters from Joseph Conrad*, p. 270.
277. *Bibliography*, p. 98.
278. *Letters from Joseph Conrad*, p. 270.
279. *Richard Curle Conrad Collection*, item 115.
280. *Life and Letters*, II, 7, 241.
281. *Bibliography*, p. 105. Wise gave a full bibliographical description (*ibid.*, pp. 98–105).
282. See pp. 201–202, above.
283. Page vii.
284. *Life and Letters*, I, 194.
285. *Letters from Joseph Conrad*, p. 54.

Indefinite as it is, the information clears up ambiguous statements of Conrad's about the story. In Curle's copy of *Tales of Unrest*, in which "The Idiots" was republished, Conrad wrote: "The Outpost and The Idiots were written in Brittany during our honeymoon. My first work as a married man" (*Richard Curle Conrad Collection*, item 32; also *Conrad Memorial Library*, p. 57). *The Rescue*, however, was Conrad's first work as a married man, but the distinction of being the first piece of completed work after his marriage belongs to "The Idiots," which preceded "An Outpost of Progress" by almost two months (see *Letters from Joseph Conrad*, p. 62).

286. Unpublished letter to Unwin dated May 28, 1896 (Beyer).
287. *Tales of Unrest*, p. ix, and *Joseph Conrad and His Circle*, pp. 37, 40. Also *Joseph Conrad as I Knew Him*, p. 38.

Jean-Aubry stressed the rareness of such inspiration in Conrad's experience: "This is the only work that Conrad ever wrote immediately after an actual experience on the spot" (*Life and Letters*, I, 164, n. 2).

288. *Letters from Joseph Conrad*, p. 54.
289. Unpublished letter to Unwin dated May 28, 1896 (Beyer).
290. *Letters from Joseph Conrad*, p. 55.
291. Garnett informed Conrad on June 2 that the *Cornhill* wanted his work and urged him to send "The Idiots" and also *The Rescue* as a serial (*Twenty Letters to Joseph Conrad*).
292. *Letters from Joseph Conrad*, p. 56.
293. Unpublished letter to Unwin written at Ile Grande and dated June 7, 1896 (Yale). Here Conrad quoted the rate at "£1.1 per page of about 450 words."

294. *Letters from Joseph Conrad*, p. 61. *Cosmopolis* apparently considered the story too long: in submitting "An Outpost of Progress" to the magazine, Conrad warned Unwin that the story was as long as "The Idiots" (*Conrad Memorial Library*, p. 62).

295. Unpublished letter (Beyer).

296. *Conrad Memorial Library*, p. 60.

297. *Letters from Joseph Conrad*, pp. 61–62.

298. *Conrad Memorial Library*, p. 62.

299. The story ran to twenty pages exactly (*Savoy*, No. 6 [October, 1896], 11–30).

300. *Bibliography*, p. 15.

301. *Letters from Joseph Conrad*, p. 72.

302. Unpublished letter to Unwin dated Monday (Yale).

303. *Conrad Memorial Library*, p. 63.

304. Unpublished letter to Unwin dated Monday (Yale).

305. *Letters from Joseph Conrad*, p. 67.

306. Unpublished letter (Beyer).

307. *Letters from Joseph Conrad*, p. 69.

308. *Ibid.*, p. 70.

309. *Conrad Memorial Library*, pp. 42–43.

310. *Letters from Joseph Conrad*, p. 71.

311. *Ibid.*, p. 103.

312. *Ibid.*, p. 105.

313. "The agreement, signed, shall be posted at noon tomorrow" (unpublished letter to Unwin dated November 5, 1897 [Yale]).

314. *Letters from Joseph Conrad*, p. 128.

315. Letter dated January 5, 1940, to the author from Mr. David Randall of the Scribner Book Store, New York City.

316. *Notes by Joseph Conrad*, p. 19.

317. *Bibliography*, p. 15. Though a full bibliographical description is found in the *Bibliography* (pp. 14–16) and the catalogue of the *Richard Curle Conrad Collection* (items 32, 33), Wise and Curle were not aware of the priority of the American edition.

Jean-Aubry's statement that *Tales of Unrest* was published in March (*Life and Letters*, I, 166) must rest on Conrad's conjecture of December 31, 1897: "Le volume de cinq contes . . . paraitra au mois de mars prochain" (*Lettres Françaises*, p. 35).

318. *Life and Letters*, I, 76. At the time Conrad's friendship with Krieger was under a severe strain (*Letters from Joseph Conrad*, pp. 119–120).

319. *Letters from Joseph Conrad*, p. 91.

320. The first edition, issued in America on November 30, 1897, as *The Children of the Sea* (*Conrad Memorial Library*, p. 38), lacks the dedication.

321. *Lettres Françaises*, p. 103. Also *Tales of Unrest*, p. ix.

322. *Life and Letters*, II, 227.
323. *Ibid.*, I, 167.
324. *Letters from Joseph Conrad*, p. 150.
325. *Notes by Joseph Conrad*, p. 38.
326. *Library of John Quinn*, I, 170.
327. *Letters from Joseph Conrad*, p. 57.
328. *Life and Letters*, I, 164.
329. *Letters from Joseph Conrad*, pp. 58–59.
330. *Ibid.*, p. 62, n. 1, and *Life and Letters*, I, 194.
Mrs. Conrad must have considerably overestimated when she declared Conrad wrote on Ile Grande "certainly two chapters of 'The Nigger . . .'" (*Joseph Conrad as I Knew Him*, p. 38). At Conrad's speed of writing he could not have written some forty-nine manuscript pages of *The Nigger* in addition to much of *The Rescue* and all of "An Outpost" and "The Lagoon."
331. *Life and Letters*, I, 164.
332. *Lettres Françaises*, p. 61.
333. *Letters from Joseph Conrad*, p. 72.
334. *Ibid.*, p. 74.
335. *Ibid.*, pp. 69–72, 74.
336. *Ibid.*, pp. 76–77.
337. *Ibid.*, pp. 77–78.
338. *Ibid.*, pp. 22, 78–79.
339. *Life and Letters*, I, 197.
340. *Nigger*, p. x.
341. *Letters from Joseph Conrad*, p. 79. *Off* is obviously a misprint for *of*.
342. *Ibid.*, pp. 79–80.
343. *Ibid.*, p. 82.
344. *Ibid.*, p. 83.
345. *Ibid.*, p. 85. Mrs. Conrad was nearly a year off in her recollection that *The Nigger* had been finished in November, 1897 (*Joseph Conrad as I Knew Him*, pp. 42–43).
346. *Letters from Joseph Conrad*, p. 22.
347. *Nigger* MS., pp. 51–56, 58, 60, 62–65, 68, 69, 75, 158, 160, 162, 163, 167, 168, 170, 171, 174, 175, 178, 182–184, 186, 194 (Rosenbach).
348. This date is misquoted as "Febry" in the *Library of John Quinn*, I, 170.
349. I, 165. In 1903 Conrad told a Polish friend that the novel had been completed in "Fevr. 97" (*Lettres Françaises*, p. 61).
350. *Letters from Joseph Conrad*, p. 23.
351. Jean-Aubry made a similar reconciliation of the contradictory dates for the completion of *Almayer's Folly* (*Life and Letters*, I, 158, n. 1).
352. *Letters from Joseph Conrad*, p. 87.

353. *Ibid.*, p. 93.
354. *Ibid.*, p. 95.
355. *Ibid.*, p. 98.
356. Thomas Beer, *Stephen Crane: A Study in American Letters, with an Introduction by Joseph Conrad* (The Star Series; Garden City, New York: Garden City Publishing Company, Inc., 1927), p. 107.
357. *Twenty Letters to Joseph Conrad.*
358. *Life and Letters*, I, 209.
359. *Letters from Joseph Conrad*, p. 105.
360. *Book Buyer*, XVI (1898), 350–352.
361. *Letters from Joseph Conrad*, p. 105.
362. *Conrad Memorial Library*, p. 31. T. J. Wise gave for the issue the less definite date, September (*Bibliography*, p. 10).

The serial and copyright edition are not entirely similar page for page. The chapter divisions of the copyright edition are like those of the first edition, not the serial. The page-lengths of the serial and copyright edition soon cease to be identical (cf. *New Review*, XVII [1897], 150, and copyright edition, p. 28). Though usually the lines in the serial and the copyright edition are word for word the same length, occasionally the length has been altered in the copyright edition (cf. *New Review*, XVII [1897], 241, and copyright edition, p. 28).

363. The description does not fit the usual copies of the first edition. The copyright edition contains 118 pages and no advertisements. The regular first English edition contains 259 pages of text and a varying number of advertisements – 20, 32, or 36 pages.
364. *Letters from Joseph Conrad*, p. 106.
365. *Ibid.*, p. 113.
366. *Conrad Memorial Library*, p. 38.
367. *Bibliography*, pp. 13–14. For a complete bibliographical description see *ibid.*, pp. 9–14, and the catalogue of the *Garnett Collection*, p. 9.
368. *Joseph Conrad: A Record*, p. 167 (Yale). For Mrs. Conrad's comments on Conrad's mottoes see *Joseph Conrad as I Knew Him*, p. 49.
369. *Life and Letters*, I, 322 and n. 3.
370. For instance *Letters from Joseph Conrad*, pp. 71, 79.
371. *Ibid.*, pp. 86–87.
372. *Life and Letters*, I, 200.
373. *Bibliography*, p. 9.
374. *Richard Curle Conrad Collection*, item 25.
375. *Life and Letters*, II, 147.
376. *Ibid.*, II, 152, and *Nigger*, p. x.

Dodd, Mead and Company blended the English with the American title inconsistently in several early copies of the novel. Mr. Keating recorded a copy dated 1899 of which the title is *The Nigger of the Narcissus: A Tale of the Forecastle*, though the running-head throughout is "The Children of the Sea" (*Conrad Memorial Library*, pp. 45–46).

Another copy, with no date on the title-page and with 1897 for the copyright on the verso, is entitled *The Children of the Sea: A Tale of the Forecastle*, but "The Nigger of the Narcissus" is the running-head on page one, though "The Children of the Sea" is the running-head on all subsequent pages (Harvard Union Library). Apparently Conrad knew nothing of such anomalies.

377. *Conrad Memorial Library*, p. 49.
378. *Letters from Joseph Conrad*, p. 117, n. 1.
379. Though the Canterbury Edition has the subtitle, *A Tale of the Forecastle*, the signed limited edition has *A Tale of the Sea.*
380. *Letters from Joseph Conrad*, p. 97.
381. *Bibliography*, pp. 9, 10, 13.
382. *Letters from Joseph Conrad*, p. 101.
383. *Twenty Letters to Joseph Conrad.*
384. *Letters from Joseph Conrad*, p. 275.
385. *Life and Letters*, I, 212.
386. *Ibid.*, I, 299.
387. *Last Essays*, pp. 137–138.
388. *Life and Letters*, II, 215.
389. *Ibid.*, I, 200.
390. *Ibid.*, I, 205.
391. *Lettres Françaises*, p. 60.
392. *Library of John Quinn*, I, 170. At the Quinn Sale the manuscript of *The Nigger* brought $4500 and the manuscript of the Preface $1100.
393. *Nigger*, p. ix.
394. *Richard Curle Conrad Collection*, item 26.
395. *Nigger*, pp. ix–x.
396. *Letters from Joseph Conrad*, p. 101.
397. MS. of the Preface of *Nigger*, pp. 7–8 (Rosenbach). The first paragraph was canceled by long lines of ink and blue pencil; the second by long lines of ink and purple pencil.
398. *Letters from Joseph Conrad*, p. 102.
399. *Nigger*, pp. xv–xvi.
400. *Letters from Joseph Conrad*, p. 102.
401. XVII (1897), 628–631.
402. *Letters from Joseph Conrad*, p. 120.
403. *Nigger*, p. x.
404. *Richard Curle Conrad Collection*, item 28.

The Hythe edition of the Preface differed somewhat in wording and contained a paragraph (the fourth in the Canterbury Edition) omitted from the *New Review.*

405. *Library of John Quinn*, I, 171.
406. *Conrad to a Friend*, p. 40.
407. *Library of John Quinn*, I, 171.
408. *Richard Curle Conrad Collection*, item 165. In *Harper's Magazine*

the Preface had new paragraph divisions, omitted sentences found in the other two versions, and, like the *New Review* version, did not contain the fourth paragraph which was found in the Hythe and the Canterbury editions.

409. *Conrad to a Friend*, pp. 16, 17.

410. *Library of John Quinn*, I, 171, and *Richard Curle Conrad Collection*, items 29, 30.

411. See the copy of the Preface inclosed with the *Nigger* manuscript (Rosenbach).

412. *Letters from Joseph Conrad*, p. 62, n. 1.

413. *Ibid.*, p. 62.

414. See the unpublished letter to Unwin written from Ile Grande and dated July 10, 1896 (Beyer).

415. *Joseph Conrad as I Knew Him*, p. 38.

416. *Ibid.*, p. 109.

417. *Conrad Memorial Library*, p. 62.

418. *Letters from Joseph Conrad*, p. 65. On the manuscript Conrad estimated the length at "9,500 words" (*ibid.*, p. 62, n. 1).

419. *Ibid.*, p. 67.

420. *Ibid.*, pp. 66–67.

421. *Life and Letters*, I, 194.

422. *Ibid.*, I, 197.

423. *Ibid.*, I, 201, and *Bibliography*, p. 16.

424. *Tales of Unrest*, pp. viii–ix.

425. *Library of John Quinn*, I, 171.

426. *Letters from Joseph Conrad*, pp. 64–65.

427. *Ibid.*, pp. 67–68. On the original typescript Conrad wrote that the story contained 5700 words (*ibid.*, p. 65, n. 1).

428. Page vii.

429. Unpublished letter (Yale). The terms seem to have been those mentioned on October 16, 1896: "On serial rights he agrees to pay me *90 per cent* of them as arranged before" (*Letters from Joseph Conrad*, p. 69).

430. Unpublished letter to Conrad from the editor of the *Cornhill* dated August 19, 1896 (Yale).

431. The story came to twelve and a half pages (*Cornhill Magazine*, New Series, II [1897], 59–71).

432. *Life and Letters*, I, 202.

433. Page viii.

434. *Tales of Unrest*, p. vii.

435. *Loc. cit.*

436. *Bibliography*, p. 16.

437. *Tales of Unrest*, p. viii.

438. *Letters from Joseph Conrad*, p. 88.

439. *Tales of Unrest*, p. ix.

440. *Life and Letters*, I, 207.
441. *Ibid.*, I, 203.
442. *Ibid.*, I, 202.
443. *Library of John Quinn*, I, 172.
444. *Life and Letters*, I, 201, especially n. 3.
445. Page x.
446. *Letters from Joseph Conrad*, p. 91.
447. Mrs. Conrad's belief that the story was begun in December, 1896 (*Joseph Conrad as I Knew Him*, p. 43) is contradicted by Conrad's statement.
448. *Letters from Joseph Conrad*, pp. 23, 91, 95.
449. *Ibid.*, pp. 91–92.
450. *Joseph Conrad as I Knew Him*, p. 109.
451. *Letters from Joseph Conrad*, p. 92.
452. *Ibid.*, p. 94.
453. *Ibid.*, p. 95.
454. *Life and Letters*, I, 204.
455. *Letters from Joseph Conrad*, p. 95.
456. *Life and Letters*, I, 234. Though Ford protested that "Karain" was Conrad's favorite early short story (*Joseph Conrad: A Personal Remembrance*, p. 180), the more trustworthy Garnett reported that Conrad never liked it (*Letters from Joseph Conrad*, p. 23).
457. Page x.
458. *Library of John Quinn*, I, 172.
459. *Letters from Joseph Conrad*, p. 97. Also *ibid.*, pp. 23–24.
460. *Tales of Unrest*, p. x.
461. *Letters from Joseph Conrad*, pp. 99–100.
462. *Life and Letters*, I, 206.
463. *Ibid.*, I, 296.
464. *Letters from Joseph Conrad*, p. 102, and *Bibliography*, p. 16.
465. *Tales of Unrest*, p. ix.
466. *Library of John Quinn*, I, 172.
467. *Letters from Joseph Conrad*, p. 95.
468. *Life and Letters*, I, 207. In addition Conrad declared on September 27, 1897, that "The Return" had "embittered five months of my life" (*Letters from Joseph Conrad*, p. 106).

The evidence is specific enough to refute Conrad's later statements in the Author's Note to *Tales of Unrest* (p. x) that he began "The Return" before "Karain" and tried to complete the former and write the latter at the same time.

469. *Letters from Joseph Conrad*, p. 98.
470. *Ibid.*, p. 100.
471. *Life and Letters*, I, 206–207.
472. *Letters from Joseph Conrad*, p. 101.
473. *Library of John Quinn*, I, 172.

474. *Letters from Joseph Conrad*, p. 103.
475. *Ibid.*, pp. 105–106.
476. *Ibid.*, pp. 107–108.
477. *Ibid.*, pp. 108–109.
478. *Ibid.*, p. 111.
479. *Ibid.*, p. 129.
480. *Sisters*, p. 1.
481. Pages ix–x.
482. *Letters from Joseph Conrad*, p. 106.
483. *Ibid.*, pp. 108–109.
484. *Ibid.*, p. 112.
485. *Ibid.*, p. 115.
486. Unpublished letter (Yale).
487. Unpublished letter dated December 11, 1897 (Yale).
488. *Letters from Joseph Conrad*, p. 26.
489. *Notes by Joseph Conrad*, p. 18.
490. *Letters from Joseph Conrad*, pp. 128–129.
491. *Library of John Quinn*, I, 172 of priced copy.
492. *Letters from Joseph Conrad*, p. 137.
493. *Ibid.*, p. 138.
494. *Lord Jim*, p. viii.
495. Later "A seaman" may have been turned into "Typhoon" or "Falk" and "Dynamite" into "The Informer."
496. *Letters from Joseph Conrad*, p. 139.
497. *Life and Letters*, I, 73, 166, 238.
498. Page viii.
499. *Rescue*, p. xii. Mrs. Conrad estimated them at only fifteen pages (*Joseph Conrad as I Knew Him*, p. 47).
500. *Lettres Françaises*, p. 62.
501. *Letters from Joseph Conrad*, p. 154. In *Life and Letters* (I, 273–274), Jean-Aubry seems to have been mistaken in assigning a letter of April 12, no year given, to 1899, and in surmising that the terms with McClure mentioned therein applied to *Lord Jim*: a letter Conrad dated "5th March '98" gave almost exactly the same terms as applying to *The Rescue* (*ibid.*, I, 230–231). In the letter of April 12 the reference to "the latest volume of my works" fits the publication of *Tales of Unrest* on April 4, 1898. Hence the letter of April 12 seems rightfully to belong to 1898 and to apply to *The Rescue*, not *Lord Jim*.
502. *Lord Jim*, p. viii. It actually ran into fourteen numbers. Though the first forty-five pages of the Rosenbach manuscript are missing, they probably were closer to the published text than is the Harvard manuscript.
503. *Richard Curle Conrad Collection*, item 35. Obviously the resolve did not come when Conrad "began this story," which was to be concerned only with the pilgrim ship, but grew up gradually in his imagination.

504. *Life and Letters*, I, 279.
505. *Ibid.*, I, 283.
506. *Letters from Joseph Conrad*, p. 157.
507. *Ibid.*, p. 159.
508. *Ibid.*, p. 169.
509. Letter to Mme. Poradowska dated April 16, 1900 (Yale).
510. Letter from Mrs. Conrad to Mme. Poradowska dated May 10, 1900 (Yale), and letter from Conrad to Mme. Poradowska dated June 1, 1900 (Yale).
511. *Lettres Françaises*, p. 40.
512. *Life and Letters*, I, 295. Jean-Aubry's statement that Conrad devoted the year 1900 to *Lord Jim* (*ibid.*, I, 167) does not fit the situation well.
513. *Ibid.*, I, 296.
514. *Letters from Joseph Conrad*, p. 154.
515. *Ibid.*, p. 156.
516. *Life and Letters*, I, 275, 293.
517. *Letters from Joseph Conrad*, p. 164.
518. *Ibid.*, pp. 171–172. He also called it "lourd comme une pierre" (*Lettres Françaises*, p. 42).
519. *Letters from Joseph Conrad*, pp. 157, 160.
520. *Richard Curle Conrad Collection*, item 35.
521. *Bibliography*, p. 19. Also *ibid.*, pp. 16–19 for further bibliographical information. Though the *Bibliography* did not give the day of publication, *Lord Jim* was listed under "Publications Today" in the London *Times*, October 15, 1900.
522. Wise gave the publisher's name in different form from the *Richard Curle Conrad Collection* (item 36) and the *Library of John Quinn* (I, 173).
523. *Richard Curle Conrad Collection*, item 36.
524. *Lettres Françaises*, p. 41.
525. *Joseph Conrad and His Circle*, pp. 9–10, 16.
526. *Bibliography*, p. 19.
527. *Library of John Quinn*, I, 172 of priced copy.
528. Sir Hugh Clifford regretted the translation: "The Malay word *Tûan* does not mean 'Lord.' Its exact equivalent in English is *Master*. . . . To raise honest Jim thus unnecessarily to the peerage appeared to those of us who were familiar with the language of the countries, in which he passed the concluding years of his life, to be a pity. It wantonly drew attention to the fact that Conrad's knowledge of Malays and of things Malayan was slender; though, in a sense, this only enhanced the marvel of the miracle which he worked in our sight" (*Lord Jim: A Tale* [Memorial Edition; Garden City, New York: Doubleday, Page and Company, 1925], p. viii).
529. *Letters from Joseph Conrad*, p. 138.

530. *Ibid.*, p. 139.
531. *Life and Letters*, I, 73, 238.
532. *Ibid.*, I, 166.
533. *Ibid.*, I, 248. The adjectives help explain the continuity and rapidity of composition.
534. *Youth*, p. xi, and *Life and Letters*, I, 65–72.
535. *Life and Letters*, I, 249, and *Library of John Quinn*, I, 173.
536. *Life and Letters*, I, 241.
537. *Ibid.*, I, 247.
538. *Ibid.*, I, 248–249.
539. Page x.
540. *Life and Letters*, I, 241.
541. *Letters from Joseph Conrad*, pp. 99–100.
542. *Bibliography*, p. 23.
543. *Life and Letters*, I, 283.
544. *Letters from Joseph Conrad*, p. 180.
545. *Bibliography*, p. 22. Though Wise did not give the day of publication, the volume was listed under new fiction in the London *Times Literary Supplement* for November 21, 1902.
546. See Mrs. Conrad's comment (*Conrad Memorial Library*, p. 94).
547. *Letters from Joseph Conrad*, p. 183.
548. *Richard Curle Conrad Collection*, item 44.
549. *Ibid.*, item 46, and *Bibliography*, p. 23.
550. *Library of John Quinn*, I, 173 of priced copy.
551. *Life and Letters*, I, 248. Mrs. Conrad set the visit "about seven months" after the birth of Borys (*Joseph Conrad and His Circle*, p. 59). Borys was born on January 15, 1898 (*Life and Letters*, I, 223).
552. *Letters from Joseph Conrad*, p. 14. The charitable negress may well have come from Conrad's reading about Mungo Park (*Last Essays*, p. 22).
553. *Letters from Joseph Conrad*, p. 150.
554. *Lettres Françaises*, p. 36.
555. *Life and Letters*, I, 265. The implications seem to be that *Blackwood's* would not accept the story, even though it was too long for one installment, until the whole was completed.
556. *Last Essays*, p. 234.
557. Consequently Conrad's statement that it was written in 1898 (*Lettres Françaises*, p. 62) was inaccurate; Jean-Aubry's statement that it "soon followed" "Youth" (*Life and Letters*, I, 167) is too vague, and his belief that by January 6, 1899, Conrad had already been working on it two months (*Lettres Françaises*, p. 36, n. 2) is not sufficiently documented.
558. *Youth*, p. xi.
559. *Bibliography*, pp. 22–23. The manuscript brought $1500 at the Quinn sale (*Library of John Quinn*, I, 174 of priced copy).

560. *Life and Letters*, I, 268.
561. *Letters from Joseph Conrad*, p. 184.
562. *Lettres Françaises*, p. 48.

CHAPTER VI

1. "Le fait même de la publication est de grande importance" (letter to Mme. Poradowska dated October 4, 1894 [Yale]).
2. *Life and Letters*, I, 208.
3. *Ibid.*, II, 83. Also *Men and Memories*, II, 66.
4. *Typhoon*, p. ix.
5. *Life and Letters*, II, 214.
6. *Ibid.*, II, 147.
7. Letter dated October 10, 1894 (Yale).
8. *Life and Letters*, II, 205.
9. *Ibid.*, II, 136, 187, *Conrad to a Friend*, p. 5, and *Lettres Françaises*, p. 49.
10. *Life and Letters*, II, 70–71, 146–147, 205; *Lettres Françaises*, p. 78.
11. Ruth Stauffer in *Joseph Conrad: His Romantic Realism* ([Boston: The Four Seas Company, 1922], pp. 102–115) gave a list of some of the articles on Conrad and his novels. She made no pretense of being exhaustive, listing, for instance, only three reviews for *Almayer's Folly*. Though the present study includes dozens of critical notices not mentioned by Miss Stauffer, it, too, is not exhaustive.
12. Letter to Mme. Poradowska dated "Lundi" and assigned by Dr. Gee to July 30, 1894 (Yale).
13. Quoted in an advertising pamphlet for *The Rover* entitled *Joseph Conrad* (London: T. Fisher Unwin Ltd., n.d.), pp. 4–8.
14. See the advertisement for *Almayer's Folly* in the first edition of *An Outcast of the Islands*. These quotations are untrustworthy excerpts from which it is impossible to judge the tone of the whole.
15. No. 3,526 (May 25, 1895), 671. Reviewed with Adeline Sergeant, *The Mistress of Quest;* W. H. Wilkins and Frank Thatcher, *The Holy Estate;* J. M. Cobban, *The Avenger of Blood*; Violet Magee, *Scholar's Mate*.
16. LXXIX (1895), 797. Reviewed with George Ranken, *Windabyne*, and John Mackie, *Sinners Twain.*
17. XI (1895), 314.
18. XI (1895), 722–723. Reviewed with H. B. Marriott Watson, *At the First Corner and Other Stories*, and Mrs. Hugh Bell, *The Story of Ursula.*
19. LXXV (1895), 530.
20. XLVII (1895), 501–502. Reviewed with Dora Russell, *The Drift of Fate*; Dorothea Gerard, *An Arranged Marriage;* Tolstoi, *Master and Man*; L. Dougall, *The Zeit-Geist;* G. R. and Edith Vicars, *A Torquay*

Marriage; Alice Maud Meadows, *When the Heart is Young;* H. D. Lowry, *Women's Tragedies.*

21. XIV (1895), 513–514. Reviewed with Eleanor Holmes, *To-day and To-morrow;* Mrs. Henry Wylde, *In Quest of a Name;* Adeline Sergeant, *Out of Due Season;* in Autonym Library, *Another Wicked Woman;* Sydney Christian, *Two Mistakes;* Mrs. Hungerford, *A Tug of War;* F. H. Underwood, *Dr. Gray's Quest.*

22. No. 1,089 (May 15, 1895), 31.

23. II (1895), 39–41. Reviewed with Frank A. Swettenham, *Malay Sketches.*

24. New Series, XVI (1895), 268–269.

25. New Series, XXIII (June 29, 1895), 481.

26. New Series, XXIII (May 11, 1895), 349 (an earlier London Letter by Waugh, evidently written before he read the enthusiastic English reviews), and XXV (1896), 335 (a notice signed Macmillan and Co.).

27. XII (1895), 353.

28. XXVI (1895), 155.

29. LXI (1895), 278. Reviewed with Gissing, *In the Year of Jubilee;* Mrs. Humphry Ward, *The Story of Bessie Costrell;* L. Dougall, *The Zeit-Geist*; Bliss Perry, *The Plated City;* George Ebers, *In the Fire of the Forge*; W. C. Scully, *Kafir Stories.*

30. LVIII (1920), 599–603.

31. XII (1895), 353.

32. New Series, XXV (1896), 335.

33. Quoted in *Joseph Conrad*, p. 4.

34. No. 3,526 (May 25, 1895), 671.

35. II (1895), 39.

36. LXXV (1895), 530.

37. New Series, XXIII (May 11, 1895), 349.

38. LXI (1895), 278. Also the *Critic*, New Series, XXIII (May 11, 1895), 349.

39. XLVII (1895), 502.

40. *Speaker*, XI (1895), 723.

41. *Bookman*, II (1895), 40, and *Literary World*, XXVI (1895), 155.

42. *North American Review*, CLXXVII (1904), 848–849. The article was condensed for *Harper's Weekly*, XLIX (1905), 59. For Conrad's acknowledgment of Clifford's criticism see *Life and Letters*, I, 237.

43. LXXV (1895), 530.

44. XIV (1895), 514.

45. Quoted in *Joseph Conrad*, pp. 4–5.

46. XI (1895), 314.

47. No. 3,526 (May 25, 1895), 671.

48. *Revue Encyclopédique* (February 13, 1897), 126.

49. No. 3,526 (May 25, 1895), 671.

50. XLVII (1895), 502. Also the *Nation*, LXI (1895), 278.

51. *Spectator*, LXXV (1895), 530.
52. XI (1895), 723.
53. No. 1,089 (May 15, 1895), 31.
54. *Saturday Review*, LXXIX (1895), 797.
55. *Bookman*, II (1895), 41; *Critic*, New Series, XXIII (May 11, 1895), 349, and New Series, XXV (1896), 335; *National Observer*, XIV (1895), 514.
56. New Series, XXV (1896), 335.
57. Quoted in *Joseph Conrad*, pp. 4–8.
58. LXXV (1895), 530.
59. XI (1895), 314.
60. XIV (1895), 513.
61. No. 1,089 (May 15, 1895), 31.
62. LXXIX (1895), 797.
63. XXVI (1895), 155. Also *World*, no. 1,089 (May 15, 1895), 31.
64. XII (1895), 353.
65. XI (1895), 314.
66. For instance *Book Buyer*, XII (1895), 353, and *Speaker*, XI (1895), 722.
67. XLVII (1895), 502.
68. For instance *Critic*, New Series, XXIII (June 29, 1895), 481, and *Saturday Review*, LXXXI (1896), 509.
69. *Weekly Sun* quoted in *Joseph Conrad*, p. 8.
70. XI (1895), 314.
71. XLVII (1895), 502.
72. No. 3,526 (May 25, 1895), 671.
73. XI (1895), 723.
74. *Conrad Memorial Library*, p. 8.
75. Letter dated May 2, 1895 (Yale).
76. *Conrad Memorial Library*, p. 11. The letter was reprinted in *Joseph Conrad and His Circle* (p. 52).
77. Letter dated May 20, 1895 (Yale).
78. Letter to Mme. Poradowska dated June 11, 1895 (Yale).
79. *Life and Letters*, I, 183.
80. The following newspaper notices were laid into Mrs. Conrad's copy of *An Outcast*. Though twenty-seven seem once to have been collected (*Conrad Memorial Library*, p. 26), only five now remain. They were identified and dated in Conrad's own hand.
81. May 2, 1896.
82. May 16, 1896.
83. May 2, 1896.
84. June 10, 1896.
85. May 15, 1896.
86. XLIX (1896), 525. Reviewed with Dora Russell, *A Fatal Past;* Lily Perks, *Gifts and Weirds;* F. M. White, *The Robe of Lucifer;* J. S.

Winter, *I Loved Her Once;* Ralph Adams Cram, *Black Spirits and White.*

87. No. 3,586 (July 18, 1896), 91. Reviewed with Justin McCarthy, *The Riddle Ring;* J. D. Hennessey, *Wynnum;* Katharine E. Colman, *The Wooing of Phyllis;* G. B. Burgin, *The Judge of the Four Corners.*

88. LXXXI (1896), 509–510.

89. XIII (1896), 376. Reviewed with S. Baring-Gould, *The Broom-Squire*, and Ralph Adams Cram, *Black Spirits and White.*

90. LXXVI (1896), 778. Reviewed with Ernest Rhys, *The Fiddler of Carne;* Sara J. Duncan, *His Honor and a Lady;* Netta Syrett, *Nobody's Fault;* Anna C. Steele, *Lesbia;* Esmé Stuart, *Harum-Scarum;* R. Ramsay, *Miss Drummond's Dilemma;* Henry Johnston, *Doctor Congalton's Legacy.*

91. CVIII (1896), 418.

92. No. 1,135 (April 1, 1896), 31. Reviewed with *Autobiography and Journals of Admiral Lord Clarence E. Paget;* W. F. Lord, *The Lost Possessions of England;* Downman, *English Pottery and Porcelain;* Timmins, *Nooks and Corners of Herefordshire; Waif and Stray: The Adventures of Two Tricycles;* Maud Vyse, *The Poetic Year, and Other Poems;* Clark Russell, *The Tale of the Ten;* Stanley Waterloo, *A Man and Woman Faithfully Presented;* Gilbert Parker, *An Adventurer of the North;* Francis Gribble, *The Things that Matter;* Sir Robert Peel, *An Engagement;* W. Pett-Ridge, *The Second Opportunity of Mr. Staplehurst.*

93. XV (1896), 680. Reviewed with J. H. Findlater, *The Green Graves of Balgowrie;* Robert Buchanan, *A Marriage by Capture;* H. G. Wells, *The Island of Dr. Moreau;* Maggie Swan, *A Late Awakening;* C. J. Mansford and J. A. Igglebright, *A Bride's Experiment;* W. L. Alden, *Among the Freaks.*

94. New Series, XVII (1896), 307. The review was copied from the *Mail and Express*, which must have been American because of such spellings as *color* and a reference to Boss Tweed.

95. XIII (1896), 537–538.

96. IV (1896), 166.

97. LXIV (1897), 287. Reviewed with P. H. Emerson, *Caóba, The Guerilla Chief;* M. Hamilton, *McLeod of the Camerons;* P. A. Graham, *The Red Scaur;* H. Pease, *The White-faced Priest;* Sarah Orne Jewett, *The Country of the Pointed Firs;* William Morris, *The Well at the World's End.*

98. XIII (1896), 537. Also *Literary News*, New Series, XVII (1896), 307.

99. May 16, 1896.

100. LXIV (1897), 287.

101. IV (1896), 166.

102. May 16, 1896.

103. May 2, 1896.

104. XV (1896), 680.
105. CVIII (1896), 418.
106. LXIV (1897), 287.
107. No. 1,135 (April 1, 1896), 31.
108. For instance *Literary News*, New Series, XVII (1896), 307, and *Bookman*, IV (1896), 166.
109. For instance *Athenaeum*, no. 3,586 (July 18, 1896), 91, and *Speaker*, XIII (1896), 376.
110. May 16, 1896.
111. XIII (1896), 537–538.
112. New Series, XVII (1896), 307.
113. LXIV (1897), 287.
114. CVIII (1896), 418.
115. No. 1,135 (April 1, 1896), 31.
116. XLIX (1896), 525.
117. New Series, XVII (1896), 307.
118. IV (1896), 166. Also the *Daily Telegraph*, May 15, 1896.
119. LXXXI (1896), 509.
120. XLIX (1896), 525.
121. LXXXI (1896), 509.
122. XV (1896), 680.
123. LXXXI (1896), 509. Also *Athenaeum*, no. 3,586 (July 18, 1896), 91.
124. Quoting Wells' review in the advertisement for *The Rover* (*Joseph Conrad*, p. 9), Unwin entirely omitted – and did not show that he had omitted – the strictures.
125. May 2, 1896.
126. XLIX (1896), 525.
127. *Citizen*, May 2, 1896. Also *Glasgow Record*, May 2, 1896.
128. LXXVI (1896), 778.
129. No. 3,586 (July 18, 1896), 91.
130. IV (1896), 166.
131. XV (1896), 680.
132. *Speaker*, XIII (1896), 376. Also *Glasgow Record*, May 2, 1896.
133. No. 3,586 (July 18, 1896), 91. Also *Daily Chronicle*, May 16, 1896.
134. New Series, XVII (1896), 307.
135. LXXXI (1896), 510.
136. *Letters from Joseph Conrad*, p. 53.
137. *Twenty Letters to Joseph Conrad*.
138. Unpublished letter (Beyer).
139. *Life and Letters*, I, 248.
140. *Letters from Joseph Conrad*, p. 49.
141. *Life and Letters*, I, 187.
142. *Conrad Memorial Library*, p. 42.
143. The following newspaper notices were identified and dated in

Conrad's own hand and laid in his copy of *The Nigger* (*Conrad Memorial Library*, p. 39).

144. February 19, 1898.
145. December 11, 1897.
146. January 7, 1898.
147. January 2 [?], 1898.
148. December 27, 1897.
149. January 3, 1898.
150. January 27, 1898.
151. December 22, 1897.
152. December 16, 1897, and January 13, 1898.
153. December 18, 1897.
154. December 30, 1897.
155. Undated.
156. December 11, 1897.
157. December 16, 1897.
158. December 19, 1897.
159. January 1, 1898.
160. December 11, 1897.
161. December 8, 1897.
162. December 9, 1897.
163. December 22, 1897.
164. December 24, 1897.
165. LIII (1898), 1–2 of Fiction Supplement.
166. CXII (1898), 50. Reviewed with W. J. Locke, *Derelicts;* Helen Craven, *Katharine Cromer*; Anne Elliot, *Where the Reeds Wave.*
167. CXII (1898), 172.
168. January 15, 1898.
169. LXXXV (1898), 211. Conrad told Cunninghame Graham: "It was Harold Frederic who wrote the criticism of the *Nigger* in the *Sat. Rev.:* He affirmed to me that Runciman had cut out the best passages. I tried to persuade him I did not care a hang, – which is true" (*Life and Letters*, I, 231).
170. XIV (1898), 425.
171. XVII (1898), 83–84. Reviewed with W. J. Yeoman, *A Woman's Courier;* Curtis Yorke, *Valentine: A Story of Ideals.*
172. LXXIX (1897), 940. Reviewed with John Oliver Hobbes, *The School of Saints*; R. D. Blackmore, *Dariel: a Romance of Surrey;* Mrs. de la Pasture, *Deborah of Tod's;* Tasma, *A Fiery Ordeal;* Francis H. Hardy, *The Mills of God;* D. C. Murray, *This Little World;* James Adderley, *Paul Mercer.*
173. April 3, 1898. Reviewed with *Tales of Unrest;* Richard Le Gallienne, *The Romance of Zion Chapel;* George Egerton, *Fantasias.*
174. XXIX (1898), 187.
175. New Series, XIX (1898), 152.

176. XVI (1898), 350–352. Reviewed with *Tales of Unrest.*

177. LXVII (1898), 54. Reviewed with *Tales of Unrest;* Mrs. Humphry Ward, *Helbeck of Bannisdale*; M. M. Dowie, *The Crook of the Bough;* D. D. Wells, *Her Ladyship's Elephant;* Paul L. Dunbar, *Folks from Dixie.*

178. VIII (1898), 91, and XXXIX (1914), 563–565.

179. (April 6 [March 26], 1898), 354.

180. Série Moderne, XXXI (1899), 265–266 (reviewed with Wells, *When the Sleeper Wakes;* Yeats, *The Wind among the Reeds;* Wilde, *The Importance of Being Earnest*), and Série Moderne, XXXIX (1901), 253.

181. December 30, 1897.

182. LXVII (1898), 54.

183. Série Moderne, XXXI (1899), 265.

184. *Illustrated London News*, CXII (January 8, 1898), 50.

185. *Glasgow Herald*, December 9, 1897.

186. *Pall Mall Magazine*, XIV (1898), 425.

187. *Illustrated London News*, CXII (February 5, 1898), 172.

188. *Glasgow Evening News*, December 16, 1897. The *News* found it superior to *Captains Courageous*, *Country Life* (January 1, 1898) inferior.

189. *Daily Telegraph*, December 8, 1897.

190. *Bookman*, XXXIX (1914), 564.

191. *Illustrated London News*, CXII (January 8, 1898), 50.

192. *Standard*, December 24, 1897.

193. *Glasgow Evening News*, December 16, 1897.

194. *Liverpool Daily Courier*, December 30, 1897.

195. *Saturday Review*, LXXXV (1898), 211. The assertion that Huish in *Ebb Tide* anticipated Donkin was based upon the fact that both were Cockney rascals; there is no other identity.

196. *Glasgow Evening News,* December 16, 1897.

197. *Speaker*, XVII (1898), 83–84.

198. *Books and News Gazette*, December 11, 1897.

199. *Standard*, December 24, 1897.

200. *Bookman*, VIII (1898), 91.

201. *Illustrated London News*, CXII (February 5, 1898), 172.

202. *Nation*, LXVII (1898), 54.

203. *Glasgow Evening News*, December 16, 1897.

204. December 8, 1897.

205. April 3, 1898.

206. *Daily News*, January 7, 1898.

207. For instance *Book Buyer*, XVI (1898), 350–351, and *Christian World*, January 27, 1898.

208. February 19, 1898.

209. CXII (1898), 172.

210. December 11, 1897.

211. LXXIX (1897), 940.
212. LIII (1898), 1–2 of Fiction Supplement.
213. *Literature* (April 6 [March 26], 1898), 354.
214. XVI (1898), 350.
215. CXII (1898), 172.
216. LXXXV (1898), 211.
217. January 1, 1898.
218. XVII (1898), 83–84.
219. *Pall Mall Magazine*, XIV (1898), 425.
220. LXXIX (1897), 940.
221. Série Moderne, XXXI (1899), 265.
222. December 8, 1897.
223. LIII (1898), 1 of Fiction Supplement.
224. January 2 [?], 1898.
225. LXVII (1898), 54.
226. XVIII (1903), 310.
227. LIII (1898), 1 of Fiction Supplement.
228. XVII (1898), 83–84.
229. *Spectator*, LXXIX (1897), 940.
230. *Book Buyer*, XVI (1898), 351.
231. CXII (1898), 50.
232. *Daily Chronicle*, December 22, 1897.
233. *Daily Telegraph*, December 8, 1897.
234. LXVII (1898), 54.
235. LIII (1898), 1 of Fiction Supplement.
236. *Bradford Observer*, January 3, 1898.
237. January 2 [?], 1898.
238. CXII (1898), 50.
239. December 11, 1897.
240. For instance *Book Buyer*, XVI (1898), 350.
241. *Star*, December 16, 1897.
242. *Spectator*, LXXXI (1898), 219.
243. For instance *Literature* (April 6 [March 26], 1898), 354.
244. *Living Age*, XXXIX (1908), 418.
245. LIII (1898), 1–2 of Fiction Supplement.
246. January 13, 1898.
247. December 24, 1897.
248. December 27, 1897.
249. For instance *Pearson's Weekly*, January 15, 1898, and *Daily Chronicle*, December 22, 1897.
250. *Literature* (April 6 [March 26], 1898), 354.
251. *Academy*, LIII (1898), 163, and *Bookman*, VIII (1898), 91.
252. December 11, 1897.
253. LIII (1898), 1 of Fiction Supplement.
254. LXXIX (1898), 940.

255. *Saturday Review*, LXXXV (1898), 145–146.

Symons found more in *The Nigger* a quarter of a century later (*Notes on Joseph Conrad* [London: Myers and Company, 1925], p. 26).

256. *Life and Letters*, I, 226. See Conrad's earlier comments on Kipling to Cunninghame Graham (*ibid.*, I, 208–209).

257. *Letters from Joseph Conrad*, p. 131.

258. *Life and Letters*, I, 228.

259. *Conrad Memorial Library*, p. 39.

260. *Letters from Joseph Conrad*, pp. 122–123. Also *ibid.*, p. 126.

261. *Life and Letters*, I, 219.

262. *Letters from Joseph Conrad*, pp. 125–126.

263. *Ibid.*, pp. 127–128, and *Twenty Letters to Joseph Conrad.*

264. *Twenty Letters to Joseph Conrad.*

Henry James wrote Edmund Gosse in 1902: "'The Nigger of the Narcissus' is in my opinion the very finest and strongest picture of the sea and sea-life that our language possesses – the masterpiece in a whole great class; and 'Lord Jim' runs it very close" (T. J. Wise, *The Ashley Library* [London: Printed for Private Circulation Only, 1936], XI, 55).

265. No. 1,245 (May 11, 1898), 33–34.

266. LIII (1898), 417–418.

267. No. 3,679 (April 30, 1898), 564.

268. LXXXV (1898), 211. Reviewed with *Nigger.*

269. LXXXI (1898), 219. Reviewed with Henry Harland, *Comedies and Errors;* H. B. Marriott Watson, *The Heart of Miranda and Other Stories, being mostly Winter Tales;* H. C. MacIlwaine, *The Twilight Reef.*

270. LVI (1899), 66–67.

271. Série Moderne, XXXVIII (1901), 262–263. Reviewed with *Lord Jim.*

272. XVI (1898), 350–352. Reviewed by T. R. Sullivan with *Children of the Sea.*

273. New Series, XXIX (1898), 328.

274. XXIV (1898), 665–666. Reviewed with A. G. Ames, *The Revelation of St. John the Divine;* R. N. Stephens, *The Continental Dragoon;* Soule, *Dictionary of English Synonymes;* The Centenary edition of Carlyle; Caroline Atwater, *A Minister of the World.*

275. LXVII (1898), 54. Reviewed with *Children of the Sea.*

276. April 3, 1898.

277. New Series, XIX (1898), 152. Included with *Children of the Sea.*

278. XXVII (1898), 428.

279. (May 11 [April 30], 1898), 507–508. Reviewed with Henry Harland, *Comedies and Errors.*

280. XXIX (1898), 204.

281. *Academy*, LVI (1899), 67.

282. *Nation*, LXVII (1898), 54.

283. *Saturday Review*, LXXXV (1898), 211. The critic included *Almayer's Folly* and *An Outcast of the Islands* in the comparison.

284. *Book Buyer*, XVI (1898), 351.

285. *Literary World*, XXIX (1898), 204.

286. *Academy*, LIII (1898), 418.

287. *Mercure de France*, Série Moderne, XXXVIII (1901), 263, and Série Moderne, XLV (1903), 831.

288. LXXXI (1898), 219.

289. LXXXV (1898), 211.

290. XVI (1898), 351.

291. LXXXI (1898), 219.

292. *Chautauquan*, XXVII (1898), 428.

293. *Academy*, LIII (1898), 417.

294. *Public Opinion*, XXIV (1898), 665.

295. *Literature* (May 11 [April 30], 1898), 507–508.

296. LXXXI (1898), 219.

297. April 3, 1898.

298. LXVII (1898), 54.

299. LXXXV (1898), 211.

300. (May 11 [April 30], 1898), 507.

301. No. 3,679 (April 30, 1898), 564.

302. XXIV (1898), 666.

303. For instance *Book Buyer*, XVI (1898), 352.

304. LIII (1898), 417.

305. (May 11 [April 30], 1898), 507–508.

306. *Literary World*, XXIX (1898), 204.

307. *Spectator*, LXXXI (1898), 219.

308. *Book Buyer*, XVI (1898), 352.

309. *Nation*, LXVII (1898), 54.

310. April 3, 1898.

311. LIII (1898), 418.

312. *Letters from Joseph Conrad*, p. 150.

313. No. 3,810 (November 3, 1900), 576. Reviewed with Max Pemberton, *The Footsteps of a Throne;* Louis Becke, *Tom Wallis;* E. Phillips Oppenheim, *The World's Great Snare;* Albert Ross, *A Sugar Princess;* Headon Hill, *The Plunder Ship;* Cutliffe Hyne, *The Filibusters;* A. S. Twombly, *Kelea.*

314. LIX (1900), 443.

315. New Series, III (1900), 215–216. Reviewed by L. R. F. O. with Israel Zangwill, *The Mantle of Elijah.*

316. LXXXV (1900), 753. Reviewed with W. S. Lilly, *A Year of Life; The Slaves of Society* by The Man who Heard Something; A. H. Norway, *Parson Peter*; Maurice Hewlett, *The Life and Death of Richard Yea and Nay;* Mrs. Campbell Praed, "*As a Watch in the Night*": *a Drama*

of Waking and Dream in Five Acts; Carlton Dawe, *The Yellow Man;* H. E. Gorst, *Fartherest South.*

317. XXII (1901), 63.

318. XIII (1901), 187. Reviewed with A. M. Barbour, *That Mainwaring Affair;* Sarah Grand, *Babs, The Impossible;* G. Knight, *A Son of Austerity.*

319. XXXVIII (1901), 437–438. The review was initialed J. B. P.

320. XXX (1901), 222.

321. LXVI, Part II (1900), 711.

322. November 3, 1900.

323. Série Moderne, XXXVIII (1901), 262–263.

324. XXII (1901), 63.

325. November 3, 1900.

326. *Book Buyer*, XXII (1901), 63. Attwater in *Ebb Tide* bears even less resemblance to Lord Jim than Huish to Donkin in *The Nigger.*

327. *Bookman*, XIII (1901), 187.

328. *Speaker*, New Series, III (1900), 215.

329. *Academy*, LIX (1900), 443.

330. *New York Tribune* (November 3, 1900).

331. *Forum*, LIII, Part II (1915), 584.

332. LIX (1900), 443.

333. LXVI, Part II (1900), 711.

334. LIX (1900), 443.

335. XIII (1901), 187.

336. LIX (1900), 443.

337. CLXXVIII, Part II (1904), 851.

338. No. 3,810 (November 3, 1900), 576.

339. XIII (1901), 187.

340. XXXVIII (1901), 437.

341. November 3, 1900. *Current Literature* (XXX [1901], 222) also knew that *Lord Jim* had been originally intended for a short story.

342. New Series, III (1900), 216.

343. *Mercure de France*, Série Moderne, XXXVIII (1901), 262.

344. XIII (1901), 187.

345. LIX (1900), 443.

346. LXXXV (1900), 753.

347. For instance *Outlook*, LXVI, Part II (1900), 711.

348. *Speaker*, New Series, III (1900), 215.

349. *Spectator*, LXXXV (1900), 753. Also *North American Review*, CLXXVIII (1904), 851, and *Forum*, LIII (1915), 583.

350. LXXXV (1900), 753.

351. LXVI, Part II (1900), 711.

352. XXXVIII (1901), 438.

353. New Series, VII (1903), 442.

354. No. 48 (December 12, 1902), 372.

355. LXII (1902), 606–607. Though not signed, the review was by Edward Garnett (*Letters from Joseph Conrad*, p. 184).

356. No. 3,921 (December 20, 1902), 824. The review was reprinted in *Literary News*, New Series, XXIV (1903), 106–107.

357. LXXXIX (1902), 827–828.

358. XLIII (1903), 280.

359. LXXVI (1903), 478. Reviewed with George Gissing, *The Private Papers of Henry Ryecroft;* A. S. Hardy, *His Daughter First;* J. P. Mowbray, *The Conquering of Kate;* J. J. Bell, *Wee MacGreegor.*

360. Série Moderne, XLV (1903), 830–831.

361. LXXVI (1903), 478.

362. XVIII (1903), 311.

363. *Nation*, LXXVI (1903), 478.

364. *Speaker*, New Series, VII (1903), 442.

365. *Spectator*, LXXXIX (1902), 828.

366. *Academy and Literature*, LXIII (1902), 606.

367. London *Times Literary Supplement*, no. 48 (December 12, 1902), 372.

368. *Nation*, LXXVI (1903), 478.

369. London *Times Literary Supplement*, no. 48 (December 12, 1902), 372.

370. *Mercure de France*, Série Moderne, XLV (1903), 831.

371. LXXVI (1903), 478.

372. LXIII (1902), 606.

373. *Speaker*, New Series, VII (1903), 442, and *Reader*, May, 1903, quoted in *Saturday Review of Literature*, IV (1927–28), 519.

374. *Academy*, LVI (1899), 67. The comment was made on the serial publication.

375. *Bookman*, XLIII (1916), 281.

376. *Academy and Literature*, LXIII (1902), 606.

377. *London Mercury*, XXII (1930), 40–43, 261–263, 350.

378. New Series, VII (1903), 442.

379. LXIII (1902), 606.

380. LXXXIX (1902), 828.

381. No. 48 (December 12, 1902), 373.

382. For instance *Bookman*, XVIII (1903), 311, and *Academy and Literature*, LXIII (1902), 607.

383. *Academy and Literature*, LXIII (1902), 606.

384. No. 3,921 (December 20, 1902), 824.

385. New Series, VII (1903), 442.

386. No. 48 (December 12, 1902), 372.

387. LXXVI (1903), 478.

388. No. 48 (December 12, 1902), 372.

389. *Speaker*, New Series, VII (1903), 442.

390. No. 3,921 (December 20, 1902), 824.

391. LXIII (1902), 606.

392. *Academy and Literature*, LXIII (1902), 606.

393. XLIII (1903), 280.

394. No. 3,921 (December 20, 1902), 824.

395. *Speaker*, New Series, VII (1903), 442, and *Spectator*, LXXXIX (1902), 827.

George Gissing advised: "Read Conrad's new book. He is the strongest writer – in every sense of the word – at present publishing in English. Marvellous writing! The other men are mere scribblers in comparison. That a foreigner should write like this, is one of the miracles of literature" (A. and E. Gissing, edd., *Letters of George Gissing to Members of his Family* [London: Constable and Company Ltd., 1927], p. 391).

396. *Academy and Literature*, LXIII (1902), 606.

397. LXXXIX (1902), 827.

398. *Life and Letters*, I, 308.

399. *Letters from Joseph Conrad*, pp. 184–185.

400. Unpublished letter dated February 3, 1903 (Yale).

401. *Richard Curle Conrad Collection*, item 43.

402. Page 126.

403. LV, 82–83. Republished with considerable alteration and excision in Edward Garnett, *Friday Nights: Literary Criticisms and Appreciations, First Series* (The Travellers' Library; London: Jonathan Cape, [1929]), pp. 73–78.

404. *Letters from Joseph Conrad*, pp. 146–147. Garnett dated the issue of the *Academy* October 18 incorrectly.

405. *Ashley Library*, XI, 55.

406. *Life and Letters*, II, 26.

407. *Ibid.*, II, 250.

408. *Ibid.*, II, 58.

409. *Ibid.*, II, 152.

410. Page xvii; see also pp. 108–109.

411. *Lettres Françaises*, p. 32.

412. *Letters from Joseph Conrad*, p. 179.

413. *Life and Letters*, II, 121–122. Also *Letters from Joseph Conrad*, pp. 264–265.

414. *Life and Letters*, II, 343.

415. *Ibid.*, II, 68.

416. Unpublished letter to Ernest Dawson dated January 3, 1907 (Yale).

417. *Life and Letters*, I, 219.

418. *Men and Memories*, II, 43.

419. *Life and Letters*, II, 151.

420. *Letters from Joseph Conrad*, p. 204, *Life and Letters*, I, 248, II, 22, 137, 229, 263, 340, and *Last Twelve Years*, p. 54.

421. *Letters from Joseph Conrad*, p. 80.

422. *Ibid.*, p. 97. Also *Twenty Letters to Joseph Conrad.*

423. *Letters from Joseph Conrad*, p. 294.

424. Page 106. *A Personal Record* itself was "indeed written for friends" (unpublished letter to Miss Harriet Capes dated May 13, 1909 [Yale]).

425. *Life and Letters*, I, 185.

426. *Lettres Françaises*, p. 32.

427. See p. 78, above. Also *Letters from Joseph Conrad*, p. 16.

428. XLIII (1903), 280.

429. *Life and Letters*, II, 53.

430. *Ibid.*, II, 147.

431. Letter dated November 15, 1938, to the author from Doubleday, Doran and Company, Inc.

INDEX

INDEX

Abdulla, 47–48
Abdullah bin Selim, 47
Academy, 226, 268, 271–74, 276, 278–79, 283, 285–89, 291, 293–95, 297, 301–2
Academy and Literature, 298–300
Aden, 60–62
Adowa, 17–18, 180
Africa, 8, 16, 59, 75–76, 85, 178, 242, 267
Aissa, 53, 104–5, 197
Ajaccio, 74
Aldington, 99
Allen, Grant, 298
Allistoun, 133, 138, 149, 286, 290
Almayer, Kaspar, 28, 35–37, 39–46, 48, 50–51, 54, 104, 113, 119, 124–29, 178, 181–82, 190, 196, 271, 273, 280
Almayer, Mrs. Kaspar, 42–43, 45, 117, 119
Almayer, Nina, 39, 42–44, 49, 52, 106, 114–15, 119–20, 123–27, 129, 182, 271, 273
Almayer's Folly, xiii–xiv, 3, 13–19, 25, 31, 35, 39–41, 44–48, 50–53, 57, 64, 78, 88, 92, 96, 103, 112–13, 115–16, 118–20, 122–26, 128, 130–32, 135, 145, 150, 174, 176–78, 180, 182–85, 187–91, 195, 198, 227, 246, 263, 270–72, 274–76, 280, 282, 285, 292, 295, 304, 308–9
Almayer's Folly MS., 36, 43, 46–47, 49, 51–52, 58, 106, 112–15, 117–21, 123–29, 146, 157, 159, 165, 178–80, 182, 189
Almayer's Folly TS., 36, 49, 51–52, 112, 114–15, 119, 121–29, 181–83, 187, 189
Ampanam, 49
Amsterdam, 46
"Amy Foster," 53, 63
"Anarchist," 29
Antwerp, 20
Appleton, 230
Archie, 54, 56
Army and Navy Gazette, 283, 285
Arrow of Gold, 8, 32, 53, 57, 106, 110, 214
Ashford, 99
Athenaeum, 186, 270–76, 280, 291, 293–94, 296, 298–302
Atkinson, Mildred, 74
Atlantic Monthly, 212
Australia, 18, 24, 60, 62, 180, 271
Austria, 9, 219
Autobiographical Sketch, 13, 22, 24, 75, 178
Avellanos, Antonia, 8
Avondale, 62
Azores, 144

Babalatchi, 48–49, 104, 190, 274, 277
Bacheller, Irving, 231
Bacheller Syndicate, 230–31
Bacon, H. L., 217
Bahasoean, Abdulla, 48
Bahassoen, Hamet, 48
Baker, 136
Bali, 49, 73
Balzac, Honoré de, *Histoire des Treize*, 10; *Père Goriot*, 272
Banjar, Sahamin Orang, 48
Banjarmassim, *see* Benjarmassim
Banjer, Mahmat, 48
Barr, Moering and Company, 16–17, 19, 179, 185
Barth, Heinrich, *Travels and Discoveries in North and Central Africa*, 7
Baudelaire, Pierre Charles, 90
Beatrix, 204

"Because of the Dollars," 53
Becke, Louis, 272, 284, 295
Bedfordshire, 99
Beerbohm, Max, *Christmas Garland*, 246
Belfast, 54, 56, 134, 138–39, 147–48
Belgium, 262
Bellessort, André, 271
Bengal, Bay of, 61
Benjarmassim, 44
Bennett, Arnold, 75, 307
Berouw, 36, 38–39, 41–42, 44–45, 47–49, 51, 53, 57–58, 104
Berouw River, 36, 44, 51
Besant, Walter, 277
Bessborough Gardens, Pimlico, 178
Beyer Collection, 155–56, 164
Birmingham Gazette, 283, 288
Birmingham Post, 271
Bishopbourne, 99
"Black Mate," 15, 174–77, 219
Blackmore, R. D., 284
Blackwood, J., 302
Blackwood, William, 81, 150, 207, 210, 251–52, 257, 259–60, 263, 265–67
Blackwood's Magazine, 77, 81, 87, 150–52, 154–56, 158, 160–61, 163–64, 169–70, 172, 206–7, 251–52, 257, 260–63, 265–67
Blue Funnel Line, *see* Ocean Steam Navigation Company
Blue Star Line, 61
Blunt, 106
Bobrowska, Teofila, 151
Bobrowski, 4, 8
Bobrowski, Stefan, 4
Bobrowski, Tadeusz, 4–5, 9, 11–12, 14–15, 24, 83, 178–80, 188; *Memoirs*, 5, 14
Boigne, Memoirs of the Countess de, 74
Bombay, 55, 62–63, 147
Book Buyer, 271, 274, 276–77, 284–85, 291–92, 294
Bookman, 271–72, 276–78, 280, 284, 287, 294–96, 298
Books and News Gazette, 283, 285, 289
Born, *see* Burns
Borneo, 15, 35–36, 38–39, 41, 43–46, 49–53, 59, 64–66, 69–71, 178, 190, 272, 277
Bradford Observer, 283
Bragg, 63
Brierly, 61, 154, 295
British India Line, 55
British Museum, 74, 236
British Weekly, 271
Brittany, 96, 200, 217, 220, 226
Brooke, Captain, 70
Brooke, James, Rajah of Sarawak, 46, 64–73
Brow, *see* Berouw
Brown, Ford Madox, 98
Bruce, James, *Travels to Discover the Source of the Nile*, 7
Brunei, 69
Brussels, 16, 19, 181
"Brute," 63
Budrudeen, 69, 71
Bugis, 49, 68, 70, 72
Buitenzorg, 39
Bulangi, 120–21
Bulungan, 35–36, 44, 49, 71
Bulungan River, 35
Burns, 37

Caine, Hall, 305
Canada, 12, 18, 180
Canterbury, 99
Cape Horn, 94
Cape of Good Hope, 55
Capel House, 99
Capes, Harriet, 98
Capri, 74, 99
Carimata Strait, 49, 51
Carlier, 241
Carlists, 10–11
Carlyle, Thomas, 284

Carter, 204
Cavalleria Rusticana, 196
Cearne, 266
Celebes, 48–49, 52, 70, 277
Cervoni, Dominic, 45–46
Champel, 24, 85, 88, 96, 179, 183, 190, 195–96, 275
Chance, 15, 90, 92–93, 109, 213, 304
Chapman and Hall, 257
Charing Cross, 112
Chautauquan, 292
Chesson, W. H., 185, 291
Children of the Sea, see *Nigger of the "Narcissus"*
Christian World, 283
Citizen, 276–77
Clark, Christopher, 217
Clifford, Hugh, 39, 110, 272, 296, 298, 301
Coleridge, Samuel Taylor, 284
Colvin, Sidney, 307
Congo, 15–16, 23–24, 59, 84–85, 96, 102, 159, 178–79, 241, 299
Congo Diary, 102, 106
Conrad, Borys, 21, 79, 87, 90
Conrad, Jessie George, 20–21, 75–76, 79, 83, 86–87, 90–91, 97, 100–1, 105–7, 117, 175, 179, 189, 199–201, 220, 229, 241, 249, 253–54, 261, 263, 266
Conrad, John, 79, 87
Conrad, Joseph
Anecdote as a source, 34–35, 57, 60–64, 74
Attitude toward critics and public, 32, 84, 173, 200, 208, 221–24, 226, 228–29, 233, 235–38, 242–43, 269, 275–76, 282, 290–91, 294, 301–6, 308–9
British merchant marine, 11–12, 16–17, 24, 59, 180
Family, 4–7, 11, 13–15, 20–21, 27, 76, 78–79, 84, 87, 90, 96–97, 101, 180, 253, 306
Finances, 10, 19–21, 75–84, 87–88, 93, 95–98, 122, 186–87, 197, 199–200, 207–8, 217, 221, 223–28, 230, 232, 239, 244–47, 251–53, 257–58, 265–66, 306
First deepwater voyage, 10, 33
Fruitless search for a berth, 16–21, 26, 76, 88, 97, 186–87, 189, 191, 193, 198, 209
Health, 3, 11, 16–17, 23–24, 59, 75–76, 83–86, 88, 91–93, 95, 97, 99, 101, 110, 179, 193, 199, 201–2, 208, 213, 216, 218, 220, 229, 250, 261, 267
Inaccuracy of recollection, 14, 102, 174–75, 177, 179, 189, 211, 219, 226, 229–30, 244, 247–48, 251
Literary career, 13, 15, 17–20, 25–27, 64, 75, 84, 91, 93–94, 96–97, 101–2, 117, 133, 135, 157, 175–76, 178, 183, 185–86, 188, 192, 199–200, 226, 228, 235–36, 261, 263, 269, 272, 274, 280, 304, 308–9
Memory as a source, 30–32, 34, 36, 74
Methods of writing, 14–15, 28–30, 33, 50, 53–54, 57, 74, 81, 86–87, 89, 91, 94–96, 99–118, 120–22, 127, 130–33, 135–36, 143, 146, 150, 154–58, 160–61, 164, 167–68, 173, 180, 182, 187, 190, 192–95, 198, 202, 206–7, 216–18, 229, 247, 249, 260–61, 267
Moods, 5, 7–8, 10, 12, 16–18, 20–21, 24–26, 31, 75, 77, 79, 84–94, 97–102, 106–7, 111, 118, 121–22, 136, 173, 180, 187–95, 197, 199, 201–4, 206–11, 214, 216, 218, 220, 225, 227–30, 236, 241–45, 247, 249–50, 253–56, 258, 261–62, 264–66, 268, 270–71, 276, 294
Observation as a source, 30, 34–36, 39–42, 44–45, 47, 49, 52–54, 57–59, 74, 178, 220
Origin, 3–4, 29, 284
Personal experience as a source,

30, 33–35, 45–46, 51, 54–59, 74, 264
Professional development as a seaman, xiv, 11–12, 15, 17, 21–22, 27, 77
Reading, 6, 14
Reading as a source, 35, 57, 63–66, 68–74
Sea, 3–4, 6, 9–10, 13, 15, 20–22, 25, 96, 98, 189, 215, 224, 236
Style, xiii, 20, 90, 107, 110–16, 118–25, 131, 133–34, 136–37, 139–46, 148–49, 151, 154–57, 159–63, 173, 187, 190, 201, 209, 212, 243, 255, 281–82, 287, 292, 296, 300
Uncertainty about technique, xiv, 18, 25, 30, 88–90, 108, 110–11, 121, 147, 163, 165, 180, 190–91, 193, 195, 197, 201–13, 217–18, 220, 227–29, 241–43, 249–51, 253–56, 260–62, 268, 282
Work in warehouses, 16–17, 179
Constitution, 69
Cools, V. A., 36, 38, 40, 44, 48–50, 58
Cooper, James Fenimore, 7, 284; *Homeward Bound*, 7; *Pilot*, 7; *Sea Lion*, 7
Corelli, Marie, 277
Cornhill Magazine, 77, 221–22, 245–47
Corporation of Pilots, 10
Cosmopolis, 77, 220–21, 241–43
Cosmopolitan, 216
Cottu, 44
Country Life, 283, 286
Court Journal, 283
Cracow, 4–6, 178
Craig, 14, 35–36, 38, 40, 44–45, 47, 58
Crane, Stephen, 231, 235, 284, 287, 291; *Red Badge of Courage*, 231, 287
Crawford, Oswald, 257
Creighton, 134, 137
Critic, 271–73, 291, 294, 296–98, 301, 308
Crocket, 277
Cuba, 112
Cunninghame-Graham, R. B., 21–23, 175–77, 209, 235, 262, 267, 269, 289, 291, 307
Curle, Richard, 32, 49–50, 55, 60, 74, 81–83, 85, 99, 110, 112, 155, 175–77, 215, 217–18, 236, 240, 263, 267, 302, 307
Current Literature, 294

Daily Chronicle, 271, 276–77, 283, 291
Daily Mail, 101, 189
Daily News, 283
Daily Telegraph, 276, 283–84, 286
Dain Marola, 49
Dain Maroola, 44, 49, 113–15, 120–22, 126–29, 182
Dain Waris, 68, 70
Dallison, Hilary, 28
Dana, Richard Henry, 284
D'Annunzio, Gabriele, *Triumph of Death*, 289
Dartmoor, 94
Daudet, Alphonse, *Fromont Jeune et Risler Ainé*, 195
Davray, Henri-D., 284, 286, 291, 294, 296, 298
Dawson, Ernest, 302
Defoe, Daniel, 284
Delestang and Sons, 10
Dent, J. M., and Sons, Ltd., 219, 263, 266
De Veer, 53, 104
Dido, H. M. S., 65
Dodd, Mead and Company, 232
Don Carlos, 10–11
Don Quixote, 6, 295
Doña Rita, 53, 106
Dongala, 48–49
Donkin, 28, 56, 133–35, 138–40, 144–50

Doramin, 68, 70–71
Dostoevski, Feodor, 298
Doubleday, Frank N., 83, 189, 217, 225
Doubleday and McClure Company, 263
Doubleday, Page and Company, 177, 188, 219, 233, 240
Douglas, Norman, 29, 34, 110, 198, 305
"Duel," 73
Duhst, 24
Duke of Sutherland, 56
Dunkirk, 55
Dutch authorities, 38–39, 127
Dyaks, 38, 72, 113
"Dynamite," 259

East Indies, 38, 45, 49–50, 60, 277
Edinburgh, 275
Egström, 168–69
Elliot, 69
Elstree, 181
"End of the Tether," 57, 101, 266
England, 11, 20, 24, 55, 65, 85, 96–97, 128, 177, 184, 188, 205, 217–18, 225–26, 231, 259, 271, 291, 294
English Review, 101
Essex, 97
Evans, C. S., 140

"Falk," 53, 57, 63, 73
Fire Queen, 69
Flaubert, Gustave, 298
Ford, Captain, 47
Ford (Hueffer), Ford Madox, xiv, 76, 79–80, 84, 91, 94, 98, 101, 103, 109, 111, 199–200, 212, 256, 260, 262
Fortnightly Review, 207
France, 10, 18, 55, 85, 185, 271, 284, 291, 294
Franklin, John, 7
Frederic, Harold, 283; *Damnation of Theron Ware*, 277
"Freya of the Seven Isles," 63
Froud, 18
Furca Pass, 10

Galsworthy, John, 28, 79, 84, 94, 111, 152, 213, 216, 232, 288, 291, 304–5; *Fraternity*, 28, 110; *Island Pharisees*, 232
Gardafui, Cape, 61
Garnett, Constance, 234, 291
Garnett, David, 7
Garnett, Edward, 13, 19–20, 22, 30, 64, 76, 80–81, 88, 91, 96, 98, 103, 144–45, 152, 178, 185, 191–97, 199–205, 208–9, 212, 216–34, 236–45, 247–52, 254–60, 262, 264, 266–68, 280, 282, 290–91, 294, 301–2, 307
"Gaspar Ruiz," 30, 73, 266
Gausseron, B.-H., 302
Geneva, 24, 179
Gentleman Brown, 68
George, Monsieur, 57, 106
Germany, 37
Getle Company, 44
Gibbon, Perceval, 83
Gillingham Street, 96, 179, 184, 190
Glasgow, 16, 21
Glasgow Evening News, 283, 288
Glasgow Herald, 275, 283
Glasgow Record, 276, 279
Gosse, Edmund, 31, 182, 303
Graham, R. B. Cunninghame, *see* Cunninghame-Graham, R. B.
Grand, Sarah, *Heavenly Twins*, 78
Grand Magazine, "My Best Story and Why I Think So," 244
Grangemouth, 20
Gray, Andrew, 36, 38–41, 53
Gray, Mrs. Andrew (Johanna Elizabeth Olmeijer), 36–38, 40, 43–45
Greenhythe, 179
Greiffenhagen, Maurice, 217
Grissee, 37

Guardian, 271, 276
Gunung Tabur, 51

Hallowes, Miss, 218
Hammersley, Hugh, 83
Hardy, Dudley, 217
Harland, Henry, *Comedies and Errors*, 293
Harper's Magazine, "Art of Fiction," 240
Harris, Frank, 207
Harte, Bret, 284
Harvard University Library, 103, 151, 157, 160, 162, 169, 260, 263
Hawthorne, Nathaniel, 292
"Heart of Darkness," 24, 28, 33, 37, 54, 57, 97–98, 102, 109, 159, 210, 260, 266–68, 298–99, 301–2
Heinemann, William, 80–81, 83, 130, 138, 140, 206, 212, 227–28, 231–32, 235, 248, 264
Henley, W. E., 223, 227–28, 230, 239, 281
Herts, 181
Hervey, Alvan, 254
Heyst, 54
Highland Forest, 23, 59
Holland, 37
Holt, Alfred, and Company, 60
Hope, Anthony, 278
Hope, G. F. W., 187, 203, 263
Hudig, 46, 52
Hudson, W. H., 98
Hugo, Victor, 277, 282, 284, 305; *Toilers of the Sea*, 6, 14
Hythe, 80, 98-99, 210, 239–40

"Idiots," 28, 53, 77, 96, 101, 108, 201, 219–23, 227, 241–42, 246, 251, 292
"Il Conde," 63
Ildegonda, 187
Ile Grande, 96, 101, 201, 240, 244
Illustrated London News, 209–11, 276–78, 283, 285–88
India, 62, 65
"Informer," 29
Inheritors, 109
"Initiation," *see Mirror of the Sea*
"Inland Sea," 109
Iris, H. M. S., 65
Irish Independent, 283
Italy, 103
Ivy Walls, 97

Jacob, Gertrude L., *Raja of Sarawak*, 65, 70
Jacques, W. H., 17, 180
Jaffer, 69
James, Henry, 28, 94, 103, 232, 292, 295, 301–3
Java, 36–38, 43–44
Jean-Aubry, G., 8, 21, 33, 36, 45, 47, 49, 56, 58, 176, 178, 203, 205, 212, 216, 226, 232, 248; *Joseph Conrad: Life and Letters*, 35, 175, 230
Jeddah, 60–64
Jeddah, 60
Jewel, 58, 72, 163, 172
Jim-Eng, 48
Johnson, 253
Jones, 54
Joseph Conrad on the Art of Writing, 240

Kamudi, 183–84
"Karain," 28, 77, 97, 106, 205, 222–23, 247–53, 257, 265, 267, 292
Kassai, 242
Kassim, 69
Katz Brothers, 52
Keating, George T., 175
Kelai, 51
Kent, 98–99, 135, 210
Keppel, Henry, *Expedition to Borneo of H. M. S. Dido*, 65; *Visit to the Indian Archipelago*, 65, 69
Ker, W. P., 83
Kipling, Rudyard, 272, 277, 279–80, 284–85, 289, 298–99; *Captains Courageous*, 289–90

Klein, *see* Kurtz
Knocke-sur-Mer, 262
Knopf, Alfred A., 240, 270
Knowles, 146
Korzeniowski, 4–5, 8, 13
Korzeniowski, Apollo Nałecz, 4, 6, 14
Korzeniowski, Hilary Nałecz, 4
Korzeniowski, Josef Teodor Konrad Nałecz, *see* Conrad, Joseph
Korzeniowski, Robert Nałecz, 4
Korzeniowski, Teodor Nałecz, 14
Krieger, Adolf P., 225
Kuching, 65, 72
Kurtz, Belgian Agent, 37

Labuan, 65
"Lagoon," 77, 96, 109, 204, 219, 222–23, 226, 244–48, 293
Lakamba, 48–49, 51–52, 113, 277
Land and Water, 217–18
Lannion, 200, 220
Last Essays, 290
Laugh, 106
Leeds Collection, 113–15, 126, 128, 183
Lena, 54
Linares, 204
Lingard, Captain Tom, 28, 38–39, 43–46, 52, 58, 127–29, 201, 259
Lingard, Jim, 45, 57–58, 71
Lingard, Joshua, 45
Lingard, Tambi, 58
Literary News, 271, 276, 278, 280, 284, 292
Literary World, 271, 274, 283, 286, 288, 292
Literature, 284, 292–93
Liverpool, 20
Liverpool Daily Courier, 283–84
Livingstone, David, *Missionary Travels and Researches in South Africa*, 7; *Expedition to the Zambesi*, 7
Lombok, 49
London, 12, 16–17, 19, 24, 56, 96, 99, 111, 177–79, 181, 184, 187, 195–96, 210, 219–20, 229, 245, 263, 266, 275–76
London Magazine, 176
London Times Literary Supplement, 60, 74, 298–300
Lord Jim (character), 28, 58–60, 63–64, 66–68, 70–73, 151, 154–56, 158, 160, 162–63, 165, 168–73, 295
Lord Jim, xiv, 3, 15, 26, 29, 35, 46, 54, 57–58, 60, 62–63, 66–73, 78, 81, 85, 87, 97–98, 101, 108–9, 112, 150, 152–58, 160, 162–64, 166–68, 170–72, 190, 208, 210–12, 226, 247, 259–64, 266, 270, 294–97, 304, 308–9
Lord Jim MS., 60–61, 69, 103, 150–54, 156–70, 172, 260, 263
Loti, Pierre, 284, 298
Lovick, J., 239
Lowestoft, 11
Lucas, E. V., 291, 294
Luton, 99

MacArthur, James, 271
McClintock, Leopold, *Voyage of the "Fox" in the Arctic Seas*, 7
McClure, S. S., 77, 207–9, 212, 259–60, 264–65
McClure, Phillips and Company, 266
McFee, William, xiii, 32
McIntyre, 21–22
M'Neil, 69–70
McNeil, 69
Macassar, 43, 46, 49, 52, 196
Macmillan and Company, 188, 271
Maeander, H. M. S., 65
Malabar, 62, 164
Malacca, Strait of, 61
Malang, 36
Manchester Courier, 271, 283, 302
Manchester Guardian, 302
Marlow, 15, 57, 59, 63, 73, 156, 159, 162–64, 168–69, 172, 294–96

Marryat, Frederick, 7, 284
Marseilles, 6, 10–12, 29, 83, 106
Masefield, John, 298–300
Matherson, 69
Matheson, 69
Maupassant, Guy de, 110, 220, 292; *Une Vie*, 200
Mavis, 11
Mecca, 47, 60
Mediterranean Sea, 10, 12, 22, 27
Mégroz, R. L., 103
Melville, Herman, 277, 284
Mercure de France, 284, 286, 291, 298
Meredith, George, 284, 287, 295
Methuen, Algernon, 212
Mirror of the Sea, 23, 31, 33, 46, 56, 109
Mohammed, 47
Mont Blanc, 10
Montpellier, 74, 85, 92
Morf, Gustav, 8, 13
Morning Leader, 283
Muda Hassim, 65–67, 69, 72
Mundy, Rodney, *Events in Borneo and Celebes*, 65, 69–70
Munro, Neil, 21
Murray, Gilbert, 83

Napoleon, 74
Narcissus, 28, 54–56, 133–37, 286
Nathan, George Jean, 299
Nation, 271–72, 276–78, 283–84, 286–87, 291–92, 298, 300
National Observer, 271–72, 274, 276–77, 279–80, 283
Newbolt, Henry, 83
Newfoundland, 20
New Review, 223, 227–28, 230–33, 239, 284
New York, 188–89, 239
New York Tribune, 283–84, 292, 294, 296
News Agent, 283, 288
Nigger of the "Narcissus," xiv, 20, 26, 31, 35, 54–57, 78, 81, 92, 96–97, 108, 112, 130–33, 135–41, 144–45, 150, 169, 199, 202–3, 205, 212, 223, 225–36, 239–40, 247–49, 252–53, 263, 270, 282–91, 294–95, 304, 308–9; Preface, 26–27, 56, 136–37, 149, 160, 232, 236–40, 284
Nigger of the "Narcissus" MS., 56, 130–33, 135–36, 139, 141–50, 157, 159, 165, 230, 233
Nigger of the "Narcissus" (*New Review*), 56, 130–31, 137–38, 143–45, 223, 227–28, 230–33, 239, 284
Noble, Edward, 105, 276
North American Review, 296
North Sea, 12
Nostromo, 8, 32, 61, 63, 73, 91, 98, 101, 103, 109, 212, 217, 303
Notes on Life and Letters, 16, 290

Ocean Steam Navigation Company, 61
Oceanic Steam Navigation Company, 61
O'Connor, T. P., 271, 274, 276
Olmeijer, Carel, 37
Olmeijer, Casper, 37
Olmeijer, Johanna Cornelia van Lieshout (Mrs. William Charles), 38, 42–43
Olmeijer, William Charles, 36–45, 53, 104
Olmeijer, William Charles Carel, 38
One Degree Passage, 61
Orleston, 99
Oswalds, 99
Otago, 15
Outcast of the Islands, 19–20, 25, 28, 30, 44, 46–48, 51–53, 64, 78, 88–89, 96, 100, 103, 107, 189–92, 194–99, 204, 222, 224, 226, 246, 263, 270, 276, 280–82, 285, 292, 304, 308–9
Outlook, 290, 294–95, 297
"Outpost of Progress," 28, 63, 77,

96, 109, 204, 222–23, 225–27, 240–44, 267, 292
Oxford Dictionary, 140

Palambang, 50
Palawan, 50
Palestine, 59, 264
Pall Mall Gazette, 291
Pall Mall Magazine, 283, 290
Pangemanan, 36, 38, 45, 58
Pantai River, 36, 45, 51, 127
Paris, 16, 197
Park, Mungo, *Travels in the Interior Districts of Africa*, 7; *Journal of a Mission into the Interior of Africa in 1805*, 7
Parsee, 62
"Partner," 53
Patalolo, 48
Patna, 60–64, 71, 159, 165, 167–69, 171–73
Patusan, 58–60, 63–64, 66–68, 70–73, 168, 170
Pawling, S. S., 80–81, 103, 206–7, 227–28, 230–34
Payn, James, 276, 283, 285
Pearson's Weekly, 258, 283
Pechet, 19
Pedro, 54
Pelewo, 70
Peneleh cemetery, 36–38
Penfield, F. C., 219
Pent Farm, 98, 210–11
Pepys, Samuel, 232
Perim, Island of, 61–62
Personal Record, 31, 39–40, 42, 47, 51, 94, 105, 178, 188–89, 304, 308
Petro, 277
Peyrol, 106
Pinker, J. B., 45, 81–83, 87, 111, 116, 130, 138, 175–76, 196, 213, 225
"Planter of Malata," 64
Po Eng Sing, 58
Poe, Edgar Allan, 29, 298
Pola, 9
Poland, 3–6, 8, 10–13, 16, 22, 27, 96, 107, 178–80
Polish souvenir album, 103; *see also Lord Jim* MS.
Poradowska, Marguerite, 16–19, 36, 84, 95, 104, 106, 113, 181–83, 185–86, 188, 193, 195, 261, 270, 275–76; *Mariage du Fils Grandsire*, 108
Primera, 20
"Prince Roman," 54, 64
Pseudonym Library, 182, 186–87, 191, 193
Public Opinion, 291, 293
Pugh, Edwin, 140
Pulman, 9
Pulo Laut, 49

Quiller-Couch, A. T., 283, 286, 290–91
Quinn, John, 177, 188–89, 196, 198–99, 203, 226, 230, 236, 239–40, 248, 253, 259, 263, 266

Radon, 179
Rajah Allang, 60, 67–69, 72
"Rajah Brooke and Joseph Conrad," 66
Razumov, 9, 82
Realm, 275
Red Sea, 61
Rescue, xiv, 20, 22, 26, 28, 30, 46, 64, 73, 77–78, 83–84, 88, 91, 93, 96–97, 99, 101, 103, 107–10, 198–221, 226, 240, 243–44, 247, 251, 253, 259–61, 264, 270
"Return," 97, 205, 222–24, 251–59, 292–93
Réunion, 61, 167
Revue des Deux Mondes, 183, 190, 275
Revue Encyclopédique, 302
Revue Politique et Littéraire, 271
Ricardo, 54
Roberts, Morley, 284
Romance, 103, 109, 111–12, 212

Romance (American Magazine), 217
Rosenbach Collection, 69, 113–15, 126, 130, 150–52, 157–58, 162, 166, 169, 179, 263
Rossetti, Christina, 98
Rothenstein, William, 83, 306
Rotterdam, 196
Rouen, 18, 180
Rover, 74, 92, 106–7, 109, 159, 177, 226
Russell, Clark, 284
Russia, 4, 8–9, 11–12

Sahamin, Daoud, 48
Saint Antoine, 11
Sakarran River, 66
Samarang, 23, 43
Samarinda, 50
Sambaliung, 44, 51
Sambir, 36, 41–42, 45, 47–49, 51–52, 105, 119–20, 124, 126–27, 272
Sancho Panza, 295
Sanderson, E. Launcelot, 87, 181, 197, 246, 248, 252–54, 290–91, 307
Sarambo, 66–67
Sarawak, 46, 64–67, 69–70, 72–73
Saturday Review, 186, 239, 270–71, 274–76, 278–83, 286, 291–92
Savoy, 77, 220, 222, 251
Scotsman, 275
Scott, Michael, 284
Scribner's Sons, Charles, 225
Scribner's Magazine, 207, 231
"Seaman," 259
Secret Agent, 28, 53, 63, 73, 103, 109
"Secret Sharer," 34, 63
Sega, 51
Seligmann-Lui, Geneviève, 185
Serebas River, 71
Set of Six, 100
Seyyid Muhammad Alsagoff, 61
Shadow Line, 33, 37, 48, 57
Shakespeare, William, 14, 59
Shaw, 259
Sherif Ali, 68
Shipmasters Society, 18
Shorter, Clement, 209, 211
"Shorter Tales," 102
Siberia, 4, 8
Singapore, 15, 23, 35, 44, 47–49, 52, 58–63
Sing Jimmung, 48
Singleton, 56, 290
Sisters, xiv, 20, 26, 53, 96, 109, 199–200
Sketch, 271, 273–74
Smart Set, 299
"Smile of Fortune," 57, 91
Smith, Elder and Company, 80, 227
Smollett, Tobias, 284
Société Anonyme Belge pour le Commerce du Haut-Congo, 16
Someries, 99
Sourabaya, 36–38, 43
Spain, 10–11
Speaker, 271, 273, 275–76, 283, 286–87, 294, 296, 298–99
Spectator, 271–73, 276, 279, 283, 285–86, 289, 291–92, 294, 297–99, 301
Spring Grove, 99
Standard, 283, 288, 291
Stanford, 98
Stanford-le-Hope, 97, 230, 254
Stanley Falls, 24, 37
Star, 283
Stein, 58, 69–71, 172
Stevenson, Robert Louis, 277–78, 280, 292, 295, 298–99, 308; *Ebb Tide*, 295
Stockholm, 226
Straits Settlements, 275
Suez Canal, 18
Sullivan, 56
Sullivan, T. R., 284
Sulu, 43, 49
Sumatra, 50, 66
Sunday Times, 283
Suspense, 73–74, 90, 109

Swettenham, Frank, 60, 272
Swinnerton, Frank, 307
Switzerland, 9, 85, 96
Syed Moshin Bin S. Ali Jaffree, 47–49
Syed Mosin, 47
Syed Reshid, 47
Syed Selim bin Sali, 47
Symons, Arthur, 220, 222, 289, 295, 307

"Tale," 64
Tales of Hearsay, 175–77
"Tales of the Sea," 6–7
Tales of Unrest, 21, 78, 80–81, 219, 222, 225–27, 234, 240, 244–48, 251–52, 256, 258–59, 263, 270, 291–93, 298, 308–9
Tamb' Itam, 68–69
Tamil, 62
Tandjong Redeb, *see* Berouw
Tandjong Sambar, 51
Templer, John C., *Private Letters of Sir James Brooke*, 65
Thames, 16, 56, 135, 179
Titanic, 248
Tit-Bits, 15, 175
"To my Readers in America," *see Nigger of the "Narcissus,"* Preface
Torrens, 17, 24, 180
Toulon, 74
Tower Hill, 56
Travers, Edith, 28
Tremolino, 11
Tristan, 182
Trollope, Anthony, 14, 75
Tuan Jim, 58, 71, 73, 157, 263
Tupper, Martin, 305
Turgenev, Ivan, 234, 292, 295; *Lear of the Steppes*, 271
'Twixt Land and Sea, 93, 269
Two Vagabonds, see *Outcast of the Islands*
"Typhoon," 63
Typhoon, 102

Ukraine, 5, 178
Under Western Eyes, 9, 63, 82, 109
Unfinished Play, 103
Union Line, 21
United States, 32, 78, 188, 198, 217–19, 225, 230–31, 233, 257–59, 263–64, 266, 271, 276, 283, 291, 294, 298, 309
Unwin, T. Fisher, 18–19, 77–78, 80–81, 115–16, 177, 182–88, 191, 198, 201, 205, 220–25, 227, 241–43, 245–47, 250–54, 257–58, 270, 275, 281, 291

Venice, 10
Verne, Jules, 29
"Victim of Progress," *see* "Outpost of Progress"
Victory, 53, 101, 109
Vidar, 15, 23, 35, 40–42, 45, 47–51, 57–59
Vinck Family, 52, 119–20

Wagner, Richard, 182
Wait, James, 28, 54–56, 105, 133–34, 137, 141–44, 146–50, 229, 231, 239, 286
Wajo, 70
Wallace, Alfred Russel, *Malay Archipelago*, 73
Wamibo, 54
"Warrior's Soul," 74
Warsaw, 15, 179
Watson, Helen, 246, 248
Watson, Marriott, 292
Watson and Company, 81–82
Waugh, Arthur, 271–72
Webster, 62
Weekly Sun, 271, 273, 276
Wells, H. G., 84, 99–100, 109, 265, 276, 280–82, 303, 307
West, Dan, 80

West Indies, 10–11, 22, 33
Weyman, Stanley, 278
Whalley, Captain, 57
Whitehall Review, 282
Willems, Peter, 28, 46, 53–54, 104–5, 196–97, 278
Windermere, 20
Wise, T. J., 176–77, 214–15, 222
Woking, 281
Wood, Mrs. Margaret, *The Vagabonds*, 192
Woolf, Virginia, 3
World, 271, 273–78, 283, 291
Wotjek, 36
Wye, 99

Yeats, William Butler, 300
Yellow Book, 257
Youth, 78, 81, 265–68, 270, 298, 301–2, 308–9
"Youth," 15, 31, 34, 50, 54, 57, 97, 101, 109, 208, 259–60, 264–67, 298–99, 301–2

Zack, *On Trial*, 295
Zola, Emile, 272, 284